# A Public Health Journey:

## My Quest to Provide Permanent Contraception

Betty Gonzales, R.N.

My Quest to Provide Permanent Contraception

ISBN: 1500883832
ISBN-13: 978 – 1500883836

# DEDICATION

TO MY CHILDREN
Who were always with me in heart and mind,
even when I was far away
working for a cause I truly believed was important:
helping to provide safe and voluntary
surgical contraception.

My Quest to Provide Permanent Contraception

# CONTENTS

My Quest to Provide Permanent Contraception

# ACKNOWLEDGMENTS

First and foremost, I would like to acknowledge all the dedicated board members of the organization that has tried to broaden reproductive choices for men and women since it was organized in the 1930s and is still working internationally under the name of EngenderHealth. While I was on staff, it was called Association for Voluntary Sterilization and later as the Association for Voluntary Surgical Contraception. I am very pleased to have worked with this group and commend them for their dedication.

Secondly, I would like to thank William R. Vanessendelft who wrote the history of AVS in his doctoral dissertation, called *A History of the Association for Voluntary Sterilization, 1935-1964.* I also want to thank Ian Dowbiggin for his publication of his book, *The Sterilization Movement and Global Fertility in the Twentieth Century.* I hope that my personal memoir about my years with the organization will help fill in some of the blanks in the records.

Finally, I would like to acknowledge the fine work of the Social Welfare History Archives at the University of Minnesota. AVS sent copious material about the work of the association to the archives from the early 70s until 1980. It is this material that has been used by many researchers. Special thanks go to David Klaassen, now retired, and Linnea Anderson, current curator at the archives center. Both were always helpful to historians looking at the sterilization movement. I am pleased to have known and worked with them.

Special mention must go to the Montville, N.J. Writers Group, whose members helped me by reviewing many chapters and offering positive suggestions about content, form and structure of the material. Special thanks go to Christine Balne who got me through the self publishing process. Without them, I doubt I would have gotten through this project. Thank you, all.

My Quest to Provide Permanent Contraception

# AVS History, 1963-1993

## PROLOGUE

It has been over fifty years since I had my tubes tied. I am at the age where reflection of one's life and achievements are possible, and I have found myself drawn to books that record changes that took place in the decades of the fifties and sixties. A book that especially impressed me was *When Everything Changed* by Gail Collins, published by Little, Brown and Company in 2009. As the book's subtitle describes it, the book relates the amazing journey of American women from 1960 to the present.

Mine was the generation that experienced the civil rights movement, the radical students and anti-war movements, the feminist movement, the sexual revolution, and the beginnings of the gay rights movement. My personal focus and participation was in the family planning movement. To my surprise and disappointment, with a few exceptions in the books about the time, I found very little mention of the organization I was affiliated with for most of my adult life, the Association for Voluntary Sterilization (AVS), now named EngenderHealth, Inc.

Even the history of EngenderHealth as found on their website (engenderhealth.org) seems to skip over the significant programs and achievements of the organization in the United States. The site discusses the early years of the association, stating, "Our first 25 years were dedicated to advocating for access to voluntary sterilization (tubal ligation and vasectomy) in the United States at a time when there was no such thing as a legal contraceptive method. With limited resources, our founders worked to educate everyone they could reach - doctors, nurses, legislators, and average citizens - about the need for and social acceptability of sterilization."

I was not too surprised that the present leadership of EngenderHealth is choosing to forget all about AVS history in the eugenics movement. I am sure they wish it had never happened. But the truth is that the organization started out with the name "The Sterilization League of New Jersey" and its objective was to reduce the number of mentally defective persons having babies. In the space of just under thirty years, from its founding in 1937 until the mid-60s, the aim of the group had totally changed.

When I was introduced to the association in 1962, AVS was increasingly shifting toward voluntarism, promoting sterilization as a choice of methods

1

for persons who wanted to end child-bearing. William Ray Vanessendelft, in his doctoral dissertation of 1978, excellently describes that period of time in his thesis, *A History of the Association for Voluntary Sterilization*, 1935-1964. It resides in the Social History Archives Center of the University of Minnesota. It is my hope that in writing these pages, I can fill in the blanks that exist in the records of social changes that took place under the auspices of this organization after 1964.

It was in the 60s that leaders of AVS were becoming concerned with over-population, some of them leaning toward compulsory limitation to a two-child family. They had been exposed to the term "The Population Bomb" used in material published by the Hugh Moore Fund and later were impressed with the ideas presented in the book by the same name written by Stanford University Professor Paul R. Ehrlich. The Sierra Club, an environmental organization, was claiming that population growth was the ultimate threat to mankind. The organization called Zero Population Growth was formed.

A shift had been made from qualitative birth control to quantitative population control. The concerns had changed from attempting to limit procreation of "defectives" to limiting all births. Instead of sterilizations being encouraged for the "unfit", clients now had to demonstrate that they were mentally "fit" enough to provide informed consent for surgery to terminate fertility.

In EngenderHealth's web-site rendition of our past, I was shocked to read that "there was no such thing as a legal contraceptive method". Surely the male methods of birth control were always available and legal. There was nothing illegal about condom use or withdrawal, the two most common methods. The "rhythm method" was not only available, but advocated by religious leaders. Early diaphragms were available, as were foaming tablets and sponges. It is true, however, that these did not have the high effectiveness that modern methods now have, but they were legal contraceptive options.

The web-site of EngenderHealth goes on to say that "by the early 1970s, surgical sterilization became – and remains to this day – the most common method of contraception in the United States, surpassing all other forms of family planning". At this point in the history, their focus shifts to "Going Global", and from that point, all references to the work of the organization were about the work overseas.

The more I read about the social changes of the fifties and sixties, the more I felt that "my" old organization had not been given full credit for all it had done. Who would set the record straight? Who is still alive who would remember the struggles? Current staff members, even those who might have been with the organization since the 1970s, had only worked with the International Project of AVS. There was no interaction with those of us who worked in the United States. When I recently checked the list of board members of EngenderHealth, the names that were familiar to me were missing. Since I am now in my 83rd year, it is reasonable to assume most have died, and their efforts have been largely forgotten by current board members and staff.

The evolution of the organization's name is interesting. The Sterilization League of New Jersey was formed to promote eugenic sterilization at a time when mental retardation and mental illness were believed to be hereditary. Between 1943 and 1964, the organization changed its name several times as it tried to clarify its work and to have its name reflect the change of focus. It was named Birthright in 1943, when its slogan was that it was every American child's birthright to a sound mind in a sound body. The next name change, in 1950, was to The Human Betterment Association of America (HBAA). It was meant to imply that sterilization could be a solution to medical, social and economic problems. In 1962, the Board of Directors decided that the name of the organization did not effectively communicate the focus of their program – voluntary sterilization. In an attempt to be more clearly understood, the name was changed to the Human Betterment Association for Voluntary Sterilization (HBAVS). In 1965, the first words of that long title were dropped, and the group became known as the Association for Voluntary Sterilization (AVS). In 1984, the title was once again changed to the Association for Voluntary Surgical Contraception (AVSC).

I was personally pleased with the later name change. In my lectures and broadcast presentations I had long referred to vasectomy and tubal occlusion surgeries as the surgical methods of birth control. It just seemed so much simpler and more understandable than having to define what "sterilization" meant. After all, outside the field of contraception, sterilization was something mothers did with the baby's formula bottles, or what they did when they were canning vegetables.

In other languages, the word "sterilization" was frequently translated as a word meaning castration. This was particularly a problem because AVS was beginning to reach out to developing countries where local languages needed to be used. While it is true that castration of either a male (removal of the testes) or a female (removal of the ovaries) would sterilize the individual, sterilizations are not castrations.

Voluntary contraceptive sterilization of either male or female does not remove the reproductive organs. It simply creates a barrier so that the sperm of the male cannot reach the egg of the woman. To clarify the situation, and to be sure that we were not discussing removal of any sex organ or gland, it seemed far better to use the term "surgical contraception".

Even in English, I had also often used the words "permanent birth

3

control" in place of "sterilization". It was not to hide the sterilizing aspects of the procedure, but to stress the permanency of the method. I was a primary spokesperson for the organization for many years so I personally felt the responsibility to be accurate. I always wanted the public and clients to understand fully the permanence of the method and that it was indeed a surgical method that was accompanied by all the risks of surgery. My aim was to clarify and educate.

For simplification, I shall use the initials AVS in this manuscript because those were the initials used during most of my years with the organization. The next change of name from AVSC to AVSC International took place in 1994, about a year after I left the organization. The latest change to EngenderHealth occurred in 2001.

Two recent books report the history of AVS. Ian Dowbiggin wrote *The Sterilization Movement and Global Fertility in the Twentieth Century* published by Oxford University Press in 2008, and Rebecca M. Kluchin wrote *Fit to be Tied: Sterilization and Reproductive Rights in America, 1950-1980* published by Rutgers University Press in 2009. Both authors were able to get much of their facts from the AVS material stored at the Social Welfare Archives of the University of Minnesota.

It is my hope that in writing these pages, I can fill in the blanks that exist in the records of social changes that took place under the auspices of this organization. I am proud to have been a part of both the social and the surgical developments. I am enthusiastic about telling my story about the activities of AVS from the time I first used their referral services until the time I left in 1993. From when I, then a twenty-nine year old woman with six children, first begged for help in obtaining a tubal ligation until I left the organization to become a consultant for a few years before settling into my retirement.

# CHAPTER 1: A BIRTH CONTROL DILEMMA

My husband, Manuel, and I were eager to start a family. Manuel had come from a background that endorsed large families, and where it was expected to have a child soon after marrying. My parents, on the other hand, had been firm believers in family planning and had decided they would wait three years before having a child. They were so successful that I was born three years and a week after their wedding day. I fully understood their reasons for delaying parenthood, but that was in 1932, when the country was in financial ruin. This was 1953, and things were looking good for us.

I was a registered nurse. I loved being a nurse, following the examples of my mother and her two sisters. The only thing I would have wanted more would have been to become a doctor. I did not see any possibility for that as it would have been financially impossible to pay for the many years of education. Also, only limited fields such as pediatrics or gynecology were apt to be open to a female doctor. I wanted to be a surgeon, but the only female surgeons I knew of were those taking out the tonsils and adenoids of their pediatric patients.

My exposure to medicine and surgery had come early into my life. My mother (divorced from my father for some years) supported my two younger brothers and me by working as an office nurse for a physician and surgeon during the Second World War, when he was the only doctor in town. We lived in an apartment above the office and Mom was on call twenty-four hours a day. If someone went into labor during the night, she would call the local police and have them pick her up and take her to the woman in labor, while the doctor was summoned from his home in another town. Sometimes she delivered the baby before the doctor arrived. Saturdays were set aside for office surgery. Mom assisted the doctor, both by serving as the instrument nurse and the anesthetist. I got the job of cleaning up the instruments and rooms between the operations.

The week that I turned fourteen, I started working as an aide in the operating room of New Jersey's Paterson General Hospital. My work included washing instruments, gloves, blood-soaked pads, reusable needles and syringes. On my first day, there was an emergency Cesarean Section. I was allowed to watch through the operating room window. How thrilled I

5

was to see that baby's head and body emerge from the bloody, draped body on the table! I continued to work every summer and most weekends in that hospital until I later entered nurse's training in that same hospital after finishing high school.

During the last year of nursing school, I met Manuel Gonzales. He was a professional welterweight boxer training and working out of Tex Pelte's gym in Paterson. Manuel was Mexican-American, born in Gonzales, Texas, He moved a few years later to Corpus Christi, where his widowed mother and siblings still resided. We met in the First Presbyterian Church in Paterson, where I was an active member.

I was attracted to this handsome man, there is no doubt. On our first date, we went to the top of the Empire State building, and while there, a couple came seeking his autograph. They had seen him fight two days before on television. Besides feeling like I was out with a celebrity, I was so happy to be with someone who was not Dutch. I had grown up in a very tight religious community where it seemed that everyone was marrying someone's distant cousin. I vowed I would never marry a Dutchman. Manuel certainly seemed a great alternative except that I did not think I could live with a boxer. Every time Manuel had a fight, I dreaded the shape he might be in when he got back home. Besides my worries, Manuel also was uncomfortable with the idea of my seeing him in the ring. He refused to have me watch any of his fights.

While sparring with a gym-mate, Fitzie Pruden, Manuel's front tooth was damaged. A day later both men left for Indianapolis for the big car-racing and sports weekend. Fitzie was going to fight Kid Gavilan and Manuel was to fight Andy Anderson at the Fairgrounds Coliseum. During Manuel's fight, he took a blow to his mouth from Andy and this time the tooth came out. This bodily damage, plus my unwillingness to marry a boxer, led to Manuel's retirement from professional boxing.

When we married, Manuel was working in the Curtis Wright aircraft assembly plant in Woodbridge, N.J. I was a registered nurse employed in the office of a leading surgeon. We had been saving money together to furnish our home. When we married, we moved into the small bungalow that we owned free and clear. We had no debts. I believed the twenties were the ages meant for childbearing, and that's what we were. Surely, we thought, we were ready to take on the responsibilities of parenting.

Manuel worked the afternoon shift, from four until twelve, getting home well after midnight. I worked in the doctor's office four days a week, plus one evening and Saturday mornings. We both used public buses for transportation to and from work. While home alone in the evenings, I sewed clothes for the baby we were expecting in late fall. During the summer, the gynecologist heard two heart beats. The preparations for the baby suddenly doubled.

I gave birth to twin boys in late September. They were premature so I was unable to breast-feed them as I had originally planned. One son could not tolerate the evaporated milk formula that was standard fare for newborns in those days. This meant that I had to prepare two batches of formulas every day for the twins, and to be sure to label the bottles so that each baby got the correct bottle. Because they were both so small (four pounds, seven ounces, and five pounds, two ounces), they could only consume one or two ounces at a time. By the time I fed one, the other was hungry.

My doctor suggested that I make a visit to his office after I had had my first post-partum menstrual period. I was eager to do this so we could initiate contraception. I believed it would be best to wait at least a year before getting pregnant again. I was fitted for a diaphragm, the best method available at the time. This method required a spermicidal jelly to be applied to the rim of the diaphragm and to the surface that would be in contact with the cervix. On our way back home with the twins in our arms, Manuel and I used the two buses necessary to get home, stopping off along the way at a drug store to get the jelly.

Much to my surprise, I did not get a period that month. Could I have misunderstood the doctor's instructions? Was the jelly supposed to have been on the outer side of the diaphragm instead of the inner side where I had put it? Maybe it was meant to kill the sperm before they swam past the diaphragm rim? My thoughts wandered to stories I had heard about unintelligent or illiterate women who were considered either too lazy or too dumb to use a diaphragm successfully. But I was smart, educated, and motivated, so what had happened?

Upon checking dates and the progress of my pregnancy, it became apparent that I was already pregnant when I was fitted for the diaphragm. I gave birth to a daughter a week before we celebrated the twins' birthday. I had had three babies in less than a year. But now I had the diaphragm ready, so surely that would not happen again.

Looking back, I remember some confusion about the use of the diaphragm. I had been instructed to insert the device well before having sex. The idea was to separate the preparation from the loving moment. The doctor and the literature of the day suggested that having to stop a romantic moment to insert a diaphragm or to put on a condom would not be kind to the man. Better to always be prepared, and then, if no love-making followed, no harm would be done. Just take it out later. After sex, however, the instructions were to wait eight hours, presumably for the spermicidal jelly to do its deed, and then to douche after removing it to cleanse oneself.

My husband was working the second shift, getting home about one o'clock in the morning. I diligently inserted my diaphragm every night before he arrived. But with two babies needing bottles, and one being breast fed, sleep was always interrupted, and love-making often happened before the eight-hour douche, reapplication of the jelly, and the re-insertion that was recommended. That is the only explanation I have for the pregnancy that would produce another baby boy fourteen months after our daughter.

This should not sound like a horror story. We were both enjoying the children. I was well organized, so things went along quite smoothly. But traveling everywhere by bus had become difficult, if not impossible. To go to church or downtown required one bus; to visit my family required two buses. But how do you carry three babies plus their diaper bags? It was time to get a car. My mother borrowed a car and taught both Manuel and me how to drive a stick shift vehicle. Then we bought a used car for two hundred dollars, so we had wheels.

During that pregnancy, we also decided that we needed to enlarge our house as soon as possible Our home had a living room and kitchen on the left side of the center hall, and two bedrooms with a central bathroom on the right side. Three cribs in the back bedroom filled it to capacity, so with a fourth child on the way, we needed more bedrooms.

We had a second story constructed with a large bedroom and a bathroom across the back of the house, and two bedrooms in the front. This enabled us to remove the wall between the front downstairs bedroom and the living room. That doubled our living space, even providing an area for a dining room table. Better yet, the back bedroom could now be used for a playroom for the children.

The re-construction went on during my pregnancy. I was hampered by a fall that fractured my left shoulder and made my arm useless. I was able to move the lower arm, thankfully, as it was needed to pick up the babies and change their diapers. I also wanted to do much of the finishing work on the house to keep costs at a minimum. We had to take out a small mortgage to have the second floor built, but did not want to owe any more than absolutely necessary, so I painted all the rooms, hung waterproof wall-covering in the bathroom, and cemented tiles on all the floors, all with my left arm hanging limply.

After this fourth baby, my husband decided he would use a condom because we had rather lost confidence in my diaphragm. That lasted a few months but one night, the condom package was empty. "That's OK", I said, "It's my safe period". Famous last words! The fifth child was born seventeen months after the last one, in the summer of 1957.

While I was in the hospital, I finally realized the size of the family we had, and the unusually brief spaces between deliveries. I was filling out the birth certificate form and answering the questions about previous births and ages. As I wrote down "3" as the age of the oldest, I realized that we had five children less than four years of age!

In spite of the large family, we were trying to give the children opportunities for educational experiences. We had traveled to Texas to visit the extended Gonzales family with our twin babies the summer before our daughter was born, and we longed to go back again. We vacationed every summer in a tent, camping in the northeast, and enjoyed that very much. During the Christmas season that year, we took the oldest ones to New York City to see the window displays. We traveled by train, to give them that added experience.

To our surprise, the children did not need a ticket for the train. The conductor said that children under five traveled free. That got me to wonder if there was any limit to the number of children that might be taken. Did it require one adult lap for every free child? Research followed, and I learned that there was no limit. The decision to take them all to Texas to visit their cousins did not take us long.

The following summer, when the baby was thirteen months old, we all made the trip. The twins were four years old at that time. Better yet, we learned that if we traveled on Monday through Thursday, we could go on the "family plan" where the wife was only charged half fare. All seven of us traveled for one and a half fares, round trip from Newark, N.J. to Corpus Christi, Texas.

To avoid having to take the children to a dining car, I packed food for the journey. Using water from the train faucet, I used dried milk and orange drink powder to make drinks for the children. Manuel and I enjoyed instant coffee made with the hot water available in the bathroom. Salads and sandwiches made with perishable meats were eaten the first day. Baby food for the youngest was easy. Then we switched to peanut butter and jam for the second day. Boiled eggs, cookies, fruit, dried summer sausage rounded out the diet.

I certainly wanted to make a good impression on the family we were going to meet. I did not want to arrive burdened down with a suitcase of dirty clothes. To prepare for the journey, I saved up old, stained or mended clothes to use on the trip. On the night we were traveling, I took the children, one by one, to the bathroom where they got washed up and changed into a fresh set of clothes for the next day. The old clothes went into the garbage. Between Houston and Corpus, I repeated the chore, thus arriving with the children all washed up and in clean, new matching outfits, and no dirty laundry after two days and nights on the train.

I repeated this on the way back home two weeks later. The only difference was that our packed sandwiches were made with tortillas instead of bread. Now these sandwiches are called wraps", but when they first appeared in fast food restaurants in the northeast, they were not new to this family.

After my fifth baby's birth, I had been visited by the town's public health nurse. She and I had become friends over the years, with her annual visit to each new baby. This time she told me she was going to change jobs and become the school nurse instead. I applied and was hired for her position, a half time job, working seventeen and a half hours a week. This had worked out well for us. I worked in the morning and got home in time for my husband to go to work in the afternoon. I started what became my occupation for the next eight years, the Public Health Nurse serving a community of about 6,000 residents in Passaic County, N.J.

Unfortunately, my husband got laid off. Airplane manufacturing had declined. Now what? We were already as thrifty as we could be, and still only had the small mortgage, but we did not want to add to that. In the absence of another position for Manuel, and with the expectation that he would be called back to work soon, I took two more part-time jobs, and he became the primary caregiver for the children.

I continued the public health work in the morning and early afternoon hours. I worked evenings from six until eleven o'clock during the week in the pediatric department of the hospital. On Friday and Saturday, I worked nights in the maternity department, either giving post-partum care or working in the labor and delivery rooms. I had worked all day Friday at my public health job and all Friday night in the hospital. I got to sleep a while on Saturday, cooking meals ahead in my awake hours for much of the week ahead. I might get a short nap on Sunday morning while Manuel took all the kids to church, but I would get to sleep Sunday night in preparation for Monday's public health job. So I existed on six sleeps a week for over a year. This schedule probably helped us to avoid another pregnancy.

When we were celebrating the youngest child's second birthday, I remember commenting to my husband that we had never had a baby at the age of two before. When the others had reached that age, there was always a younger one. I asked Manuel if he thought he would ever like to have a sixth child. He responded "Of course!" Well, I thought, if we were going to round it off to a half dozen, we better do it now. I did not want the kids all to be in school and then have to start all over with a baby again. Manuel was happy to oblige.

The next day was bedlam. Everything that could go wrong went wrong. The children all threw up, spilled milk, failed to make it to the potty in time, wrote on walls, etc, etc. I said to Manuel "We must have been out of our minds last night to think we wanted more of this!" But it was too late. Using contraception for the rest of the month did no good. It soon became obvious that I was pregnant. Even worse, I had to break the news once again to my parents who had been so much more successful at using contraception back in the 1930s.

This turned out to be a stressful pregnancy. Not because I had any trouble with the pregnancy, but because the twins had started school and brought home every communicable disease they encountered. And the children at home caught it from their brothers. It took a detailed schedule to keep track of all the separate periods of quarantine. We dealt with measles, German measles, scarlet fever, and chicken pox. Vaccines for these childhood illnesses were not yet available, but the children had all been immunized against whooping cough so at least we did not have to deal with that.

It was during this difficult pregnancy, I begged my doctor to schedule a post-partum tubal ligation. I had suffered from dangerous episodes of phlebitis with every pregnancy and had even had bilateral saphenous ligations to remove varicose veins, with twenty-two scars on my legs to prove it. After each delivery I had to be treated with anti-coagulants and elevated legs to prevent dangerous blood clots. But the doctor, in agreement with the vascular surgeon, said I had only proved that with proper care, I could survive another pregnancy. Sterilization could not be done as I did not have sufficient medical reasons for it, they claimed.

I then begged "Please deliver my baby by Cesarean Section and secretly tie the tubes while you are in my abdomen". I knew that doctors often tied tubes of women during Cesareans, even without their knowledge, so I was sure that could be done, but "No!" was again the reply. Then was when I really had my "Aha Moment", my epiphany, my sudden realization of reality. It was medically possible for doctors to take out pieces of tubes when it was their idea, or when they deemed it appropriate. But it was not permissible for a woman to decide what she wanted done to her own body!

In those days, most towns were still requiring placards to be nailed on the houses where anyone had a communicable illness. I believed it would have been a far better plan to have the nurse (me, in this case) visit the families and teach them how not to spread the disease, rather than have a card nailed to their doors. I had been trying to convince our Board of Health that it was time to change that policy but I had not yet succeeded. As a result, our house had one card after another tacked on it.

We were in isolation. No visitors could come to the house. No babysitters could be used. As a family, we could not go anywhere because there was always someone in quarantine. But at least the kids had each other to play with. At the end of my pregnancy, we were dealing with chicken pox. One of the twins developed viral encephalitis from the varicella (chicken pox) virus. He was hospitalized in a coma. It was in this situation that I went into labor a few days later.

I gave birth to our baby girl by the next morning. That day, no one mentioned our critically ill, comatose son who was in the pediatric department one floor below me in the maternity section. I was too afraid to ask how he was. The next day, I got the news that he was beginning to respond and had opened his eyes. It seemed the crisis had passed and he was now expected to live. A few days later, we all were discharged. In addition to the new baby I had a six-year old son who was not yet able to walk and needed to be carried.

The good news was that we were out of quarantine, at least. I was so happy that our son was improving and we had a new baby to show off, that I immediately baked some cakes for expected family and guests we assumed would be arriving soon. But this break did not last long. The next week, the kids got mumps. Back to more placards on the door!

I thought about going to Puerto Rico for a tubal ligation. I had learned that it was easily obtainable there. But how could I leave six young children to travel to a strange place alone and risk surgery by an unknown doctor? How long would it take to make the arrangements without knowing anyone there to help? What if I died and left my husband with six young children to rear by himself?

The Federal Drug Administration had just approved "The Pill", the first hormonal contraceptive. I considered it but was really worried about the possible long term effects of manipulating hormones. I had twenty years of fertility ahead of me yet and the drug had not been tested that long. I also counted the cost. The early pills were not cheap and not covered by any insurance. The cost over the next two decades would far exceed the cost of surgery even if it had to include a trip to Puerto Rico. Even better, we had insurance that covered surgery.

Manuel and I discussed how we should handle the birth control issue. I was still trying to find a way to have the surgery. Manuel expressed his willingness to have a vasectomy, but I knew his heart was not in it. He would only be doing it because I felt so strongly about not ever wanting to be pregnant again. I could not, in good conscience, let him make a permanent decision to have his body altered to protect me. I believed then, and continued to counsel others in the future, that a decision to be sterilized should be a very 'selfish' one. The person who feels most strongly that he or she never wants another chance to reproduce should be the one to have the surgical termination of fertility. Manuel would have welcomed six more children and loved them all. We never can be sure what the future will bring. There may be a future change of circumstances. If Manuel were ever to remarry, I would not want him to regret not being able to have more children. After all, in our case, I was the one who had suffered the pregnancy risks. I had the repeated threats of blood clots in my engorged veins. It was I who insisted that I could not handle one more pregnancy, therefore my responsibility.

We seemed to have hit a dead end. Perhaps I gave up. Maybe I just did not care enough anymore. Whatever the situation was, a year later I was pregnant again, but this time I was not going to let it continue to term. I sought out an abortionist. The Roe vs. Wade Supreme Court decision that legalized abortion was still thirteen years in the future. I would have to seek out someone who might do it secretly, though I knew that might be fraught with added risks. I even asked policemen that I knew quite well where an abortion might be obtained. I figured that if anyone knew where it was being done, surely the police would know. But the safest one they knew had retired, so I failed there.

There seemed no choice but to do it myself. I will spare the details, but I will report that I had access to an autoclave so I could sterilize the equipment. I borrowed a set of instruments from someone (not a doctor nor a nurse). He never admitted it, but he must have been doing some illegal abortions himself, or why else would he have gynecological instruments including one to dilate the cervix?

My subsequent hemorrhage and emergency surgery finally convinced my gynecologist that I was serious about not wanting another pregnancy. Of course, the subject of my abortion was never mentioned. He was decent enough to pretend to believe me when I said it was a spontaneous miscarriage. But he had noticed the cervical damage from the instruments I had used, so he knew the truth even if not the details.

During a follow-up visit to his office, he told me about a Doctor Guttmacher, in New York City, who was helping people get their tubes tied. I wasted no time calling his office and was pleasantly surprised that Dr. Guttmacher took the time to speak to me directly. He told me that I did not need to travel to New York for the operation. The Human Betterment Association had a referral service. They could refer me to a surgeon who would perform a tubal ligation if my application were to be approved by a panel of three gynecologists. He supplied the necessary address and phone numbers so I could request an application.

I subsequently learned that Dr. Alan Guttmacher was a distinguished obstetrician-gynecologist and leader in reproductive rights. He served as president of the Planned Parenthood Federation of America as well as a member of the board of what was then called The Human Betterment Association, one of the early names of AVS. As such, he advocated voluntary sterilization for those wishing to terminate their fertility by surgical means.

The association's panel of gynecologists approved my application. I was referred to a surgeon in another county, about fifteen miles from where I had been refused. The doctor gruffly told me that he did not care why I wanted the operation. He was not going to ask about my morals or make any judgments, he said. He had only one requirement and that was that he wanted to be paid up front.

I certainly was not impressed by this man, but I had checked his surgical credentials so decided I would overlook his manner and his opinions. I paid the man and scheduled the surgery, which was done under general anesthesia, using a long incision from my navel down to my pubic bone. I was hospitalized for a week, but I finally got my tubes tied!

*1964 Family Photo.*

# CHAPTER 2: SHOWING GRATITUDE

My surgery went as expected, and recovery was uncomplicated. Soon I was back at work, serving as the Public Health Nurse for my community. At that time, it was my responsibility to visit the home of every newborn to be sure that the mother was recovering and the baby was developing normally. The county health department expected me to make regular visits for almost a year, checking that the baby had received all the recommended immunizations for tetanus, whooping cough, diphtheria and typhoid. Policies within the health system were a bit outdated, in my opinion. In our town, all the mothers had a doctor who was caring for the baby, so my mandatory visits were becoming less important because I was often duplicating the work of the pediatrician. But in another way, I took advantage of another shift in policy. Social workers had historically been forbidden to discuss birth control methods, and public health nurses were usually hesitant to get involved unless asked. I thought it was about time to change this pattern.

My relationship with many of the mothers had become that of personal friendship. It was not unusual for a mother to express her concern about the number of children she had or to ask about new developments in birth control methods. Many were quite open about telling me that the last child (or children) had been unplanned, and had caused stress, both emotionally and financially.

Having gone through the lengthy process of obtaining my tubal ligation, I now felt more comfortable discussing voluntary sterilization as an option for those who had already had the number of children they wanted. I was aware of the issues that women were facing during the decision-making process. I had empathy for the mothers trying to control their fertility. Mothers who wanted temporary methods could get what they needed from their gynecologists, but few doctors at that time would discuss voluntary sterilization. I was not hesitant to talk about it. I also had the resources of AVS at hand. I was able to refer women to the organization for referrals to a surgeon if putting an end to their fertility was what they wanted.

I was also better prepared to discuss other birth control options. The Pill had recently been approved for use by the Federal Food and Drug Administration (FDA). Dr. John Rock, a Roman Catholic gynecologist, was a long time advocate of family planning. He had helped develop the Pill and had been responsible for the clinical trials. Rock hoped to gain approval by the Catholic Church by first presenting the Pill as a menstrual regulator. He intentionally connected the Pill to the menstrual cycle by including a week of placebo pills in one month's supply of the hormonal pills. During that week, menstruation would occur. Rock hoped that in time, the Church would approve the Pill as a contraceptive.

Pope Pius XII had approved the use of the Pill to treat menstrual disorders in 1958. This was two years before FDA approved the Pill for contraception, recommending it especially for younger women who were spacing their pregnancies. I remember many of my Catholic public health mothers telling me that they planned to take the Pill to regulate their periods so that when they used the Catholic-approved rhythm method, they would have better success. The Pill was reported to have the same effectiveness as sterilization. Failures were less than one percent. For women using the Pill to "regulate their periods", the rhythm method of periodic abstinence also enjoyed an improvement in effectiveness.

The intrauterine contraceptive device (IUCD) also had become an option. The Lippes Loop, developed by Dr. Jack Lippes, was first distributed in 1962, a year after I had been sterilized. It was expected to have an effectiveness rate similar to the pill, but it was unclear how many years a woman could safely use an IUCD. Potential side effects were also unknown. As the Public Health Nurse for the community, I had an obligation to keep up-to-date on the medical facts in order to be able to counsel clients, but neither of these methods was freely available over the counter. They were both dependent upon the personal physician or gynecologist caring for the woman.

Looking back, I suspect that had the Loop been an option for me, I would have had reservations about wearing a foreign object in my uterus for twenty years, just as I was not willing to use hormones for such an extended time period. Although current IUCDs have been improved, and birth control pills with lower hormone levels have become safer, I will always believe that for those who are looking for a permanent cessation of child-bearing, a simple, safe, one-time surgical procedure might be the best method.

Given my experience, and my medical background, along with a willingness to be open about my sterilization, it was a natural step for me to want to share my knowledge with others. I began to meet with groups to discuss the surgical method of contraception. I spoke to women's clubs, church groups, and family planning clinics. Public presentations were usually announced in a local newspaper. In this way, I became a source of information about voluntary sterilization.

Most importantly, I wanted to help the work of the Human Betterment

Association of America (HBAA). I made an appointment to meet the executive director, Ruth Proskauer Smith to discuss possible ways I might be of assistance to the organization. I told this lovely, sophisticated lady that I was so grateful for their assistance in locating a surgeon for me that I wanted to do something in return. Her first idea was that I should try to disseminate information to other nurses through the Public Health network so that other home-visiting nurses would be better informed and able to help their patients. She also suggested that I join the organization and begin to attend the annual membership meetings and their conferences.

Mrs. Smith also suggested that I look for any opportunities to write about voluntary sterilization in newspapers. This activity was not a new concept for me. As a young teen, I had remembered reading newspaper clippings that had been saved by my mother. In the late 1920s, when Planned Parenthood was in its infancy, my father had been an activist in promoting birth control. He regularly wrote to newspapers that had a "Letters to the Editor" or "Reader's Forum" section. He would advocate use of contraception, and tell of the local services available. When readers would respond, he replied. In this way, news about family planning spread at no cost to him or to Planned Parenthood. Now, I was being asked to do a similar job for voluntary sterilization. It seemed like a natural progression for me.

Mrs. Smith had been active in the Massachusetts Planned Parenthood chapter in the 1940s, moving to New York in 1953 where she managed the family planning service at Mount Sinai Hospital. Two years later, she became the Executive Director of the Human Betterment Association (later to be AVS). She lived in a two-bedroom apartment in the Dakota, the hotel on Central Park West and 72nd Street, where John Lennon and Yoko Ono later joined her as tenants. A few years ago, I learned that she died at the age of 102, having continued to use the buses to travel to City College of New York, teaching a class about the history of the Supreme Court until she was 101. In the words of her son, she "died where she wanted to, when she wanted to, and as she wanted to". That seems appropriate for the daughter of the woman who was one of the founders of the Euthanasia Society of America.

Mrs. Smith's focus had been on individual's choices for health and reproduction. Hugh Moore, unlike Mrs. Smith, was not concerned with women's health or reproductive rights. He was a major contributor and an influential member who was focused on international population control efforts. Moore believed that population growth would lead to more international conflict. He supported legalization of euthanasia and the repeal of abortion laws, all with the goal of limiting population growth. Moore was playing an increasing role in AVS. The more the board of directors followed Moore's persuasive arguments, the more money he contributed to the financially strained budget of the organization. With Hugh Moore came his contacts with more large donors. As his power grew in the organization, Mrs. Smith's declined to the point where she withdrew, saying she wished to devote more of her time and efforts to the repeal of abortion laws.

John Rague, who had been Mrs. Smith's assistant, was promoted to Executive Director of HBAA after her departure in 1963. Rague had become active in the World Federalism movement after serving in the Army in the Second World War. He had been that organization's executive director for New York State for a while. I believe it was through Rague's contacts with his fellow World Federalist friend, Hugh Moore, that he was brought into AVS. I once asked Rague what positions or occupations he had before coming to AVS. He told me that since college, all the jobs he had were as the director of the organization that had hired him. I was quite impressed.

Rague developed a plan to increase public knowledge of voluntary sterilization. Until then, Doctor H. Curtis Wood had been the primary spokesperson. Dr. Wood was a long-time crusader for voluntary sterilization. As an obstetrician in Pennsylvania, he had to deal with the guidelines of the American College of Obstetrics and Gynecology. Most hospitals at that time had rules that would not permit voluntary sterilization for a woman twenty-five years of age unless she had or would have five living children after her present pregnancy. Dr. Wood asked such questions as "What if a woman has only two children and that is all she feels they are able to care for? If she is under twenty-five, must she produce three more unwanted children before she can obtain a sterilization operation?"

Dr. Wood was a strong and vocal advocate for post-partum tubal ligation. In the few hours after delivery, the uterus and tubes are high in the abdomen, at about the level of the navel. At that time, a doctor needs only a small incision to be able to reach the tubes and tie off a small segment, thus preventing future pregnancies. The hospital stay for the woman would not be more than an extra day, if any. In those days before laparoscopy, this was a big advantage. Most of Dr. Wood's messages focused on these facts. He also brought these issues to the attention of medical associations and hospital boards, urging obstetricians to initiate an educational discussion with their pregnant clients early enough in their pregnancies so that the woman would have plenty of time to decide before her delivery date.

Dr. Wood was my role-model for most subjects related to family planning in those days. I looked up to him with great reverence. I thought he was the ideal country family doctor who was really concerned for the families in his care. Over the years, we became good friends and I felt I could discuss any issues or subjects with him. He was very interested in nutrition and had written a book entitled *Overfed but Undernourished*. Facts in the book are still relevant today when we have such a high incidence of obesity and so many people consuming junk food.

Dr. Wood also believed that asparagus had anti-cancer abilities. He recommended four tablespoons of canned asparagus, blended into a pulp with the juice, to be taken daily for prevention of cancer. He claimed that double that dose had cured cancer in patients. I so respected him that after my mother had much of her colon removed because of cancer, I treated her for many years with daily asparagus. I thought it could do no harm and might even help. She remained cancer-free.

Rague would soon expand the public outreach program of the association to increase public awareness of both the organization and the surgical methods of contraception. In 1964, he hired Donald Higgins as the Public Relations Director for the organization. They then brought in Courtland Hastings as a public speaker. In this same year, Hugh Moore was elected President of the Association for Voluntary Sterilization. These four men had been friends and had worked together in the United World Federalist movement. This group had been formed by persons who feared that the United Nations organization, like the League of Nations, might not be successful in preventing wars. They strove to form a world government. They believed that there could not be international peace without such a world government.

I have to admit that at that time, I was not at all aware of the growing concerns about world peace or world government. Nor was I aware of the shift in power on the Board of Directors and the significance of the change in leadership. I was only slightly familiar with population growth. As a volunteer trying to show my appreciation to the organization for its help to me, I was unaware of what was happening in the board room. My interest was limited to family planning for the sake of the individuals in each family.

Hugh Moore was the founder of the Dixie Cup Company, originally manufacturing disposable paper cups to replace the common dipping ladles for fountains or tin cups in public bathrooms. In 1944, Moore founded the Hugh Moore Fund for International Peace. The fund published Moore's pamphlet "The Population Bomb" in 1954, the title of which later was used by Paul Ehrlich for his book. Moore was also chairman of the board of the Population Reference Bureau, vice-president of International Planned Parenthood Federation, and co-founder of the Population Crisis Committee.

Courtland Hastings had no medical background and as a father of a single child, had no personal interest in the cause that I was aware of. I can still picture Court, as we called him, in my mind's eye. He always wore a dark grey or black suit, white shirt and a black bow tie. He was quite somber. I remember thinking that he looked like an undertaker. Hastings was excellent at remembering facts. I never shared a speaking engagement with him so never heard him, but I was told that he could quote population figures and miscellaneous facts, making an impressive speaker. He had three major fields of interest in addition to over-population. He had frequently been a guest on late night radio shows discussing world government, unidentified flying objects, and extra-sensory perception.

Under Rague's leadership, Public Relations Director Don Higgins formalized the letter-writing activities of members. Those of us who were participating were named "The Correspondence Committee". Soon after, trying to publicize AVS, I wrote a letter to a New Jersey newspaper in which I described sterilization as a permanent method of birth control. In it, I also suggested that this surgical method ought to be offered, along with the other methods, to all adults in the Federal Aid to Dependent Children program. Because my name and address were published, I received letters and phone calls from readers.

I learned that there was a great deal of misunderstanding in the minds of the readers. I decided to write another article to clarify facts and clear up any misconceptions. It was published under the banner 'Sterilization Facts'. In the article, I made four points. First, I described the surgical procedure. I reported that over 100,000 Americans every year choose this method and that a Gallup poll had showed that sixty-four percent of the population approved of voluntary sterilization.

Second, I discussed the legal status. At the time, voluntary sterilization was legal in all fifty states, but restricted to cases of medical necessity in Connecticut and Utah. My third point was that voluntary sterilization was not castration, and that it had no harmful side effects and that authorities in the field of psychiatry had stated that voluntary sterilization can contribute to mental health.

The next paragraph reported that both Catholic physician John Rock, developer of the 'Pill', and Dr. Jack Lippes, inventor of the Lippes Loop IUCD, were on the AVS Board of Directors and fully endorsed voluntary sterilization as a permanent method for those sure they wanted no more pregnancies.

Finally, I provided information about AVS' program, including its referral service. I concluded the article by mentioning that the US Department of Health, Education and Welfare (DHEW) and the Department of Defense (DOD) endorsed the method and that thirty-two states had included voluntary sterilization in their Medicaid program. I then strongly urged local hospitals to review their out-dated limiting regulations, and to make voluntary sterilization easily available to those who chose it under professional guidance. I would like to believe that my publicity efforts helped hasten the changes that occurred in hospital policies in my part of the state.

AVS subscribed to a clipping service that screened publications nationwide for articles containing such words as 'sterilization', 'vasectomy', 'tubal ligation'. Along with other AVS records that showed the ongoing changes in this country's history of social welfare, the boxes of clippings that accumulated over the next years were eventually donated to the Social Welfare History Archives at the University of Minnesota.

In an early attempt at national news coverage, AVS made a thirty-three and a third rpm phonograph recording that was sent to radio stations for use in their broadcasting. Its title was "Voluntary Sterilization and the Population Crisis". It featured three to six minute interviews with eight persons. Stations were free to pick and choose any or all of the recordings for airing on their programs. Recorded on one side were Arthur Godfrey; H. Curtis Wood, MD; Betty Gonzales, RN; and Courtland Hastings.

Arthur Godfrey was a popular radio personality. He starred on the CBS network program, *The Arthur Godfrey Show* for twenty-six years. He was an avid aviator and environmentalist. Godfrey edited a book, *The Arthur Godfrey Environmental Reader*. He frequently spoke about his vasectomy. Because his voice was distinctive and he was so fervent about overpopulation, it was felt that his segment of the recording would be aired more frequently than someone lacking such notoriety.

On the other side of the record, there were talks by four other individuals. One was Paul Ehrlich, PhD. He spoke of the issues he had written about in his book, *The Population Bomb*. Also recorded was U.S. Senator Robert Packwood, from Oregon. Two years before Roe v Wade, he had introduced the Senate's first abortion legalization bill. His pro-choice stance earned him the loyalty of many feminist groups.

Mrs. Janet Stein was the third speaker. When she was a twenty-seven year old mother, pregnant with her third child, she had been advised to have a post-partum tubal ligation for medical reasons but the hospital refused to allow it. With the help of the New York Civil Liberties Union, she filed a lawsuit requesting that the hospital provide the medically-indicated procedure. She also requested that the restrictive hospital rules about sterilization be eliminated, and that the hospital pay her $250,000 in damages.[1]

The final recording was by the Rev. Rodney Shaw, a United Methodist clergyman who had devoted twenty years to advocating nuclear arms control. He had become convinced that overpopulation and its related evils were a more immediate threat to mankind. A father of three, Shaw had a vasectomy. He felt that the husband has a moral responsibility for birth control, and that vasectomy would accomplish that most effectively.

In 1964, I was asked to serve on the AVS Board of Directors. I was pleased to be able to participate on this level even though most major decisions were made by the Executive Committee that met more frequently. I learned much about the art of conducting a meeting from Hugh Moore, who had just become President of the organization. I have followed his example in many organizations in subsequent years. Moore made it very clear that he had limited time for any chit-chat. He expected the secretary to have prepared an agenda that would include, in addition to the usual reports, a time slot for itemized unfinished issues. It was then that any pending issues were finalized. Then there was time for new business. He expected everyone to have all the background for these new items in advance. I remember Moore saying once that if a business meeting could not be done in an hour, the planning was poor. I took that to be directed at the secretary whose job it was to organize it all. From that time on, in every organization I was part of, I offered to be the secretary. It seemed that was the real power behind the throne. Moore also said that a good secretary could have the minutes written in draft before the meeting, needing only to fill in the final votes or details afterward. I have indeed done just that.

In 1966, there was a popular radio program recorded in New York City, hosted by Tex McCrary, a pioneer of the 'talk show' genre of broadcasting. Tex wanted to discuss the subject of voluntary sterilization on his radio show but wanted a sterilized woman to add a personal tone to the discussion. He contacted Don Higgins, AVS Public Relations Director. Higgins contacted me, remembering my offer to assist the organization in any way I could. Of course, I agreed.

The response of the public was a surprise to the AVS staff. Where letters following radio or TV presentations were often addressed "Dear Doctor", now letters were pouring in addressed "Dear Betty". It seemed that the public could relate to another person who had walked in their shoes. It did not take Rague long to capitalize on this new finding. He soon added my name to those of Wood's and Hastings' on the AVS Speakers Bureau list. I was described as a nurse who had been sterilized after having six children. Higgins included the biographical sheets in the many nationwide mailings sent out to print and broadcast contacts.

The goal of the public information office was to educate the public. But there was also a need to inform the media and the communications industry that voluntary sterilization was a valid and timely subject, one that was appropriate for public discussion. Some program directors were a bit uncomfortable with medical or surgical subjects. They were unsure how to air a subject with sexual overtones. Only a few years earlier, 'pregnancy' had had to be referred to as 'in the family way'. It was still considered risqué to use words such as 'erection' or 'menstruation' on the air. Non-medical speakers had to be cautious to keep the subject from sounding crass. Neither Dr. Wood nor I had any difficulty with this. As medical professionals, we could comfortably explain that vasectomy would not have any negative effect on a man's ability to have an erection. We could explain that after a tubal ligation, women would continue to have normal menstrual cycles.

I remember one example of a woman client Higgins hoped to use to speak about her experience obtaining her sterilization surgery. During her first program, while on the air, she wanted to tell about why she did not want any more children. She announced that "giving birth is like trying to pass a pumpkin". Needless to say, that person was not used again. AVS could not take a chance on offending the public.

In addition to serving as a speaker, I had begun to take exhibits to medical and social work conventions. I was awarded the title of Nurse Consultant, and I was provided with business cards. I also represented AVS at various meetings of related organizations, including Planned Parenthood Federation of America (PPFA), The American Public Health Association (APHA), and the American Civil Liberties Union (ACLU).

In my presentation to the Board of Directors at their meeting in March, 1971, I reported that from 1966 until 1969, I had totaled forty-two appearances. In 1970, I took part in forty-six programs, and in the first months of 1971, I had already done eighteen more shows. As an example, my 1970 activities included twenty radio shows in nine states, ten TV shows in six states, twelve speeches before live audiences in five states, a presentation to the American Nurses Association Convention in Florida, and a phone interview for a program in Gary, Indiana. Additionally, I wrote and published an article about voluntary sterilization for the *Journal of the American Nurses Association*. The news about the surgical, permanent method was spreading. By the time I joined the staff in June of 1971, I had been the guest on over a hundred programs, helping to make known the benefits and availability of voluntary sterilization.

The early interest of AVSC in eugenic sterilization had faded. Selective sterilization of the "unfit" was increasingly frowned upon. Negative reactions to the compulsory sterilizations that had taken place in Nazi Germany had a large part to play in the shift toward voluntarism. Family planning advocates such as Margaret Sanger[2] and leading gynecologist Robert Latou Dickinson[3] were early proponents of making sex information and birth control available to everyone.

Sex therapists such as Alfred Kinsey[4] and marriage counselors such as Paul Popenoe[5] were beginning to see the benefits of voluntary sterilization. The original thrust of the organization had been to promote the idea of sterilization as a way to reduce the chance that a mentally ill or developmentally disabled person might be burdened with children they could not adequately care for. That focus was giving way to promotion of voluntary sterilization as a birth control option for anyone.

For surgical birth control to become a viable option for anyone, it was critical to correct the rampant misinformation of the time. The public also had to be advised that the method was legal in all fifty states. Only Utah and Connecticut still had laws restricting sterilization to those of 'medical necessity'. AVS and other family planning proponents were trying to remove these laws. The public needed to be informed that sterilization should be available without arbitrary age/parity limits to those adults who chose to end fertility and that AVS would assist them if they were denied service by a hospital. They needed to know that while it was best if a couple made a joint decision for one partner to be sterilized, the law did not require a spouse's consent.

Doctors also needed correct information. Many doctors were still fearful that they might be sued by a spouse or criticized by a medical board if they performed a sterilization without a medical reason. Some feared they would be accused of 'medical mayhem', an old term used to indicate willful and permanent crippling, mutilation, or disfiguring of any part of another's body. Providing correct information was a major goal of AVS.

I had begun to notice changes in the attitudes of the public as I traveled around the country and as I participated in 'call-in' radio programs. The public was becoming more positive about permanent birth control and more knowledgeable about the methods. Questions raised were becoming increasingly more specific. There were questions now about the various surgical techniques, the different ways that surgeons were approaching the tubes, and the chances of reversal. There were special concerns about costs. People asked if insurance plans would cover the expense. They were also beginning to ask if public funding such as Medicaid would cover the costs.

A second change I had noticed was an increased concern with ecological problems that prompted audiences to comment on the role of sterilization in preventing over-population. Although global issues were not my area of expertise, I had to be prepared to answer questions and respond to such comments. Fortunately, I had access to information as a result of interaction with the organization called Zero Population Growth (ZPG).

ZPG had sprung to life in 1968 having been incorporated by Connecticut lawyer and activist, Richard Bowers. Bowers had been attempting to call attention to the population issues for some time. His primary concern was the interrelationships between population density and quality of life. He wrote and distributed many newsletters to that effect. He had received a National Conservation Award from the Nature Conservancy for volunteer efforts as Chairman of the Connecticut chapter of the Nature Conservancy in 1964. In late summer, 1968, his article discussing optimum human population levels was published in the *Defenders of Wildlife News*. Its title was "A Proposal for Local Action Programs".

Paul Ehrlich had recently published his book, *The Population Bomb*. While the contents of this book were shocking to most readers, it was just what Bowers had been trying to say. Bowers, who knew Ehrlich from his time at

Stanford University, suggested forming an organization to address the issues of over-population. The goal would be to form a national association with local chapters to work toward reaching what he had called an optimum population level. Professor Charles Remington, from Yale University's Department of Biology, who knew of Bowers' work in Connecticut, was the third founding member.

When trying to decide the name of the group to be formed, Bowers proposed the words Zero Population Growth, a term that had been coined by Kingsley Davis[6] a year earlier. Demographers understood the concept behind the words, but Ehrlich was afraid that the public would think it meant 'no people'. Bowers met with Rague and Higgins at AVS and they encouraged him to use the title and to use "ZPG" as the acronym. Later, Ehrlich admitted that it was a brilliant choice.

The organization was incorporated by Bowers, and he used the address of his law office in Mystic, Connecticut, as the address of the new group. Ehrlich was the president and primary spokesman; Bowers was executive director, secretary, and editor of the newsletter. Early planning meetings of ZPG were held in the offices of AVS. It was by way of this connection that I became knowledgeable about these ecological issues.

A third change I noticed was in the attitude of the public toward large families. A year or two before, while on a vacation with our children in Montreal, Canada, my husband and I were being patted on the back with a "God bless you!" by total strangers who saw the six children. In 1970, on a number of speaking engagements, the audience actually booed when I was introduced as the mother of six. One of these incidents was on national television when I was being interviewed by David Frost[7]. Although this caused some personal embarrassment and feelings of guilt for having "over-populated", I believed that the change in public attitude was good to see. I believed that the world would not truly be on the way to the stabilization of population growth until large families became socially unacceptable. If demographers were correct in saying population control was necessary for all to benefit, then families themselves had to decide to have fewer children.

*Speaker for Voluntary Sterilization: Betty Gonzales, R.N., Mother of Six*

Notes

1. The Stein lawsuit served as the impetus for AVS to initiate "Operation Lawsuit" with the American Civil Liberties Union and Zero Population Growth. The goal was to help other women obtain sterilizations they had been denied. AVS publicized the activity and investigated claims of denial. ZPG spread the word through their chapters and newsletters. ACLU lawyers handled the legal actions. With the threat of lawsuits, hospitals began to drop their restrictions.

2. Margaret Sanger (1879-1966) was an American birth control activist, sex educator, and nurse. She popularized the term 'birth control', and opened the first birth control clinic in the United States. Like the early founders of AVS, she was a eugenicist. She believed that women wanted their children to be free of poverty and disease and that birth control could limit the number of children and improve their quality of life. She supported sterilization for the mentally ill and the mentally impaired, as did the AVS founders. In 1921, Sanger founded the American Birth Control League, which later became the Planned Parenthood Federation. In 1952, she established the International Planned Parenthood Federation. Sanger is widely recognized as the founder of the modern birth control movement. Seeking a "magic pill", Sanger recruited Gregory Pincus, a human reproduction expert, to develop an oral contraceptive. Working with Dr. John Rock, their research yielded the first contraceptive pill, which was approved by FDA in 1960. Sanger lived to see another important reproductive rights milestone in 1965, when the Supreme Court made birth control legal for married couples in its decision on Griswold v. Connecticut. She died a year later, leaving numerous women's health clinics that carry her name in remembrance of her efforts to advance women's rights and the birth control movement.

3. Robert Latou Dickinson was a native of New Jersey, born in 1861. He was a surgeon, obstetrician, gynecologist, maternal health educator, research scientist and medical illustrator. He was responsible for many advances in obstetrics (advocating tying off the umbilical cord after birth before severing it) and in gynecology (using cautery in an office setting to sterilize a woman). Dickinson was one of the first doctors to obtain detailed sexual histories of his patients, collecting over 5,200 sexual case histories. His work was the inspiration for the later sexologist, Alfred Kinsey.

4. Alfred Kinsey was a noted sexologist who founded the Institute for Research in Sex, Gender, and Reproduction. He is best known writing *Sexual Behavior in the Human Male* and *Sexual Behavior in the Human Female*, better known as the Kinsey Reports.

5. Paul Popenoe was a pioneer in the field of marriage counseling. For many years, he had a column in the popular *Ladies Home Journal* entitled "Can this marriage be saved?" In earlier years, he had been an authority on eugenics. In the mid-1920s, Popenoe began working with E.S. Gosney, a wealthy California financier, and the Human Betterment Foundation to enact California's first compulsory sterilization law that allowed sterilization of the mentally ill and mentally retarded persons.

6. Kingsley Davis was an internationally recognized American sociologist and demographer. He coined the term 'population explosion' and is also credited with first using the term 'zero population growth'. He was known for his expertise in world population growth, global resources, and population policy.

7. Sir David Frost is an English journalist, writer, and media personality, known for his interviews with various political figures. He had a number of television programs in the United States, including *'That Was the Week that Was' (TW3)* and *'The David Frost Show'* (where I was once interviewed). In 1977, he met with former US President Richard Nixon to do a series of interviews for American television.

# CHAPTER 3: VOLUNTEERING

I believe it was in 1963 that I was invited to speak at an AVS meeting about my personal attempts to obtain my sterilization. It was the first time the leaders and donors of the organization had an opportunity to hear from a client. This invitation to tell my story was a result of my having spoken to Mrs. Smith about my willingness to help AVS.

Shortly after this first meeting with the leaders of the organization, I was invited to become a member of the Board. I was quite impressed with the "up-town" manners of the ladies on the Board. For example, in their identification of themselves, they all used their husband's names instead of their own, even when their own maiden names carried clout in the social and financial world. It was Mrs. Philip Bastedo (not Helen Wilmerding Bastedo), Mrs. Robert M. Ferguson (not Frances Hand Ferguson), Mrs. John K. Howat, (not Anne H. Howat), Mrs. Harvey McClintock (not Beatrice Kellogg McClintock), Mrs. James P. Mills (not Alice DuPont Mills) and Mrs. Lloyd Morain (not Mary Stone Dewing Morain).

The exception to this pattern was in the names of those who served on the Medical and Health or the Legal and Social Scientific committees of the Board. There the women used their own names. Included were luminaries in their fields, including Mabel S. Ingalls, PhD, a bacteriologist serving as the liaison officer between the World Health Organization and the United Nations; Beryl J. Roberts, DPH, a consultant to the World Health Organization and to the Population council of New York; Anna L. Southam, MD, who worked under the auspices of the Ford Foundation's Population Office, conducting research and lecturing on population control; and Emily Mudd, PhD, founder and Director of the Marriage Council of Philadelphia, consulting editor of the Kinsey Report on the Human Female, and President of the American Association of Marriage Counselors. Even though I had no opportunity to interact on a personal level, I was proud to be affiliated with these notable women.

There were two other professional women that I had many opportunities to work with over the next years as my activities with AVS expanded. One was Dr. Helen Edey, a philanthropist and psychiatrist active in the field of women's reproductive rights. After having four children, Edey graduated with a medical degree from New York University.

27

She practiced psychiatry and psychoanalysis in Manhattan. She supported organizations trying to control population growth, solve environmental problems, and control nuclear arms. Dr. Edey was a long-time member of the AVS Executive Committee, serving as Chair and as long-time Treasurer. When AVS opened the first vasectomy clinic in 1969, Dr. Edey screened all the potential clients.

The other professional that I enjoyed working with and held in admiration was Harriet F. Pilpel, LLB. During her career, Pilpel played a role in twenty-seven cases that were heard by the Supreme Court of the United States. Pilpel was involved in the birth control and the pro-rights movements, helping to establish the legal rights of minors to abortion and contraception. She handled Planned Parenthood's *amicus* brief for *Roe v. Wade*. Pilpel served on the boards of the Guttmacher Institute, the ACLU, NARAL and the National Coalition against Censorship. She served as legal council to AVS and was the person behind any legal matters AVS encountered. I am very pleased to have had many opportunities to work closely with Harriet Pilpel.

My name appeared on the published documents and AVS Board of Director's lists as Mrs. Betty Gonzales, RN, apparently a combination of the two groups mentioned above. I did not think about how the names appeared until I was seated next to Mrs. Howat at an annual meeting that I attended in the early 60s. During our casual conversation, I had given her my business card. She wondered if it might be socially acceptable for her to have a card printed with her name on it instead of her usually printed Mrs. John K. Howat. I believe it was twenty-five years or more before her name appeared as Anne H. Howat.

I do not mean to imply that the leadership of AVS was only female. There were many notable men that I was very pleased to meet also. For example, as a Public Health Nurse, I had certainly heard of Homer Calver, Executive Secretary of the American Public Health Association. Now I was a fellow Board member with him for AVS. I particularly appreciated getting to know and work with Joseph Fletcher, STD, and originator of the concept of situational ethics, which I fully endorsed as the model for my own life. Later, when I was on staff, I had the pleasure of lunching with him each time he visited AVS, giving me time to interact with him personally. I also enjoyed meeting Algernon D. Black, the leader of the New York Society for Ethical Culture, who once invited me to speak to his congregation about voluntary sterilization.

There were two men I had the pleasure of meeting even though I did not have much personal contact with them. One was Rabbi Balfour Brickner, the first rabbi I had the pleasure of meeting. He was a leading rabbi in the Reform Judaism movement, a political activist, and involved in the civil rights struggle. He served on the boards of the National

Association for Repeal of Abortion Laws (NARAL), Planned Parenthood, and AVS, supporting reproductive rights.

When I was a young girl living with my Dutch conservative Calvinist grandparents, they would listen to radio broadcasts featuring the Reverend Harry Emerson Fosdick. Little did I think I would get to meet the noted minister, but I did, and enjoyed being able to put a face on the voice I had remembered. Fosdick served on the AVS Clergymen's Committee. An interesting note is that the committee consisted of ten men. There were no women clergy at that time.

It was after an annual conference in 1963 that I thought I was being gracious and helpful when I offered to drive some of the ladies to their homes after the program was over. My mother and I had driven into the city from New Jersey in the family van that seated at least eight passengers. I thought I was doing the ladies a favor by offering to get my vehicle from the near-by garage to take them home. After all, I thought, it would be nice for them to ride with me to their door, rather than to have to take a bus or an expensive taxi. How naive I must have seemed. Some of the women politely declined but three of the ladies graciously accepted and I delivered them to their addresses on Fifth and Park Avenues. I later wondered how they felt, climbing out of a van. What did their doormen think they were doing?

In addition to my participation on the Board and my speaking engagements, there was one special task I was asked to do for AVS. It was to review the referral system then used to assist men and women who were seeking sterilization. Old records show that a Miss Poletti had been the full time social worker on staff, assisted by Mrs. Gilmore, a part-time social worker. I have no recollection of these individuals and am not sure if either was still at AVS when the Executive Directorship changed from Mrs. Smith to John Rague, but whoever had been doing the referral work had left the job, and there was no staff member who knew the system being used for referrals. John Rague and the Public Relations Director, Donald Higgins, decided to turn to me for help. Because I had been a client in 1962, I knew the steps I had gone through and believed I could be of assistance to them.

My first step was to look up my own records. I had kept copies of all correspondence to and from AVS during my application process, and there were additional notes in the office files. This enabled me to envision the steps usually taken and to develop guidelines to be followed. All requests for referral were answered with a letter and an application form. The form inquired about medical and obstetrical history as well as miscellaneous details about their situation such as the number of both live and deceased children, age, income and religion. There was also a space for the applicant to explain in his or her own words why sterilization was being requested. The vast majority of applications were from women, and they all had children. Many had also had abortions, which were illegal at the time. Sometimes these were recorded as 'miscarriages'.

The next step was for the completed application form to be copied and sent to a panel of three gynecologists for female applicants. Applications from men were sent to urologists or surgeons who performed vasectomy using local anesthesia outside of a hospital setting. These doctors did not meet; they each responded directly to the AVS staff person. If the three determined that permanent sterilization was suitable for the individual, the applicant was referred to a doctor on AVS's list of doctors who had indicated that they would accept referrals from us. All attempts were made to find a doctor near the area where the client lived.

In a few days, I had systemized the social work office procedures and written a procedure book that was used to guide the next staff person to be hired for the position. The director believed it would be appropriate to hire an experienced social worker to handle the client counseling and referral service. Mrs. Evelyn Bryant was employed in 1965.

Even though I had been called in to clarify the steps to be followed, and not called upon to make any changes, I did make a suggestion that was implemented. I thought that as the requests were increasing, and there was no funding available for poor clients, we ought to seek help for the neediest ones. I did this by drafting a letter to go to all the doctors on our list, asking if they would be willing to do some procedures at no cost to the client. The letter asked how many such unpaid operations they would do. The response was favorable, and the answers were varied, such as "I will do one a month." or "I will do one vasectomy each week." or "I will do three tubal ligations a year." In response to this request, 135 doctors in thirty-two states pledged 2,100 voluntary sterilizations at no cost to the needy clients we referred.

This list of "cooperating" surgeons had developed over a period of years. I am sure that Dr. Wood regularly asked for names of willing doctors as he met with medical groups all over the country. I know that over the years, as I was taking AVS exhibits to medical groups, I always had a pad to take names and addresses of surgeons who would accept referrals or who would contribute a free operation if we had a financially needy client in his or her area.

As the public was becoming so much more aware of sterilization, it seemed that the three-doctor panel was a step that would no longer be needed. I believe that this was a significant step in moving from the concept of "physician-approved" or a "doctor-recommended" operation to a woman's free choice issue. With a skilled social worker now on staff, she was able to watch for information in the applications that might indicate that the client had not thought through the decision, and needed counseling or further information before being referred. A large number of application forms or letters of request were followed by personal phone calls from the staff social worker who was well suited to counsel clients.

I clearly remember the day Mrs. Bryant got the first request from a couple who did not want any children, and the wife wanted to have her tubes tied. After an extended phone conversation, it appeared that the client and her partner were making a well-thought out request. At that time, there was only one doctor who was willing to do the surgery: A. Jefferson Penfield,[1] an obstetrician/gynecologist, in Syracuse, NY. The client was sufficiently motivated to make the trip. Penfield was a firm believer that arbitrary rules were not appropriate for sterilization candidates. He was willing to consider a single, young or childless adult woman who was requesting a sterilization, and if he was convinced that her decision was well-thought-out, he would do the surgery for her.

In the summer of 1972, the Planned Parenthood Center of Syracuse, under Penfield's medical directorship, initiated an outpatient sterilization program for women. By March of 1976, laparoscopic sterilization under local anesthesia had been performed on 1,200 in that outpatient setting. His analysis of the first two hundred patients provided the impetus for many other outpatient centers to begin such services.

Women whose husbands could not or would not give consent for a sterilization operation posed a challenge for the referral program of AVS. Many hospitals were still requiring any female surgery on the reproductive system to have the husband's approval. While women were beginning to be recognized as individuals rather than chattel, it seems their reproductive organs were the last to be set free from male dominance.

Some doctors feared a possible lawsuit from the spouse should they do the surgery on the wife. In most of these cases, as I recall Mrs. Bryant's reporting, the husband was often a missing person. Women would report that they had no idea where the husband was, or that he had not supported the children already born to them. Gradually, doctors on the AVS referral list were willing to take on these more difficult cases and consider their merits on an individual basis.

Perhaps there is a relationship to be noted here: when the day would come that women could use their own name on their calling cards, perhaps they could also control their own reproductive organs. Until then, they were under the control of their husbands.

Many books and articles published about surgical contraception have included the subject of involuntary sterilization or coercion. While I had known of AVS's early interest in eugenics, in all the years I was affiliated with the organization (from 1962 until 1993) there was never any staff person who had ever endorsed the concept of trying to talk someone into a sterilization operation. All efforts were made to be sure that the client had full knowledge of the permanent nature of the operation, and to be sure that the request was not a hasty one, but one that had been carefully considered. A regular part of counseling a prospective sterilization applicant would include asking such questions as, "How do you think you would feel about this permanent decision of you were to lose a child?" or "What would you do if you remarried?" These kinds of probing questions uncovered any possible doubts or hesitation on the part of the client, and would indicate that perhaps the client needed to think through the options further before being referred for surgery.

Certainly, in those early years of AVS's referral program when the staff had direct contact with clients, the availability of sterilization was limited. A woman had to be really motivated to be able to find a doctor or a hospital that would permit the elective operation. Many hospitals were still limiting tubal ligations to women who had medical reasons that made another pregnancy a danger to her health. Others followed the recommendation of the American College of Obstetricians and Gynecologists (ACOG), commonly called the "120 rule".

This arbitrary guideline suggested that doctors multiply the mother's age by the number of children she had. If the resulting number exceeded 120, ACOG thought most hospital review committees would consider her appropriate for sterilization. If the number was under 120, ACOG expected she would be denied. Thus, a thirty-year old woman with four children would theoretically be approved. A woman of thirty-seven with three children would be denied because 3x37=111. Theoretically, a woman who wanted to stop after only two children would have to be sixty years of age, long past the age of menopause.

Shortly after I had my sterilization, I was contacted by a frantic family who had heard that I had had my tubes tied. The woman's husband had come home from work and found his wife (the mother of seven young children) with all the gas jets of the stove and oven turned on, and his wife's unconscious head lying on the oven door. She had attempted to get her tubes tied at a local hospital that had a screening committee, but she had been refused as a patient for sterilization. She felt that suicide was her only option. When she was revived and the family assessed the situation, she called me, desperate for information about how I had obtained the surgery. I was able to tell the family about AVS and their referral service. She was subsequently sterilized and I still get an occasional note or call from her, thanking me for helping her at such a desperate time of her life.

Pronatalism was surely a factor in these restrictive policies. In spite of the strides made in the women's movements of the 50s and 60s, most still saw women primarily as wives and mothers. Some hospitals did not want to provide tubal ligation for fear of offending their Roman Catholic obstetricians and gynecologists. The hospital where I had obtained my nursing degree, and where my doctor was affiliated, simply limited tubal ligation for serious medical reasons. But as obstetrical care was improving, more and more women with medical complications were surviving pregnancy. As my doctor had told me, my repeated bouts with phlebitis put me at considerable risk, but each delivery was proof that medical skill and knowledge could get me through another one – even if I might have to spend the nine months in a bed.

Men seeking vasectomy were not subjected to these rules and regulations. Vasectomy was a simple procedure, done under local anesthesia, usually in an office setting, rather than a hospital. It was primarily a task of finding a doctor who was willing. There would be no committee approval that would be required as there were for women in so many hospitals. While women were usually expected to be able to produce their husband's consent to her sterilization, it was a rare occasion when a urologist would demand the wife's consent for her husband's vasectomy.

In the decade of the 60s, sexuality was being more openly discussed in public, and there was no secret about a man being interested in enjoying a sex life while unmarried. For those who wanted to be sure they did not ever become an unwilling father, vasectomy was the permanent solution to their problem. A slogan sometimes heard or read in the magazines was "Vasectomy means never having to say you're sorry".

The first single vasectomized man I knew was Stephen Keese, who worked as a vasectomy counselor at the Boston Family Planning Clinic in Massachusetts. Even before he decided to have a vasectomy himself, Steve had approved a young unmarried man who came to his clinic for a vasectomy. The man was a rock musician who was headed out on a tour, expecting to have sex with lots of fans. He did not want then or ever to have children and had thought a lot about it. For him a vasectomy was the responsible thing to do. After much discussion, and in spite of a near rebellion by the older women at the clinic, Steve agreed with him and was able to provide the vasectomy.

After Steve's vasectomy, he joined the Speakers Bureau at AVS and helped spread the news to other men. He served for a while on the Board of Directors and later on the staff, always a strong voice for male participation in control of unwanted fertility.

By 1967, many changes were taking place. The Department of Defense decided to permit sterilization as a family planning service and was allowing it to be performed in military facilities. Medicaid was covering voluntary sterilization in most of the states that had begun the assistance program. Blue Cross and Blue Shield Insurance Plans were paying for voluntary sterilization in most states. There was still a lot to do to educate the public. There was insufficient knowledge as well as a lot of misinformation about the permanent method of birth control. AVS looked for opportunities to increase awareness and spread correct facts about voluntary sterilization whenever possible.

In 1968, a week in October had been declared "Health Week" by the city of New York. Rague and Higgins conceived of the idea of placing an informational booth on Fifth Avenue in Manhattan. It was to be an exhibit booth declaring "This is Health Week". Under that, a banner stated "Family and Community Health Includes Effective Voluntary Sterilization". Below that was a streamer reading "Association for Voluntary Sterilization". Information about AVS and about the availability and legality of voluntary sterilization followed. A staff member and I were in attendance to distribute pamphlets and answer questions.

The exhibit took place on October 23rd. It was admittedly provocative with regard to its location, directly across the street from St. Patrick's Cathedral. It certainly had an element of gimmickry, but it was an example of AVS efforts to reach and inform the general public. Sometimes it took attention-getting action to get publicity. Publicity increased public awareness, so the end justified the means.

During the day of this exhibit, a photographer from the Associated Press came, collected some literature, and took a photograph. The photo was sent, along with a feature story on voluntary sterilization to two thousand newspapers across the land. The article and photo was released the week of November 10. The Encyclopedia Britannica press release and used it in an extensive section on population in their annual *Year Book of 1968*. Their article included the photo of my colleague and me in front of the booth.

On that busy street corner I spent the day giving out literature and answering questions. The reactions of the passers-by varied. Some people were very interested in getting more details and a referral to a doctor. Others were not so supportive. I will always remember one man. He was not happy with the subject of the exhibit, apparently. While waiting to cross the street, he loudly asked me "Have you been sterilized?" I tried to ignore this personal question but he persisted, even more loudly, "Have you been sterilized?" I felt I had to answer. I certainly had been talking about my personal experience freely for many years, so I was not really shy. I was just a bit taken aback by his angry approach. I answered, "Yes, I have". He replied, "Good! Your mother should have been!" I could not help but admire his quick mind. This story has been told many times over the years, and I still chuckle at the adventures that day, trying to promote permanent birth control in the face of the Roman Catholic Cathedral.

Speaking engagements, as well as radio and television broadcasts continued to keep me traveling and meeting the public. I never kept an accurate list, but thanks to what notes I do have, I can list some of the programs. Many were call-in programs and some were quite lengthy, allowing many aspects of the subject of voluntary sterilization to be covered on air. Sample names of the shows were: *The New Yorkers, Girl Talk, Hot Line, Sound Off, Roundtable, Frankly Speaking, In Touch, Perspectives,* and *Talk of the Town.* I was a guest on an early talk show headed by Barbara Walters; it was called *Not for Women Only.*

Other programs were better known by the name of the interviewers. For example, Casper Citron, Barry Farber, David Frost, Phil Donahue, and Walter Cronkite. There were also many of the magazine format programs across the country. For example, titles like Good Morning, Chicago, or Good Day, New York.

Interview programs were not a challenge for me. Prior to the date of broadcast, the interviewer had time to read AVS material. The questions were likely to have been developed from information I was very familiar with. Some interviewers felt they had to invite a person with an opposing view, so on occasion I would be sharing the questions with someone who did not approve of sterilization. Call-in programs were more challenging. We never knew what was coming. I had to be at ease with any related topic, and prepared for comments that might be accusatory, disapproving, or off on a tangent.

Surprisingly to me, I was more comfortable with TV than radio. Having to sit in a still position in front of a microphone was more strenuous than the comfortable TV format where a small mike was attached to my shirt or hung overhead. For my first TV show, I wore a black and white narrow striped dress that was a disaster. The contrast of the colors gave the appearance of vibrating waves! From then on, I stayed with simple patterns and plain, clear colors.

Speaking at public meetings continued for me during these years. There were engagements at a number of nursing schools, colleges, universities, churches and ethical culture societies. As a freshman in high school, I had taken one semester of public speaking, but I never thought I would do any. As time went on, I became quite comfortable, primarily because I was so at ease with the subject. There was not an issue that could throw me off guard. I had dealt with all kinds of unexpected subjects being raised on the talk shows.

One night, I was to participate in a lengthy radio program. The plan had been for me to be interviewed briefly first, and then the host would open the program to calls. The program began with the host introducing me and immediately asking me to tell the listeners about voluntary sterilization. I thanked him for inviting me and started to speak. He handed me a note that said "coffee break" and he left the room. I was alone, speaking for twenty minutes before he strolled back and took part. During that time, I could see him through a glass window, relaxing with his coffee and probably wondering how long I could go before he felt he should return. I was still talking comfortably when he got back to the microphone.

I will always remember one pleasurable trip to South Dakota. I had been invited to address a group at the State University at Brookings. Accommodations had been arranged at nearby cabins, where I rented one for about eight dollars a night. That evening, as I went into the office cabin to get some ice for a cold glass of water, there were a few truckers sitting outside. I was invited to pull up a chair and join them in "slappin' skeeters".

For the next hours, I listened to them telling stories about local customs followed in different parts of the country where these fellow travelers had lived or worked. Mostly, I learned about various wedding customs. I learned that in one area, it was customary for the bridegroom to give his new wife a ride in a wheelbarrow down the main street of town. In other rural areas, the return of the bride and groom after the honeymoon to their new home was a cause for local fun. When the lights went out, all the neighbors would encircle the home with pots, pans, whistles, or other noise-makers. They would make a racket until the newlyweds opened the doors and let everyone in for a treat of cookies or cake. This was a totally pleasant exposure to customs I knew nothing about and always will remember fondly. Little experiences like this made up for the inconveniences and loneliness of traveling by myself.

The public information program was progressing under the direction of Donald Higgins, and the service program was growing under the direction of the social worker, Evelyn Bryant. Early plans were developing to reach professional groups at their annual conventions. My notes indicate that the first AVS exhibit was shown at the National Conference of Social Workers in 1963. The exhibit probably focused on the AVS referral services and offered fact sheets about male and females sterilization that could be distributed to social workers and used by their clients.

In 1964, AVS exhibited at the 92nd Annual Meeting of the American Public Health Association in New York City. The display featured a two-panel sign indicating basic facts about voluntary sterilization. Free literature was offered, including a *"Digest of United States Sterilization Statutes"* prepared by the association's legal counsel. This mixed message reflects the confusion about how AVS saw itself. The older "Human Betterment" board members were still interested in improving human life through many venues: abortion, euthanasia and sterilization of the mentally "unfit" and the poor. The newer board members wanted to focus on voluntary sterilization. It was a period of self-evaluation for AVS.

In 1965, AVS had tried very hard to get an exhibit into the American Medical Association (AMA) convention. The display panels that had been used at APHA were to be used again, but the title banner was "The Physician and Voluntary Sterilization". Free literature included the above-mentioned *"Digest"*, but also such articles as *"The Place of Sterilization"* by a gynecologist; *"The Legal and Medical Aspects of Vasectomy"* by a lawyer and a doctor; "*Voluntary Sterilization as it Relates to Mental Health*" by Robert W. Laidlaw, MD (a psychiatrist) and Medora Bass, MA (a specialist in mental retardation); "*Legal Status of Therapeutic Abortion and Sterilization* in the U.S." by a lawyer; and "*Sterilization of the Incompetent – Opinion of Herman M. Moser*", Judge of the Supreme Bench of Baltimore, Maryland.

The AMA secretary requested copies of the digest of statutes and the opinion of the judge about sterilization of incompetent persons. Sometime after, AVS (then still called HBAVS) received a letter stating that the Scientific Exhibit Committee of the Council on Postgraduate Programs of the AMA, with the input of special consultants, had "carefully evaluated" the application and regretted, however, that it was impossible to take advantage of the organization's contribution. I believe AMA did not want to associate itself with sterilization of incompetent persons.

That same year, however, the American Urological Association did accept an AVS exhibit at their annual meeting. AVS offered brochures about voluntary sterilization that doctors could use for reading material in their waiting rooms, or could be given to patients who were interested in a permanent method of birth control. Patients were then able to take the informative material home to discuss it with their family or friends. Another goal was to use this opportunity to meet with doctors to add more names to the referral list.

Acceptance of AVS material at professional meetings gradually increased. I believe that dropping the distribution of pamphlets about sterilization laws for incompetent people was a significant factor. State and regional meetings first accepted, followed soon after by national meetings. In 1967, we finally were permitted to exhibit at the American Medical Association. In 1968, AVS had exhibits at the urologist's and osteopathic doctor's conventions.

I remember that the first professional exhibit I handled for AVS was at the Washington, D.C. Nurses Association Conference in 1968. It was a good opportunity to exchange stories with other nurses about what they were observing about the changes in the practice of gynecologists regarding voluntary sterilization. It also gave me an opportunity to familiarize nurses with vasectomy.

While in medical school, doctors learned how to do a vasectomy in conjunction with a prostatectomy, using general anesthesia. Similarly, hospital-based nurses were also limited. Vasectomy had not yet become a recognized method of voluntary birth control, so medical personnel had little knowledge of the procedure or the ability to perform it using a local anesthetic. The AVS exhibit began to change that level of knowledge.

In 1969, we were at the American Nurses Association conference. We were again at the AMA, but this time, it was really a scientific exhibit, not just a promotion of literature. We presented an exhibit demonstrating the disappearance of sperm from the ejaculate after vasectomy. It provided guides for instructing post vasectomy men how long they had to use contraception until their post-surgical semen was clear of sperm. The exhibit was based on studies done by Doctors Mathew Freund, a physiologist, and Joseph Davis, a urologist, both affiliated with the New York Medical College. Freund and Davis collaborated on other issues, also. They studied frozen sperm and were proponents of sperm banking to offer fertility to men that would undergo vasectomy.

The presence of AVS at professional meetings had another important benefit. The organization was becoming known as a clearing house for all information regarding voluntary sterilization. More and more, AVS was gaining professional recognition.

Notes

1. On a personal note, I will add that "Jeff" Penfield was such a calm and gentle physician that when his wife decided she wanted to end her child-bearing capacity, she would not consider anyone but her husband to do the surgery. He did it, calmly and without incident, in his office. I met Jeff soon after I joined the AVS staff at the time he was going to begin his office surgery. Together we established procedures to be followed in outpatient centers, including emergency equipment and skills that should be in place, such as a ventilator and access to an emergency vehicle. Jeff and his wife, Kathy remained my friends until he died in 2011. Incidentally, Jeff's father was Wilder Penfield, MD, an internationally respected neurosurgeon who worked at the Neurological Institute of New York. There he carried out the first operations on the human brain to control epilepsy, destroying nerve cells in the brain where the seizures originated. I salute them both as medical pioneers, both groundbreaking researchers and highly original surgeons.

*1966 Family Photo.*

# CHAPTER 4: POLICY CHANGES

The legislative record of the 89th Congress was outstanding in the matters pertaining to health. It served from January 3, 1965 until January 3, 1967, during the third and fourth years of Lyndon Johnson's presidency. Amendments to the Social Security Act were passed on July 30, 1965, including Title XVIII (Medicare) affecting individuals over the age of sixty-five, and Title XIX (Medicaid) affecting medically needy families.

The first group to benefit from these changes was the senior citizens, those persons whose age already made them eligible for Social Security benefits. A Senate Subcommittee had been studying aging and health issues of the elderly. They released a report that stated that private health insurance was unable to provide the large majority of Americans with adequate hospital services at reasonable cost. Representative Wilbur Mills introduced a bill entitled "Social Security Amendments of 1965". This was the birth of Medicare.

The Office of Economic Opportunity (OEO) had been formed in 1964 as part of President Johnson's War on Poverty to assist families who were not covered by any health insurance and who were in need of financial assistance. This Office had wanted to fund family planning programs for married women with children. Funds were intended to be used to cover the one-time cost of getting a permanent method of birth control: vasectomy or tubal ligation. But, in 1965, under the leadership of R. Sargent Shriver, Jr., OEO prohibited funding for voluntary sterilization in their family planning programs in the United States. The response of AVS was to pledge to "hammer away" at the ban until the "court of public opinion demanded an end to the usurpation of the right of the people to free choice".

Medicaid was a health insurance program established primarily for low-income persons, regardless of age. The program was jointly funded by the federal government and by the states. To participate in the plan, states were required to offer Medicaid to all persons on public assistance. Family planning was among the services that were covered by the plan.

By 1966, Medicaid coverage was expanded to include Native Americans.

OEO allowed Indian tribes to receive direct funding, much of which went into community action programs that focused on education. Health clinics were also funded. Also in that year, the Department of Defense decided to permit sterilization as a family planning service and stated that it was permissible to perform the surgery in military facilities for service men and women. Yet, OEO continued its ban against public funding of voluntary sterilization.

The American Civil Liberties Union (ACLU) protested the funding ban, claiming that it was discriminating against the poverty group. That year, Congressman Gerald Ford and Senator Everett Dirksen supported AVS in urging a bipartisan investigation of OEO's ban. Unfortunately, it was not until 1971 that the OEO lifted its ban and permitted funds to be used for voluntary sterilization.

The National Medical Association (NMA), the oldest national organization representing African American physicians in this country, had always been committed to improving the quality of health services among minorities, disadvantaged people, and medically underserved populations. Writing about the start of Medicaid in the January, 1967 issue of the *Journal of the National Medical Association*, its President John L.S. Holloman, Jr. discussed the significance of this program in the President's Column of the journal.

Holloman wrote, *"The end of the so-called 'free clinic', as we have previously known it, is clearly in sight. It is now possible for a medically indigent patient still to be treated with courtesy and afforded human dignity. This is the visionary promise of Title XIX as yet unfulfilled. No longer must a person who happens to be poor, and too frequently a black man, be reduced to the level of an 'interesting case', or 'clinical material'. No longer must he become an uninformed clinical volunteer to the unsympathetic, dispassionate clinical researcher, interested primarily in clinical statistics with frank distain for the human dignity of the poor. No longer must a man suffer as the 'placebo' treated control, while his disease progresses even to fatality in the interest of academic medicine and science. No longer must a man suffer as an involuntary experimental control as various doses of new therapeutic agents are tried."* He concluded, *"There is an important human rights factor in Title XIX which makes it meaningful, and promises to extend the democratic process to the health care which is afforded the poor. It may help the medical profession to serve truly the society which it is licensed to serve."*

I felt that it was an honor to be able to work with Dr. Holloman. One such opportunity had been in 1966 when AVS held a National Conference on Voluntary Sterilization and Human Rights. Dr. Holloman served as moderator of a panel discussion and he invited me to be a panel member. Others who served on the panel were Fay Bennett, executive secretary of the National Sharecroppers Fund; Mrs. Sophia Yarnall, treasurer of the American Civil Liberties Union; Harriet F. Pilpel, LLB, AVS legal counsel, and Stephen J. Plank, MD, Assistant Professor of Population Studies at Harvard University School of Public Health.

The Foreign Assistance Act of 1967 provided $35 million for voluntary birth control programs abroad. Congressman Zablocki, a staunch Roman Catholic, added an amendment banning voluntary sterilization under that Act. The next year, 1968, that amendment was repealed, thus allowing voluntary sterilization among the birth control methods provided with foreign assistance funding. This fueled the interest AVS had in working toward the eventual development of an overseas program.

Back in the spring of 1964, I had attended the First International Conference on Voluntary Sterilization organized by AVS and held in New York City. The purpose of that meeting was to explore prospects for a world movement to promote voluntary sterilization. Participants concluded that there was a need in many developing countries for information about sterilization – both about the surgical techniques and about the means to publically promote and publicize the benefits of voluntary sterilization. The perception was that organizations could follow the example of the work done in the United States. The International Planned Parenthood Federation, at their meeting in Singapore the year before, had made it clear that they would not include sterilization in their programs, so it seemed that AVS was destined to take the lead. The Conference participants concluded that it would be premature to establish an International Association for Voluntary Sterilization at that time but that establishing an International Fund would be an appropriate first step.

When, three years later, foreign assistance funding seemed probable, Doctor Sripati Chandrasekhar, Minister of Health and Family Planning of India, accepted the chairmanship of the new International Association for Voluntary Sterilization. Other active officers, in addition to AVS President Hugh Moore, included AVS members Brock Chisholm, former director of the World Health Organization; Homer Calver, Public Health and Welfare Committee; and John C. Cutler, director of the Population Division and Professor of International Health at the University of Pittsburgh. Details of development of the global outreach programs of AVS, and the formation of the World Federations of Associations for Voluntary Sterilization are carefully and fully detailed in the excellent book by Ian Dowbiggin, *The Sterilization Movement and Global Fertility in the Twentieth Century*. (Chapter 7, Oxford University Press, 2008)

As a volunteer speaker for AVS, I was not involved in these actions, so I take no credit. Nor am I an expert about what was happening behind the scenes that made these social welfare changes. Donald Higgins kept the volunteer speakers well informed of all AVS activities and policy shifts so that we were always prepared to speak publically and knowledgably as representatives of the organization. I remember getting the happy news from AVS every time another positive change had occurred that would expand choice for individuals and groups of persons.

While voluntary sterilization was gaining popularity, findings about the contraceptive pill were causing concern by the users and some medical investigators. In the first ten years of marketing the Pill, from 1960 to 1970, its use had escalated so that an estimated eight to nine million U.S. women were using it. Concerns had arisen, however, about the side effects of the hormones utilized in the medication. Among those most commonly encountered by women were weight gain, breast tenderness, and a change in sex drive, whether increased or decreased. Of far greater seriousness was the formation of blood clots in the leg veins (thrombophlebitis). A feminist author, Barbara Seaman, was responsible for calling the public's attention to the side effects of the method. In her book, *The Doctor's Case against the Pill*, she described a long list of problems that Pill users were reporting, including blood clots, stroke, migraine headaches, diabetes, liver ailments, breast cancer, and rheumatoid arthritis. As a result of this publicity, congressional hearings were held in Washington, D.C. in January, 1970. A Senate committee was formed under the leadership of Wisconsin Senator Gaylord Nelson. His concern was that women should be informed about all aspects of the use of the Pill so that they would be able to make an informed, personal decision about its use.

The most significant finding to emerge from these congressional hearings was that doctors were prescribing the hormonal contraceptives, refillable indefinitely, without careful, periodic evaluation of the patient. Not enough attention was paid to careful evaluation of the client's medical histories that may have included contra-indications to the use of the Pill. The Food and Drug Agency decided to develop an informational leaflet that would go directly to the women purchasing the Pills, thus making them independent of their doctors. The American Medical Association (AMA) was not happy with this. They considered the informational leaflet to be interfering with the doctor-patient relationship. The drug producers were not happy with the warnings either. As a compromise, a watered-down leaflet was printed.

This attempt at client education about medications coincided with general changes in the medical profession that were happening at this time. Once, the doctor had been the person who knew it all, who told the patient what to do. This included "choices" about non-emergency medical options, such as contraception methods and voluntary sterilization. Clients, now armed with information they had gathered themselves, would go to their medical providers seeking the treatment or procedure they had already decided upon. It was a difficult time for some doctors who did not want to give up their position of authority, or as the one in charge.

Meanwhile, researchers developed safer versions of the Pill, using reduced doses of the hormones to reduce the risks. The original high-dose contraceptives were pulled from the European market in the early 1970s but they continued to be available in the U.S. until 1988. How relieved I was to know that I had been able to avoid all the risks associated with the Pill by having my tubes tied back in 1961. Because of my frequent episodes of phlebitis with every pregnancy, I would have been at a very high risk for serious blood clot complications, including stroke.

Finally, the American College of Obstetricians and Gynecologists dropped their "120" rule, evidenced by the fact that the 1969 edition of their manual, neither a mother's age nor the number of her pregnancies was mentioned. It was now a personal choice to be decided by an informed client with her physician.

The National Welfare Rights Organization (NWRO) had been started in 1967. Their early concerns were about women being forced or pressured into sterilization. Most members of the group were receiving welfare for the support of their children. The majority were women of color. They worried that welfare recipients would be forced to stop bearing children because their children would need further public funding.

NWRO concerns were not unreasonable. Five states were considering bills designed to have certain recipients of welfare submit to sterilization. Indiana wanted its sterilization law extended to cover women on welfare who had born an illegitimate child. Illinois offered incentives and New Hampshire was adding an incentive to its law. Ohio and Tennessee would make sterilization a prerequisite for state aid for women with two or more illegitimate children.

Shortly after its founding, I met Ms. Johnnie Tillman. Under her leadership, the NWRO expanded their goals. In addition to their efforts to stand up to any pressure that might be placed upon welfare recipients, they now saw the need to insist on women's rights to control the number of children they had. They began to advocate for every woman's right to control her own reproduction, including the right to choose sterilization when she was ready to stop having children.

I am proud that I was able to relate so well to this organization. I think they knew me as a woman who shared their personal beliefs. This excellent working relationship and mutual trust enabled AVS to work with NWRO in 1973 when the Relf sisters, two teen-aged, reportedly mentally or developmentally-challenged girls in Alabama were sterilized. Under the directorship of Charles Faneuff, AVS was able to issue a joint statement with NWRO against forced sterilization. In it, we decried involuntary sterilization as an assault on human dignity and a violation of human rights to which everyone is entitled. (I suspect there were more than just a few of the old AVS members and contributors that squirmed in their chairs at this turn of events.)

This action on the part of AVS marked its public shift from the early eugenic policies of the organization. There had been attempts to pass laws that would allow sterilizations to control physical, mental and social disease. As AVS went through name changes over the course of those formative years, so too did the focus of the Board of Directors gradually shift from selective sterilization to voluntary sterilization. Upon reflection, however, I am left feeling that among AVS leadership, as well as at USAID, there remains the belief that "some people" really should not be having babies.

I was not involved with that larger picture or with any grand aims to see sterilization as a benefit to "society" or to the world. My interest in voluntary sterilization was limited to ensuring the rights of the individual to control one's own body and reproductive system. My Speakers Bureau engagements and presentations on radio and television reflected my convictions. I had a responsibility to keep informed about policy changes that would curtail an individual's access to service. I needed to be alerted to any action or policy change that would remove an obstacle for anyone seeking to put an end to his or her childbearing. I had to be able to respond to questions or comments from the audience. Regardless of policies, my focus was always on the personal level.

# CHAPTER 5: CHANGING SEXUAL ATTITUDES

There can be no doubt that interest in voluntary sterilization in the 50s and 60s was about more than just preventing pregnancies. It was also an acknowledgment that people wanted to be able to control their own bodies and to have the right to do so. The sexual revolution had been taking place. The right to control one's own fertility was a part of that larger picture.

When Alfred Kinsey's studies in the early 50s showed that half of American women had had sexual encounters before they were married, it came as a shock to many. The culture in which I had been reared taught that women were to remain virgins until their wedding night. "No man wants damaged goods", we were told. I was convinced that once a girl had been intimate with a male, she would have to marry him. The girl was expected to be the one to control the sexual urges of her boyfriend. It was her responsibility to say "No!" Everyone seemed to accept that it was normal for a young man to want to have sex, but only "bad" girls would want to take part in such behavior.

The fear of pregnancy was another factor. Lack of over-the-counter contraceptives added to the risk. The only way to obtain a diaphragm was to have a doctor measure her and prescribe it, and there were very few doctors who would do so for an unmarried girl. Condoms were not easily obtainable. They were kept in the back of the prescription department and had to be specifically asked for by the purchaser. If an unfortunate girl got pregnant, she either got married or "went away," ostensibly to visit an aging auntie in another state. While she was away, the baby would be born and given up for adoption. In some cases, the girl went to live in a home such as one of the Florence Crittenden Homes. Their goal was to shelter "wayward" or "fallen" unwed pregnant women.

When Manuel and I married in 1953, it was not uncommon for men to expect their wives to be submissive and docile homemakers. This was certainly the case with our friends, most of whom were professional boxers. Although I treasured these friendships, I never felt I fit into their lifestyles. All the wives were slim, stylish, and beautiful. I was a "middle-weight", pregnant, and used only lipstick. They had free time to visit beauty salons, shop, or decorate while I worked at my nursing profession well into my first pregnancy.

Women who had taken the place of men in factories during the Second World War were encouraged or pushed into giving up their jobs when the men returned. They were expected to go back to being housewives. Television shows such as *"I Love Lucy"*, *"Leave it to Beaver"*, and *"Father Knows Best"* showed what society thought of a woman's role in the home.

After the war, housing development changed as large areas of vacant land were turned into rows of almost identical homes for a growing number of young couples. Most women not working outside the home filled their days with housework, having coffee with the neighbors, and upgrading their appliances. Obtaining a new washing machine or refrigerator was considered an answer to a woman's prayer or a dream come true. The idea of a "girl's night out" was apt to be a 'Tupperware Party' where the neighborhood women would gather to have coffee and sweets while they bought plastic kitchen products.

But the "baby boomers", children born after WWII, were coming of age. They did not want to be limited to the lifestyles of their parents. Families were beginning to get a taste for two incomes as more employment began to open up for women. Because of the many numbers of "boomers", they were able to make drastic changes. Among the ideas they challenged were attitudes towards sex and sexuality.

As women became confident that they could avoid pregnancy with the Pill, they were better able to consider additional years of education. Young ladies were no longer planning to go to college just to get an 'MRS' degree. They wanted higher degrees, perhaps becoming a doctor instead of a nurse, choosing to be a lawyer instead of a secretary, or a professor rather than a teacher. But in these years, while parenthood was being postponed, an increasing number of women wanted the same opportunities as men to explore sexual activity. Wanting to postpone parenthood did not mean they wanted to postpone sexual satisfaction.

By the time Helen Gurley Brown wrote her book, *Sex and the Single Girl*, in 1962, I had already had six children, one abortion, and a tubal ligation. I had not yet had an orgasm. I felt I had been cheated. Why didn't I have the same right to enjoy sex as men did? It seemed unfair to me.

The changes in sexual attitudes and practices did not come suddenly. The 'revolution' that began in the early 50s is still going on in many areas. It was in 1952 that beautiful, blue-eyed Christine Jorgenson had appeared in public as a tall blonde woman. She had been born a male and had "come out" as a female, having had sex reassignment surgery. Christine was the first to make her experience public. While she was not the first example of transsexual surgery, hers was noteworthy because her treatment was the first to include hormone therapy, which added to the success of the reassignment.

During the following decade, homosexuality was under consideration the American Psychiatric Association. Thinking was shifting away from calling homosexuality a mental disorder but the change in actual terminology in their textbooks was not recorded until 1973. Homosexual acts, by then, were no longer being considered "unnatural acts" or "crimes against nature" by the mental health profession. The research studies done by Alfred Kinsey and his colleagues had convinced an increasing percentage of the public to think of homosexuality as a normal variant of human sexuality.

Today, in our country, most Americans believe that permitting gays and lesbian couples to marry is the right thing to do. This is evidenced by three consecutive annual Gallop poles since 2011. Only a decade ago, homosexual conduct was still a crime in many states. Gay marriage is already legal in thirty-two states, and that number is expected to rise.

The decade of the 60s were the years when sexual activity was considered quite safe. Antibiotics were available to treat sexually transmitted diseases (STDs), previously called venereal disease (VD). The human immunodeficiency virus (HIV) and the auto-immune disease syndrome (AIDS) had not yet emerged. Combined with the newer contraceptive methods, risks associated with sexual activity had all but disappeared.

Sadly, there was a period of time while people were still enjoying unprotected sex, before AIDS had been widely recognized as heterosexually transmittable, that many people risked HIV transmission by their activities. As public awareness spread, however, behaviors began to change. It was then that entertainment halls such as "Plato's Retreat" and gay bath-houses were closed. Orgies and free sex with strangers risked death. The three popular, risqué Erotic Baker shops in New York City, operated by Patrika Brown and Karen Dwyer, closed their doors. Even eating anatomically-correct breads and cakes was no longer just fun.

Seeking sexual fulfillment outside of a marital relationship was always a temptation for a portion of the population. A factor that might have constrained some people was a fear of pregnancy. Dependable contraception surely prevented many unwanted pregnancies that might have occurred outside a marriage. Voluntary sterilization was one of those dependable methods. Surgery was not a method of choice for young persons for obvious reason, but for older persons, who had already had their families and who had terminated their fertility, it may have been an added benefit. I feel sure that some extramarital affairs were spared from embarrassing pregnancies as a result of a tubal ligation or a vasectomy.

Capitalizing on the increasing transparency about sexual matters, AVS created a vasectomy pin that could be worn as a lapel pin or a tie tack. It was in the shape of the universal symbol for male: a circle with an arrow extending outward from the "2 o'clock" position of the circle. The circular part had a small section removed, indicating the interruption in the vas.

Printed on the pin was the word "Vasectomy". Orders for a single pin came into AVS from vasectomized men. Larger quantities were ordered by doctors and clinics who presented them to their vasectomized clients after their post-surgical sperm count had shown the surgery had been successful.

This pin had two uses, the primary purpose being to stimulate open discussion about vasectomy during this period of AVS' intense public information campaign. It was successful, as many newspaper articles included photographs of the pin. It is true that this was a bit of a gimmick, but it did help open discussion about permanent male contraception during a time when most people thought that pregnancy prevention was a woman's responsibility.

*Various versions of the Vasectomy pins.*

The second use of the pin was not advocated or promoted by AVS. Some men, in this era of open sexuality, wore the pin as if to proclaim, "Look! I'm safe!" Whenever I had an opportunity to discuss the pin or respond to comments about it in media interviews, I always stated clearly that the pin came with no promise or guarantees. If a potential sexual partner wanted assurance of sterility, a better idea would be to check the laboratory report of the semen analysis to verify sterility.

John Rague, the Executive Director, and Donald Higgins, the Public Relations Director of AVS, then decided to have a similar pin made for women. When they asked for my opinion, I replied that I did not think women were going to want to proclaim their sterility or "safety", even in those days of increasing equality in sexual matters and increasing sexual freedom. The men went ahead with their plan. The female pin, much larger than the vasectomy pin, was indeed ugly! Shaped like the universal symbol for female, a cross suspended from the circle at the "6 o'clock" position, it had the words "Voluntary Sterilization" emblazoned on it. I doubt any clients bought any, but they were worn by a few doctors or family planning workers who wanted to use it as a discussion stimulant. In that case, it was not much different from the labels we sometimes see now on grocery clerks' jackets reading "Ask me about our new detergent".

*Original large pin for women and later smaller versions.*

In the early 70s, Ellen Peck wrote *The Baby Trap*, which quickly attracted a lot of media attention. It served as a focal point in what became the non-parenthood movement. Women as well as men were questioning whether for them adulthood was synonymous with parenthood. An increasing number of adults were considering sterilization as the way to make their decision permanent. For a man, in particular, his dependence on a woman to have an abortion in case birth control failed put him in a vulnerable position. If he supported her right to control her own body, he could not compel her to have an abortion. He could end up being a father against his will.

When Peck's book resulted in an avalanche of letters from people all over the US asking about support groups in their area, she decided there needed to be an organization to connect people. AVS member, Stephen Keese, a single, vasectomized young man, attended the initial planning meeting in New York City where he was elected the Treasurer of the new National Organization for Non-Parents (NON). Soon after, Steve became the Chair, taking over the organizing duties so that Peck could continue her promotional activities.

NON enjoyed a lot of national publicity, including significant articles in the New York Times and the Washington Post. Steve did a lot of public speaking to mother's groups, adoptive parents groups, infertility support groups and others. As public acceptance of childfree lifestyles grew, there seemed little need for support groups. As a result, the organization disbanded in the 80s and gave its archives to the University of California, Santa Cruz.

Through my activities with AVS I had the opportunity to interact and work with persons such as the Reverend Joseph Fletcher, the author of *Situation Ethics*, Betty Friedan, author of *The Feminine Mystique*, Mary Calderone, founder of the *Sex Information and Education Council for the United States (SIECUS)*, and Gloria Steinem, co-founder of *MS* magazine. All were important figures in changing sexual attitudes.

As noteworthy as these individuals were, I thought no one was more outspoken about the role of voluntary sterilization in making sexual freedom more possible than Dr. Lonny Myers. I am pleased to have been able to develop a close friendship with her over many years.

Lonny, (nee Caroline Rulon) was an anesthesiologist in Chicago when she heard Paul Ehrlich speak about overpopulation. Lonny became actively involved with Zero Population Growth, AVS, and the National Association for the Repeal of Abortion Laws (later named National Abortion Rights Action League). With her friend, the Reverend Don Shaw, and with some funding from AVS, she opened the Midwest Population Center (MPC), performing her first vasectomy there in 1970.

Lonny's reputation as "The Vasectomy Doctor" in Chicago spread quickly. After she had done the surgery on one fireman or on one police officer, it seemed he would return to his firehouse or precinct and tell others. Soon co-workers were coming in for their vasectomies. Everyone seemed to want Lonny.

At the time, I knew of no other female doctor offering vasectomy. I asked Lonny if she had any idea why she had so many more clients than male doctors in the Chicago area. She thought that it was "natural preference", explaining that she thought most men would prefer to have female hands on their scrotum because that was what they were used to.

The concept of "open marriage" was being discussed in the 60s and 70s. There was definitely more acknowledgement of sexual activity within the privacy of an extended family group, but it also happened in more public situations. There were specifically organized groups or clubs for "swingers". Suburbia had its share of "pool" or "key" parties where the house keys were tossed into the pool and the man who recovered a set went home with the owner of the keys. For men and women who took part in such a lifestyle, birth control was a necessity, and voluntary sterilization, either vasectomy or tubal ligation, had an important role to play. Lonny embraced this. In 1975 she and her close friend, Hunter Leggitt, M.Div., published a book called *Adultery & Other Private Matters*.

Lonny was on the Board of Directors of AVS. Her outspoken ideas and comments were often shocking to the formal ladies and gentlemen who made up the Board. But there was no doubt of Lonny's firm conviction that all people should have the right to control their bodies, to satisfy their sexual desires, and to end their fertility if that was their wish.

# CHAPTER 6: CIVIL RIGHTS

I was introduced to discrimination on a very personal level. My family, including my parents, had all been born in The Netherlands. They and all my friends were blond, fair-skinned, and blue or green eyed. Frankly, I was bored with the sameness, so when I met Manuel Gonzales, the handsome tan boxer who attended my church, I felt an immediate attraction. Fortunately, so did my family, so we had no problem there. We also had the full support of the minister, the Reverend Ernest Ackerman, who had been my spiritual advisor at the First Presbyterian Church in Paterson, N.J. for a few years and who knew me well.

I was shocked, however, to find that others raised so many objections when we announced our plans to marry. They asked me why I was marrying outside my race, or why I didn't want a nice Dutch man. I was surprised that those thoughts had been brewing in the minds of my friends. The idea that a man of Spanish and Indian background would be labeled as another "race" had not even entered my mind. Nor would it have mattered. It was only a few years since I had presented a case in favor of mixed marriage while enrolled in a college sociology class. My theory was that if we truly believed in equality, racial or ethnic background would not matter in a relationship. I still believed that, sincerely.

It was in the summer of 1954 that Manuel and I decided to visit his family in Corpus Christi, Texas. We had ten-month old twin boys, and we wanted the family to see them. I was also eager to meet my new family, as I had only met his brother Ruben, the best man at our wedding. Manuel was not at all worried about the reception we might get from his family, but as we were planning the journey, he became increasingly worried about public reaction to his arriving with a blond wife, especially one who was already very pregnant with another child. "I may have to fight for your honor", he warned me. He feared that some Mexicans would accuse him of trying to "marry up" to raise his own status. Others, he thought, might think of me as "low class" or "white trash" for being with a Mexican.

Until then, I had not realized that such old concepts of racial inequality might still be in people's minds. After all, I rationalized; the Supreme Court had just handed down its landmark decision in the case of Brown vs. the Board of Education[1]. Surely, the American population had gotten beyond prejudice, I naively believed.

I experienced, first hand, our wanting to go to a restaurant in Corpus Christi, and finding a sign on the front window reading "No Mexicans". Public places, especially bathrooms and eating areas were still segregated, separating people of different colored skin or backgrounds. As we walked in the downtown area, I was aware that Manuel was very tense, keeping a constant watch over his shoulder in case he, or we, should be attacked.

Usually when people spoke to us when we were with the twins, there would be a comment or question about how Manuel had fathered a blond baby. Our twins were fraternal, one looking like my side of the family, and the other looking more like Manuel. As time passed, he was able to treat such comments with humor. Often, when we each held one of the twins, he would choose to take the blond boy just to get reactions.

When racial unrest was at its peak in the mid 60s, I had another personal experience. I was then working weekend nights in the hospital. A nurse who worked with me was black. She lived in Paterson, NJ, and did not have a car. She would have needed to take two buses to get to the hospital. I offered to pick her up at her home at 10:30 p.m., as I could drive through her area on my way to the hospital.

One night, as I was stopped at a traffic light, we were suddenly shocked by a loud crashing sound and the noise of breaking glass. The back window of my Volkswagen Microbus had been smashed in. A black man was running away from my vehicle, with a large crowbar in his hand. A few people were nearby, but no-one approached to give aid. We went to the police station to report the incident. The police told me that, more than likely, it had been the sight of a black and white woman sitting in the front seat of the vehicle together that irritated the culprit.

I often reflected on this incident over the years; it was not a white man who had attacked my car because of a black passenger. It was a black man, in a black neighborhood, attacking me presumably because I was an outsider. Perhaps the crowbar-wielding man thought I should not have been in his neighborhood. If I had been black, I am convinced this would not have happened. I was in the minority here; a white person being discriminated against by a black man. In addition, I had the temerity to be sharing the front seat with a black person. What were they afraid of? Perhaps it was simply social changes that were frightening. We are an astonishingly change-resistant species. The changes that were equalizing people of different races and backgrounds were threatening to some, it seemed.

I was determined not to let this incident change my way of life or my attitude toward others. My nurse friend offered to take the buses instead of having me pick her up on my way to the hospital. That was out of the question for me. If I had done that, the racist black man would have won. I continued to stop in her neighborhood and we continued to drive together in the front seat, through the same streets, stopping at the same traffic light, looking back at the people lurking at the corners.

In the mid-60s, family planning clinics were coming under suspicion. Militant blacks were accusing government-funded clinics of promoting "black genocide". In Cleveland, Ohio, a family planning clinic was firebombed and several others were closed in response to threats from Black Power advocates. Cultural conservatives affiliated with the Catholic Church were likely to support the action against the family planning clinics.

Activists in Pittsburgh, Pennsylvania forced the closing of a family planning clinic in the primarily black Homewood-Brushton neighborhood of the city. Although Planned Parenthood had been serving the local citizens without incident for many years, in 1966, when the Office of Economic Opportunity began to subsidize services, the local Citizen's Renewal Council requested a grant of money to pay for the local clinics. The Pittsburgh branch of NAACP interpreted this as an instrument of genocide and feared that federal funds would be used to exterminate Negro people.

The leaders in Pittsburgh were two black men, Dr. Charles Greenlee, chairman of the health committee of the Pittsburgh NAACP, and William "Bouie" Haden, leader of a black militant organization called the United Movement for Progress. These men allied themselves with Father Charles Owen Rice to lead an anti-birth control campaign. They threatened to fire-bomb the center unless it closed. Women members of the Welfare Rights Organization objected to Haden's lead. "Who is he to tell us about having babies?" "He cannot speak for us!" It was clear that the women using the services did not look upon the clinic as a genocidal plot. Nevertheless, as a result of the efforts of the black militant men, Pittsburgh rejected federal funds for birth control clinics, the only major city to do so. The clinic was closed under threats of riots if it were to be reopened.

It was while the clinic was closed that AVS got a call from a television station in Pittsburgh, asking for a representative to discuss contraceptive sterilization on an early morning live television program. I was the volunteer speaker chosen for that "honor". The next day, the Pittsburgh Planned Parenthood Association called AVS, urging they reconsider the idea of sending someone to talk about what they believed was an inflammatory topic in the midst of such a racially charged environment. They were concerned that AVS might not be aware of the volatile mood in Pittsburgh and wanted to warn the organization and the speaker what might lay ahead.

AVS gave me the opportunity to back out of the engagement. My family worried about the trip and the dangers that I might face. If I were to be fatally harmed, I would be leaving six children. But my inner voice kept reminding me that speaking up for individual choice and reproductive freedom was not wrong. I remembered the words of Edmund Burke, who said 'The only thing necessary for the triumph of evil is for good men to do nothing'. Furthermore, I believed those words. I did not feel uncomfortable with the subject or my messages, so I continued with plans for the trip. My family prayed for the divine protection they depended on when I was facing risky situations.

Fortunately, the trip went without incident. I had been supplied with a spray canister of mace that I carried hidden in my pocket, having been instructed not to travel without it at my fingertips. Because of heavy rain, my evening flight from New Jersey was delayed. I arrived at the hotel in the wee hours of the night, with only a couple hours to rest before the early date at the TV station. There was some concern, even at the studio, that an angry black activist might recognize me after the live program and attack me on my way back to the airport. But I took a public cab, which happened to have a black driver, and got safely back to the airport, into a plane, and onward to home with no personal attack, mace still intact in my pocket.

The battle was really between the Black Power male activists who were interested in gaining political power and the black women who were concerned with their personal welfare and that of their children. This was exactly the way I had always viewed sterilization. It was a personal choice that should be available without restrictions for anyone seeking it, and who understood the permanence of the decision. I had no discomfort discussing voluntary sterilization as an option that should be available to women in Pittsburgh, even in this charged environment.

A day or two after the broadcast, I was extremely gratified to learn that the black women who had been previously served by the Planned Parenthood Clinic in Pittsburgh were successful in having their wants and needs heard. The protests of the black women had more effect than genocide claims of the men. The city reversed its position and accepted the federal funds for their clinics. While the Black Power males suspected that there might be a white plot to control the black population, black women knew that they could use birth control for their own advantage. They believed that the decision regarding if and when to have children must be left to women. It should not be an issue that men might turn into a political battle.

Note:
Brown v Board of Education, 347 U.S. 483, 74 S. Ct. 686, 98 L. Ed. 873 (1954)

# CHAPTER 7: JOINING THE STAFF

The primary goal of AVS during the decade of the 60s was to raise public awareness and acceptance of voluntary sterilization as a birth control method. Because I wanted to help, I began to take college courses to improve my ability to assist their public relations activities. I studied publicity, press release techniques, advertising, and communications. By the time I joined the staff in 1971, I also had five years of broadcast experience, having dealt directly with radio and television producers, directors, program managers, and interviewers. When John Rague told me that AVS was planning to hire a staff person to run the Speaker's Bureau, I was ready.

When I joined the staff, my youngest child was eleven, and the other five were all in their teens. I felt I was ready to take a full time position, all previous work having been on a part-time basis. Getting up early to take a bus from Morris County, N.J. to Manhattan was one of the more difficult adjustments, but I was motivated and excited about the new challenges ahead.

I had never worked in an office setting before. My eight years as a public health nurse had been a half-time position and my schedule was flexible, based on my husband's availability to care for the children while I worked, and the needs of the people of the community. My work in the hospital also was during the hours my husband was at home. Now, because Manuel had changed jobs and no longer worked evenings, we would both be working during the day. Most of that time, the children would be in school. I thought they were responsible enough to be alone a few hours after they got home.

The many trips I made while on the Speakers Bureau had prepared my family to carry on while I was away for a few days at a time. The children all had their special talents. One of the twins was very talented in electronics, so it was his job to repair things, change the electrical fuses when they blew, etc. His twin could be counted on to make decisions that were well thought out, in my opinion, so I trusted him to be in charge of the younger boys and to serve as their overseer. Our daughter was very capable in the kitchen and had been preparing meals for many years. She seemed perfect for the role of housekeeper-in-charge. She would also look after her younger sister, the eleven-year-old. The two youngest boys posed the largest worry. They were at the age where they were subject to temptation and mischief. They needed the most attention from their elder brothers and the most attention from their dad when he got home after work.

My career with AVS was about to begin. I was excited. My salary was to be $4,200 for the six months remaining in 1971, about half of the annual salary being offered. Even better, I was given papers to fill out that would enroll me in what John Rague described as AVS' retirement plan. If I set aside three percent of my salary in the plan, AVS would contribute an extra 14%. That seemed incredible to me. I wasted no time in writing my name on the line to start benefiting from this plan. Until then, Manuel and I had not been able to establish a retirement account.

For a few years before joining the staff, I had been a member of the Board of Directors. I had not heard anything about staff or salary matters because such issues were handled by the Executive Committee. Financial matters were handled by the treasurer, then Fifield Workum. Mr. Workum was a graduate of Harvard Law School and a partner in a Manhattan law firm. He and John Rague had a close working relationship regarding the AVS budget and expenditures. Some months later, after I learned that the 3/14 ratio was something that no other organization was offering, I was informed that Rague had a medical condition that prevented some insurance coverage. To compensate, Rague and Workum had set up the retirement plan to provide additional compensation to Rague. But Rague could not be treated differently than the rest of the staff, so all employees would benefit from the plan.

While I was setting up my office, I noticed there were a few items that were not available in the room I was assigned. Other than the desk and a typewriter, there were none of the other usual tools such as a stapler or tape dispenser. I was told that because AVS was dependant upon donations, we had to conserve money. If I wanted such items, I should buy them myself. Since I had been a modest contributor to AVS, and believed in the cause they were working for, that seemed reasonable. I bought the office items I would be using. I still have my stapler and tape dispenser on my desk at home. After many years of using them in the office, I wanted to take these two items as a reminder of my days at AVS.

When I started my work, I was expected to follow the example that had been set by Donald Higgins, the public relations director. He had been the person in charge of fulfilling speaking engagements for radio and television programs. His procedure had been to send out letters offering a speaker who would address the subject of voluntary sterilization. Enclosed with the letter was a biographical sheet describing Dr. Wood, Courtland Hastings, and me, Betty Gonzales, the nurse and mother of six who had chosen sterilization.

When Higgins got replies to his mailings, he tried to send the speaker who had been requested. But replies were coming from all over the country, and requests were for different speakers. In my opinion, there was wasteful spending, with someone flying to California, as an example, just for one program. If Higgins could, he would try to fit in a second appearance along the way.

As I began my mailings, I believed I could streamline the system and make the Speakers Bureau much more cost-effective. Because I had been in so many stations as the guest speaker, and generally understood the pecking order in the broadcast world, I thought the communication should be with the program directors directly. I truly believed that AVS had an important message to offer. I believed that the talk programs needed speakers and that they should be grateful to interview a guest for whom they did not have to pay transportation or lodging. With that in mind, I made the proposal to Rague that I switch from letters to phone calls. I further believed that a less formal, more personal conversation would be more effective than the rather stiff letter format.

I had three valuable resources to use. The first was a publication called *TV Publicity Outlets - Nationwide*. The second was *The National Radio Publicity Directory*. The third was *Broadcasting Yearbook*. These reference books listed stations and specific programs that entertained guest speakers. They listed talk programs, call-in shows, women's or home-maker programs or formal interview formats. All were suitable for my purpose. Using these references, I knew before I called what format I would be discussing, who the program director was, details about the show, the time it aired, and some indication of the popularity of the program in terms of the audience it reached.

The next step for me was to plan an area to cover in the course of one week. I would plan a Sunday night or Monday morning departure for Wood or Hastings. I would select an area of the country using the airport city as a start. I would try first for the most popular TV program near the airport. Of primary importance were any live shows. Programs that were to be taped could fill in the hours between live programs. I would have the speaker rent a car to go to the next appointment. I tried to schedule two or three shows every day for four or five days "on the road".

When I telephoned the stations, the approach I used was to inform the program director or station manager that I was planning an itinerary that would have an excellent speaker in their area on a given week and that I could book that speaker (Wood or Hastings) with his program immediately. I worked with a six week time frame, knowing that stations needed some lead time, and also to make sure I had the travel plans well worked out for the speakers. I was not offering a choice of speakers. I was offering the one who was going to be sent to that part of the country. I was not begging for air time. I knew we had an important message to offer, and a skilled spokesperson to deliver the message for the station. I believe that my approach made a significant difference. It also made travel costs much more efficient. For every dollar spent on phone calls, air fare or car rental, we were reaching many more thousands of listeners.

My plan would have them return at the end of the week, giving them hardly time to repack their clothes for the next trip to another area of the country. Because I was now in the office every day, my participation in the Speakers Bureau had officially ended, but I could still do the radio shows that were done by phone hookups. Some of these were call-in shows, many of which ran at night, so I could take part in those programs from my home.

By the end of 1972, after I had been on staff for eighteen months, sterilization had been the subject of programs in every one of the fifty states. I believed that we had saturated the airwaves. The goal of making sterilization a subject of common knowledge had been achieved.

When the Correspondence Committee of the 60s had been at work, it was difficult to get a word that referred to sex on the air. It made interviewers uncomfortable to have a speaker say that after a tubal ligation, women would continue to have normal 'menstrual periods' or to say that after a vasectomy, men would still be able to have normal 'erections' or 'ejaculations'. Later such language no longer shocked anyone, and all methods of birth control could be freely discussed in public.

I remember one incident that made me realize how much public knowledge had increased. I was at a medical conference in Washington D.C. with an AVS exhibit, and was staying at the Shoreham Hotel. At that time, Mark Russell was the featured political satirist who entertained with two performances in the lounge every night. One evening, between shows, I placed a small gold vasectomy pin on his piano. When he returned for the second show he spotted it as he started one of his musical routines, and immediately went into an entire discussion about vasectomies! There was no need to explain anything. The public knew what a vasectomy was and it was no longer a shocking subject. That, for me, was a turning point. I knew we had done much of what we had set out to do to increase public knowledge and understanding.

Since the first vasectomy clinic had opened in N.Y. in 1969, other clinics had opened around the country. In 1971, vasectomies made up 60% of all voluntary sterilizations in the United States. AVS estimated that of the 554,000 vasectomies that year, 39,000 had been done in clinics, 24,000 in military facilities, and the rest, 478,000, by private practitioners. Vasectomies that year outnumbered female procedures by a 60/40% ratio.

Other events were also taking place. Laparoscopy had been introduced as a less invasive surgery for female sterilization requiring a reduced hospital stay. Population growth and high birth rates were of greater public concern. Overpopulation problems were featured headlines of publications and discussed on nightly TV talk shows. After a twenty-year baby boom, journalists and politicians were treating population growth as something that needed to be tamed. The U.S. Agency for International Development (USAID) had shown an interest in funding an international program to provide surgical contraception in the developing world and AVS was being considered as the agency to spearhead that movement. We were in the midst of all these changes.

AVS had, until then, focused on public information and advocacy. In my opinion, it was time for the focus to shift to professional education. My concern was whether the medical community would be prepared to respond to the demands of the public, now that individuals were increasingly requesting permanent birth control procedures. My opinions did not carry much weight with Rague and Higgins. They lacked vision for anything beyond trying to increase the numbers of people getting sterilized.

The first frozen sperm bank in New York had opened by the Idant Corporation. Rague was attracted to the concept of the sperm bank as a back-up for men who might like to keep an option open after vasectomy. He and AVS Board President, urologist Joseph E. Davis, M.D. believed that more men might agree to a vasectomy if they could be offered an opportunity to have a future child using frozen semen and artificial insemination.

I was not enthusiastic about this. I was concerned about possible electric failure and how hundreds of men would feel when their stored sperm perished in the thawed semen. How would men in the underdeveloped countries feel if sterilizations were being offered in developed countries where sperm could be frozen, but where equal opportunities were not available to them? Research at that time had not convinced me that sperm would survive long term freezing. More studies were needed, in my opinion. More importantly, I truly believed that sterilization should be reserved only for those who were prepared for a permanent procedure. I always counseled clients "When in doubt, don't!"

Operators of commercial sperm banks were presenting the idea of freezing semen as "fertility insurance" to be utilized by men anticipating vasectomy or who wanted to insure their future fertility against injury, illness, or possible radiation therapy that might make them sterile. This back-up plan was accomplished by storing three sperm specimens in vials, or "straws", that would be sealed and stored in liquid nitrogen tanks maintained at a temperature of minus 321°F. In addition to the initial fee for depositing, there would be an annual fee for the continued storage.

I had no doubt that freezing tissue such as sperm or embryonic tissue could have many benefits in the scientific and biological world. I just did not like the idea of featuring the use of frozen sperm to give the idea that vasectomy could be offered as a "temporary" method of fertility control.

In 2012, I learned that veterinarians were injecting DNA from endangered species of animals into the egg cells of domesticated animals. The domesticated animal then could serve as the surrogate mother and give birth to a newborn of the rare species. This work was being done at the Audubon Center for Research of Endangered Species in New Orleans and is an example of one of the many wonderful ways that frozen cells may be used to save species on the brink of extinction.

In the years of my work, William B. Shockley, who shared a Nobel Prize for the invention of the transistor, was making news about his concerns that less intelligent people were having more children than those with higher IQs, and that a drop in average intelligence would ultimately lead to a decline of civilization. Capitalizing on the ability to freeze sperm, Californian Robert K. Graham opened the Repository for Germinal Choice in 1979. Donors were men whose IQs were over 140, William Shockley being among the more frequent donors.

My personal thoughts about this were that if I wanted to increase the chance of having a genius child, I would opt to have the sperm of the father of the genius implanted in me rather than that of the genius himself. After all, the father's sperm has already created a genius. The genius has not yet proven his worth.

Many years ago, I read Roald Dahl's wonderful book *"My Uncle Oswald"*. It is an imaginary story about collecting, unbeknownst to the donors, semen specimens that would then be quickly frozen and offered for sale to women who were willing to pay high prices for the frozen sperm of famous men. I think this is the most humorous book written about this particular time of my life.

John Rague, with his experience in media outreach, started working with the Idant Corporation, guiding their publicity activities. While the Board could not dictate the extent to which Dr. Davis was involved, they did question whether Rague should be spending his efforts on Idant while he was employed by AVS. Staff members, although not questioned by the Board, were well aware of the large percentage of his office time spent on promoting Idant.

By early 1972, some questions had also arisen about staff spending. There were large bills every month for restaurant dinners, reportedly for meals with media persons such as journalists, authors, or broadcast personalities. During the first few months of my employment, I had frequently been asked by Rague to stay after work to discuss some issue or plan, with the explanation that he had not had a chance to discuss the idea during the day. He would take me to a restaurant, the Four-Forty Club in a building adjacent to our office at 14 West Fortieth Street. When the bill came, he whipped out his credit card, which I had naively assumed to be his own.

But I began to worry when I mentioned the dinners to my mother. She said that if her contributions might be going to pay for any staff meals, she would no longer contribute. She worked hard for every five dollar bill that she sent in. I found the idea shocking. After all, I thought, I had to buy my own stapler and tape dispenser. Surely, the leaders would not be wasting money. But I began to look at expenses being submitted and got increasingly suspicious. I declined any invitations to stay late to discuss anything outside the office after that.

The bookkeeper was Mildred Mayers, a very meticulous person when it came to her financial responsibilities. I would see her with her hand-operated adding machine, making sure that every penny was accounted for. With Mildred, there was no such thing as "petty cash". She needed a receipt for every cent she recorded and made sure the columns balanced every month. But it was not her role to question or report on the specifics, such as the names of the journalists reportedly being taken to dinner.

During the Christmas season, while Mr. Workum was away, the assistant treasurer, Mrs. Beatrice McClintock, reviewed the bills and probed for more documentation. She found little to support the expenses for the reputed guests and reported her findings to the Executive Committee. While there might have been such a need to attract writers in the early days, AVS had become the recognized "go-to" place for any information about sterilization; there should be little need to wine and dine anyone.

Both issues, staff involvement in a sperm bank and excessive spending, contributed to the termination of Rague's employment. Additionally, the Board recognized that Rague's expertise in publicity had run its course. It was time to move toward professional education. The Executive Committee of the AVS Board of Directors hired Charles T. Faneuff, an educator, to replace John Rague.

Unlike Rague, Higgins, Hastings, and Chairman of the Board Hugh Moore, and some other Board members, Faneuff had not been affiliated with the World Federalist movement. He had no desire to be a part of a world government. He seemed honestly concerned with overpopulation and was eager to work in that field of occupation. He had developed a pilot model for teaching population dynamics in Mysore, India, and went on to earn his doctorate on the subject of population growth at the University of North Carolina's Population Center.

Since the departure of Ruth Proskauer Smith in the early 60s, the focus of AVS had shifted from trying to limit childbearing by the "unfit" toward trying to limit childbearing by everyone. The Zero Population Growth organization had spread, mostly with college chapters opening across the states. From a beginning of about one hundred members to over 25,000 in eighteen months, it seemed apparent that young people were supportive of limiting family size. This was evidenced by the requests coming into AVS for referrals to doctors. Clients were requesting sterilization at younger ages and with fewer children.

In 1972, AVS received funds from USAID, and Ira Lubell, M.D. was hired to lead that international program. It was called The International Project of AVS (IPAVS). His goal in that leadership position was to start organizations similar to AVS around the world. IPAVS would work with medical communities to help them offer voluntary sterilization as an additional family planning option.

Ira Lubell was a native New Yorker who received his M.D. from Brooklyn's Downstate College of Medicine. Lubell went into research rather than private practice. His background was broad. He had gone to the Soviet Union in 1962 and instructed Soviet doctors how to use dialysis as a treatment for kidney failure. He set up a mobile outpatient clinic in Brooklyn when he returned. He was aware that poor people only went to a doctor when they were very ill. Lubell believed in bringing health care to the community. He spoke six languages, so was deemed by the AVS directors to be well prepared to direct the International Project.

The result of these hiring decisions, unfortunately, was to form an organization with two heads. Faneuff felt responsible for the money granted to AVS, yet Lubell had been hired as the executive in charge of the International Project. Lubell did not feel he should have to go to Faneuff for approval or supervision of funds. Faneuff felt the responsibility was his. In his six-month report to the Board of Directors, Faneuff expressed his concerns. He recommended that the Board decide on one director and adjust the structure of the organization accordingly. As a result, Faneuff was let go and Lubell became the director of both the national program and the International Project.

The International Project (IP) was located in a separate building a few blocks away from the national office. There was no interaction between the staff members. Expenses for IP were covered with the USAID funding while the national work continued to be privately funded by private donors.

The Public Relations Director had left soon after Rague departed AVS. I was not surprised. During the years I had known them, I never saw any evidence that Higgins had done anything without close collaboration with Rague. They even had a "working lunch" at La Fortuna, a nearby Italian restaurant, almost every day.

With that change, I became the head of the information and education work of the organization. Under the tutelage of Faneuff, a natural teacher, I had honed my writing skills and was improving my editing abilities. I had been writing and editing the AVS News that went quarterly to members. With Faneuff's encouragement, I began publication of the AVS Biomedical

Bulletin. Each issue dealt with a scientific aspect of sterilization.

There was no more need for public relations or publicity because AVS was widely recognized as the depository for all accurate information about male and female sterilization. Although we did not need to reach out, we did need to respond to all the writers and publicists who came to us for help. It was time to hire someone to handle these tasks so that I could focus on the professional education activities.

Ever since I joined the staff, I had the responsibility of checking all articles being written by medical writers. This fell to me because I was the only staff person who had a medical background. I kept aware of all changes and improvements in both the surgical techniques and the instrumentation used. I took part in surgical training programs so that I could be well-informed about all techniques.

I was increasingly more occupied with attending medical conferences, exhibiting at scientific and professional meetings, and serving as the medical and technical staff person to respond to any authors writing a book or article about sterilization. I was also the staff person to meet with other organizations with whom we were working, such as Planned Parenthood, the American Civil Liberties Union, Zero Population Growth, and others who were concerned with reports of involuntary sterilization, such as the Committee to End Sterilization Abuse (CESA).

Plans to increase our professional education activities continued under Lubell's directorship. I was finding it increasingly difficult to keep up with all the new responsibilities while still handling the scheduling of public speaking engagements, distribution of educational brochures, requests for referrals, and the publication of the AVS Newsletter.

I found a great person to join the staff and work on publications and the informational aspects of our work. Miriam Ruben had been a secretary under Rague, but then had moved to Great Britain for a few years. She was ready to return to the states, and because her writing skills were exceptional, I felt she would make an excellent addition to our team.

The employment of Miriam as Public Information Officer left me free to focus on professional education, which included the spreading of new and improved surgical techniques in the United States. Dr. Lubell concentrated on the international activities, and I became the point person for national issues such as exhibiting at medical meetings, responding to reports of involuntary sterilizations and representing AVS in the development of sterilization regulations. My working title became "Director of Professional Education".

Lubell relocated both the AVS office and that of the International Project. We moved to the corner of Third Avenue and Forty-Fourth Street where we could share a space but great care was taken to keep activities and related expenditures separate. For example, we in the National unit had separate venders to supply our office materials and we used different printing companies for our publications. The IP had a rapidly improved library with the beginning of computerized publications but the National staff was forbidden access to it. Fortunately for me especially, that policy changed when William Record was hired as the professionally trained librarian. He pointed out that because the library had been funded by public funds, it had to be open to the public. Without that library, my work would have been much more difficult. I would no longer have to visit the medical library at a nearby Medical College for information.

If there had not been such an intentional effort on Lubell's part to keep the national work and staff totally apart, the International Project could have benefitted from learning how we spread the word about voluntary sterilization in the United States, and perhaps could have followed our example. They could have done a lot more to create a public demand for services in other counties had they thought about public relations and publicity rather than education. Lubell had a nurse educator, Marilyn Schima, working as his second-in-command for IPAVS. She was also the director of any international public Information and Education (I&E) activities. Schima had no experience in the kind of outreach that AVS had successfully achieved under the direction of Rague.

After I retired from AVS, I served as a consultant to the Family Planning Association of Nigeria. There I was able to teach a group of outreach workers how to reach out using media to spread the news of their services. That was twenty years after the International work of AVS had started.

In 1976, Lubell met Merrie Spaeth, who's political and lobbying activities interested him. At the time, there was a great deal of media attention to the development of sterilization regulations. This media attention needed to be handled by AVS staff. I was primarily occupied with the introduction of improved surgical techniques in the U.S. at the time. Lubell decided to hire Spaeth so that he would not have to deal with national issues. His heart and mind was with the International Project and he was overseas at least half of the time. Merrie Spaeth's presence would give him more freedom to travel.

Working with Merrie Spaeth was a strange experience. She had been an actress as a teenager, playing a major role in the movie, *The World of Henry Orient* and she reminded us of this frequently. On her birthday, staff was urged to attend a screening of the old film at her apartment. In her office, she had stuffed animals on the chairs and the sofa so that when she called a staff meeting, some of us had to sit on the floor. A large smelly poodle often accompanied her to the office. It was not unusual, even during a staff meeting for her to accept calls from her male friend, who she called her "teddy bear", even though he was a very prominent newspaper mogul with the New York Post. She remained at AVS for about eighteen months before returning to college to pursue a degree in business. She subsequently served as a White House Fellow assigned to the Federal Bureau of Investigation. Ultimately, she moved to Dallas, Texas, where she became a political and public relations consultant.

*1973*

Upon Spaeth's departure, I again became the Director of the National Program of AVS, reporting directly to Lubell. Because of the growing number of staff in the International Project, the office was moved to a larger space at the corner of 42nd Street and Lexington Avenue. Diagonally across the corner from the Chrysler Building and just a short distance from Grand Central Terminal, it was a wonderful location, and even had two small balconies for short breaks.

In the late 70s, even while the international work was progressing, there was a considerable level of discontent among the staff of IP. Because the national staff was ignored by Lubell and Schima, we were unaffected. Sara Seims, who was serving as a coordinator for evaluations at IP at that time, has described the situation in her 2004 interview by Rebecca Sharpless in a Population and Reproductive Health Oral History Project, Sophia Smith Collection, Smith College. She described IP as *"the most dysfunctional workplace I had ever been in. The two founders (Lubell and Schima) were absolute tyrants. And there were about five of us hired on the same day; three people were fired immediately thereafter. And the working environment was so poor that, shortly after I left, the workforce unionized and went out on strike. When AID visited, the founders were fired and new leadership was brought in and it all had a happy ending. But after a few months there, I decided life is too short, and I got a job at the Alan Guttmacher Institute as a senior research associate."* Sara Seims, at the time of this writing, 2014, is listed on the EngenderHealth Board of Directors.

A board member, Hugo Hoogenboom, interviewed the IP staff about working conditions. When Lubell was discharged in 1980, Hoogenboom applied for and was awarded the position, taking over as the Executive Director. He planned to reorganize the entire staff by creating a Medical Division that would deal with all medical issues both in the U.S. and in our overseas programs.

In this interim, after Lubell had departed and before the new Medical Director had been hired, the press began writing about long term effects of vasectomy in primates, creating a concern for men who had had a vasectomy. The studies had demonstrated that vasectomized monkeys had developed anti-sperm antibodies. Men also had been found to develop anti-sperm antibodies. Because I was the only medically trained person on staff at the time, it was my responsibility to handle this sensitive situation.

I was very grateful for the help I received by two specialists in this field. Dr. Nancy J. Alexander was the primary investigator who had conducted the studies at the Oregon Regional Primate Center. She was always generous in giving her time to keep me well educated and up-to-date on the studies and to guide me in the interpretation of the findings for the public and press.

Sherman J. Silber, MD, the foremost surgeon working with vasectomy reversals which was a related issue in the news at the time. He was also very ready to take my calls and to volunteer information about the most current techniques in both vasectomy and its reversal. This was especially critical because of the fear that antibodies in men might interfere with the success of a reversal.

I appreciated the significant help from these experts and think fondly of them both. The manner in which I handled this national medical issue might have led to Hoogenboom's conclusion that I had an important role to play in the future Medical Division.

Libby Antarsh was employed to direct the national activities. Schima left soon after Lubell, so Terrance Jezowski was promoted to be Director of the International Division. Douglas Huber, MD, MPH, was hired as the Medical Director, and I became the Deputy Director of the Medical Division.

# CHAPTER 8: FUNDING

The recorded histories of AVS by authors not directly involved with the organization have not always been kind. Books written about the years during which we were trying to expand sterilization services in the United States have too often mislead the readers to believe AVS was trying to subject poor people into having a sterilization operation against their will. Part of this is because of the history of AVS itself. In the 1960s, board members were quite vocal about wanting to promote sterilization as a "solution" to poverty, welfare, and overpopulation. Add to this the eugenic interests of the early founders, and it is easy to see how AVS was misunderstood in subsequent years as they struggled to gain public funding for persons unable to afford an elective surgical procedure.

Before any public funds became available for voluntary sterilization, AVS had provided "loans" to some people unable to afford the surgical expense of tubal ligation. The first offer to fund surgery for indigent women came from a Philadelphia lawyer, Graham French. After hearing his friend, Dr. Wood, speak about the virtues of sterilization and how such surgery for the poor would reduce welfare costs, he offered AVS $10,000 to subsidize sterilizations for poor persons. To the best of my knowledge, all the recipients of these funds were women. Between 1957 and 1960, five hundred and eight operations were paid for by this "French Fund". Because French had said there should be no pressure applied to have the "loans" repaid, these were actually gifts. I have no memory of any reports that might have indicated that any were ever repaid.

Some critics of AVS have implied that sterilizations obtained through these "loans" were perhaps not really voluntary choices. I am absolutely convinced that there was not one woman, who upon hearing about the available funding, said to herself, "Oh, I think I'll get sterilized because it's free!" A more likely scenario would be a woman who had wanted to stop having more babies, and now she was finally able to get a sterilization operation because money had become available to help her achieve her goal.

A second attempt at funding sterilizations for indigent women was initiated by AVS board member, Alice DuPont Mills, at the Fauquier County Hospital in Virginia. Mrs. Mill's money had enabled the hospital to open a contraceptive clinic, and in 1960 it began to offer information about sterilization to patients with three or more children, including a free tubal ligation should the woman wish one. By 1963, two hundred and three women had taken advantage of the offer.

While AVS was not officially involved with this funding offer, Mr. Mills and Dr. Stinson, AVS member and later its president, were on the board of the hospital. John Rague, AVS Executive Director, saw the clinic as a publicity opportunity and arranged a tour of the hospital for the press. The sterilization program caused an unexpected reaction, probably because two thirds of the clients had been African-Americans.

Protests came from Billy Graham, who called sterilization a "crippling of a vital body function". Some rabbis, representing both the Union of American Hebrew Congregations and a Reform congregation, said that sterilization was "reprehensible" and a "violation of moral law". The leading attack, however, was Patrick O'Boyle, Washington, D.C.'s Roman Catholic archbishop. The tour of the facility had backfired.

Members of the AVS board had not expected this reaction. They had moved away from earlier beliefs in eugenic sterilization, and by the early 60s really were primarily concerned with providing what they called "a hand-up, rather than a hand-out". The majority of AVS members and leaders saw sterilization as a way to break the chain of poverty by helping underprivileged persons to have fewer children.

There was one more attempt at private funding of sterilization for the poor that involved AVS. Jesse Hartman donated a total of $35,000 to AVS to fund sterilizations in the mountainous area of Berea, Kentucky. There, a female doctor and the area's only pediatrician, Louise Hutchins, was providing contraceptive information as she traveled to her patients by horse-back, by Jeep, or on foot.

She and Hartman had hoped that their project would be taken over by Johnson's "War on Poverty", which was in early development at that time. In its first year, the Hartman Plan paid for seventy-six women and thirty-nine men to be sterilized, almost one hundred percent Caucasian clients.

Hartman subsequently tried to set up a fund in Florida in 1965. He wintered in the Broward and Palm Beach County every year, so was interested in that area. However, there was a large African-American population in that area. The program seemed to be targeting that minority, and as a result, the project never was initiated. AVS was, by this time, more interested in public funding than in individual grants of a "loan" program.

In the mid-60s, AVS was heavily involved with the initiation of out-patient vasectomy clinics and with attempts to gain funding from Federal sources and by private insurance companies. Dr. Wood had been meeting with heads of hospitals in the New York area, trying to encourage them to open a vasectomy clinic as a demonstration model for what AVS hoped would become a widespread service for men. He had been unable to convince a single hospital to do so. Finally, someone suggested he try "those Margaret Sanger people" and he did.

The result was that, with AVS funding, the Margaret Sanger Research Bureau opened the first vasectomy clinic in lower Manhattan in 1969. The clinic was very popular, and news coverage of it was praiseworthy. It was not long before vasectomy clinics were opening all across the nation, many with sliding scale prices from $50 to $175. Vasectomy soon became an affordable option for men.

Vasectomy was a less-invasive surgical procedure than female sterilization, and was suitable to be performed in a free-standing clinic. Women did not have an equivalent out-patient procedure available to them. A tubal ligation would require an abdominal operation with all the expenditures and risks of major surgery, including the costs of a hospital stay and perhaps, child care.

While wealthy women have always seemed to be able to avail themselves of any sort of medical care they might choose, poor women have not had that option. That seemed to me to be discriminatory, with less fortunate women being denied a service they felt they needed. This inequality is what made it so important for AVS to struggle to obtain public funding for poor women. It was why insurance carriers needed to be persuaded to cover voluntary sterilization. It had nothing to do with trying to target poor persons.

In the early 1950s, while I was a student nurse, there were no federal funding programs to provide medical care to poor people. If one could not afford a private doctor, he or she went to a free clinic based in a charitable hospital. It was common for persons confronted with a medical emergency or sudden illness to go to an emergency room where immediate care could be obtained. For follow up, we would refer the patient to the appropriate clinic.

For example, if a person had a wound repaired in the emergency room, we would have them return to the surgical clinic for removal of the stitches in ten days. If a child had been brought in with a severe respiratory infection, the family would be referred to the pediatric clinic for follow-up and any additional health checkups the child might need. Patients with heart or circulatory problems would be sent to the medical clinic. Persons with broken bones would have the healing fractures checked and casts removed at the orthopedic clinic.

There were also maternity clinics that cared for pregnant women, and "well-baby" clinics that would follow newborns, administer all the immunizations, recommend feeding changes, and monitor the growth and development of the infant. These clinics were staffed by interns and residents under the supervision of the teaching medical doctors. Care, in my opinion, was excellent, even though the patients might be sitting out their appointment time on benches in a hall rather than in a nicely furnished private doctor's office.

Similarly, poor patients were admitted to a ward if they could not afford a private or semi-private room in the hospital. I am not advocating that we go back to "good old days". But I want to point out that although there was care for poorer populations, this care was for medically necessary assistance and treatment. It did not cover an elective procedure such as a tubal ligation any more than it would have covered a face lift or liposuction.

To be sure, there was a down side to being cared for in clinic. The patients were part of the doctor's training, so the care-givers were not as experienced as a private doctor would be. Also, if a new treatment or medication were to be tried, it was more likely to be done in the clinic rather than in private practice. There might be the risk that surgical residents could be tempted to encourage surgery rather than a medical or mechanical treatment because that would give them more experience in the operating room.

My family had a friend who had acquired tuberculosis (TB) when he was sixteen years of age. He had been in the hospital ever since. My mother was the head nurse in the unit where Willie was a patient. His TB was considered hopeless. I was told by my mother that when a new drug was going to be tested, the doctors would say, "Let's try it on Willie". The doctors and Willie's family all thought it was worth the risk. They had nothing to lose, because Willie would not get better anyway.

As a side story about Willie, I will say that he had a remarkably positive attitude in spite of being the TB guinea pig for the hospital. He wanted to become a watch-maker. My grandfather was a watch-maker and was able to help Willie get training books from the Bulova watch company so he could study in bed. Willie had an over-head mirror above his bed so that he could see the reflection of what was on his chest. He would lay out the watch parts on a tray on his chest, and practice this new trade. He became an accomplished watch-maker.

One of the experimental drugs given in large doses to Willie damaged the nerves in his ears to the point that he lost his hearing completely. Not only that, but the TB had not been cured by the experimental drug. Years later, scientists developed new medications that rid Willie of the contagious bacilli, and Willie was discharged at the age of fifty-three, no longer contagious, in 1957. He already had a heart condition, but he was able to open a small watch-repair shop in Newark, N.J., where he felt his dream had come true.

My positive attitude in general toward clinic-based care remains. Some years ago, I developed a neurological problem that affects my walking and balance. I have gotten the best care imaginable at the Neurological Institute of the Columbia Presbyterian Hospital in New York. Yes, it is a clinic, and each July, I meet the new neurology residents who will assist in caring for me. And yes, I sit in a rather bare room with no niceties, but I am more than happy to get my care there.

When the Margaret Sanger Research Bureau started the trend of vasectomy clinics, men suddenly had a place where they could undergo an elective (that is, not medically necessary) surgical procedure at a reasonable cost. There was not yet a counterpart for a woman who wanted to terminate her child-bearing.

The first step toward getting public funding was taken in 1964, as part of President Johnson's War on Poverty. Congress established the Office of Economic Opportunity (OEO). It was headed by a staunch Roman Catholic, Sargent Shriver, John F. Kennedy's brother-in-law. Dr. Paul Bryant was the Director of the Office of Health Affairs.

The Office of Health Affairs initiated the Family Planning Program in 1968 naming Dr. Gary London, as the director; London was soon replaced by Dr. George Contis. Dr. Warren Hern joined the team as the Chief of the Program Development and Evaluation Branch under Contis in March, 1970.

Encouraged by his wife, Eunice Shriver, the OEO's Director Sargent Shriver was influenced by their religious belief that artificial contraception was immoral. As a result, the social programs for family planning were fraught with limitations. Only married women living with their husbands could qualify for birth control services. Sterilizations for either men or women were not permitted with family planning funds. Abortion funding was also prohibited, but that was to be expected because abortion was still illegal (and would continue to be illegal until the Roe v Wade Supreme Court decision in 1973).

While AVS was optimistic about this program, the organization was very displeased with the OEO War on Poverty Office's prohibition of funds for voluntary sterilization. In 1966, the Board of Directors and the Executive Director, John Rague, pledged to "hammer away" at the ban until the "court of public opinion" demanded an end to the usurpation of the right of the people to free choice. These quotations are taken from my verbatim notes made at that time.

In 1967, public funds for family planning became available. The Department of Defense (DOD) decided to permit sterilization as a family planning service. DOD further stated that the procedure could be performed in military facilities. This partially explains why, when the first vasectomy clinic opened, some servicemen had already been talking about their having obtained one while they were in service.

Also in 1967, there was a change in the Title V program. Funds for the Aid to Families with Dependent Children (AFDC) program were allowed to be used for family planning. The initiation of family planning services to welfare recipients also occurred at that time. One draw-back, though, was that funds continued to be denied for both abortion and sterilization, much to the disappointment of AVS.

I remember the political thinking at that time. It was thought that it would be economically better for funds to be spent to help families control their fertility than to have to pay for more and more unwanted children who might otherwise be born to that family. President Lyndon Johnson, in addressing the United Nations on its twentieth anniversary in 1965, had said "Let us act on the fact that less than five dollars invested in population control is worth one hundred dollars invested in economic growth".

Congressman Clement John Zablocki, a liberal Democrat from Milwaukee, Wisconsin, had initiated an amendment to a bill that would ban voluntary sterilization under the Foreign Assistance Act of 1967. A year later, the House Senate Conference Committee defeated that bill. As a result, the Foreign Assistance Act set aside $35 million to provide birth control abroad, and it permitted voluntary sterilization to be funded. The U.S. Agency for International Development (AID) added family planning to its overseas aid program. Soon after, AID set aside $2.7 million to combat overpopulation abroad. This opened the door for what would later assist the international work of AVS.

That same year, AVS recorded that in the twenty-seven states with Medicaid, at least twenty-two states used the Title XIX funds to pay for voluntary sterilization. With regard to private insurance funding, by 1969, Blue Cross and Blue Shield paid for elective sterilization in most states. Voluntary, permanent surgical methods were finally becoming more accessible for the middle class, at least.

Richard Milhous Nixon became President in 1969. His administration encouraged both the OEO and the Department of Health, Education and Welfare (DHEW) to allocate more funds for family planning grants. Title X of the Public Health Service Act was signed into law by Nixon in 1970. When he did so, Nixon commented, "No American woman should be denied access to family planning assistance because of her economic condition. I believe, therefore, that we should establish as a national goal the provision of family planning services…to all who want but cannot afford them".

The regulations promulgated by Sargent Shriver were being called into question. The American Civil Liberties Union (ACLU) was one of the groups that was protesting OEO's ban of funding for surgical contraceptive services. They believed the ban discriminated against the poverty group.

It was generally agreed that the ban on abortion funding was consistent with the conscious intent of Congress, and besides that, abortion was still not legal. Objections, however, were increasingly being raised about the ban on funding for voluntary sterilizations.

Dr. Warren Hern, the young public health physician who was serving as the Chief of the Program Development and Evaluation branch of OEO at the time, reported an increasing interest in vasectomies, especially because use of that procedure had been spreading across the country in the new out-patient vasectomy clinics that were proliferating.

When Frank Carlucci was the assistant director of OEO in 1969, he had approved the removal of the bar against sterilization. However his boss, director Donald Rumsfeld, did not act upon the request. After Rumsfeld left the agency, Carlucci became the director and was in a position to review the request for the removal of the ban.

Carlucci agreed to delete the prohibition, influenced to a large degree by complaints from women who were wondering why family planning was only a woman's issue. They were encouraging a program that would include men, for example, by funding vasectomy programs.

In 1970, sterilization was able to be funded by DHEW and by the Public Health Service (PHS). Along with the availability of funds came a realization that there should be some parameters set for providers in order to ensure that all procedures were, in fact, voluntary. AVS had already taken a stand against any form of compulsion in sterilization, whether direct or implicit. There had been some situations reported in California where punitive sterilization had been proposed. There were also some concerns that non-English speaking clients might not know all they needed to make a fully informed decision.

In May of 1971, the italicized words in the following quotation were removed from the regulation that had been in effect since 1965: "No project funds shall be expended for any surgical procedures intended to *result in sterilization or* cause abortions." Once the new policy had been established, Dr. George Contis, the physician serving as Director of the OEO Family Planning Division, notified the health center directors that sterilization services were not to be initiated until precautionary safeguards had been prepared by his assistant, Dr. Warren Hern.

While DHEW's family planning program (Title X) and Medicaid (Title XIX) funds permitted sterilizations, OEO funds would not be available until Hern could develop guidelines. This brings us to the next phase in the work of AVS: ensuring free choice.

# CHAPTER 9: ENSURING FREE CHOICE

I do not think it is possible to report on the development of sterilization guidelines to ensure free choice without mentioning the valuable work of Dr. Warren Hern. Hern was head of the Program Development and Evaluation Branch of the Family Planning Division, Office of Health Affairs at the Office for Economic Opportunity (OEO) when it first initiated a family planning program for the poor as part of Johnson's "War on Poverty". His job had been to help set priorities for the family planning program, to design programs, and to evaluate them.

Dr. Hern was a public health physician with experience in women's health issues, not only in the United States, but overseas. He had served in the Peace Corps in Brazil, worked in the Peruvian Amazon as a third year medical student, and did his internship at Gorgas Hospital in the Canal Zone. He was especially moved by the suffering of large numbers of Latin American women who were dying of illegal abortions and lack of reproductive choices.

Hern's superior at OEO was Dr. George Contis, Director of the Division of Family Planning. Contis assigned Hern the responsibility of developing sterilization guidelines. The guidelines had to be approved and in place before any sterilization could be funded by OEO. Contis wanted to be able to field-test the guidelines by September, 1971.

Dr. Hern had been instrumental in changing the governmental policies to permit funding for voluntary sterilization services for those who wanted and needed services but were unable to afford them. With his experience and background, he was well-suited to take on this responsibility. In his own words, he was *"convinced that the development of guidelines was a significant step forward, not only in government policy, but the recognition of a fundamental need for people that had not been fulfilled, especially for the poor"*.

Hern worked in concert with AVS as well as Dr. Louise Tyrer, then the Medical Director of the Planned Parenthood Federation of America. I was the participant who represented AVS because I had long been the association's advocate for counseling as a pre-requisite for voluntary sterilization.

Hern worked diligently over the summer, his work strongly supported among health officials in the government and among non-governmental organizations. He was determined to produce a document that would have the approval of all the family planning and social welfare agencies. The process took more time than had been allocated. This delay was because so many agencies wanted to participate.

Some reviewers were adamant about extended waiting periods between the time of consent and the time of surgery. I was the vocal participant who kept insisting that there was no magical removal of risk by the simple passage of time. I insisted that counseling had to be a part of the process to assure that the decision to sign the surgical consent form had been thoroughly thought through. In all my presentations, both in public speaking engagements, media interviews, or to professional audiences, I tried to explain the difference between "informed consent" to any medical procedure, including voluntary sterilization, and an "informed decision" about a permanent change in reproductive capacity.

Over recent years, there had been a few lawsuits brought against surgeons by patients that had been sterilized. They fell into two categories. First, a doctor could be held liable if he or she caused a surgical injury while performing a sterilization operation or while providing post-operative care. A sub-set of these cases involved doctors who had failed to recognize that they had caused an injury and therefore did not treat the injury promptly. These, I referred to as "complications of the complication". Such unrecognized or untreated injuries deserved medical mal-practice compensation for the patient. Fortunately, these cases were very rare.

The other situation in which a doctor could be sued and be expected to lose his case was where the patient had not been fully informed about the procedure. Perhaps the patient had been under sedation in preparation for a Caesarean Section or delivery when the consent form was presented to her. Perhaps the doctor did not make it clear that the tubes could not be easily "untied" at a later date. These cases were generally resolved in the client's favor.

Doctors had become quite aware that to protect their professional reputation (as well as their bank account) they had to obtain an "informed consent" to the surgery. My contention was that simply giving facts to the client was not sufficient for sterilization surgery. Counseling should be offered to make sure the client had given full consideration to the non-medical components of the decision.

Hern labored over the guidelines during the summer of 1971 however they were not completed until December 27, three months later than originally expected. The guidelines drew the approval of everyone in the field. Besides getting the support of family planning agencies, Hern had walked the document through the government bureaucracy including the Office of Management and Budget. OMB finally granted their approval of the necessary "management information" forms, removing the last obstacle to publication and distribution.

The guidelines were finally printed on January 11, 1972. Included in the document were instructions that clients must be "informed enough to make a meaningful choice". Furthermore, they limited any services provided by OEO to those individuals who had *"the legal capacity to consent for surgery"*.

Once the guidelines had been finalized and approved, Hern submitted them to the American Journal of Public Health for publication. They were accepted for publication in that prestigious journal and Hern received a galley or page proof including the listing of the guidelines in the table of contents for an upcoming issue. At the last moment, the publication was cancelled, and Hern was told that it was at the demand of the White House. Upon reflection, years later, Hern felt that he should have gone public with this censorship, or suppression of information, about such a critical matter.

Although the guidelines had been printed, they were not distributed. Dr. Leon Cooper, an active member of the National Medical Association (the equivalent of the American Medical Association, but for black physicians) had become the new director of the Office of Health Affairs. His position was in authority over Dr. Contis' Family Planning Division there.

In my reviewing these events with Dr. Hern in December, 2013, he wrote, *"The conflict between Cooper and Contis was apparent from the moment of Cooper's arrival at OEO. It appeared to many of us as a basic power struggle, but these two men had starkly different views of the world and professional agendas. They didn't like each other, and they didn't like each other's politics."*

Dr. Cooper was opposed to the distribution of the guidelines for two reasons. He was personally uncomfortable with the idea of contraceptive sterilization, perhaps because he feared that black women might be targeted. He was also afraid that provision of voluntary sterilization surgeries would put a strain on his agency's budget. The result was that at the end of January, Cooper stopped the release of the new policy document.

President Richard Nixon condoned cancelling the distribution of the guidelines. He feared that his authorization of voluntary contraceptive sterilization would result in a Catholic backlash that would harm his re-election. As a result, the 25,000 copies of the guidelines were transferred to a warehouse in Washington, DC. I am sure I was not alone in thinking that the documents would be released and distributed after the election.

It was maddening to Hern that the process of issuing guidelines could be derailed in such an arbitrary and capricious way for reasons that he could not understand, of which he was not completely aware, or which were outrageously disconnected from the people whose needs he was trying to meet. He was encouraged by other family planning workers to hold a press conference to denounce the process. Instead, he resisted, thinking that he should follow a straightforward path and try to get the system to respond. He was also warned that he would jeopardize his career in government health services if he took any such action.

At the beginning of February, 1972, the start of the re-election season, the President's agents concluded that Nixon's well publicized opposition to abortion might also mean he would not want the government paying for voluntary sterilizations, which, like abortions, were contrary to Roman Catholic doctrine. His advisors included Paul O'Neill, an official at OMB, John Ehrlichman, Director of the new Domestic Council, and James Cavanaugh, who had responsibility for the health issues coming before the Council.

On February 2nd, Cooper advised Hern that the guidelines would not be issued. The White House wanted an "executive policy review", he explained. Two days later, the two hundred copies that Hern had set aside for distribution to the press were confiscated and lodged in a safe at OEO. The rest remained stored in cardboard boxes at the warehouse.

In discussions with Hern, while this manuscript was being drafted, he wrote to me, "*I was personally furious with Cooper and felt that our highly professional and comprehensive approach to the role of reproductive health care in the general context of health care for the poor was exactly right. It was what people said they wanted, and we were successful in many ways in meeting those needs. I sent Cooper several memoranda concerning the need for this program, and we got no reasonable response.*"

At the end of March, he sent another memo to Dr. Cooper, expressing his strong belief that the suppression of the guidelines placed the OEO programs in jeopardy. Funds were reportedly being used for services in some areas even in the absence of guidelines that were meant to ensure proper administration and supervision of the program.

Hern and Contis continued to try to force the release of the guidelines. They felt Cooper was abusing his power and letting politics override good public policy and public health administration. Hern tried to contact the White House counsel, John Dean, but only got to speak to Fred Fielding, Dean's assistant. Hern simply wanted the real reason the guidelines were being held back. He did not believe that the decision to withhold the guidelines had been a White House call, even though that was the excuse being used. Cooper did not appreciate Hern's going over his head to the White House.

Hern tried to reason with Cooper from a basis of facts and human need but to no avail. The profound disagreements about fundamental issues continued between them until June 2nd, when Hern resigned in protest of Cooper's mismanagement, incidentally the week of the Watergate break-in.

Nixon was re-elected in November. With George McGovern as his

Democratic opponent, he probably would have received the votes of many Catholics regardless of what OEO was doing about the guidelines. Besides, the Department of Health, Education and Welfare (DHEW) was already funding sterilizations – exactly what Colson, Cavanaugh and Cooper were so determined to prevent OEO from doing.

Nixon's second administration immediately dismantled OEO. Family planning programs were consolidated within DHEW. The guidelines were never used. They would have limited non-therapeutic sterilizations (not required for medical reasons) to those who were over twenty-one years of age, legally competent, and who had given their informed consent. Additionally, there would have been review committees and judges to watch over and assure adherence to the guidelines.

The National Family Planning Forum said the federal review requirements would create undue hardship for prospective patients, parents, or guardians. Dr. Carl Shultz, deputy director under Dr. Louis Helman at DHEW, pointed out that the guidelines would not be fully effective anyhow because DHEW lacked the surveillance and policing capabilities. This reinforced my belief that counseling by sensitive professionals was a better alternative to ensure free choice.

When the news broke about two Alabama teenage sisters having been sterilized became public, Hern was no longer employed at OEO. I remember, however, his reaction. If the guidelines we had worked on had been released as planned, these girls would not have been able to be sterilized.

AVS Executive Director Charles Faneuff was at the end of his six months of leadership, and Ira Lubell had not officially taken charge of national activities, concentrating instead on the AVS International Project. So I was the person who took the phone call in June of 1973, reporting that Minnie Lee and Mary Alice Relf had been sterilized. Coincidentally, Charles Pratt, the Director of the Alabama Council for Voluntary Family Planning, happened to be in my office at the time. I taped the entire phone conversation but unfortunately the cassette was lost over the years. The story I will relate is what I was told at the time before the story became a national media headline. Other versions of the incidents have been reported, such as "forced" sterilizations of girls whose parents were uninformed. Following is what I believe was the accurate reflection of the circumstances.

To understand this case, it is helpful to be aware of the changes that were taking place in birth control methods. There had recently been a policy change regarding the use of the injectable hormonal contraceptive, Depo-Provera. The drug had been commonly used for young women who were sexually active or presumed to be at risk for unwanted pregnancy. This method required a clinic visit for an injection every three months. It provided a safe and effective method, as do the progesterone methods we have available today. It was considered especially beneficial for sexually active girls who were not apt to be faithful in taking a daily oral contraceptive.

The injectable contraceptive had been the method chosen earlier by Mrs. Relf for her daughters. She had expressed her concern about boys "hanging around" the girls and she wanted to be sure they did not become pregnant. The method was satisfactory to every one concerned. According to the staff person who related the news to me, Mr. Relf was an absent father, never participating in decisions about the girls.

When the Food and Drug Administration decided to withdraw the use of the three-month injectable progesterone method pending further study, the family was faced with the need to select another method for the girls, who had been considered "slow" or retarded, and therefore unable to handle other methods such as the diaphragm, or other barrier methods. In addition to an intrauterine device (offered and provided for an older sister), sterilization was an option for mentally limited or disabled females whose guardians approved.

As I received the story, Mrs. Relf had been fully informed of the permanence of tubal ligation, and she was happy to sign approval for the girls. It was important for Mrs. Relf that her daughters not become pregnant and bring more possibly retarded children into the already stressed family. The surgery was done for both girls in a hospital. As I was informed, it was after the surgery, when the girls were ready for discharge from the hospital that Mr. Relf appeared with a religious worker from the local Roman Catholic Church. It was then that the "story" developed about how no one knew that the girls were going to be sterilized when they went to the hospital the day before.

Various books and articles have included the Relf saga, usually stressing involuntary, coercive sterilization of the girls, and assigning blame to the family providers serving the Relf family. My memories are different, but I believe I was getting the correct information at the time it was all happening. Regardless, it became clear that regulations were needed to assure that no involuntary sterilizations would be done in the future. In the meantime, there was a halt on all such funding.

# CHAPTER 10: THE ROLE OF THE COUNSELOR

During the years that the Federal guidelines were being developed, there were two factions at work. Some focused on the need to protect women from being coerced into a sterilization operation without the client's complete understanding of the surgery. They were the ones who were insisting on a waiting period between the time of the informative visit and the surgery. The other group focused on the need to provide the surgery without delay so that the number of consultations would be fewer, and travel arrangements might be easier for those women who lived some distance from the surgery site.

I understood the dilemma posed by these two opposing views, but I did not agree totally with either side. I spoke openly at every opportunity about where I stood. I did not believe that there was anything magical about a waiting period that would protect a woman from involuntary sterilization. I insisted that unless the woman had access to counseling during that period, the wait would be in vain. I began to address this subject in all my interviews with persons seeking comments from AVS about the issue.

I stressed the missing counseling component at all the meetings with other agencies who were involved with the development of the guidelines for federally funded sterilizations. There was a significant period for organizations such as AVS, Planned Parenthood, American Public Health Association, American Civil Liberties Union, and many others, to offer suggestions and comments. I am pleased that some of what I had to offer on behalf of AVS was considered during that process.

I was a lone voice for some time. A few years later, when the AVS librarian William Record was researching articles in the Population Information Program's internet library (Popline), he found that all of the articles, papers, and presentations that mentioned counseling had been authored by me. At the time of the drafting of this manuscript, I was proud and gratified to learn that EngenderHealth was still emphasizing their counseling program activities.

I continued to emphasize the need for counseling as an important component in the informed consent process. I took every opportunity to encourage discussions with clients about their personal situations rather than to simply read or recite a list of facts about sterilization before a client was presented with a consent form to sign. I did not believe that facts, however helpful, were enough to ensure a well-thought out decision. I feared that without personal discussions as an integral part of a counseling session, the forms would eventually become a routine without much meaning or significance.

My first significant presentation to a broad professional group that was involved was at the 105th annual meeting of the American Public Health Association held in Washington, DC, October 30 to November 2, 1977. I will include here the paper, verbatim, as I presented it to the group.

*The Role of the Health Professional in Counseling*

*The Association for Voluntary Sterilization (AVS) estimated that by the close of 1976, nearly nine million persons in the United States had chosen to terminate their fertility by means of a surgical procedure – voluntary sterilization.* [1] *According to the National Fertility Study of 1975, sterilization is now the single most popular method of birth control for couples married ten years or longer. Among couples who have had all the children they want, 43.5% have elected sterilization.* [2]

*It is clear that voluntary sterilization is now recognized not only as acceptable, but as a desired means of contraception. Yet, much recent publicity has focused on the issue of abuse i.e. coercion, especially of those who are dependent upon the public sector for their health care. There are numerous incidents of improperly obtained consent under duress, during labor, at the time of delivery, or under other stressful situations.* [3] *Similarly, AVS has in its files letters from individuals documenting the refusal by health and medical professionals to provide them with either information or services because of arbitrary restrictions of age, parity, religious or socio-economic criteria, particularly in rural or non-urban areas.*

*If the role of the health professional in counseling were to be defined succinctly, it would aim to prevent sterilization abuse that occurs when the procedure is performed without the patient's informed consent, and to ensure that the individual's right to obtain information and services is upheld. In order to eliminate all possibilities of abuse, guidelines must be developed and followed by those health professionals involved with persons in the decision-making process concerning this permanent, and at present, irreversible surgical method of contraception.*

*Standards of the Department of Health, Education and Welfare already govern the provision of sterilization services in federally funded facilities. They include a list of the various elements that constitute "informed consent" together with instructions for the safeguarding of patients' rights and other benefits.* [4]

*Bio-medical standards have been approved by both the Association for Voluntary Sterilization and the Planned Parenthood Physicians that mandate medical and surgical safeguards to protect the health of the patient. These address themselves to the qualifications of the surgeon and surgical assistants, the required equipment, recommended laboratory tests, etc. But there is not yet one clear-cut, uniform set of regulations or guidelines for sterilization counselors. What qualifications should they possess? What*

82

*role must they play?*

*One primary prerequisite for sterilization counselors should include a sympathetic attitude toward the concept of sterilization as an appropriate method of birth control. Implicit in the word "counselor" is the obligation to remain non-judgmental and objective. A good counselor will have the ability to recognize his or her own personal preferences and prejudices with regard to child-bearing, sexual anxieties, and satisfaction with another contraceptive method, and will guard against their intrusion into the decision-making process of the patient.*

*There is a growing movement today toward consumer medicine that urges greater involvement of patients in their own care – taking the responsible for decision-making. Second opinions are not only being sought, but encouraged before undergoing surgery. A reproductive health professional who is counseling prospective sterilization patients therefore has the responsibility to be thoroughly knowledgeable about all the available techniques so the patient can select the one with which she feels most comfortable. The direction and content of any interview will be influenced by several factors, for example, marital status or lifestyle of the prospective candidate, and accessibility to specific procedures in the particular area.*

*Counseling for partners in a stable relationship in which there are children will obviously vary from counseling for single persons or childless couples. With respect to surgical procedures, is it realistic, particularly in rural areas, to discuss a variety of surgical techniques when in fact only one laparoscopist or one general surgeon is within a 100 mile area? In such a case, choice will be limited to what the community can provide and, to a degree, may even determine the choice of candidate for the procedure. A situation of this kind may be seen as coercive, and needs to be approached cautiously to minimize any feelings of regret.*

*Post-partum sterilization can be done conveniently shortly after delivery through a small incision near the umbilicus. The ideal situation for this method would include patient counseling and arrangements made well in advance of the onset of labor.*

*Can a mechanism be established that will permit an individual to obtain a postpartum sterilization while protecting her from being influenced toward sterilization by even a well-intentioned physician? Can we meet the needs of rural women who may be forced to return to a hospital 150 miles from home for a desired sterilization and at the same time concern ourselves with minority women in municipal hospitals in urban settings where there may be a communication gap between the physician and the patient?*

*We hope both voluntary and government regulations can be flexible enough to design such a mechanism. It might include a provision for waiving a standard waiting period. A second opinion from another physician might be advisable, especially if the patient did not initiate the request for the sterilization. There might also be a required consultation with a specially trained patient advocate, ombudsman or social worker.*

*Even when the decision for postpartum sterilization is made early, the patient must be assured that she may cancel the surgery if she has any reservations about the birth or condition of the baby. She may wish to proceed with the sterilization regardless of the health of the infant, but she should certainly be given the opportunity to explore her feelings about this during counseling.*

*Should the counseling include a discussion of the neonatal death rate? It may not be of concern to a person who already has more children than planned, but if the prospective patient is one who is planning a postpartum sterilization after the birth of a second child because a two-child family is the goal, this could be critical.*

*Specialized counseling is also valuable when delivery is to be by Caesarean section. In these instances, when the patient is more than likely to be under general anesthesia, she will not be able to make a last minute change of plan. Prior arrangements should have been made about whether or not to proceed if the condition of the baby seems questionable.*

*A sterilization procedure may also be combined with abortion, but is suitable only in those instances where fertility termination was under consideration prior to the accidental and unwanted conception.*

*Interval tubal sterilization is unrelated to pregnancy and allows a woman unlimited time to carefully weigh her decision and schedule the operation at her convenience. However, these interval sterilizations also present special considerations for the counseling health professional. Myths and misconceptions are prevalent in many areas. Tube tying may be understood as a procedure after which the tubes could be "untied" at will, or tubes that will untie themselves after a period of years. How does the patient interpret the term "band-aid surgery" – a phrase often applied to laparoscopic tubal sterilization? Do such non-medical labels appear as simple, no-risk, no complication procedures? Patients must be made aware that though seemingly minor, these procedures carry the dangers and problems of all major abdominal surgery.*

*Minilaparotomy (called minilap) is a recently introduced procedure that offers the advantage of a simple sterilization techniques without the rare hazards associated with laparoscopy (e.g. hemorrhage from perforation of vessels by the instruments or from electrical burns). Although minilap is widely used in developing countries, it is only available in the U.S. on a very limited basis. Recent publicity [5] has described minilap as an ideal procedure to be done in free-standing clinics under local anesthesia. Costs are expected to be considerably less than in-hospital sterilizations. Removal from the hospital setting ensures that the procedure will become patient-initiated, thereby effectively reducing some of the situations conducive to sterilization abuse.*

*If female sterilization us going to be performed under local anesthesia, the patient will have to be prepared for the possible discomfort – or even actual pain – that might occur. It is essential that the patient be told about each step of the procedure and what discomforts she can expect during its various stages.*

*In meeting with prospective sterilization patients, the counselor must be alert to indications of special need for in-depth discussions. Such indications would include the individual who has a physical, mental or emotional condition which, it is assumed would be improved by the sterilization. For example, the vasectomy candidate who is troubled with impotence or other sexual problems may see vasectomy as the resolution to his difficulty; couples in an unstable marital relationship may believe that sterilization of one or the other may terminate not only their fertility, but their marital difficulties as well. Counselors are obligated to direct the person's thinking away from such unrealistic expectations.*

*Any evidence of coercion should be seen as a contraindication to sterilization. This can range from subtle pressure exerted on a man by his wife "for the sake of her health", to open coercion in the case of government-ordered compulsory sterilization as a solution to the problems of overpopulation.*

*Individuals considering sterilization because of economic problems might later regret their decision should their financial status improve. Young, single or childless persons may, at some later date, wish they had not taken the permanent step of fertility termination. Certainly, those persons counting on a possible reversal of the sterilization, or those who insist upon banking sperm before vasectomy, need special attention, and present particular challenges for counselors.*

*In recent years, correlated with the increased numbers who have undergone sterilizations, the number of requests for reversal of sterilizations has increased. In our opinion, this is not to be construed as poor judgment on the part of the patient, faulty counseling, or even unrealistic attitudes toward the procedure. Of the patients seeking restoration of their fertility, the vast majority are doing so because their family and/or marital relationships have changed.*

*How does a counselor present the arguments against successful reversal in individual cases while at the same time making it clear that reversals are increasingly successful? The counselor must present the total situation honestly, with the built-in tension factor of the strong possibility of unsuccessful reversal surgery. The prospective patient should be informed that there is ever-increasing surgical technology that may offer broader success than that possible today. Having done this, the counselor must then back away and let the patient make the final decision.*

*No one, no government, no institution can guarantee perfect decision-making, free of regret. No mechanism and no set of restrictions exists that will ensure this. Our objective is to see that the patient understands the risks and benefit, the possibility of change, and believes that he or she has made the right choice under present circumstances.*

*Based upon logical and reasonable considerations, most healthy people make the best possible decisions at a given time.*

1. *AVS, Estimate of the Number of Sterilizations Performed in the United States, Nov. 1977.*
2. *Westoff, C.F., and Jones, E.F., Contraception and Sterilization in the United States: 1965-1975, Family Planning Perspectives, Vol. 9, No.4:153-157, July/August, 1977.*
3. *American Civil Liberties Union, Reproductive Freedom Project Legal Docket, June, 1977.*
4. *DHEW, Federal Register, Vol. 39, No. 76, April 18, 1974.*
5. *Minilap Reduces Sterilization Risks, Family Planning Perspectives, Vol. 9, No. 2: 85-86, March/April 1977.*

In 1978, DHEW published the Federal Guidelines for Sterilizations in the November 8 issue of the Federal Register. There was a mandatory waiting period but no mention of counseling with the clients about his or her personal situation. The guidelines included a very extensive list of facts that had to be covered during the information-giving session prior to obtaining an "informed consent" from the client.

The idea that a patient had to sign a consent form stemmed from the time when all surgery was done at the recommendation of a doctor or surgeon. It was routine for all procedures to be performed. But times had changed and it was now the clients who were requesting the surgery. The terminology now seemed a bit backward to me. In my mind, if the client wanted to be sterilized and was requesting the service, it should be the provider who would consent to do it. For a client to "consent" to a permanent end to child-bearing, suggests to me that it was someone else's idea, thus perhaps not entirely voluntary. It might have been better if the client had to sign a request that included a statement about her having had all her questions answered to her satisfaction. Then the surgeon would sign the request form to indicate his or her willingness to provide the requested service.

# CHAPTER 11: FEDERAL REGULATIONS

Before 1973, DHEW had funded voluntary sterilizations among other family planning services. After the cases of coercion raised in July, the Department responded by imposing a moratorium on Federal funding for persons under age twenty-one or legally incapable of consent. The Department then began rulemaking proceedings that led to the adoption of interim rules in April 1974. These rules required the client to be over age twenty-one and mentally competent under State law. Further, there was a mandatory waiting period of seventy-two hours from the time of consent until the sterilization procedure. These rules were to remain in effect until Federal Regulations were finalized in 1978.

There were a number of situations that did not lend themselves to an inflexible rule. One such situation was the question of some mentally impaired persons who were sufficiently aware of their limitations and wanted to be sure not to create a child that perhaps could not be cared for. Another situation was whether or not an institutionalized person could be granted a sterilization procedure. While institutionalization lends itself to possible coercion, there are conceivably times when a physical problem that requires institutionalization, the incapacitated person should be free to make a decision about contraception. It had always been the policy of AVS that mentally or physically impaired persons should be able to enjoy sexual activity even if they could not cope with parenthood.

In preparing the regulations, the Department was fully aware of these touchy situations but they were faced with the need to build safeguards into the Federal programs while at the same time building a strong and effective enforcement program. Dealing with these conflicting viewpoints required the Department to make difficult judgments, however, the proposed regulations were hoped to be a workable balance between conflicting ideas. Wanted was a workable balance in which no one consideration was given so much weight that another was not achieved, and in which the overall goal of providing federally-funded sterilizations to those who voluntarily choose this service would be realized. The regulations dictated the adoption of policies that minimized exceptions, that did not make subtle or individual distinctions, and that were susceptible to verification or documentation.

The proposed rules were made public and comments were encouraged.

The preamble to the Notice of Proposed Rulemaking identified several major issues on which public comment was particularly solicited. Specifically, they were asked to define "sterilization". They were asked to comment on the appropriateness of the thirty day waiting period, the appropriateness of the age twenty-one minimum, and the provisions relating to the sterilization of mental incompetents and institutionalized individuals. The Department was also seeking comments about the effectiveness of the informed consent procedures of the proposed rules, and the appropriateness of excluding hysterectomy as a family planning technique. Revision of the proposed rules was organized around these major issues.

The *Federal Register*, published Volume 43, No 217, on Wednesday, November 8, 1978. It reported the final rules and regulations prepared by the Department of Health, Education and Welfare. They relate to federally financed voluntary sterilizations. The quoted sections that follow are from that publication.

**Definition of "sterilization"**: The text of the proposed rule read "Sterilization means any procedure or operation for the purpose of rendering an individual permanently incapable of reproducing". Several comments pointed out that it is possible to sterilize by administering certain drugs or x-rays and the definition as proposed would not cover such cases. The definition was accordingly modified to include "treatment" (by drugs or x-rays) for the purpose of inducing sterility.

It should be emphasized that the definition does not cover medical procedures which, while they may have the effect of producing sterility, have an entirely different purpose, such as removal of a cancerous uterus or prostate gland. In such a case, there is no reasonable alternative to the procedure so the rationale for imposing the requirements does not apply.

**Thirty-Day waiting period:** the proposed rule was simply that "programs or projects shall perform or arrange for the performance of sterilization of a mentally competent individual only when at least thirty days have passed between the date of the informed consent and the date of the sterilization. Comments pointed out that a similar waiting period would not be required for persons who could fund their own sterilizations so this would discriminate against the poor. Comments also pointed out that the wait would create a hardship for sterilizations for residents of rural areas, migratory workers, and many low-income individuals who might have difficulty obtaining services.

The majority of comments received that addressed the thirty-day waiting period advocated provision for waiver of the waiting period for special circumstances. Specifically, imposition of an inflexible requirement in cases of premature delivery or emergency abdominal surgery would be medically unsound as the client would have to undergo two surgical procedures with concomitantly increased risks. Several of these comments recommending a waiver suggested nevertheless that at least seventy-two hours should pass from the time of consent until surgery.

The text of the final rules stated that "programs or projects to which this subpart applies shall perform or arrange the performance of sterilization of a mentally competent individual only if the following requirements have been met: at least thirty days but no more than one hundred eighty days have passed between the date of informed consent and the date of the sterilization, except in the case of premature delivery or emergency abdominal surgery. An individual may consent to be sterilized at the time of premature delivery or emergency abdominal surgery if at least seventy-two hours have passed after he or she gave informed consent to sterilization. In the case of premature delivery, the informed consent must have been given at least thirty days before the expected date of delivery."

**Minimum age of twenty-one:** The final rule was basically unchanged from the proposed rule. "Programs or projects shall perform or arrange for the performance of sterilizations of individuals only if the individual is at least twenty-one years at the time consent is obtained". Some comments suggested a lower age to coincide with a state's age or consent, which might be eighteen. This would cause an administrative problem. It would not be feasible to have different minimum ages in each state. Other comments suggested a higher age in the hope that there would be fewer incidences of regret. Considering the comments on both sides of the issue, the final decision was to retain the proposed twenty-one year old age requirement.

**Sterilization of mentally incompetent individuals:** The proposed text for the rule prohibited sterilization of any person declared mentally incompetent by a Federal, State or local court, or a person who "is in fact mentally incompetent under Federal or State law". This last portion posed difficulties for a great number of reviewers. Many comments questioned what the proposed test of "incompetent in fact" meant. One attorney stated that since the parameters of legal incompetence differ from state to state, the term "incompetent in fact" was so vague as to be meaningless. Another attorney suggested that since under many State laws persons are presumed competent until adjudicated incompetent, the term and the application of it mandated by the proposed rule would require persons such as physicians and social workers to perform a judicial function they have no legal authority to perform.

AVS was the group that had most information and experience with sterilization of mentally challenged individuals. Even after AVS's early involvement with eugenic sterilizations had ended, there continued to be a significant portion of the membership and board of directors who believed that mentally ill or mentally retarded individuals might, in spite of their limitations, be able to understand that having a method to end the risk of pregnancy might enable them to have a normal sex life. One board member, Mrs. Medora Bass, who also had been the president of the Planned Parenthood Association of Philadelphia, was the most outspoken proponent of offering sterilization to those mentally challenged individuals who were none-the-less mentally able to understand the risks and benefits of surgical birth control.

AVS had developed many informational brochures about voluntary sterilization. They were mailed to individuals seeking either general information or answers to specific questions about voluntary sterilization. The brochures were also sold to doctors and clinic who wanted to put them in their waiting rooms for patient information. Among these brochures was one that addressed contraceptive sterilization for mentally disabled persons who could understand and make a choice. I believe that this material developed by AVS played an important role in the discussions that resulted in the rules pertaining to sterilization of mentally ill persons.

After an extensive review of the public comments, the Department finalized the rule. The text that resulted stated, "programs or projects to which these rules apply shall not perform or arrange for the performance of a sterilization of any mentally incompetent individual". A related requirement defined a 'mentally incompetent individual' to be "a person who has been declared mentally incompetent by a Federal, State or local court of competent jurisdiction for any purpose unless he or she has been declared competent for purposes which include the ability to consent to sterilization".

**Sterilization of institutionalized individuals:** The proposed rule generally would have prevented sterilization of persons in an institution, but it set forth a number of conditions, under which sterilization might be obtained. After the many comments were reviewed, the Department decided they would not permit any exceptions because of the 'inherently coercive' nature of institutions. There would be no federally funded sterilizations of institutionalized individuals.

They went on to define such persons. "An 'institutionalized individual' means a person who is (1) involuntarily confined or detained, under a civil or criminal statue, in a correctional, or rehabilitative facility including a mental hospital or other facility for the care and treatment of mental illness, or (2) confined under a voluntary commitment, in a mental hospital or other facility for the care and treatment of mental illness."

This definition covers all institutions where persons are confined as a result of a court order. It also covers all facilities such as half-way houses regardless of whether the person has been civilly committed or has voluntarily signed him or herself in as a patient. The definition does not cover health care institutions, such as acute care hospitals, which are not primarily residential and which provide medical services.

**Informed Consent Procedures:**   The purpose of spelling out the details of what would constitute an "informed" consent is clearly legal in nature. The carefully worded definition was to protect the doctor as much as the patient. Some accusations of involuntary sterilizations had to do with whether the surgeon had enough evidence to back his claim that the patient had been aware of what was being offered. Some persons who later regretted their decisions for sterilization tried to accuse the doctor of not informing them of the consequences of the surgery. For example, there had been stories of patients who thought that if they had their tubes "tied", they could just have them "untied" at a later date.

Many of the comments offered during the review process suggested expansion of the counseling process to include individual sessions not only to provide informative details about the surgery but to help the client clarify his or her feelings about a permanent contraceptive. I was a vocal advocate for this inclusion, but in the final wording, this counseling component was omitted. While the Department admitted that such additional procedures would be desirable, and encouraged them when possible, they were rejected as being "administratively infeasible."

The text of the final rule regarding the informed consent requirement follows. "Informed consent does not exist unless a consent form is completed voluntarily and in accordance with all the requirements of this section.

(a) An individual who obtains an informed consent for a sterilization procedure must offer to answer any questions the individual to be sterilized may have concerning the procedures, provide a copy of the consent form and provide orally all of the following information or advise to the person who is to be sterilized:

(1) Advice that the individual is free to withhold or withdraw consent to the procedure at any time prior to the sterilization with out affecting his or her right to future care or treatment, and without loss or withdrawal of any federally funded program benefits to which the individual might be otherwise entitled;

(2) A description of available alternative methods of family planning and birth control;

(3) Advice that the sterilization procedure is considered to be irreversible;

(4) A thorough explanation of the specific procedure to be performed;

(5) A full description of the discomforts and risks that may accompany and follow the performing of the procedure, including an explanation of the type and possible effects of the anesthetic to be used;

(6) A full description of the benefits or advantages that may be expected as a result of the sterilization; and

(7) Advice that the sterilization will not be performed for at least thirty days except under the circumstances specified in paragraph 50.203(d) of this subpart.

(b) An interpreter must be provided to assist the individual to be sterilized if he or she does not understand the language used on the consent form or the language used by the person obtaining consent.

(c) Suitable arrangements must be made to insure that information specified in paragraph (a) of this section is effectively communicated to individuals to be sterilized who are blind, deaf, or otherwise handicapped.

(d) A witness chosen by the individual to be sterilized may be present when consent is obtained.

(e) Informed consent may not be obtained while the individual to be sterilized is:

(1) in labor or childbirth

(2) seeking to obtain or obtaining an abortion, or

(3) under the influence of alcohol or other substance that affects the individual's state of awareness.

(f) Any requirement of State and local law for obtaining consent, except one of spousal consent, must be followed."

The final text goes on to include specific details about certifications of signatures of the various persons involved. I did not think all these details needed to be spelled out here, but there was one related requirement that was critical to include. *"Programs or projects to which these regulations apply shall perform or arrange for the performance of sterilization of a mentally competent individual only when the following requirements have been met: the individual has voluntarily given his or her informed consent in accordance with all the afore-mentioned procedures and at least thirty days, but no more than one hundred eighty days have passed between the date of informed consent and the date of the sterilization".*

The remainder of the Department's publication of the regulations dealt primarily with sample pamphlets that could be produced to give to the public and to prospective sterilization clients. I can quite proudly say that information in these samples came primarily from AVS, where I had been constantly adding to the pamphlets we made available to both individuals and to providers of service. They described vasectomy for men, the various approaches to the female tubes, including abdominal or vaginal surgery or laparoscopy. They covered post-partum and non-pregnancy-related timing, and issues to consider when thinking about permanent birth control.

# CHAPTER 12: ADVANCES IN FEMALE STERILIZATION

In 1880, Dr. S.S. Lungren, in Toledo, Ohio, performed the first tubal ligation for a woman having a cesarean section. Until this time, removal of the ovaries, with subsequent menopause, would have been the accepted procedure to permanently prevent another pregnancy. Lundgren was convinced that the surgical risk would be reduced by simply tying off a segment of the Fallopian tubes, and that the same result would be accomplished. This forward-thinking man started a series of advances in the surgical techniques that have been used over the ensuing years to provide women with safer and simpler methods of achieving permanent sterility.

After Lungren's demonstration that removal of the ovaries was not necessary to ensure sterility, the simpler ligation of the tubes still required a large incision, general anesthesia, and a hospital stay of at least two days. There were a few doctors who were using a vaginal approach to the tubes. That had the advantage of leaving no abdominal scar, but it still required general anesthesia and up to three days in a hospital.

The desire to view the cavities of the body was reported centuries ago. Early in the nineteenth century, urologists were attempting to view the urinary bladder with a "viewing tube". They used a candle and series of mirrors. It did not find favor among surgeons because it was impractical, but it probably served as an inspiration to future inventors.

To view internal abdominal organs, there has to be a light source, a way to inflate the abdomen so that structures can be moved about, and instruments to operate. In 1938, Janos Veress, in Hungary, had invented a needle with which he could inflate the body cavity with a gas, usually carbon dioxide. Originally, that "Veress needle" was used for inflation of the chest cavity. The needle was later used for inflation of the abdomen for laparoscopy. The primary difficulty that persisted was the lack of an effective light source.

When doctors first thought of using the laparoscopic approach for female sterilization, the question to be solved was deciding the method to occlude the Fallopian tubes. With traditional open incisions, the doctor had his "fingers in the belly" so he was able to tie a ligature around a loop of the Fallopian tube and remove the section. If the procedure were to be performed instead with no fingers, but "an eye in the belly", the occlusion would have to utilize an instrument that could be manipulated through the viewing tube, the laparoscope. The use of electrical current seemed the practical answer.

In the early 1960s, French surgeon Raoul Palmer described his adaptation of biopsy forceps to electrocoagulate the tubes. He used high-voltage generators that required the use of a grounding plate under the patient. The electric current traveled down the unipolar forceps, coagulated (or cooked) the segment of each tube that was grasped by the forceps, and then exited the body via the ground plate. There was a risk of sparking from the electrical current, and when that occurred, there was potential serious damage to nearby abdominal organs. In spite of these difficulties, surgeons were excited about the benefits that could follow being able to visualize the pelvic organs and structures for the first time without the need for a large incision.

In those early attempts to operate through a scope, lighting continued to pose a major problem. A small filament lamp on the tip of the scope provided only a dim red light to view the abdominal structures. Later, Palmer began to transmit light by the use of quartz rods. These were very hot and could potentially burn the patient's tissues, but they provided better illumination. To cool the rods, a vacuum system was used, adding to the difficulty of the operation. Another problem was that the vacuum cooling system was so noisy that the operators could not hear each other in the room.

Karl Storz, in Germany, was an early innovator who had been producing bronchoscopes for throat specialists in the mid 50s. In 1960, he set out to introduce very bright, but cold light into the body cavities through use of a laparoscope. By 1965, the development of fiberoptic bundles had improved the visibility to the extent that surgeons were increasingly documenting their surgery by means of photographic images. Storz' contributions were an important step for the advancement of laparoscopy.

Palmer, who spoke five languages, was able to teach many other doctors. He worked with his physician wife, Elisabeth, in hosting visiting surgeons from many counties. Meanwhile, Patrick Steptoe was initiating advances in laparoscopy, with his physiologist colleague Robert Edwards, at the Oldham Hospital in Great Britain. Edwards and Steptoe hoped to visualize the act of ovulation, which was still a mystery, never having been seen.

In Germany, Hans Frangenheim was practicing laparoscopy, publishing his data, and making improvements in laparoscopic techniques in Konstanz. He was a fertility specialist and envisioned laparoscopy as a tool to treat infertility. At the same time, Kurt Semm, in Stuttgart, began to imagine eventually being able to conduct an increasing variety of surgical procedures through the laparoscope. He could be considered the "father" of minimally invasive surgery.

Robert Neuwirth, working at St. Luke's - Roosevelt Hospital in New York, has been credited with bringing laparoscopy to the United States after having worked with Palmer in France and Steptoe in Great Britain in the mid 60s. When he returned to the United States, he approached the American Cystoscope Makers, Inc. (ACMI) in New York, encouraging them to begin manufacturing laparoscopes so that American surgeons would not have to depend upon the two West German companies, one owned by Dr. Karl Storz (trading as Karl Storz Endoscopy) and the other by Dr. Richard Wolf. In time, Wolf established an American distributing office in Illinois for North and South America, called Richard Wolf Medical Instrument Corporation.

Also 1968, Canadian Dr. Jacques-Emile Rioux went to Paris to study with Palmer. He had completed his medical training in Quebec and subsequently had advanced surgical training at Johns Hopkins. Fascinated by Palmer's technique, he (like Neuwirth) bought a Wolf telescope and a light source. He had also obtained the equipment needed to inflate the abdomen with gas, a necessary step in laparoscopy. The gas enables the surgeon to manipulate the abdominal organs and to separate one internal structure from another.

Before returning to Quebec, Rioux stopped in Baltimore to visit his former professors and surgical resident colleagues. When they learned that he had with him all the necessary instruments and equipment to perform a laparoscopy, they invited him to demonstrate the surgical procedure at Johns Hopkins, which led to that hospital's becoming a leading training center for laparoscopy.

Ray (Reimert) Ravenholt, an epidemiologist who fervently believed that world-wide overpopulation was a critical matter to be dealt with, had been named head of the new Population Branch of the U.S. Agency for International Development (USAID) in 1966. His idea was to saturate the developing countries with contraceptives, especially the Pill, which had become available by then. He obtained pills from various manufacturers, depending on the lowest bidder for the contract, without regard to the doses and side effects of the pills that were coming to light.

In the early 70s, Ravenholt was in communication with AVS regarding potential funding of a program that would promote sterilization services overseas. AVS obtained funding for its International Project in 1972. Johns Hopkins was also named as a potential training center for female contraceptive methods, particularly laparoscopy. Johns Hopkins began its Program for Information and Education in Gynecology and Obstetrics

(JHPIEGO) in 1974 under the leadership of Dr. Theodore King.

Meanwhile, inventors William Knepshield and Russell Lampman started a company (KLI) to manufacture a laparoscopy system especially designed to be used for tubal sterilization. Unlike a laparoscope that could be used for a variety of surgical procedures, the KLI laprocator was only suitable for occluding the tubes. A trained doctor might be able to visualize a woman's tubes to diagnose endometriosis, for example, but would not be able to treat it through the laprocator. Similarly, one might diagnose an ectopic pregnancy, but not remove the misplaced embryo as could have been done with a laparoscope. The advantage was that the laprocator was far less expensive, so USAID was very much in favor of its use in the international programs they were supporting.

In order to simplify provision of safer services in rural areas or in out-patient facilities, there were efforts to substitute Silastic bands applied to the tubes instead of using electrical current to coagulate the tubal segment. Dr. InBae Yoon, who had started his studies in Korea, introduced the method in the US in 1972 when he continued his clinical investigations at Johns Hopkins. His technique was to place either one or two tiny bands around a loop of each tube. The tissue caught in the loop would scar the tube and result in obstruction much the same way sutures would seal the tubes after a ligation. The non-electrical method appealed to USAID. With their backing, by the late 70s, the laprocator with the Yoon bands had become the most used technique in the international programs. Doctors completing a study course with JHPIEGO were provided with a free laprocator.

Jaroslav Hulka, MD, of the Department of Obstetrics and Gynecology at the University of North Carolina wanted to develop a clip to be applied to the tubes. With a bioengineer, George Clemens, of Chicago, they designed what became known as the Hulka-Clemens clip. The clip had two hinged plastic jaws that were locked in place by a gold-plated and stainless steel spring that would apply continuous pressure. This clip required a special clip applicator, so although it became a common technique in the United States and other developed countries, it was not a part of the USAID-funded programs.

In Nottingham, England, Marcus Filshie, MD, developed another style of clip made of titanium with a soft silastic lining. Unlike Hulka's, this clip did not have potentially dangerous teeth in the jaws. Nor did it require a spring to hold the jaws together. Once applied, the Filshie clip lining maintained pressure on the tube, resulting in eventual necrosis at the clip site. The system required a specially designed applicator, depending on whether the clips were being applied through an open abdominal incision or by laparoscopy.

The Filshie Clip System became accepted as the "Gold Standard" for female sterilization around the world, and offered women the best chances for potential reversal because so little of the tubes were damaged. Because of lengthy tests demanded by the U.S. Food and Drug Administration (FDA), the Filshie clips were not commercially available for sale in America until the 1980s. Unfortunately, like the Hulka Clip, it was not suitable for the international programs funded by USAID because of the costs. While a surgeon in the developed world might not mind a cost of forty dollars for a set of clips, that amount would be prohibitive in the poorer countries of the world.

The American Association of Gynecologic Laparoscopists (AAGL) was founded in 1971 by Dr. Jordan M. Phillips. This medical association was dedicated to research and advancement of all kinds of minimally invasive gynecologic procedures. It grew to over 5,000 members, world-wide. AAGL was interested in establishing a relationship with AVS, and I became the link between the two groups.

In 1973, I was invited to participate in one of AAGL's laparoscopy training courses, held in Quebec. It was at this meeting that Dr. Rioux demonstrated his new invention, a bipolar forceps. This innovation was expected to reduce one of the serious risks of electrocoagulation in that the current would only flow down one jaw of the forceps, through the grasped tissue, and back up the other jaw of the instrument. This eliminated the need for a grounding plate and would avoid any spark-gap injuries to adjacent organs.

Unfortunately, production and distribution of the Rioux Bipolar Tubal Forceps did not go as well as expected. Despite patents having been secured for Canada, the US and twenty-five other countries, the patents were not properly defended. That resulted in other instrument makers being able to make and market bipolar forceps with impunity.

As the use of bipolar forceps increased, so did the questions about the most effective technique for coagulating the tubes. There were numerous articles and medical discussions about whether the surgeon should coagulate one, two, or possibly three sections of each tube. While unipolar coagulation had been codified, with specific instructions regarding electrical current to be used, those issues were unclear with regard to bipolar electrocoagulation.

In the US, about that same time, Dr. Stephen Corson, in Pennsylvania, had also designed a bipolar forceps that was manufactured by the Cameron-Miller Company, owned by John Martin in Chicago. Corson's instrument had a pistol grip and insulated jaws that were able to both coagulate the tubes and then cut across the desiccated area to further separate the ends.

By 1976, FDA (which had a medical device division under its power) had identified too high a number of failures with bipolar methods. The agency demanded much larger studies of efficacy. They wanted multiple sites with a large number of surgeons and many patients in each group. The costs of such an undertaking were prohibitive to Cameron-Miller as the number of sales did not justify the expense and time of such a large study.

By the time bipolar electrocoagulation had lost favor, the clips were becoming more common. Less of the tube was damaged during the procedure, so if there were ever to be a request for a reversal of the surgery, there would be a better chance at successful rejoining the separated ends of the tubes.

Many of the founding members of AAGL offered their services as trainers to other countries. Dr. Clifford Wheeless of Johns Hopkins University was an advocate for using an "operating laparoscope", one that had a channel for auxiliary instruments. This required only one opening into the abdomen, as compared to the earlier scopes that required two openings: one for providing the light through its lens system, and the other channel for the operating instruments. Wheeless took this technique to Nepal, Thailand, El Salvador and India. Dr. Kanti Giri, who had learned it from him in Katmandu, provided the procedure to the people of the mountains of Nepal, but she used only local anesthesia because there were very few anesthesiologists in the country.

Along with innovations in laparoscopy came new capabilities for photographing tissues as seen through the scope's lens. The first meeting of AAGL that I attended was held in New Orleans in 1973. Hans Frangenheim, from Konstanz, Germany, had been the featured luncheon speaker. He had attached a camera to the lens of his laparoscope and had been photographing his findings. He showed the first film of human ovulation ever photographed. We could see the egg as it was being exploded out of the follicle, followed by the extruded liquid and detritus that accompanied the ova. Never before had a human eye witnessed this miracle. Frangenheim got a standing ovation and I was left with a permanent image of the event in my mind.

It was in November, 1977, when AAGL met in San Francisco, that Patrick Steptoe reported his successful fertilization of the ova of Louise Brown in a Petri dish. At the next meeting, we saw photos of the baby born in July of 1978, the first successful in vitro fertilization resulting in a successful pregnancy and live birth. Again, an unforgettable experience I had as a result of my association with these leading laparoscopists.

I continued to be the liaison between AVS and AAGL. I was invited to their conference every year, and often was given an opportunity to take part in one of their roundtable discussions or to present a paper at a plenary session. In turn, when any of these laparoscopists wanted information about any aspect of sterilization besides surgical technique, I was able to provide it. As a result of this affiliation, I maintained, on first name terms, a relationship with the world's leading laparoscopists, continuing to attend the annual AAGL conferences long after I retired from AVS.

To celebrate the one hundred years of advances in female sterilization since Lundgren's first tubal ligation, I proposed that AVS sponsor a Centennial Conference. The idea was approved by the AVS Executive Committee, and the Conference was successfully held in Monterey, California, in June, 1980. We were joined in this enterprise by the Planned Parenthood Federation of America (PPFA) under the leadership of Louise Tyrer, MD, and the Association of Planned Parenthood Physicians (APPP) under Johns Hopkins' Theodore King, MD, who was able to provide continuing medical education credits for the participants.

Countless innovations and new instruments had occurred over those one hundred years. Various changes in the approach to the tubes expanded from laparotomy to laparoscopy, colpotomy, culdoscopy, mini-laparotomy and hysteroscopy. Tubes, which once had to be cut and tied, could be coagulated, banded or clipped. Experiments were also being conducted to find ways to plug the tubes. Conference attendees were brought up to speed on the more recent developments in female sterilization. It had been a century of great changes in gynecology.

Innovations are on-going, and surgical procedures will continue to improve as time goes on. Shortly after the Centennial Conference, a solid state video camera was used during laparoscopy. With that equipment, the operating surgeons and assistants were able to visualize the operative field on a video monitor. In 1983, the first appendectomy was performed by Kurt Semm, who had predicted such procedures many years before. In 1987, the first gall bladder resection was done using the laparoscopic approach. The era of minimally invasive surgery had truly arrived.

# CHAPTER 13: INTRODUCING MINILAP

Sterilization surgery for women was always a surgical procedure fraught with more risks than vasectomy for men. While the vas is easily accessible through the scrotal skin, the oviducts are within the abdominal cavity, necessitating an incision through layers of muscle. Before the advent of laparoscopy and minilap, traditional tubal ligation at a time not associated with childbirth usually resulted in a four to five inch scar with an equal number of days recovering in a hospital. The medical term for this abdominal surgery is 'laparotomy'. The incision was usually done in the midline from umbilicus to the pubic bone, with the large scar leaving a visual reminder of the woman's sterility. When surgeons began to work through a much smaller incision, the name of the abdominal procedure became 'mini-laparotomy', or minilap.

The uterus is an inverted pear-shaped organ. The tubes extend on each side from the upper, rounded fundus toward the ovaries. Each tube ends in a fringed opening called the fimbria. This finger-like structure is adjacent to the ovary. It helps to capture the ova as it is expelled from the gland, and aids its journey down the tube where fertilization takes place. From the tube, the embryo travels to the uterus where it can grow and be nourished.

The fimbriae are important identifiers during surgery for sterilization. Two other structures, the round ligament and the ovarian ligament, are adjacent to the oviducts. A surgeon planning to occlude the oviduct will follow the tube to the fimbriated ends to assure the proper tissue has been grasped.

Post-partum sterilization was easier from the standpoint of the surgeon. It required only a small incision near the umbilicus. Through that opening, the oviducts, which had been displaced during pregnancy, could be grasped and ligated. Because the enlarged uterus brought the tubes so near the surface, they could be visualized and accessed with less difficulty. An additional advantage was that the woman needed only to add a day or two to her stay at the maternity hospital. Postpartum tubal ligation never became popular in the United States, perhaps because maternity units were not set up to provide elective surgery at an unscheduled date. It would not have been convenient for the operating room staff.

In Japan, Dr. Hajime Uchida began to work with smaller incisions many years before anyone else. Uchida owned and operated his own hospital so may have had more latitude in trying new techniques or making surgical innovations. His interest was to reduce the size of abdominal incisions. Tubal ligation was an excellent procedure to practice his refined surgery. To better reach the tubes, he developed an adaptation of a urinary catheter that he inserted through the cervix, into the uterus. By manipulating this instrument he would be able to bring the tubes closer to the abdominal wall. That made it easier to grasp the tubes and to remove a segment.

Uchida began his work in the 1940s but his earliest publication was not until 1961. He was probably the first person to describe the smaller incision as a mini-laparotomy, or 'mini-lap'. He continued into the late 70s. By then, he had reported doing over 20,000 tubal sterilizations without a failure. His technique was to remove the entire fimbriae, thus guaranteeing successful sterility. He also used general anesthesia for his procedures. As other doctors began to follow his example of small incisions and his manipulation of the uterus, they did not follow his practice of general anesthesia or fimbriectomy.

During that decade, I had numerous occasions to meet Dr. Uchida at medical conferences. At one of the international meetings we both attended, I gave him one of the AVS pins for women and he gifted me with a beautiful pearl and gold stick pin. My interactions with this "father of minilap" were always a joy. He was an important figure in the history of gynecologic surgery and I was flattered that he always knew who I was. I had many pleasant conversations with him.

Doctors in Thailand did a great deal for the advancement of minilap surgery. Dr. Vitoon Osathanondh and Dr. Pramote Rattakul, both in Bangkok, were early promoters of minilap. As is common in Thailand, they were usually known better by their first names, Doctors Vitoon and Pramote. They were the developers of the prototype instruments later used internationally in minilap sterilization.

When laparoscopes were developed in the early 70s, gynecologists were eager to use the new technology. The technique was to become the method of choice for tubal sterilization in developed countries by the middle of the decade. Doctors in less developed lands, however, increasingly used the minilap method because it did not require all the electrical equipment necessary for the lens system of the scope or the coagulation forceps used to occlude the tubes. Nor did it require the abdomen to be inflated with gas as laparoscopy needed. Not only was minilap cheaper in terms of supplies, but it was more adaptable for transporting to rural facilities.

It was interesting to me that early innovators of refined surgery were people who had the dexterity to use chop-sticks to pick up a small grain of rice. The same fingers that used fine brushes for their writing or to create detailed paintings seemed more capable of working with tiny instruments, whether through a mini-lap or through a laparoscope. Their precise finger movements seemed to me to be a natural talent, not found in much of the world where the people were accustomed to eating with their fingers, without implements.

Vitoon designed an instrument to mobilize the uterus. Unlike Uchida's catheter-based instrument, Vitoon's was malleable metal. When this 'uterine elevator' was inserted into the womb, the surgeon could lift the organ closer to the abdominal wall. Turning it from side to side would bring first one tube into view, and then the other, so that a loop of each tube could be ligated and the segment removed.

Pramote worked on facilitating access to the tubes by using a small proctoscope to hold the incision open. Others used a very small vaginal speculum. This did away with the need to have a surgical assistant to hold retractors to hold the incision open during the surgery. It also helped the surgeon visualize the tubes without the need for as much manipulation of the uterus. By 1973, articles about minilap were beginning to appear in the medical literature, but in the United States, doctors were more enthusiastic about their new toy, the laparoscope.

An organization in Seattle, Population Dynamics, produced 'loop' films showing the minilap procedures done by Vitoon and Pramote. They were interested in spreading the technique in the U.S. so that it might be used in outpatient settings such as Planned Parenthood clinics or the "Surgicenters" that were sprouting up all over the country. Laparoscopy carried more serious risks than minilap. Complications included the possibility of puncturing a major vessel with the sharp instrument used to enter the abdomen, or burning the intestine with the coagulation forceps. Either could be fatal, especially if it were to happen in a clinic without full emergency equipment and skills.

At AVS, in the mid-70s, I had become the Director of Professional Education and as such, I was eager to spread the news about minilap to American doctors. I obtained copies of the two films produced by Population Dynamics in cooperation with Vitoon, and purchased a portable projector that would repeatedly play the films as a continuous loop. I also had scripts outlining the details of every surgical step of the surgery. I took the AVS exhibit, the films, the script and a variety of patient-education materials to as many medical conferences as my schedule would permit.

I met with doctors at such meetings as the American Medical Association, the National Medical Association, the American College of Surgeons, American College of Obstetricians and Gynecologists, Medical Student associations and the American Association of Gynecologic Laparoscopists. It was not uncommon to have six to ten doctors crowded around the projector at each repetition of the film, discussing the technique and asking technical questions. In this way, minilap became known to

American doctors.

Vasectomy clinics had been widely used since the first one opened in 1969, and the Planned Parenthood Federation was interested in providing a similar clinic procedure for women. In 1972, Dr. A. Jefferson Penfield, Medical Director of Planned Parenthood of Syracuse, began to provide laparoscopic sterilizations as an out-patient procedure under local anesthesia. After Penfield learned of the minilap procedure, he opted to perform it both in his private office setting and in the family planning clinic. He was a firm believer that even though he had not had any surgical accidents providing laparoscopy, he did not want to risk any potential harm to a patient from blindly inserting the sharp trocar necessary for laparoscopy.

Laparoscopy requires that this trocar, a sharply pointed instrument encased within a cannula (a tubular sleeve), be inserted into the inflated abdomen. Once in, the tubular cannula is left in to provide the opening into the abdomen. The sharp trocar is then removed and the scope is inserted. Additional openings are made in a similar manner for operating instruments to be inserted. The reason the abdomen is inflated is to avoid internal damage to organs or vessels as a result of the insertion of the sharp trocar.

Dr. Harrith Hasson, in Chicago, shared Penfield's concerns about the potential for harm. In 1970, he began to avoid having to plunge a sharp trocar into the inflated abdomen by making a small one-inch incision in the lower rim of the umbilicus. Through that opening, he inserted the laparoscope. He called his procedure 'open laparoscopy'. Penfield also utilized Hasson's open technique when he wanted to use the laparoscope for any abdominal procedure.

In Texas, Dr. Frank Stubbs began to provide minilap under local anesthesia. Unlike Penfield, who tied off and removed a loop of each oviduct, Stubbs used electrical coagulation to occlude the tubes. His patients were able to leave the clinic in less than four hours. Tubal sterilization was becoming a true outpatient procedure. Stubbs reported on his experience at the 1974 annual meeting of the Association of Planned Parenthood Physicians. I credit both Penfield and Stubbs for advancing the use of minilap in America and for encouraging Planned Parenthood to include provision of voluntary sterilization in their services.

The AVS International Project was also promoting minilap for its overseas programs. Doctors were being trained in the procedure in Thailand under the leadership of Dr. Vitoon. At the Ramathibodi Hospital in Bangkok, he was already training Thai physicians in the hope of having over three hundred outpatient centers in Thailand. AVS' International Project was funding these activities and providing assistance in the development of training manuals.

Other minilap training centers in the U.S. were at the Johns Hopkins

University in Baltimore, the University of Pittsburgh Western Pennsylvania Hospital, the Washington University at St. Louis, Missouri and the American University in Beirut, Lebanon. USAID recognized that minilap held promise as a simple, quick, low-cost method of sterilization that could be especially useful in developing countries. The agency provided funding to assemble a 'minilap kit' that would contain the special uterine elevator developed by Vitoon and a uterine tubal hook used to pick up the loop of tube. These kits became available for use and distribution to training programs in early 1975. Every physician would be given a kit upon completion of minilap training.

In the mid-80s, AVS set about to produce instructional films to be used in training physicians to perform minilap surgery, both immediately post-partum and at an interval not associated with pregnancy. I had been named the Deputy Director of the Medical Division of AVS in 1981, and was the person selected to oversee all the medical and surgical components of the film. It was critical that a film intended to be used to train new providers of service be without flaws.

The films were to be produced in Kenya, where AVS had an office and staff for the East African programs it supported. Their medical doctor on staff was to take a leading role as a spokesperson and trainer. Unfortunately, that doctor spent most of his time overseeing program issues and not doing any surgery. In previous visits I had made to Kenya, I had the pleasure of working with another doctor who had excellent surgical skills and operated regularly at a family planning clinic. He was extremely gentle, and seemed to have magic fingers that could identify the tubes and ligate them with no discomfort for the woman who was wide awake during the surgery. With the help of the film editor, we were able to feature the staff doctor in the distant or broad scenes, but when the film showed the surgical details, the gloved fingers were those of the expert surgeon.

While serving in the medical division, I continued to participate in surgical training programs for minilap as well as laparoscopy. It was critical for me to maintain my skills and knowledge in all the newer surgical modifications and instrumentation. Much of my continuing education was possible through my membership in the American Association of Gynecologic Laparoscopists. They treated me no differently than doctors except that because I was not a physician, I did not take part in the actual surgery. I was introduced to new techniques and inventions even before they were commercially available, and had the rewarding experience of seeing them through the stages of development.

The international division of AVS was in need of training manuals and curriculum materials for training in minilap. I introduced the concept of training medical teams instead of just doctors. I felt it was important to involve the entire team, especially the nurses and aides who would be responsible for the sterilization of the equipment, preoperative and postoperative care of the clients, and prevention of infection.

I monitored the development and progress of guidelines and curricula in sub-Saharan Africa, Asia, Central and South America and the Caribbean. I wrote the medical components for the curricula. Its modules included preoperative assessment, surgical techniques and procedures, local anesthesia techniques, postoperative care and follow-up, prevention, diagnosis and treatment of complications, record-keeping, case studies, and analysis of complications and mortalities.

I was proud to be the medical author of curricula used internationally, and of my role in introducing minilap to the world.

# CHAPTER 14: INTRODUCING NO-SCALPEL VASECTOMY

'Vasectomy' is the term used to describe the surgical procedure that produces permanent sterility for men. The word incorporates the word 'vas', the duct through which the sperm travel from the testes to the urethra, and 'ectomy', the medical term for surgical removal of tissue. Until the mid-80s, vasectomies were done with the use of a scalpel to make either one midline incision into the scrotum, or two small incisions, one on each side, through which the vasa were lifted, sections removed, and ends tied off, cauterized, or had a clip applied.

The technique of no-scalpel vasectomy (NSV) came to the United States almost accidentally. AVS had learned about Dr. Li Shunqiang, of the Chongqing Family Planning Scientific Research Institute in Sichuan Province, China. He was doing male sterilizations by injecting a chemical combination of phenol and cyanoacrylate into each vas through the skin. The phenol component was a corrosive agent that caused damage to the inner surface of the vas. The cyanoacrylate served as a tissue glue that resulted in a permanent bonding together of the vas surfaces. Dr. Douglas Huber, AVS Medical Director, thought this percutaneous method warranted investigation.

An international team was assembled in 1985. Participating with Dr. Huber were (alphabetically listed) Dr. Mahmoud Fathalla, from Egypt; Dr. Phaitun Gojaseni, Thailand; Dr. Marc Goldstein, U.S.; Dr. Jack Lippes, U.S.; Dr. Mary Rauff, Singapore; and Dr. John Sciarra, U.S. AVS staff member, Keekee Minor, accompanied the group. As the Deputy Director for the AVS Medical Division, I stayed in the office to "man the fort" while the Director was absent.

During the visit, while Dr. Li was demonstrating the chemical technique, he encountered difficulty injecting one client with the chemical. Dr. Li simply told the group would proceed to do his usual vasectomy instead. What followed amazed every participant in the group. Dr. Li did not use a scalpel to reach the vas! Instead, he anchored the vas under the skin with a tiny clamp, being sure no other tissue was in his grasp. He then punctured the tissue with the closed tip of a sharp forceps. The next step was to use the small forceps to stretch the scrotal skin open, lift the vas through the opening to excise and seal a section. By stretching the opening in the scrotal skin instead of incising it, he did not cut across any small blood vessels, significantly reducing the risk of any bleeding or bruising. He proceeded to extract the second vas through the same opening. Everyone was impressed with the lack of blood or trauma.

Interest in the chemical method waned. Although that had been the reason for the investigatory team, it was not deemed to be appropriate for AVS at that time. Approval by the U.S. Food and Drug Agency (FDA) would require too much research. Additionally, the feat of injecting the chemical into the very thin vas was a feat that required great skill and a considerable amount of training. Dr. Li, however, continued to utilize this method in China. A few months after the visit by the team, an article was published, written by Dr. Li, reporting his experience with over 500,000 percutaneous chemical occlusions done in China between 1972 and 1984.

Unknown to the rest of the world, Dr. Li had developed his refined surgical procedure and had used it routinely since 1974. By 1988, it was estimated that ten million men in China had received a vasectomy by his no-scalpel method. Working with Dr. Li was a young physician, Dr. Philip Shihua Li (not related). Philip had done over five thousand no-scalpel vasectomies himself in China, though he was only twenty-five years of age.

One of the team members, Dr. Phaitun, introduced the no-scalpel technique in Thailand upon his return from the trip. Another member, Dr. Goldstein, who was affiliated with New York Presbyterian Hospital – Weill Medical College of Cornell University, began performing the procedure at his Center for Male Reproductive Medicine and Microsurgery at Cornell. He was also instrumental in arranging a postdoctoral fellowship in male reproductive medicine and microsurgery for the young Dr. Philip Li at Cornell. In a joint arrangement with The Population Council, Cornell also offered Philip a scholarship.

When Philip Li arrived in America, he had no family or close personal friends here. I welcomed him into our family circle, which was especially appropriate because I had recently lost a son. When, a few years later, Philip returned to China to get married, we included his wife. Two daughters followed and they have all been part of our extended family group ever since.

AVS was eager to use Philip's expertise to help train other physicians to do this refined vasectomy technique. The goal was to teach the chief urologists in medical schools how to extract a segment of the vas through the scrotal skin without using an incision. Once the chief was trained, we were sure he would train the interns and resident physicians that were working under him. We also wanted to train the surgeons working at the major vasectomy services in the country. The plan was similar to the plan

AVS used to introduce the use of local anesthesia for female sterilization surgery. It was the most effective way to introduce a new method in our country.

In 1986, Dr. Li Shunqiang and Dr. Goldstein traveled to Bangkok to work with experienced vasectomists from Bangladesh, Nepal, Sri Lanka, and Thailand. Dr. Apichart Nirapathpongporn of Thailand was trained at this time. Dr. Goldstein and Dr. Apichart then trained other surgeons in their home countries. Clinical training subsequently expanded to other countries. In several countries in Africa, where vasectomy was just being introduced, doctors who had never performed a vasectomy were trained only in the no-scalpel technique.

When Philip came to serve as a training consultant for AVS, there were no written materials available. There was no equipment or model with which to practice. In my capacity as Deputy Director of the medical division, I was the person to accompany Philip on his early training missions in the U.S. It soon became obvious to us that hands-on training would be necessary. The instruments were held in a manner slightly different from the normal way they were used for other procedures. The trainees had to become comfortable with that alteration.

In Philip's first attempts to describe the technique, I offered the hem of my skirt and a rubber band to him so that he could demonstrate the grasping technique. When we got back to New York, we began to experiment with materials we could use with the trainees. My favorite traveling skirt had enough tiny holes that had been stretched even larger as Philip showed how to extract the vas (rubber band) from the opening. We settled on using layers of gauze to simulate the skin, and a segment of very thin rubber tubing to serve as the vas.

In another aspect of my work at AVS, I was going to be serving as an advisor to the country of India for a microsurgery training program they wanted to start. In India's efforts to control their population, vasectomy had been promoted. They had since realized that there were times when it would be appropriate to attempt to reverse the procedure, especially if someone had been sterilized without full understanding of the permanence of the procedure. To help me guide them, I wanted to be trained and had been accepted into the microsurgery class at the University of Louisville Medical School as a trainee. My goal was to learn how to set up a microsurgery laboratory and to learn the basic microsurgical techniques.

The textbook we used had impressed me. It illustrated every step to be followed to connect two segments of a vessel. The illustrations showed every change in position of the operator's hand. It was extremely helpful. Looking down at the illustration on a table was the same as looking down on the actual procedure. When I operated on my first live animal, I followed the illustrations step-by-step. I severed the aorta and then reconnected it successfully, with no significant loss of blood. The mouse survived.

When planning the initial training for no-scalpel vasectomy, I was convinced that we needed to create such a manual for our trainees. We would use Philip as the expert, and a medical illustrator who had experience in drawing male anatomy. It took a while for the completion of this publication. The staff of the AVS' international division wrote the proposal for funding the project for our overseas work. Two other staff members assisted in the development of introductory pages of the manual. I was responsible for the technical content. Meanwhile, no-scalpel vasectomy training was progressing. Philip, then twenty six years old, was teaching the technique to the senior urologists in the U.S.

In 1988, in Thailand during the King's Birthday Vasectomy Festival, AVS had an opportunity to test the no-scalpel technique and to compare it with the conventional method using an incision. Two long outdoor operating areas were set up. The shelters were tents, each with a long row of cots that would serve as the operating tables. A doctor and an assistant were stationed at each table. In one tent, the doctors were to provide no-scalpel vasectomy (NSV); in the other, they would perform the incisional method. The men who were coming to receive their vasectomies were lined up outside where the preliminary screening was done and consent forms signed. As a table became available, the next man in line entered the tent. In this way random assignment to either no-scalpel or incision eliminated any risk of bias in the study.

Over 1,203 vasectomies were performed by twenty-eight surgeons in a single day. Conventional vasectomy was performed on 523 men while NSV was performed on 680. The doctors doing the conventional method performed an average of thirty-three cases each, while the doctors doing NSV did an average of fifty-seven each.

Neither conventional nor NSV is time-consuming. However, during this large festival, we learned that NSV took forty percent less time to accomplish than the incisional technique. More importantly, because no blood vessels were severed during NSV, these procedures resulted in almost ten times fewer hematomas. Infections, which often begin in residual blood at the surgical site, were therefore also fewer. Men undergoing NSV reported less pain during the procedure because Dr. Li's technique of administering the local anesthetic had included injection of the tissue around the vas as well as the skin. All the trainees had followed his example.

Field experience in the U.S. had shown that even experienced vasectomists had difficulty teaching themselves the no-scalpel method. Manipulating the special instruments and developing the eye-hand coordination would be easier with the proposed manual, but we felt that would not be sufficient. To test our theory, we conducted a one-day orientation on NSV in 1990, inviting a group of experienced vasectomists to hear a lecture, observe a procedure and practice on a model. Three months later, Philip conducted site visits to watch the trainees perform. He learned that the physicians were still lacking the refinements of the technique that would reduce the amount of bleeding. Consequently, we concluded that hands-on training using the trainee's clients was essential to fully master the NSV technique. Future training included clinical practice.

The AVS manual was published in 1992, titled *No-Scalpel Vasectomy: An Illustrated Guide for Surgeons*. I was proud to have my "baby" come into being. It has been used in all AVS training since then. Over a thousand doctors were directly trained by AVS in the U.S. Those doctors, in turn, trained thousands of others.

The manual has been translated into other languages and has been used for training doctors in over forty countries. Because of the ongoing demand for the publication, AVS, now called EngenderHealth, has updated the content and expanded on the surgical technique described in the manual. It now includes more than the approach to the vas, which was the focus of the original work. Once the doctor had the vas in his or her hand, we did not direct the method of occlusion. The newest edition includes recommendation for cautery of the vas segments and positioning fascia between the segments of the vas to decrease the risk of accidental reconnection of the vas. The newest edition is therefore a broader version of an already useful book.

As a result of AVS' NSV training efforts, the technique has become the 'gold standard' for vasectomy. According to a publication by Cornell's team in 2005, over fifteen million men had already obtained an NSV. In the U.S. alone, over a million men have had the procedure and more than five thousand physicians have been trained. More than a thousand doctors were trained in AVS programs overseas with hundreds more having been trained by those original trainees.

The World Health Organization has reported that the no-scalpel technique has helped to increase acceptability of vasectomy worldwide. In Latin America, NSV has been credited for a four-fold increase in the past decade. Many countries in that region have promoted vasectomy in mass media campaigns much as AVS did in the US for sterilization in the 60s.

The Indian government launched an NSV project in 1998 in collaboration with the United Nations Population Fund. Under that project, four thousand doctors were trained in NSV, and there are now over a hundred trainers across the country.

A country report on the population and family planning program in the Islamic Republic of Iran stated that between 1993 and 2004, NSV training courses were conducted, resulting in 460 doctors being trained in the technique. The result was that 350,000 Iranian men had the procedure.

NSV continued to expand options for male involvement in family planning in many countries where contraception had only been considered to be a woman's concern. One example is the Philippines. According to a report about their Safe Motherhood Enterprise, the number of men choosing a vasectomy rose from twenty per year in 2000 to about two thousand per year by 2007.

Dr. Philip Shihua Li has worked with Dr. Goldstein for over twenty-five years. He traveled to Austria in 1990 and to Spain in 1991 to introduce NSV to Europe. He is currently an Associate Research Professor of Urology and Associate Research Professor of Reproductive Medicine at Weill Cornell Medical College of Cornell University.

In summary, the NSV technique is now used in more than forty countries and has become the standard method around the world. My "baby" is developing nicely.

# CHAPTER 15: HABEMUS PAPAM

*"Habemus Papam!"* In English, "We have a Pope!" So announced that the conclave of Cardinals had elected the man to serve as the 266th head of the Roman Catholic Church in March of 2013. The announcement continued with "The most Eminent and Reverend Lord Jorge, Cardinal Bergoglio, who takes to himself the name Pope Francis." The former janitor, nightclub bouncer, and teacher seemed to be announcing to the world that he aimed to model his papacy on the humble saint from Assisi.

Early the next morning, Pope Francis, the new 'keeper of the keys to the kingdom of heaven', reported at the front desk of the hotel where he had been lodged, and turned in his room key, personally paying for his hotel stay. It seemed to many that there might be changes in store for the many Roman Catholics of the world.

I found myself thinking back to the brief papacy of John Paul I, who had been named Pope in August of 1978, and who died suddenly on September 28, just thirty three days later. Those of us who were working to expand family planning services had been so encouraged by the willingness of Pope John Paul to meet with delegates from the U.S. State Department to discuss artificial birth control.

The Catholic Church's opposition to family planning methods had been in the news since 1951 when Pope Pius XII approved the rhythm method. In that decade, Catholic doctor John Rock was developing the contraceptive pill, soon commonly known as 'The Pill'. In the hope that the Catholic Church would accept use of The Pill as a dependable regulator of menstrual cycles, he intentionally developed the daily pills to include one week of placebos, pills that had no hormonal content at all. He wanted women to continue having menstrual periods during that week. If religious beliefs forbade hormonal contraception, the women could depend on effective periodic abstinence, avoiding sexual activity during their fertile days.

At the end of his papacy, in 1963, Pope John XXIII created the Papal Commission on Population and Birth Control. Again, those of us who were working for reproductive choices were enthusiastic about the anticipated outcomes of the proposed study. We hoped it would result in the Church's acceptance of The Pill, which the U.S. Food and Drug Administration had approved for use three years earlier. Dr. Rock was a participating member of this commission, favoring The Pill's use for Roman Catholics. Surely, we thought, the Church would not put such effort into studying birth control if there were no chance of a change in policy.

My church, the Presbyterian Church, U.S.A., had affirmed contraception as a right of married couples in 1960. Five years later, the General Assembly of the Presbyterian Church urged the government of the United States to assist countries who requested help to develop voluntary family planning programs.

In the decade of the sixties, human sexuality was being scrutinized by Masters and Johnson, the contraceptive pill was freeing women from fear of unwanted pregnancies, and women were taking a stand for more equal treatment in employment. At the same time, there were factions in the Catholic Church seeking changes in its canon laws. There were priests urging an end to the rule of celibacy. Some groups were suggesting that women should be permitted to serve as priests. There were many hoping the Church would change its stance on divorce, abortion and homosexuality.

Pope Paul VI inherited all these issues when Pope John XXIII died in 1963. Five years later, in 1968, the *Humanae Vitae* was published. Pope Paul had decided to ignore the advice of the commission that had urged loosening the restrictions on birth control methods. He declared that only abstinence and the rhythm method were acceptable and that there should be no impairment to procreation of human life. This rigid declaration resulted in great disappointment for many of us in family planning.

It seemed that once a Pope had declared artificial birth control was a sin, the rule could not be changed without jeopardizing the concept of Papal infallibility. It was reminiscent of the Roman Catholic stand on Galileo's discovery of a heliocentric solar system. Once the Church made a pronouncement, no matter right or wrong, it was set in stone.

Millions of women ignored the encyclical and continued to use The Pill or whatever method they had adopted. Many used menstrual complaints as an excuse for a hysterectomy to avoid another pregnancy. Others turned to tubal ligation with the belief that they would only commit that sin one time, ask for forgiveness, and then enjoy a future without fear of unwanted children. The percentage of Catholic women seeking referral to an AVS sterilization provider in those years was disproportionally high compared to the percentage of Catholics in the general population.

Local priests were also conflicted, and some were more lenient than others. I recall many women "shopping around" for a priest who would absolve what Pope Paul had called a sin. They avoided the priests who were denying absolution for using birth control. The encyclical was creating a division in the church. Many lost faith and became members of what we might call the "Church Alumni".

The Vatican had gained control of the *Instituto Farmacologico Serono* (Serono Pharmaceutical Institute) in 1952, after the death of its founder, Italian chemist, Cesare Serono. The company was developing hormonal drugs, starting with the infertility drug, marketed later as Pergonal. This drug uses follicle-stimulating hormones (FSH) to increase the number of ova produced by the ovaries each month. These ova are used for in vitro fertilization, commonly called "test-tube" babies. FSHs were harvested from the urine of post-menopausal women. What could be more symbiotic for the Vatican-controlled company, Serono? With the approval of the Vatican, they obtained the urine collected by the older nuns in the convents. These religious women, devoted to chastity, were helping to make pregnancy possible for infertile women while adding to the coffers of the company.

To reduce the risk of public attention to the investment, Pope Paul VI decided to stop naming any directors to the Board of Serono. In 1968, the year that *Humanae Vitae* was published, he also decided to reduce investments in some Vatican-owned companies. In addition to Serono, the Vatican Bank held interests in the Beretta handgun company. The Pope wanted to reduce the risk of public awareness of the Vatican's investments in controversial companies.

Serono relocated to Geneva in 1977 because of the social tensions in Italy at that time. It later merged with Merck to become a major provider of hormonal contraceptives. Reports that the Vatican was benefitting from the sales of birth control pills have been denied, but Vatican spokesman, Christophe Lamps, did admit to the Associated Press that the Vatican held stock in its Rome subsidiary in the late 60s and early 70s.

The future Pope John Paul I, Albino Luciani, was born in 1912 to a mother who was already rearing two small children from her husband's first wife. Soon after, another son was born, and then a girl. His father struggled to find employment, working in any capacity, including bricklaying and mechanical work. He sometimes worked far away from his family, leaving his wife, Bortola, to care for the children while she also supplemented the family income by working as a scullery maid. Albino entered the seminary at the age of eleven. At that time, his father, Giovanni, was working in France, a factor that undoubtedly was the explanation for Bortola's failure to have more babies.

It is conceivable that his family's struggles led to Albino's willingness to be open to possible changes in the church doctrine against birth control when he became a Bishop under Pope John XXIII, and a Cardinal under Pope Paul VI. When Albino Luciani was elected to be Pope following the death of Pope Paul VI in 1978, he took the name of his two predecessors, choosing to serve as Pope John Paul I, the first Pope to take two names.

At that time, U.S. Congressman James Scheuer was serving as head of the House of Representatives' Select Committee on Population; he was also the vice-chairman of the United Nations Fund for Population Activities. He had become aware of Pope John Paul's less than enthusiastic support of the *Humanae Vitae* decrees on birth control. Scheuer prompted the American embassy in Rome to contact the Vatican and inquire if the new Pope would be open to a meeting to discuss population and family planning issues. Once again, those of us working in that field had our hopes raised. Might there be a possibility of change in the church rules? How excited we were to learn that Scheuer's delegation would have an audience with the Pope on October 24, 1978.

That meeting never took place. Pope John Paul went to his room about nine o'clock the evening of September 28, and was found dead by five o'clock the next morning. The cause of death was attributed to a heart attack, but an autopsy was never performed to verify that diagnosis. The most detailed account of the life and death of Pope John Paul I can be found in David A. Yallop's well-researched book, *In God's Name*. After three years of investigation by Yallop into the death or murder of the Pope, the book was published by Bantam Books in 1984.

In summary, there are many similarities between Popes John Paul and Francis. Both were elected when many were calling for financial reforms of the Vatican Bank. On August 27, 1978, the new pope John Paul instructed his secretary of state to initiate an investigation of the entire financial operation of the Vatican. He was acting on his firm belief that the Roman Catholic Church should be the church of the poor.

Similarly, in June, 2013, Pope Francis established a five-man commission to investigate activities of the Vatican Bank. The Vatican Bank had just issued a report on money laundering, an apparent attempt to improve its financial transparency. This was a result of a claim by Antonio Nicaso, an expert on organized crime in Italy, that underworld gangsters frequently paid for local church repairs or feast-day celebrations in exchange for Catholic officials keeping quiet about their illicit deeds. In speeches, this Pope has been quoted as saying that a Christian "who gives to the church with one hand but steals with the other hand from the country, from the poor, is unjust".

Both these popes are known for their simplicity, humility and willingness to change things at the Vatican. John Paul was never crowned; he never wore the papal tiara. Francis, also, turned down sartorial splendor by choosing to live in a guesthouse rather than in the Apostolic Palace and by refusing to wear the red shoes as his forerunners had done. John Paul tried to avoid the *sedia gestatoria*, the ceremonial throne used to carry the pope. Pope Francis has often chosen to use a bus rather than a limo. While John Paul was open to discussing family planning, Francis seems open to considering family life and sexuality. While he says "no" to abortion and same sex marriage, he does not want to focus on the issues he calls "teachings of the church" as opposed to "the word of God". This, to me, is a significant change for the better.

# CHAPTER 16: BOARD AND STAFF RELATIONSHIPS

Over the thirty year period that I was affiliated with the Association for Voluntary Sterilization, the role of the board of directors changed significantly. The board was originally a group of like-minded persons interested in encouraging sterilization. As such, they wanted a hands-on relationship with the staff. The board members and their friends were the primary financial contributors to the organization, and that probably led to their feeling that they were entitled to direct the activities of the staff. It is understandable that they wanted to be part of the action; to be able to feel that they were part of any success or social changes that might occur.

I believe that the first people leading the group, Secretary Marian S. Norton (1937 – 1948) and President Dr. H. Curtis Wood Jr. (1945-1961) probably received small compensation for their work. I know that when Ruth Proskauer Smith took on the task of Executive Director (1961-1963), she earned a salary. The leadership had definitely become a paid position by the time I became actively involved with the group. John Rague was hired in 1963 as Executive Director and was the employee who had previous experience in directing an organization. Some of the board members were members of the World Federalist's Movement, so knew of Rague's abilities from the years he had directed that program. Rague and his assistant, the Public Relations Director, Donald Higgins usually enjoyed their complete confidence.

A few of the other board members continued to interact with staff. Medora Bass continued to communicate directly about issues related to sterilization of mentally challenged individuals. Helen Edey, a psychiatrist, was doing vasectomy screening at the newly opened vasectomy clinic at the Margaret Sanger Center in NYC. She continued to interact with AVS staff doing counseling and referrals. Beatrice McClintock would stop in from time to time to offer encouragement and to press for more public outreach, evidence of her devotion to the work we were doing.

Rague served until 1972, about a year after I had joined the staff. In that year, Dr. Ira Lubell was hired to direct the International Project and Charles Faneuff was chosen to take over the U.S. program.

During the brief period of time I had the pleasure of working with Faneuff, we initiated a new publication, *The Biomedical Bulletin*. I had reported to Faneuff that AVS had covered radio and television programs in every one of the fifty states, and that I thought it was time to concentrate on professional education. I wanted to be sure that when the public approached their doctors or counselors, the professionals had the latest information. During Faneuff's tenure, the first of these bulletins was published. Each issue dealt with a new surgical technique, or specific concern related to sterilization. From the broad range of professionals and experts in the field that I knew, I would select the best qualified person to write each issue. They all worked without payment. We had the support of the AVS Medical and Scientific Committee behind us.

Six months later, in the summer of 1973, Faneuff advised the board that they had inadvertently created an organization with two heads. Lubell was directing the overseas program but the funds from the U.S. Agency for International Development had awarded the money to AVS. Faneuff felt he had the responsibility to oversee the funds, but Lubell felt that he had been hired to make the decisions and that he should be the person responsible for deciding the allocation of those funds. As a result, Faneuff was terminated and I took over the leadership of the domestic program, reporting to Lubell.

Until Dr. Lubell arrived, I had been the only staff person with a medical background. For many years, I had been the person to take AVS exhibits to medical conferences. Over that period of time, I had gotten to know the major doctors working in the fields of gynecology and urology. Laparoscopy was increasingly playing a large part in provision of female sterilization and the newly formed American Association for Gynecological Laparoscopy had accepted me as one of their experts in the field. I was invited to their training courses and invited to take part in their panels at annual meetings. The leading innovators in new surgical techniques were always easily available to me when I had questions. Likewise, they knew they could count on me for any general questions about trends in the practice of sterilization. Many would send me their manuscripts to be checked for accuracy before publication.

Dr. Lubell had little, if any, interest in the national program. While he met with the board at their monthly meetings, he was far more involved with the group he had helped form, the International Committee. Because the funding from USAID was so much more significant than the contributions of the board members, their voices became less important. The organization was likened to a large tail wagging a small dog. The board's work was shifting from directing the staff and all the domestic activities of the organization to being a group of persons selected either because of their financial support or for recognition of their names in professional circles.

One committee that continued to be involved on a regular basis with staff activities was the Information and Education Committee. The board members on this group continued to want a hands-on relationship with staff. I remember two specific situations that demonstrate the involvement of this committee.

In 1972, the numbers of vasectomies peaked. Female sterilizations were increasing as laparoscopic sterilizations were becoming more available. But the I & E Committee wanted to know why the numbers of vasectomies were not continuing to rise. They proposed to do a survey of doctors to ask them why more men were not requesting vasectomies. In my opinion, this seemed a total waste of effort. How would a doctor know why a man did not come to him? It took quite a bit of persuasion to convince the committee that a better purpose for a survey would be to assess the level of knowledge the public had about both male and female voluntary sterilization. With such knowledge, we could then focus our public information activities on the gaps in awareness of details.

Dr. Edey, a very active AVS board member, was a friend of George Gallup. With help from his polling group, AVS was able to conduct a public survey. The results showed that the public was indeed quite knowledgeable in general about both male and female operations that would result in permanent sterility. There was less knowledge about specific details, an important finding for our staff. We then knew we had to develop educational material that was far more specific. We produced a series of brochures to supplement the general ones already being mailed to persons who inquired of AVS or were being distributed by doctors and clinics.

Another example of the board's involvement in the work of the staff occurred in 1980 when the I&E committee was being consulted about the possibility of AVS placing advertising cards above the seats in buses and subways, a common advertising method in those days. We needed board support because unlike the International Project that had money from the US government, we in the national office depended upon our donors to fund any project. We had obtained an offer of pro-bono assistance from the New York Advertising Council. They were willing to donate the services of an advertising specialist to help AVS get a message to the public in a variety of ways. The bus/subway cards were one example. Magazine ads were another. It was our task to decide on the message.

The board members on the committee were very enthusiastic about this advertising campaign. They wanted to tell the world how popular voluntary sterilization was, and urge others to follow the obvious suggestions in the ads. It was a "Get on the band-wagon" concept, in my mind, and one with which I did not feel comfortable. I suggested instead we develop a notice that would deal with the current concerns at that time. Forced or coerced sterilizations had been in the news since the mid seventies so I wanted a notice to say something like "Stop and think about sterilization. It is permanent. For information, contact AVS at..." Or "When in need of permanent birth control, contact..." Even "Don't let anyone decide for you. Sterilization is voluntary and permanent. When in doubt, don't!"

I lost this argument. The I&E group could not be dissuaded. I think they believed that if no one mentioned the possibility of uninformed clients, the matter would simply go away. The advertising campaign announced in its headlines "12 Million Americans have chosen permanent birth control over all other methods". It featured three photographs, the first of which was a couple with two small children in a campground setting. The quotation was "We decided that our family was complete and wanted to enjoy each other in a more relaxed way. So we selected permanent birth control."

Another photo showed a young gentleman in a tuxedo. He is quoted as saying "I never wanted to be a father. And I didn't want to incur any risk of having children. That's why I decided on permanent birth control." The third photo showed a young black business woman at a desk saying "I've made a strong commitment to my career. So even if I were to get married now I wouldn't want to have children. Permanent birth control was the perfect solution for me". Beneath the photos was this message: "Over 1 million Americans each year choose contraceptive sterilization over all other methods of birth control. It's a safe, efficient way to prevent unwanted pregnancies permanently. If you've ever considered permanent birth control and would like more information contact the Association for Voluntary Sterilization". The address and phone number followed. The final message was "Permanent Birth Control: the most widely chosen method in the world".

Public reactions varied. The phone number listed on the cards was very active for some time. AVS was able to provide information and assistance to many interested persons who might not have been able to get it otherwise. On the other hand, there were reports that many of the subway or bus cards had been pulled down or torn up. Miriam Ruben, the staff person then handling public information, was reported in a newspaper article as saying sterilization is "obviously a sensitive subject. The city is made up of minorities, and it has been a sore subject with minority groups. Minorities fear sterilization may be used to eradicate their nationalities or races; that bigots may talk unwitting illiterate men or women into having the operation, or might sterilize them without their permission. These things have happened. And every time it happens, it sets us back". I continued to regret that AVS had missed an opportunity to announce its protective stance against sterilizations being done without full knowledge of the client.

This campaign was probably the last staff activity in which the board of directors played a role. Hugo Hoogenboom had become the Executive Director and it was clearly his intention to separate the board and staff. He had been an active member of the board when the staff of the International Project had become so dissatisfied with working conditions under Lubell and his assistant, Marilyn Schima, that they had formed a labor union. Hoogenboom was selected by the Board to interview staff and solicit information later used to terminate Lubell. Hoogenboom was also selected by the board to become the successor to Lubell. It would follow that Hoogenboom would not want fraternization between board and staff, or for staff to be able to communicate with the board about him.

As the new leader of the organization, Hoogenboom restructured the group. Lubell's assistant, Marilyn Schima, was terminated soon after, but the rest of the leadership of the International Division was retained. Terrence Jezowski was the Director of the International Project, assisted by Lynn Bakamjian. The senior staff met monthly with the board's executive committee. International projects that required private funding were presented by staff to the international committee. By then, the International Project staff was overseeing regional offices in Dhaka, Bangladesh; Bogota, Columbia; and Nairobi, Kenya. They were planning another in Nigeria. Later, another opened in Tunisia.

Hoogenboom selected a new leader for the National Division. Libby Antarsh, who held a doctorate in musicology, was a person he hoped would be more active in lobbying activities. Dr. Douglas Huber, an epidemiologist, was hired as the Medical Director. For the next six months, I worked for both these new employees, helping them by sharing all my past experiences and knowledge with them. At the end of that period, I was very pleased to accept the position of Assistant Director of the Medical Division.

I was delighted to work with Dr. Douglas Huber. His judgment on medical issues was carefully made and always one with which I concurred. Our styles were complimentary. I always thought this as one of the reasons we worked so well together. As an epidemiologist, Huber was tempted to want more information before making a decision. I, in the manner of an emergency medic, was usually quicker to come to a conclusion. As a result of having studied time management at NYU, I would look at items in my in-box and immediately decide to either do, delegate, or dump. Huber would grow piles on his desk. When he went away on a field trip, he would return to a clean desk. Because we had the same medical standards and because I knew what concerns were foremost in his mind, there was never a problem.

In 1989, the program staff wanted to introduce Norplant into their services. This was a new contraceptive method that was developed by the Population Council with clinical trials in Chile. It used six silicone rods, each filled with a dose of levonorgestrel, introduced under the skin of a woman's arm in a fan-like configuration. The rods were designed to work for six years and were said to be highly effective. One of the problems, however, was that they were difficult to remove. The U.S. Food and Drug Administration had not yet approved the method.

While we were evaluating the possibility of using this method, Dr. Huber learned that there were actually two types of Norplant being studied at the Population Council. The one being offered for use in family planning programs was actually the less effective version. In addition to the difficulty in removing the rods, there was evidence that many women were not returning after five years to have them removed. As the blood levels of the drug declined, these women would be at greater risk of pregnancy.

There was also evidence that the lower effectiveness rods were associated with higher risk of ectopic pregnancies, especially in heavier women in the third and fourth year of Norplant use. In both my and Huber's opinions, subjecting poor women to any increase of risk of death from an ectopic pregnancy was unacceptable. In poor counties, an ectopic pregnancy was tantamount to a death sentence. Ectopics would require immediate diagnosis and surgery, not likely to be available.

The international staff was really pressing for approval to go ahead with introduction of the method. They saw this as a surgical procedure that would come under the new name of the organization: The Association for Voluntary Surgical Contraception (AVSC). They complained to Hugo Hoogenboom about Huber's hesitancy. As a result, Hoogenboom, who had once been a director at the Population Council, decided to terminate Douglas as the Medical Director.

The applicant for the position that was decided upon by Hoogenboom was Dr. Amy Pollack, who had served one year as assistant to Dr. Louise Tyrer, Medical Director of the Planned Parenthood Federation. I found a bit of humor in this because Dr. Tyrer had first offered that position to me! Becoming AVS's Medical Director was, in my opinion, a huge step up for a person with no significant international or leadership experience. But the decision was Hoogenboom's after senior staff had interviewed all the candidates.

During my interview with Dr. Pollack, I found her attitude toward me was hard to understand. She was direct in telling me that she felt she would never be able to work with me. I asked, "Why?" Her response was that because I had worked so closely with Dr. Huber, and had been loyal to him, she would never be able to trust that I would be loyal to her. I tried to let her know that my characteristic of being loyal would be beneficial, but to no avail. Pollack was hired as the new Medical Director in 1991.

When the next time came for annual evaluations of staff, I was given a poor review by Pollack. This was hard to comprehend because I had been given a meritorious service award at the last review. I had not changed, nor had my dedication or quality of work, in my opinion. I realized that my future at AVS was not apt to be pleasant. I began thinking about retirement although I was only fifty-nine.

I reflected about the role of the Board at this time, and thought of the examples of staff activities that went unnoticed by the Board since I had joined the staff. First was the retirement deal that Rague had made with the Treasurer. Then the abuse of the expense accounts by Rague and Higgins who pretended all those restaurant and bar bills were used to treat publicists. I thought about the poor choices the Board made in simultaneously hiring both Faneuff and Lubell, creating a two-headed organization. I remembered how the Board was oblivious to the poor management skills of Lubell and Schima, which resulted in a very dissatisfied staff and formation of a labor union. Now a skilled and dedicated doctor had been discharged without good cause.

By early 1993, when I took a medical leave for a fractured leg, I offered to work from home. I got a box of material to complete what had accumulated while I was on an assignment in the Philippines. After that, Dr. Pollack advised me to enjoy my medical leave. No further work assignments or contact with me followed, although I was perfectly able and willing to take on some tasks that would not require walking in my large cast. I "got the message" so when my cast was finally removed, and I returned to the office, I put in my request for an early retirement.

Not quite ready to go from full-time work to full-time retirement, I decided to do consulting for a while. A major assignment came from the Family Planning Association of Nigeria. I was to be the team leader or organizer of a group of clinic workers who would develop a manual of standards for all the procedures of clinic, country-wide. It was a task I found very rewarding and one I would not have been able to do if still at AVS. Although I missed some of my co-workers, I had a new and exciting life ahead.


Postscript

A year later, Hoogenboom resigned and Pollack moved up to be the head of the organization, taking the title of President instead of Executive Director. During her tenure, in 2005, the organization, then called EngenderHealth, was the subject of an investigation by the Office of the Inspector General (OIG) of USAID, for improper management of government funds. They denied wrongdoing but entered into a settlement with the OIG to repay $3.3 million to the US government. Also, the organization had to enter into an Organizational Integrity Agreement with the OIG and work with an independent monitor to oversee compliance.

Amy Pollack left in 2005 and was replaced by Ana Langer. In 2007, the OIG concluded that EngenderHealth was in full compliance and withdrew the oversight.

Douglas Huber continued his dedication for international health, working with Management Services for Health, and other agencies. In 2014, he received the annual Champion Award by the Christian Connections for International Health (CCIH) organization. The award recognizes an individual who has dedicated his or her life to global health from a Christian perspective and made significant contributions in the field.

"Dr. Huber has been a global health advocate and dedicated volunteer to the cause of serving those in need across the globe for many years," said CCIH Executive Director, Ray Martin. "He has generously devoted his time and medical expertise to improving maternal and child health, and promoting family planning in a way that is sensitive to the faith traditions of communities. As a reproductive health expert with a strong personal faith, he has helped many denominations and faith-based organizations appreciate the tremendous value of family planning, sometimes called child spacing, for improved maternal and child health."

"Dr. Huber has worked in international health for forty years with a focus on reproductive health, research and innovative community program implementation. He designed and led community-based family planning programs in Bangladesh from 1975 to 1979 that helped guide the national family planning program. As a missionary for the Episcopal Church from 2002 to 2004, Dr Huber served as the HIV/AIDS advisor to the council of Anglican Provinces of Africa, which served 42 million Anglicans in 25 countries. From 2006 to 2008 he designed and directed the Afghanistan Accelerating Contraceptive Use project, which has been replicated nationwide by the Afghan Ministry of Health."

When Douglas Huber was removed from his post at AVS, the rest of the world was the beneficiary. In November, 2014, Douglas received the "life-time achievement award" from the International Health Section of the American Public Health Association at their annual conference in New Orleans. To have worked with this talented and dedicated doctor was the highlight of my career. I am grateful to AVS for having given me the opportunity to do so.

It is easy to see that the role of the board had definitely changed over the years. The board of directors was no longer a hands-on group. They were not consulted about any management or operational issues as they once had been. They were not engaged in the hiring of staff under the level of executive director or president. The role of the executive director had greatly expanded to be responsible for the leadership once held in the hands of the board.

# INTRODUCTION

My travels for AVS began in 1976 and continued until my retirement in 1993. During that time, I made it my plan to write notes about my experiences to share with my children, family members and close friends. Once I became the Deputy Director of the Medical Division in 1981, my travels increased significantly, and the notes became even more important to me and those who read them.

The chapters that follow are basically the same as they were written at the time. I have edited them a bit for publication, but the content tells of situations that existed at the time of the visit. I hope that some things have improved over time. Sadly, there were additional trips when I was too busy to write any notes, or where I had visited a country so many times that I had no new information.

My first trips for AVS were to attend our International Conferences. I attended the first overseas meeting in Geneva in 1973 but did not make any notes about that first experience abroad. The second international journey was for the conference held in Tunisia, when I started the written notes. The third trip was to take part in the Korean International Conference held by AVS.

Some of the journeys were made to deliver a prepared speech at an international gathering such as the Congress of Medical Law in Belgium, or the First International Convention on Medico-legal Aspects of Disability and the National Conference of the Society for Rehabilitation of the Disabled, both held in Israel.

There were many assignments that required me to help establish counseling services in AVS overseas programs. I had been AVS' primary spokesperson on that topic in the US, so it followed that I could help our foreign counterparts with their programs and trainings. Sri Lanka, Nepal and Thailand were examples of places where I was very involved in their counseling programs.

As I became more involved in the work of the Medical Division, many of the trips were for the purpose of conducting medical needs assessments. Some site visits were required to address a series of complications or to evaluate surgical practices. Guatemala was the first of such assignments. Other Central American countries and Asia followed. During my later years, I spent considerable time in Africa.

Occasionally, I was involved in the investigation of a death of a client. Every death was carefully looked at, usually by Dr. Huber or Dr. Khairullah (a medical program officer based in New York, usually assigned to conduct medical visits in the Middle Eastern countries). It was critical for AVS to know what led to the death so that steps could be taken to reduce the risk even further.

All of these trips necessitated an official written report for AVS with a copy going to the US Agency for International Development. Back in the early days, before we had computers, the reports were typed by a secretary. I never kept a copy. Only my personal notes, written in long hand script, were saved by me. I duplicated them to share. It was many years later that I bought a personal computer and typed all the trip reports into it while spending a winter in the south in a motor home.

As AVS began opening regional offices, I began to work with regional staff, teaching medical staff and consultants how to conduct medical site visits. I was also able, frequently, to identify a skilled surgeon who might serve as a trainer of other doctors.

As AVS International Division staff was developing training materials for both male and female sterilization, I was usually the person to oversee the medical and surgical components. Likewise, as countries started to develop their own materials, I was regularly called upon to assist with the technical medical sections. In Kenya, I served as the medical overseer of surgical training films AVS was making.

My final two trips for AVS were to Nigeria and the Philippines and were both part of a plan to develop or test a curriculum. When the Family Planning Association of Nigeria was ready to go ahead with their plan, they hired me as the consultant to oversee the project. By that time, I had retired from AVS and was happy to take on the task.

These journeys, while giving me a wonderful opportunity to see many parts of the world that would otherwise have been unknown to me, were not always pleasant. There were many difficulties and lonely hours, but I would not have given up any. The good that I was able to accomplish far outweighed the inconveniences. I am very grateful for the confidence that Dr. Huber, AVS Medical Director, had in me, and the wisdom he shared.

# CHAPTER 1: TUNIS, EGYPT, ITALY, LONDON, JAN – FEB , 1976

In 1964, AVS held its first International Conference in New York City, under the directorship of John Rague. The Board of Directors and the International Committee had helped him prepare the agenda and select the invited participants. At that time, there was no work being done outside our own country. I was pleased to have been one of the persons invited to that initial conference to consider expanding the work of AVS to other lands.

When the AVS International Project was in its infancy, in the early 70's, Dr. Lubell and the international staff organized the Second International Conference, to be held in 1973 in Geneva, Switzerland. The primary goal was to establish key contacts with surgeons and family planning directors from developing countries. If those countries requested aid in offering voluntary sterilization services, AVS might be able to assist with funding, training and surgical supplies. The cost of this conference was covered by the grant AVS had received from the United States Agency for International Development (USAID).

Now, in 1976, the Third International Conference was to be held in Tunis, Tunisia. Interacting with family planning workers from other lands was critical for our expanded work. Even though I was primarily concerned with the domestic work of AVS, I was pleased to be able to attend this third conference, especially since I was the only staff person who had attended both the earlier ones.

**TUNIS:** The first leg of the trip, from JFK to Rome, was more than two hours late - due to some bolt having come off the engine, we were told. It was almost midnight by the time we departed, and dinner was served an hour later. The in-flight movie was "Jaws". It was not as frightening as I had anticipated, but not a movie I would have selected for viewing while over the ocean. Soon I was watching the sunrise. From the air, the Alps looked like piles of dirt, some snow-covered, but not particularly impressive. We arrived at noon, only one hour late.

I was traveling with other staff and we were carrying many cartons of supplies for the conference along with our personal luggage. In Rome, where we had to change aircraft, we experienced some difficulties checking on our cargo. We finally were able to verify that all the cartons had arrived and were being properly transferred to Tunis. This task took some of the five hours we had until our next plane. We watched the sun go down as we left Rome, arriving in Tunis about twenty hours after we left New York.

An AVS staff member and driver met us. We discovered that one of our packages of conference material was missing but all else seemed to be in order. We reported our lost package and were then taken to the Tunis Hilton where we all had dinner together while we reviewed our assignments.

Tunis is nestled in a valley near the bay but the Hilton Hotel, where the conference was to be held, was on a hill some distance from the city. As I was having breakfast in my room, I could look down on white stucco buildings and lush green foliage. I could see groups of women walking across the fields, dressed in their haiks, the large outer wrap common in North Africa. A man on horseback rode across the fields in another direction. The modern Hilton seemed out of sync on the fringe of a city that did not appear to have changed much in two thousand years.

Eight of us had dinner in town the following night after working fourteen straight hours. I enjoyed a great bouillabaisse in a tiny Tunisian-French restaurant named Chez Slah. The next day I worked all day with time out only for a bowl of carrot soup. Our work days continued to be fourteen hours each. After the first days of preparation for the conference, I was pleased to help register the participants because it gave me the opportunity to meet and welcome many old friends and former associates.

The next evening, we attended a formal reception given by the President Director General of the Office of National Family Planning and Population, Mizri Chekir. A huge ice mold shaped like Roman arches was the centerpiece. Local delicacies were served but the cocktails were questionable. I requested a gin martini at the open bar, and was given a tall glass with ice and a splash of gin in it. The rest of the glass was filled with Martini & Rossi sweet vermouth.

I had dinner with friends, doctors I knew from the American Association of Gynecologic Laparoscopists. Included were Jordan Phillips, Louis Keith, Jaroslav Hulka, and Ingmar Joelsson. Others were Lise Fortier (Medical Director of Los Angeles Planned Parenthood), George and Martha Dennison (directors of Population Dynamics), and Mrs. Ann Howat (AVS Board member). We went to La Chateau in the Medina and listened to Arab music that sounded like bag-pipes, played on instruments made with goat-skins. A beautifully-clad belly dancer performed, wearing a full skirt and a sari-like top. We had a fantastic evening.

After five long and busy days, I finally got to wander around the town. Co-worker Terrence Jezowski and I sneaked away from the conference late one afternoon to shop in the souks. We walked around looking for a restaurant for dinner and found "The Orient", where the chef showed us raw whole fish for our approval before cooking it. The sea bass was an outstanding treat. I purchased a few small items at The Artisanat, a shop that specialized in local crafts and fabrics.

The conference finally ended. After the tired AVS staff spent the morning packing conference materials, I went on a tour of Carthage and Sidi Bou Said. It was great to get out. I will never forget seeing the ruins of ancient Carthage, where there still was the sacrificial stone pillar on which parents placed their first-born child and any twins to be killed by the priest. There was also an excavated room filled with clay jugs, each of which held the remains of a dead infant.

*Sacrifice stone in Carthage.*

As I was packing my suitcase the night before leaving Tunisia, I opened the sliding bedroom door and was surprised to find the night filled with sounds of barking dogs. People in the city must have left their pets all out at night. The clear air carried the noise for many miles. I thought of the noisy animals as bidding me farewell.

Three other staff members and I had decided to request vacation time after the conference to visit Egypt. The impetus for my visit was in part to visit with my daughter's in-laws in Alexandria. Her brother-in-law was going to be my guide and driver. One of my companions, Aida, would travel with me. Phyllis and Lorraine made their plans for the week in Egypt on their own. We had an early morning flight with a stop in Libya.

We were not permitted to exit the aircraft in Tripoli, but a few of us stepped out onto the stair case to get some fresh air while waiting to board more passengers. I had my camera and decided a photo of the airport would be interesting. Suddenly a soldier came up and instructed us all to get back in the plane. He followed me to my seat and angrily started questioning me, in Arabic, about my camera. I played dumb and repeatedly said, "I only speak English". He finally gave up and, to my relief, did not confiscate my film.

**EGYPT:** Entering Cairo was a terrible experience. There was no semblance of order. There were no lines at the immigration counter. Crowds of people were pushing and trying to step in front of each other. I had my passport in my hand but another passenger grabbed it from me and passed it forward. I could not see the man at the desk until he got up and left. Someone heard him voice his distress with the crowd as he walked away, leaving all the passports on a pile. What followed then can only be described as bedlam. Everyone was trying to find his or her own passport from the pile. When we finally got our document back, we had to go to another counter.

My son-in-law's brother, Essam, was waiting with his friend, Sailu, to greet us when we finally got through the immigration area. Aida and I were to drive in Sailu's car to Alexandria for the first part of our stay. Phyllis and Lorraine went on their way independently.

The trip to the coastal city of Alexandria was an education in Egyptian driving habits. Every driver blew his horn at every opportunity, even approaching an intersection, "to let the people in the cross streets know we are coming through", according to Sailu. Cars also sounded their signals when they faced a car coming from the opposite direction. The result was a constant cacophony of horns.

Along the way, there seemed to be something wrong with the car engine. The two men got out to check under the hood without any explanation to us. They were searching for something in a tool box. I finally asked what it was they needed. The response was one I learned was typical in the Arab culture. It was not a woman's business and clearly they did not feel they should inform us what was going on. When Essam began to signal other cars, I finally pressed him to tell me what was wrong. He replied that they needed a screw driver. I produced one from my purse, surprising the male chauvinists, and we were soon on our way.

We toured Alexandria and then had dinner at the home of my daughter's new in-laws. The wife's daily activity was to shop for the ingredients for the main meal that was served in the late afternoon. This day, she had prepared scrumptious stuffed baked artichoke hearts that I will always remember, the likes of which I never had again and the recipe for which I never obtained.

Aida and I had reservations at the Palestine Hotel on the grounds of King Farouk's former palace. In the morning, we toured the grounds and the palace, which had been considered ultra-modern in the forties and fifties. The building contained the best white Italian Carrara marble, exquisite tapestries and Iranian carpets. The queen must have had poor taste because her bedroom was quite tacky. Cobalt blue mirrors were used for baseboards and the trim around all the windows and door frames. The top surfaces of all the dressers and tables were also blue mirrors.

The last night in Alexandria, I suggested we celebrate my forty-fourth birthday by going to a nice restaurant for dinner. But our guide selected another place. Essam took us, with a few of his friends, to a dimly-lit, empty hall that sold refreshments. I was beginning to feel that having a guide, while helpful, was also limiting.

The next day we traveled to Cairo by train with Essam continuing to serve as our guide and manager. The trip took us through primitive farmland. It seemed that hand tools and animals were used to do all the work. I saw no evidence of machinery. Upon arrival, we walked around, stopping for a meal while looking for a hotel for Aida and me. Essam was planning to stay with a friend. He chose the Victoria Hotel for us in what seemed like a seedy section of the city.

The hotel had only the barest necessities for sleeping securely. There was no way to close and lock the door. There was only a hook-and-eye lock that was aligned improperly so the door had to be slightly open for the hook to enter the eye. Anyone could simply insert a finger or pencil, lift the hook, and gain access. Aida and I noticed that many of the rooms were occupied by men who left their doors open, so we decided we would not worry about security either. When in Egypt, do as the Egyptians do.

The Cairo Museum with the effects of King Tutankhamen was an eye-opener of unbelievable splendor. The art work and portraits on the mummies were fantastic. I wondered how many days of labor were involved in the preparation of the mummified bodies for the afterlife.

That night we saw the pyramids for the first time. It was dream-like to see them in the moonlight. We followed that experience with a dinner where the entertainment was provided by female belly dancers and a male musical group from Upper Egypt.

The next day we visited the Cairo Tower with its open latticework design intended to look like a lotus, the symbol of the Pharaohs. We visited the Manial Palace and Museum and then went back to see the pyramids and Sphinx in the daylight. We even rode on camels at the pyramids. From there, we went to the Khan El Khalili, the old souk with its narrow paths and stalls of craftsmen and hawkers. I needed to use a bathroom and was taken to a hidden corner where there was a hole in the floor.

The final night in Cairo, we went to a nightclub on the Nile, and watched as a belly dancer performed with a lighted candelabrum on her head. We had our last opportunity to thank Essam for his helpfulness. He had carried cameras and jackets, and had done all the bargaining for prices for us. He had taken us to parts of the city we never would have seen otherwise.

Leaving Cairo was easier than entering. No-one questioned the twenty four carat gold bracelets I had purchased. We met Lorraine and Phyllis and looked forward to continuing our travels together.

*Belly dancer with candelabra.*

**ITALY:** Upon arrival in Rome, we immediately set off to walk to the Trevi Fountain, and tossed the obligatory coins into the water to guarantee a return trip. We saw a women's liberation parade that must have been a mile long. Women of all ages and types filled the entire width of the road, carrying banners and shouting for the freedom to work outside the house. Some were also carrying signs in favor of the right to abortion.

Our hotel room was overpriced but we were all grateful for lots of hot water and towels. There had been a short supply of both in Cairo. It was almost strange, however, to not see the donkey carts, sheep and camels, horses and dirty children we had become accustomed to in that city.

Our first sightseeing trip was to the Coliseum and the Roman Forum. The lower level of the Coliseum was visible, so we could see all the corridors and rooms that had held the lions and Christians. The Forum reminded me of my high school Latin classes. I felt like I had stepped into a bit of history.

Saint Peter's Cathedral was much more impressive than I had imagined it would be. The Pieta was not available because it had been sent to New York for the World's Fair. We climbed to the top of the dome of St. Peter's and were exhausted by the end of that invigorating experience.

I had expected the Sistine Chapel to be a thrill, but it was not as great as I had anticipated. The room seemed to me to be a big barn of space with a flat ceiling. For some reason, I had envisioned an oval-shaped dome. I don't believe the ceiling was ever intended for the public to be craning their necks to see. It was done for financial reasons by a hungry artist, Michelangelo, who knew that the priests and cardinals who would be looking at it had as much artistic sense as a barrel of monkeys. It is a confusing, swirling mass of figures that somehow culminates in the scene of the last judgment at one end of the hall. Perhaps that signifies the end to all earth's confusion, when the final day arrives.

The next day we moved on by train to Florence. Wherever our eyes wandered, there was beauty. Magnificent doors and statues were everywhere. Many were priceless treasures, open to the elements and risks of damage. I found myself with tears in my eyes when I saw Michelangelo's works in marble. So many were unfinished. Or maybe he just abandoned the marbles because he had already captured what he wanted. What a shame that he had to go off and paint for the priests, for money. Why couldn't his sponsors have seen that he was primarily a sculptor? To stand in the Medici Chapel, designed by Michelangelo and containing seven of his works, in the location he, himself, chose for them, was a thrill beyond compare for me.

Before settling in at our small hotel for the night, we climbed to the top of the Giotto Bell Tower, over four hundred steps. The exhilaration I felt was hard to describe. Somehow, it seemed symbolic of the heights we can reach if only we try.

In the morning, we spent time in the Pitti Palace, to see many fabulous paintings, many by Rubens and Raphael. What a treasure in one gallery! From there, we walked to the Borgello Museum for some more sculpture before we went to the train station to continue on our trip to Pisa.

The stairs of the leaning tower beckoned us. We had already climbed to the top of Saint Peter's in Rome, the Bell Tower of Florence, so now the Tower of Pisa was irresistible. Climbing these stairs was a dizzying experience because as we climbed the circular stairwell, gravity caused us to lean first toward, and then away from the walls. There was no railing or banister, except for the top level. Standing on top, with the Alps in the background, the view was breath-taking. When I had seen photos of this site taken by soldier friends during the Second World War, I never dreamed I would visit there.

The people of Pisa appeared to me to be more plebian than the residents of Florence. The most handsome men and the most smartly dressed women of Italy must live in Florence. Unfortunately, however, many women have dyed their hair a reddish shade that looked more like Oxblood shoe polish. It was really horrible. Italy could use better hair colorists, for sure.

**LONDON:** After our day in Pisa, we took the train to the Rome airport to conclude our trip with a visit to London. We arrived in time to enjoy a fish and chips supper and to attend an English play. It was typically British – dull and droll.

Our 'culture shock' had almost made a complete circle. London's Piccadilly Circus and surrounding Soho district looked much like Times Square in New York, preparing us for our return. There were sex films, massage parlors, "hippy" types and an assortment of odd characters, the likes of which I had not seen in all of Tunis, Egypt, or Italy. It stands as a sad commentary on "civilization".

The highlight of the trip to London was not the English breakfast of kippers, nor the lunch of steak and kidney pie, but the visit to the British Museum to see the Elgin Marbles. These magnificent figures were taken by Lord Elgin from the Greek Parthenon. This museum was the only one I ever encountered that permitted flash photography, so I took advantage of that by finishing all my film with photos of the marbles. On the Acropolis in Athens, there is one statue missing. It stands in the British Museum. I made sure to capture that image on one of the photographs. I hoped to see the rest in Athens some day.

*Elgin marbles.*

The visit to the museum rounded out the historical knowledge gained on this trip, having been exposed to Greek, Egyptian and Roman works of art from ancient times, in addition to the Italian Renaissance. How I wished I knew more ancient and world history. It created in me a wish to learn more. I certainly recognized that my Christian Academy education omitted a great deal.    To have lived these last three weeks in the land of the Pharaohs, to have walked the same roads as the Roman Senators, Julius Caesar and Brutus, to have seen the works of the masters of the Italian Renaissance, have all been experiences I will never forget.

# CHAPTER 2: SEOUL, KOREA, 1979

AVS was to hold its Fourth International Conference on Voluntary Sterilization, and I had been invited by the International Project to represent AVS with regard to our work in our own country. I had attended the three previous international meetings and was delighted to be part of this fourth gathering. One more such meeting was eventually held in Santo Domingo, in the Dominican Republic, and I took part in that one also.

The leadership staff of the International Project, under the direction of Marilyn Schima, scheduled all the working hours of staff who would be attending. As a result, we had very few moments to see anything outside of the conference rooms. We were prepared for this. It had been much the same in Geneva and Tunis. But an added order was that no staff could add a vacation to the trip, so we had no opportunity to make a stop either on the way to or from the conference. We would miss any opportunity to see a bit of the world along the way.

In Seoul, we had one free period to visit the city. There were temples everywhere one could see. All, of course, had been built after the Korean War, but were of the same construction as those that were there before. The gardens around the temples and at other tourist sites seemed to me to be unorganized. They did not appear to have any style. Unlike the formal English gardens, which I did not expect, and unlike the wild-flower gardens that have equal charm in another way, these seemed to me, like Topsy, to have just grown up.

One day, when we were set free in the late afternoon, a group of staff members decided to go into the "old City" to wander around and have supper. I enjoyed the sights, smells, and sounds of the crowded city alleys, the raw fish stalls, the strange fish and vegetables for sale, and the garlicky, very spicy, fermented cabbage dish called KimChi that was an important part of the dinner we enjoyed.

I don't remember why brass was a particular bargain or specialty in the area, but it seemed to be. Because I wanted a souvenir of my first trip to Asia, I bought an outrageous number of candlesticks as souvenirs. They eventually ended up in the screened patio of my weekend retreat house in Sussex, NJ, until one year they were stolen. What I remember most was the weight of the luggage I had to carry home from Korea.

One evening, all the conference participants were invited to an evening reception given by the Korean government. There was a fabulous buffet and liquid refreshments. An ice sculpture was the centerpiece, and I had never, nor since, seen such a skilled ice carving. Later, we were all transported to a show. To our surprise, the performance was probably an imitation of what Asians had seen in Las Vegas, with topless show girls and lavish costumes. All the show girls were American, we were told, because Asian women would not be willing to show their bodies in such a fashion. There was a part of the program that featured local musicians, so at least we had that introduction to Korean entertainment.

This was my first visit to Asia, and I would have liked to add a bit of a vacation along the way. To my surprise, when I returned directly to the office, as instructed, I learned that other staff had ignored the commandment of "Thou shalt not vacation elsewhere". They had, in fact, gone to another country on the way to or from Korea.

*Korean temple.*

# CHAPTER 3: BELGIUM, AUGUST, 1979

The purpose of my trip to Belgium was to present a paper at the prestigious Fifth World Congress on Medical Law. Because this meeting would be attended by members of both the legal and medical professions from all over the world, I considered it quite an honor to have been invited to present my topic: "Voluntary Sterilization Counseling as a Pre-requisite to Informed Consent".

The Congress was scheduled for the 19th to the 23rd of August, in Ghent. I had flown into Amsterdam and planned to travel to Ghent by train. That allowed me to take a break in Antwerp along the way. I had traveled by trains in this part of Europe before, so was familiar with the arrangements for storing my luggage while in Antwerp.

Luckily for me, the Royal Academy of Art was having a special exhibit of the works of Rubens and Rembrandt. Seeing those paintings served as a wonderful reminder that in the seventeenth century, women were not expected to be thin. The models used by these masters all had a bit of extra flesh to cover up the bones and make pleasant curves.

Middleheim Park, also in Antwerp, was an open air modern sculpture garden. The park covered many acres, so it took quite a while to see the works on display. Some were very unusual; others were more understandable; all were beautiful. Most of the photos I took were with my three dimensional camera. The statuary seemed to call for other than a two dimension photo.

The architecture of the railroad station in Antwerp was attractive, as were so many in this part of Europe. It was a surprise to find the entrance to the Antwerp Zoo right in the heart of the city, next to the central railroad station and bus depot. How convenient for the citizens, I thought, but I did not have time for a visit to the zoo.

In Ghent, I visited Gravensteen Castle, which dates back to the thirteenth century. Being in the presence of such old structures always puts me in awe of what the people of those days could build without the tools and equipment we have today. Also, newer buildings cannot be expected to remain in use for so many hundreds of years.

I stopped in the large church in the center of Ghent to see the renowned altarpiece called the *Adoration of the Mystic Lamb* (or briefly, *The*

*Lamb of God).* This painting was an early fifteenth century treasure that had been taken out of the country by the Nazis during the Second World War. Two years later it was found and returned by the "Monument Men", a small group of artists assigned to rescue stolen art and to return the pieces to their home counties. This polyptych was so much larger than I had imagined; I was very pleased to have the opportunity to view it.

Before I left Belgium, I was able to visit Bruges, again traveling by train. I had heard so much about this beautiful city from my father's wife, Helene, who was born and reared there. I was also very fortunate to have Helene's niece, Angele, accompany me on this side trip. She made a wonderful guide. I had first met Angele fifteen years earlier when she was in the US for an extended stay and it was nice to see her again after many years.

One of my first stops in the city was at the Church of Our Lady, to see Michelangelo's depiction of the *Madonna and Child.* Like the altarpiece of Ghent, this sculpture had been removed from the church in 1944 with the retreat of the German soldiers, who smuggled it to Germany enveloped in mattresses in a "Red Cross" truck. Like the altarpiece, it was returned by the "Monument Men".

Bruges was known for its lace-making. Angele and I visited one of their schools where the women sat on straight-backed chairs, with a large, round padded work board on their lap. It was on this board that the lace was pinned while it was being made. The craftswomen must keep track of the dozens of bobbins of thread that get manipulated to create the lace.

*Lace makers.*

The canals of Bruges were beautiful. All along the canal, as we rode in a boat on a tour of the area, we could see flower boxes on the shore line filled with geraniums or other colorful plants. That extra touch made the sight memorable.

At noon, we had freshly fried flounder in a restaurant near one of the canals. It was a great meal, but the vision that I have retained was the bathroom. There was one such room. As I entered, there were sinks and urinals against the walls. Further on, there were stalls. I had not expected to have to walk past men who were urinating in order to sit in a stall beyond them.

It was a very pleasant trip, and the final plus came in 1982, when the paper I presented at the World Congress was published in *Medicine and Law 1:29-32*. The abstract of *Voluntary Sterilization: Counseling as a Pre-requisite to Informed Consent* follows: *A summary of legal and medical aspects of voluntary sterilization. With the widespread use of sterilization as a contraceptive device, there is an increasing need for public safeguards to eliminate sterilization abuse. While it is difficult to pinpoint a body of information that will exclusively and exhaustively assure an informed decision, it is recognized that there are many components of the counseling and advising process that have universal as well as specific applicability to consenting persons. This information must be neutrally and sensitively conveyed in order to assure a truly informed client. It is this realization that must dictate the approach to securing informed consent, and is precisely the consideration that is most abused. The question of gaining informed consent from a mentally impaired person is even more complex because legal statutes are all but nonexistent. No one should be categorically denied voluntary sterilization either because of his or her confinement in a mental institution, or having been judged to be mentally incompetent. The merits of each case should decide whether the individual is able to understand the implications of sterilization and to choose for himself or herself.*

# CHAPTER 4: ISRAEL, FEBRUARY, 1981

Valentine Day of 1981 was departure day - the day that the big TWA 747 left JFK airport for Israel, carrying me to attend two meetings in Tel Aviv. Because I was scheduled to deliver a paper at each of two conferences, there was to be quite a bit of free time for me on this trip. In the week between my presentations, I was entirely free to go on sight-seeing side trips, including a visit to Jerusalem. I had no prearranged side trips; I planned to use local tour service buses, scheduling some starting out from Tel Aviv, and others starting in Jerusalem.

It was mid-afternoon the next day when the plane landed in Tel Aviv. I purchased some shekels at the Tel Aviv airport as soon as I arrived. After being in Israel for a few days, I realized that had been an unnecessary nuisance. The reason was that the shekel was daily going down in value while the American dollar was escalating. Visitors in Israel could get more value paying in dollars, and shopkeepers preferred being paid in dollars. By holding the dollars a few more days, they would be worth more.

Local cabs seemed to be the mode of transportation from the airport to the beach area where I had a reservation at the Diplomat Hotel. I always found it a bit risky to enter a taxi in a new country. There was the wonder whether a bus might have been a better option - especially if the hotel was forty miles away, as in Israel. Also, there was the fear that I might be taken on some "joy ride" to build up the fare before reaching my destination. But all went well. The fare was only about ten dollars. That was half of the cost from my office in mid-town Manhattan to the JFK airport.

The drive from the airport to Tel Aviv was not inspiring. We drove through areas that were in a bad state of disrepair. Many buildings were empty and windowless. I was sure they had been abandoned and boarded up, but later I learned that they were very much occupied. Unfortunately, the need for security panels (either against the elements or for blackouts - I was not sure) created a feeling of despondency. There was little indication of happy carefree living. I later learned the reason so many buildings were being rebuilt. They had been erected in haste with cheap materials about forty-five years before. The salt air had been destructive to the cement, plaster, and paint. Consequently, large areas were now being torn down. Renewal projects would gradually replace what appeared to me like bombed

142

areas.

The first conference opened the next morning. I had been invited to speak at the First International Convention on Medico-legal Aspects of Disability. My topic was the medico-legal aspects of sterilization for mentally disabled persons. Ten days later, a National Conference of the Israel Society for Rehabilitation of the Disabled, with a different membership, was also to be held in Tel Aviv. I had been invited to address that group about sterilization as an option for disabled persons. The content of these papers overlapped, so I can summarize the content of both papers as one, as follows:

*The commitment to make voluntary sterilization available to all has generally not included the individual who is mentally disabled. Examples of such persons would include those who recognize that his or her mental or emotional level of ability is already strained, and the responsibility of rearing a child might be more than could be managed. The dilemma of mentally retarded persons or of those judged to be incompetent provides a clear example of our greatest failure in achieving the ideal: the availability of contraceptive sterilization without coercion as well as without the exclusion of any individual or group.*

*World-wide, too few countries have taken a legal stand or have exact legal rulings on the issue. Those that do so recognize the rights of parents or guardians to request sterilization for their mentally incompetent wards. Generally, permission is granted on any of three grounds: parental request, for eugenic purposes, or incapacity of responsible parenting.*

*In the United States, only twenty-four states provide for legal sterilization of mentally disabled persons. The statutes vary in their provisions, allowing various agents to initiate sterilization proceedings, and in some cases making no distinction between mental illness and mental retardation. The US Department of Health and Human Services has not satisfactorily come to terms with this difficult question. Instead, they have chosen to simply refuse federal funding for sterilization of anyone judged to be mentally incompetent, a decision that discriminates against indigent persons with mental disabilities.*

*AVS has recently prepared a model voluntary sterilization act aimed at permitting voluntary sterilization for all adults capable of giving informed consent (done under the leadership of Harriett Pilpel and her colleagues who served as AVS' legal advisors). The question of informed consent, however, is problematic and has not been resolved to anyone's complete satisfaction. The AVS model statute authorizes voluntary sterilization only, and does not apply to institutionalized individuals. Counseling is an integral part of this process.*

*The case of minors is considered particularly sensitive. Minors are not considered to be candidates for sterilization because intervening years and growth may either alter former assessment of mental capability or improve the possibilities for growth and change in the potential of mentally disturbed youth. AVS has gone on record urging the development of guidelines that would be specific to this group, available where wanted, imposed on none.*

The full text of the paper delivered at the first meeting, the International Convention, was later published as a chapter in *Disability*, edited by A.

Carmi, E. Chigier and S. Schneider, Berlin, Springer-Verlag, 1984, pp 238-243.

The following notes are about my travels in Israel and not related to any work for AVS. I covered the costs of these trips personally, as I considered the time between conferences to be a vacation.

My first journey was to Cesarea, Acco, and Hanikra, the area north along the Mediterranean Sea toward Lebanon. The tour bus drove north, toward Natanya, through the area called the "Sharon" district. Strawberry farms were the chief source of income. They were the largest, most succulent berries I ever tasted. At the beginning of the twentieth century, this area was all swamps, and malaria was rampant. To decrease standing water, Israeli pioneers planted eucalyptus trees in the swamps. In addition to the beneficial water absorption, the oil from the sap of the trees was used to make cough syrup and to make lotion to ward off mosquitoes. Natanya was named in honor of the American philanthropist, Nathan Strauss.

The first stop in Cesarea was at a Roman theater. From there, we tourists went to see Crusader ruins, an aqueduct, an olive wood factory, tile painters, the Rothschild winery, and banana farms between Mount Carmel and the sea. Cypress rows protected the bananas from high winds. Plastic was used to cover the ground plants in winter months. We passed an Arab village where small buildings clung to the slopes of the mountain. The tour director told us that Arabs were entitled to all of the rights of Israelis, but were exempt from military service because of fear of treason.

We passed caves where remains of prehistoric men had been found. The bones were estimated at more than 40,000 years. In Haifa, a Carmelite monastery had been built above a cave said to be significant in the Biblical stories about the prophet Elijah. Twelve miles away was another cave where Elijah once hid, and on the promontory was the place where Elijah challenged the god Baal to bring fire.

We passed over the Kishor River, named in the Bible, on the way to Acco. Here, a visit to the Crusader fort was exciting. It had been built in the twelfth century and held by crusaders for about two hundred years. On display was one of the granite catapult balls used by Egyptian Mamelukes when they destroyed the castle. Far below the ground level we trod through tunnels that were part of the Crusader's hidden storage areas and escape routes. The passageways were narrow and required us to bend over as we walked. I was glad I was not wearing armor.

A walk through the old city of Acco revealed stairways that were only about eighteen inches wide, leading to upper level apartments. I was able to glimpse into some ground floor rooms and enjoyed speaking to some of the beautiful little children playing around doorways and in the narrow alleys. The souks appeared to be only for local residents to shop. There was no calling to tourists or begging. The one small gift shop was located at the bus stop. The buildings in Acco were cement-colored, blending right in with the color of much of the ground. I remembered that the colors in Egypt were similar. Everything seemed to be sand-colored.

Rosh Hanikra, located just below the Lebanese border, was the northern-most stop on this journey. Some shooting was occurring in this area, so we were under the watchful eyes of the army as we moved about. We were able to take a cable car down to the shore and to enter caves that had been carved out of the mountainside by the waves. It was a combination of pleasure and tension that I experienced.

The next trip I took was a taxi ride to the old city of Joppa, now called Yaffo. In the higher areas of the landscape I could see many ancient walls, arches, domes and minarets. Every time I climbed a level, I would find another one higher up and farther out. High up on the highest spot near the water, the terrace's white chairs reflected the sun streaming through the white arbor. It was beautiful. I sat at a table on the edge of the terrace of the Mediterranean Restaurant, with a two-foot thick stone wall at my side. Beyond was the break-water that held the tides and waves out of the buildings down on the edge.

Looking around, I could see the old buildings, very much still lived in, with their delicate grill rails surrounding several small domed roofs. Through an open door of one of the buildings, I could see a plasterer smoothing a wall from which the corner had been cut into an arch formation. The building was one of the highest, but nearby there was a mélange of single rooms of different heights, and from most of them sprung small terraces. Looking directly down from where I stood, clothes were strung to dry in an air shaft no more than ten feet long and four feet wide. There were three or four levels of clothes lines.

Behind where I was sitting on the terrace, there was an old man wearing an Arab headdress, sitting on a stone railing. He was filing a white sculpture that appeared to be many white balls all connected to form a cornice. The primary sounds I heard for the two restful lunch hours were the waves splashing on the rocks beyond the jetty, the barking of seals on the outer rocks, and the rasping of the sculptor's file.

That evening, with other registrants of the conference, I visited the cafe of Omar Kyam in old Joppa. The cafe itself was an ancient building with arches and niches. The star performer was a fifty-four year old woman who had been drafted into the Israel War for Independence where she joined a military band. Since then she entertained the troops at the front of every battle. Her name was Yaffo Yarkoni but she was known as the "War Singer". I have since learned that she died at the age of eighty-six, in 2012, after having taken a public stand criticizing the Israeli Defense Forces for its treatment of the Palestinians. She sang songs of every country represented at the conference.

The next tour I was able to schedule was to Masada and the Dead Sea. The tour bus traveled on an excellent highway from Joppa to Jerusalem. About half way was an area called Sha-ar HaGay (also referred to as Beit Me'ir). Along the road, there were memorials for the many Jewish boys killed in the 1948 War for Independence. These commemoratives consisted of damaged Jeep and car chassis painted a rust color and marked by plaques. They reminded me of some of the modern art I have seen in museums.

The bus continued through the town of Abu Gosh, the traditional resting place of the Ark of the Covenant in Biblical history. Soon after, there was a settlement of apartments high on a hillside. It was there where Israeli immigrants lived for six months while they learned Hebrew. I thought that would be an excellent idea for the USA to copy. "Mt. Joy" was said to be the location of Saul's and of Samuel's graves. It was a holy place for both Jews and Muslims. From the hill I had my first look at Jerusalem. Seeing pictures of Jerusalem had not prepared me for the excitement of seeing the old walled city and domes. It was a sample of what would lie ahead for me in the coming week.

I had been reared in a Protestant conservative environment and had attended Christian schools where the Biblical stories were stressed as an important part of our religious education. The tour bus had a guide who pointed out all the locations that were mentioned in both Old and New Testaments. One was the city of Bethany, the home of Mary and Martha and the place where Lazarus was raised from the dead. Another was the supposed site of the Inn of the Good Samaritan, on our way through the Judean desert.

The desert sands were tinted green, thanks to the recent rainy weather. As we descended from the peaks of Jerusalem to the Jordan Valley, the temperature rose. Off came the raincoat, then the jacket, followed by the sweater. Soon the air conditioner in the bus came on. We stopped briefly to see the Caves of Qumran, where the Dead Sea scrolls were found by two Bedouin shepherd boys in 1947. Nearby, beautiful white ibises were grazing on small green plants.

We passed through En Gedi, an oasis, on our way to Masada, the site where Jewish zealots hid around the years seventy to seventy-two CE. It had formerly been King Herod's palace. From a distance, the high plateau looked quite like many others, but once on top, viewing the rooms, cisterns, bath-houses, and guest houses, it suddenly seemed to me more like a fairytale.

On towards Mt. Sodom, we stopped for a swim in the Dead Sea, which was great fun. It was almost impossible to stand in such salty water. We returned by way of Beer Sheva, driving through Bedouin territory. Instead of tents, some people were now living in permanent sheds. The auto had replaced most camel and donkey transportation. There was still no electricity, but many had battery-operated television sets. There was a special school for Bedouin children in the area.

My next tour took me to Nazareth, Tiberius and Capernaum. Our guide spoke eight languages but only English and German (for the one family from Holland) were needed. We learned from our guide that forrell is a hybrid trout/carp raised here to large sizes, developed because indigenous trout ate each other after they reached 250 kg. In the language of the Netherlands, the word for trout is forel. Perhaps that was the origin of the name for the new fish.

*Capernaum temple.*

The Valley of Yizreel was the next stop. It was mentioned in early Egyptian hieroglyphics, cuneiform writing, and in the Bible stories about Deborah and Gideon. The valley has been known as the most continuous battlefield. This is the area referred to as Armageddon. Across are the hills of Nazareth. King Saul used this road as a caravan trail. Horses traveled this route after they had been purchased in Egypt to be sold in Mesopotamia. A chain of chariot towns had been established along the way. Megiddo was one of those stops. The book, *The Source*, by James Mitchner, was based on the history of this area.

Nazareth lies northeast of Megiddo. We were shown the cave where the angel appeared to Mary. We also saw Mary's well, which still supplied the village water, and the home of Joseph the carpenter, where Jesus lived as a boy. Of course, none of these sites could be documented, but why visit and look at these sites if you don't take in the tales that go with it?

Lunch on the shore of the Sea of Galilee consisted of fish named "St. Peter's fish", after the apostle fisherman. (We know it as tilapia.) Leaving Tiberius, going northward, we continued to Capernaum. This city was one of our guide's favorite sites, so we had a very enthusiastic tour. A bit south of Capernaum was the site where Jesus instructed Peter to "Feed my sheep. Feed my lambs". Not far away was the hill where the multitude was fed from two fishes and seven loaves. We saw the area where the Sea of Galilee feeds into the River Jordan. Along the banks of the river, we had an opportunity to go to the water. It was interesting to see everyone bending down to wash their hands in the water or splash water on their arms and faces. An enterprising preacher could do a box-office business here offering re-affirmation of baptismal vows.

I had no more tours scheduled while in I was stationed in Tel Aviv. Any free hours were spent visiting shops along Diesengoff Street, art galleries on Gordon Street, walking to the Town Hall Plaza, library, museum, and Ben Gurion's home. One afternoon, I stretched out on the beach for an hour or two. Too chilly to swim, but fine to relax, listen to the waves, and read. It was quite peaceful until a young man, probably in his late twenties, strolled by and started a friendly conversation about the beach, staying on to talk about life in Israel. He complained about their Prime Minister, talked about politics, asked many questions about life in America, and discussed problems associated with discrimination against various people. It turned out to be an interesting visit. I especially got a kick out of his telling me that Israeli women all have dark hair covering their legs ("Ugh!" he said.) Then he told me he suspected I had not shaved my legs. I had not guessed that my hairless pale legs on the beach were such a novelty.

Living in a kosher environment was a new experience. No hot meals were available in the hotel from Friday evening until Saturday night because lighting fires on the Sabbath was forbidden. I was surprised to learn that even smoking was not allowed. Fortunately, not all the restaurants follow the religious laws.

Between the two conferences, I moved to Jerusalem so that I could take some tours from that area. I shared a taxi from Tel Aviv to Jerusalem and checked into the Intercontinental Hotel on the Mount of Olives. I strolled outside for a magnificent view of the eastern wall of the old city of Jerusalem, with the silver and gold domes of its two famous mosques shining in the afternoon sun. I was approached by a twenty-year-old Muslim, Mahmoud, who sold me a two foot wide picture of the view with identifying information about the major sites. He then convinced me that an independent guide, himself, could show me the old city far better than a tour bus. It sounded good, so we made a date for the next morning. He invited me to call him Mike.

To my surprise, Mike's brother Bassem ("Sam") showed up instead. He said he was substituting for Mike who had been called to work. Later, I learned that it was actually a late night out carousing with the girls that caused Mike to stop by his brother's house at five o'clock and ask him to fill in. It was to my advantage. Bassem was twenty-two, married, expecting his first baby, and an excellent guide. We started down the path directly in front of the hotel, where Christ walked on Palm Sunday. We passed the Tomb of the Prophets (Zachariah, Haggai and Malachi). We proceeded to the Garden of Gethsemane with its many grottos, basilicas, and tombs, up to the Sheep Gate of Jerusalem. The name refers to the Bedouins who have long been bringing their sheep, donkeys, camels, and various livestock to this gate every Friday morning for sale or barter.

We followed the footsteps of Christ, on the Via Dolorosa. Some people were making a religious procession. Others were doing their daily shopping for food and clothing. Still others were just wandering tourists. Walking through the narrow alleys, I was reminded of the Khan El Kalili in Cairo, the souks of Tunis, and the mercados of Latin America. Stalls lined the narrow pathways. Clothes and other saleable items were hung in the lanes and overhead. Shopkeepers tried to encourage business by any and all means. It was not uncommon to hear "Let's make a deal" or "No charge to look", and all sorts of greetings. The shopkeepers had learned enough of many languages to be able to communicate with almost any passerby. It was amazing to see how they seemed to be able to pick the correct language for each. It seemed that Americans were especially easy for them to identify.

The many smells in the old city were a treat all by themselves. Walking along, I could smell spices, then freshly ground coffee, then bakery products, butcher stalls with the slight odor of raw meat and blood, barbecued shish-kebab, donkeys and people.

After a full day, I welcomed Bassem's invitation to visit with his uncle for a cup of Turkish coffee. Uncle Abed was a caretaker for the Jewish cemetery adjacent to the Intercontinental Hotel. He served as watchman, grave digger, monument maker, stone engraver, and wall builder. He was in his late forties but had the weather-beaten face of a man almost double that. His house was a metal shed with a cot, two chairs, a cabinet, a sink, and perhaps a toilet hidden somewhere unseen. The coffee was brewed on a sterno stove in the middle of the floor. Mike joined us, so there I was - one Christian female with three Arab men, drinking Turkish coffee in a Jewish cemetery.

Before I left New York, I had agreed to deliver some medicine to the parents of one of my instructors at Pace University. When I called Mrs. "G" upon arrival on Sunday, she insisted on having me to dinner the next day. I arrived to find my instructor's brother, his wife and their three children also there for the occasion. Mr. and Mrs. "G" were most cordial, and my having a touch of home life was a pleasant break from hotel life.

The religious service at the end of the meal was the most irreverent one I have ever seen. Prayer books were distributed with an effort to give me an English translation, but with no guidance as to the starting place. The grandson, Adam, was trying to imitate his father and grandfather, with his mother constantly telling him to slow down because she could not keep up. Meanwhile the father and grandfather rushed along mumbling many sentences so quickly that no meaning could possibly be gotten. Finally, Adam admitted he had lost his place, only to be told he had been reading too slowly. Adam blamed his mother, and I thought a fight would bring the "worship" to a close. Actually, I don't know how it ended. They all just seemed to wind down as casually as they had gotten wound up.

The weather turned very windy and by late evening the rain had begun. It continued the next morning, so there was no temptation to walk outside. Fortunately, the museum was open late, and a guided tour in English was scheduled for four o'clock that afternoon. Afterwards, I made a visit to the Shrine of the Book. This was a display of the ancient scrolls found in the Qumran caves near the shore of the Dead Sea. I wanted to try to go by city bus to the Damascus Gate of the walled city of Jerusalem, but it required either a transfer or a long walk from where the first bus dropped me off. I got directions from another passenger, but apparently the language barrier caused a problem and I could not locate the area I was looking for. After wandering down many streets in the rain, I finally gave up and hailed a taxi. I had dinner in a restaurant called Hasson Effendi, in the Arab quarter. Dinner started with eighteen salads and pita bread, and it continued with chicken roasted in a crepe-like crust, lamb chops, kebabs, a sweet pastry and Turkish coffee. What a feast to end this second day.

Instead of taking two bus tours, I arranged with Bassem to go by car to four nearby areas: Bethlehem, Bethany, Qumran and Jericho. I was curious about the kind of junk we would be riding in, and certainly did not expect the $50,000 Mercedes that pulled up to the curb promptly the next morning. Bassem had said he would get his friend to drive, but did not tell me his friend was a taxi driver. We traveled in class.

In Bethlehem, the Church of the Nativity stands on the spot where Jesus is said to have been born. In a small room, a star on the floor signified the spot, and in a small nook two or three feet away there was a manger. We next drove to Shepherd's Field and saw many caves that were used for shelter for thousands of years. We entered one that was typical of many, and I felt that the simplicity of this site gave more feelings of authenticity than the large churches built over other sites.

We stopped in Bethany to see the places where Jesus visited with Mary and Martha, but the most memorable experience for me was to enter the tomb of Lazarus. A church commemorates this spot also, but it is adjacent to the tomb rather than on top of it. To enter, one must go through a small door, and down a flight of old narrow stairs. Then, even further down on narrower, older steps to the tomb, quite far below street level. The condition of the ancient tomb removed my fear that this was just a tourist trap. Once again, the feeling of being a part of a historical and spiritual experience was overwhelming.

When we went to Qumran, I was expecting to go inside some caves, but the main attraction was an excavated village where a group of Essenes once lived. The walls of the structures were high enough to get a fairly good idea what life in that area had been like. The climate overlooking the Dead Sea was arid, so much of the Essene settlement consisted of cisterns and aqueducts. There seemed also to be one large dining room, indicating a communal style of living. It was the Essenes who, when fearing the Romans were about to attack, hid their scriptures in the caves where those "Dead Sea" scrolls were found a mere thirty-four years before my visit. The primary occupation of the Essenes seems to have been serving as scribes. The scriptorium was a central room of the village.

Traveling north, we approached Jericho. The first surprise was to have the driver pull up to the side of the road, and calmly say, "This is the sycamore tree that Zaccheus sat in so he could see Jesus when he passed." It was the only sycamore tree in the area, and certainly was massive and old. It had branches that spread out, starting about six feet above the ground, so it was very easy to picture a short man being given a boost so he could climb high enough to see over the heads of the crowd. But was it the same tree?

We drove a bit beyond the city proper to a site at the base of the Mount of Temptation. From there, we could look back upon the remnants of the old city walls that fell at the sounds of Gideon's trumpets. Even more impressive was the "ghost town" of Jericho. Hundreds of cement, glassless windowed, box-like shelters were lined up, row after row, just outside the city limits. These were the barren homes built by the United States for the influx of Jewish immigrants. Gradually, as the people were absorbed into various communities, the homes were left unoccupied. Recently, those abandoned buildings had been used again by Arabs. As the tension in that area progressed, the local "squatters" ran into Jordan where they planned to bide their time until they felt safe to return to Israel.

The city of Jericho was a vacation spot for many Israelis because of the cooler climate. The hills are beautiful, fruits and vegetables are lush. One type of orange unique to the area was grown, and apparently much sought after. The guide and driver each bought a big sack to take home. Lunch was delicious, served in a restaurant with lovely gardens surrounding it. We ate humus, pita, and all the other local goodies I was by then considering to be normal fare.

Driving anywhere in Israel, one could expect to be stopped and questioned by the authorities. One such road-block was about a mile outside of Jericho. A young Israeli soldier questioned us all, asking place of birth, checking my passport and the ID cards of the others. We were permitted to pass when he verified that all was in order. The driver was obviously annoyed with the procedure, although he meekly submitted to the interrogation. As we drove, he expressed his thoughts, "I was born in this country, and so was all my family for a thousand years back. This young soldier, who is probably a new Jew in the land, is checking my papers to see if I can move from place to place!" The irony of history illustrated by this will stay in my memory.

It was mid-afternoon and a beautiful sunny day when the taxi dropped me off at the hotel. Too early to quit, it seemed like a perfect opportunity to walk to the Kidron Valley, past Absolum's Tomb, Zachariah's Pyramid, and the other tombs in the valley between the Mount of Olives and the walled city of Jerusalem. From the hotel's location atop the Mount, Absolum's Tomb had seemed small. Only the upper third had been visible, so when I approached it, I was immediately impressed with its massive size. Then my mind focused on the authenticity of such an old monument, and the capabilities of ancient builders and architects. Seeing such things gives meaning to the old phrase about travel being broadening - especially for Americans who have so little exposure to examples of the ancient past.

*Kidron Valley*

Walking in the valley, I could see the homes up on the hillside. It was clear that some dwellings were still adaptations of caves. Rectangular sand-colored houses were stacked up on the steep slope. Some children were playing near the road. One came asking for a shekel. I told him that if he would pick up his little lamb so I could take his picture, he would earn one shekel. He took off immediately, but the lamb was even faster. Up the slopes they raced, stumbling boy in hot pursuit of a sure-footed animal. By luck and a short cut, the boy lunged for the lamb and caught a hind leg. Then the fun began. The lamb, standing on hind legs, was about as tall as the boy struggling to pick him up. So he decided to dance the lamb down the hill, expecting the animal to walk backwards. An older boy came to the rescue, picked up the lamb and placed it in the boy's arms. The proud boy came beaming toward me, had his picture taken, and received the shekel.

Walking on, suddenly there was a loud splat behind me. As I turned around, I saw another piece of soft fruit or tomato hit the ground a few feet away. Looking up toward the firing range, I caught a glimpse of a boy on a balcony being spanked by his father. It seems he had been caught in the act.

Near the Gishon spring, and the Pool of Siloam, there was a small shop where a local resident was selling antique oil lamps. Some dated back thousands of years. They were accompanied by certificates of authenticity. At less than twenty dollars, they could be considered a real bargain, but what would I do with an antique lamp? The shopkeeper urged me to have coffee with him, and proudly showed me an issue of the National Geographic magazine from 1968 that featured him. To prove he was the man in the photo and article, he whipped off his head covering and explained that his hair had turned grey.

These small contacts with local residents are examples of the experiences that I so much enjoy. I pity the tourists who never mingle with the people who live in the lands they visit. They miss the benefits of such interchange. It is also why, whenever I can, I will travel on my own rather than with a tour group. I want to communicate with the residents of an area rather than just associate with other travelers.

Turning direction, to go up the other side of the valley, toward the temple mount, I was in the area called the Ophal, the location of the actual City of David. Excavations were underway outside the southern wall of Jerusalem and ruins of the old city were clearly visible. There was a great deal of excitement about the dig as new light was being thrown on old theories about David's city.

My next journey to Elat, on the Red Sea, was about two hundred miles each way and required two days. To add to the experience, and to break up the long ride, stops along the bus route were scheduled. The first unexpected pleasure was a stop at Avedat, a Nabatean city high on a hill in the Negev desert. Once, this area had been a flourishing farm and vineyard, thanks to the Nabatean people's industriousness and their system of water collection for irrigating the fields. While I visited, young farmers were working at the base of the tell, trying to duplicate the efforts of those earlier people, and they were succeeding in helping the desert to blossom.

The Nabateans utilized arches in their structures, and the craftsmanship of that era was remarkably modern. Walls were thick, providing insulation against the cold and heat. Cisterns were plentiful, but most interesting to me were the troughs on the building roofs and in the middle of the streets to carry the water to the cisterns. There they were - perfectly visible and in working order. Peering down into one of the cisterns, I could not see the bottom.

We were traveling through the desert at a fortunate time. For only about one week of the year, small purple flowers sprout up from the sand. A few days later, the weather gets warmer, and the plants wither until the following year. The road we were to travel on, according to the tour book, was closed to all traffic, so we took a longer route past an area where there were signs of nuclear energy activity. We could see three large cooling towers not far from the road. Because all information or discussion about military activity was forbidden to the tour guides, and because absolutely no explanation was given about the reason for the detour, I thought it was safe to assume the army had closed the road. That was understandable because the Jordanian area of conflict was not far away.

Just north of Elat, we visited Solomon's Pillars where we were told that Solomon once had his copper mines. I had never heard of this story. Massive rocks took over the entire horizon. About ten years earlier, Elat had been no more than a small police station. It had since been attempting to become the "Miami Beach" of Israel. It was a bit of a disappointment to me. There were a few three-star hotels, and in each, guests were sitting in a large "parlor" watching about a hundred other tourists looking back at them. Not very exciting or tempting. Dinner was served in a crowded room where strangers shared tables in mess-hall style room.

A visit to the cocktail lounge was no improvement. While I was sipping an over-priced drink, I heard the manager scolding someone on the phone. It seems a guest in the hotel had requested room service and it had not arrived, there being some error in the room number. Instead of a courteous attempt to rectify the situation, the guest was told that the manager never made mistakes, so the person calling for the service must have given the wrong room number. In no uncertain terms, the guest was told that the staff had more important things to do than to go knocking on doors to find the right room. I concluded that if Elat were really going to become a tourist attraction, some things were going to have to change.

Before departing the Red Sea area on our way back Tel Aviv, the tour bus traveled further south into the Sinai Peninsula. This land was scheduled to be turned over to Egypt the following year, 1982, in accordance with the terms of the peace treaty. On our drive, we saw a movie set in the middle of the desert emptiness, where US style western movies were being made. It was a humorous sight to see the big sign, "Texas Ranch" and an entire frontier town in the middle of nowhere. As the drive continued, we could see Coral Island, holding the ruins of Crusader and Mameluke castles. Further south, we refreshed ourselves at a palm-fringed inlet, called the Fjord.

Returning to Tel Aviv to deliver my second presentation, I settled down comfortably in a hotel near the conference center. On my last day, I chose a familiar restaurant for my last dinner, the Safari, which was identified by a huge stuffed gorilla sitting above the door. In the week I was gone, the weather had gotten warmer. Potted plants had been set in the square, and patio chairs were now enlarging the dining areas of small restaurants. It was time to turn my mind and heart once again to the United States.

# CHAPTER 5: GUATEMALA, JUNE, 1983

This was the first time I was assigned to do a medical site visit to one of our programs without the Medical Director, Dr. Douglas Huber, at my side. As the Deputy Director of the AVS Medical Division, one of my responsibilities was to review all mortality and morbidity reports from our international programs. I had noted a significant number of post-surgical complications being reported from Guatemala. Now I was to visit the program, accompanied by Dr. Michael Kafrissen, an epidemiologist who worked at the Centers for Disease Control. Our assignment was to investigate the complications following mini-laparotomy surgery. Dr. Kafrissen had never been on an assignment for AVS before so we were both eager to take on this assignment.

Upon our arrival, we went directly from the Guatemala City airport to the US Embassy to get the required country briefing. We were told to request indoor rooms at the hotel they had selected for us. We were not to be able to be seen from the street, because there were frequent shootings during this time of civil unrest. We were told to stay away from all crowds, street activities, or situations of political action. We were then driven to the hotel in an armored car, under guard by a Marine officer with a machine gun. But once established in our inside rooms, we were left to walk to and from the family planning office every day to work.

APROFAM was the name of the non-profit organization that provided comprehensive health services, with a focus on sexual and reproductive health. Affiliated with the Planned Parenthood Federation, it was headed by Dr. Galish. AVS was providing funding for the sterilization program, making us responsible for medical quality oversight. The organization had been doing excellent work, and our purpose in visiting was to help them solve their problems, not to admonish them. They were as interested in making improvements as we were.

When I first met Dr. Galish, I was struck by his resemblance to my husband's Mexican uncle, the Reverend Samuel Ramirez, our "Tio Sam". I mentioned this to the doctor and his response was immediate: "Well, call me Tio, and I will be your uncle here in Guatemala." From that day onward, that was how I addressed him. Over the years, we worked well together, having a special bond.

We started our work at the APROFAM office. Kafrissen, in the manner of an epidemiologist, suggested we review all the records and make charts to show the various types of complications and any recurring factors that might be associated. We found an excess of perforations of the uterus. We also found that they were taking place during training sessions. So we had our first clues about what to investigate. We would observe surgery, observe training sessions, look into the background of the trainees, and visit some of the doctors who had completed training and were now conducting services at their home base. I had been in many operating rooms and had attended many surgical training sessions so was probably more comfortable with this part of the assignment than was my epidemiologist partner.

Almost every day, we were awakened by the sounds of marching men. We were fairly near the central plaza, and the military were probably just practicing, but it was unnerving. It was not a pleasant way to wake up, bearing in mind that we had been driven to our hotel under the protection of an armed Marine. When we went on our field trips to Mazatenango, Chiquimula, and Escuintla, we were often stopped by gun-wielding troops in tanks and by interrogators at the road blocks. After questioning, checking of records, inspection, etc, we were allowed to proceed.

One morning, at one of these checkpoints, there were vendors in the road taking advantage of the delay to sell snacks to the travelers. Dr. Galish encouraged me to have a turtle egg for breakfast. I have always liked eggs so I accepted, thinking that all eggs taste pretty much the same. But to my surprise, the egg was raw, and hiding in a small glass of tomato juice. As I drank the juice, the egg slipped down. No taste of the egg at all!

The fruits of this country deserve special mention. Papayas were the size of a watermelon, and just as sweet. Cactus fruit was served in our hotel dining room for breakfast. It was bright purple-red, succulent, and delicious. Juicy ripe mangos were also available. The food in general was great. The corn tortillas were always fresh, coming off the cast-iron *comal.*

There were few opportunities to take photos because we had so little free time and because of the restricted movement that the Embassy advised. I was concentrating on the medical aspects of this trip so my photo memories were primarily of operating room scenes. One exception was the day we detoured through the Lake Atitlan area with its peaceful neighborhoods, beautiful views, and great weather. Guatemala would be a fine vacation spot if there were not so much unrest.

We were particularly interested in observing the surgical procedure called mini-laparotomy, frequently shortened to 'mini-lap'. The word stems from 'laparotomy' which means a surgical incision into the abdomen. "Mini' indicates the smaller incision that is used to reduce recovery time and which results in a much smaller scar near the 'bikini' line. In order to reach the Fallopian tubes (oviducts), the doctor manipulates a long thin instrument inserted vaginally, through the cervix and into the uterus. In that way, the tubes can be elevated, bringing them close to the abdominal wall where they can be grasped and ligated.

We found some things we would like to change in the surgical program. First, the trainers had assumed that the trainees already had experience inserting an instrument into a uterus. We found this not to be the case, so a change was made to allow the trainees to develop this initial skill before they would proceed to learn the surgery.

Another practice we found was that the patients were placed in an extreme hip-elevating position for the surgery. It is standard to tilt the head of the table down so that the abdominal organs fall away from the operative site, thereby making the tubes easier to grasp through the tiny incision. We observed that in many operating rooms the woman's legs were so high in stirrups that her neck was bent. This added to breathing difficulties for clients who had sedation and some analgesics prior to surgery. Even without medication, I would have had trouble breathing in this position. I encouraged the doctors and nurses to imagine themselves in the position of the client. Sometimes making minor changes can result in improved client safety and satisfaction.

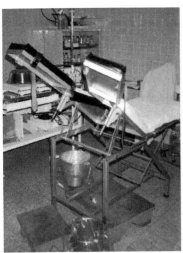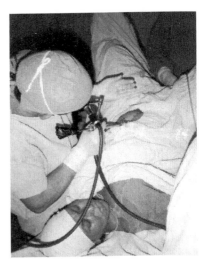

*Laparoscopy*

I had an opportunity to observe vasectomies being performed at APROFAM by Dr. Escobedo. The technique he has developed was refined, bloodless, painless, and effective. I immediately began thinking about his use as an international trainer for doctors from other countries, and planned to follow up when I return to AVS.

# CHAPTER 6: AROUND THE WORLD TO SRI LANKA, 1984

This assignment was presented to me at a horrible time in my life. In mid-March, just as I was planning to take a week-long spring vacation, my youngest daughter was killed outright in an automobile accident. I spent the week planning a memorial service and dealing with emotions that only another grieving mother can understand. I returned to work determined to concentrate on the very positive memories I had of the wonderful twenty-three years I had had with my daughter, but I was suffering.

On my first day back, my Medical Director informed me that our International Division needed a counseling consultant to assist the Sri Lanka Association for Voluntary Sterilization (SLAVS). I was the only staff member with such experience. It would take about two weeks to get my visas and make travel arrangements. I thought about the timing of this assignment and decided it would probably be a good idea. By immersing myself in activity, my grief could not immobilize me.

While discussing travel arrangements, I learned that because Sri Lanka was half way around the world, I could choose to travel either in an easterly or westerly direction. Also, because of the long flights, I was allowed to have one night of rest in each direction. I chose to travel west all the way so that I would circumnavigate the world. I confess to a bit of nervousness. I had never traveled to such strange places alone.

**FIRST STOP: SINGAPORE.** My destination in Singapore was the old Raffles Hotel, the place where so many famous people once gathered, and where the bartender had created the drink called "the Singapore Sling". My room was really a suite. When the hotel was built in 1887, visitors arrived with steamer trunks, planning to spend an extended period of time there. The room was huge, full of closets, dressers and tables with chairs. There was a sitting room up front and a dressing room in the back with a large bathroom. Ceiling fans cooled the rooms. The entire unit reminded me of a movie set.

I only had one day free so I made arrangements with a taxi driver to show me some of the highlights. We went to a batik factory and to a craft center where "paintings" were made entirely with chips of semiprecious stones. The driver next took me to the Tiger Balm Gardens, a large park full of statues depicting old myths and legends. There I had my first taste of coconut juice, drinking from a large green coconut that had the top cut off with a machete as though it had been scalped. The vender then poked a straw in the small opening, allowing me to sip the slightly sweet refreshing liquid. I was surprised how full it was, having only been exposed to the dry brown coconuts in our supermarkets.

After my taxi tour, I ventured into town and took a boat ride in the harbor. I enjoyed seeing the small work boats, some with families living aboard. Ocean liners were at the piers, evidence that Singapore was one of the busiest seaports in the world.

What impressed me most about Singapore was the orderliness. People waiting for a taxi stood in rows at designated corners. Every driver signaled before changing lanes. No one exceeded the speed limit. No wonder that in this island community, the people were also regimented in the number of children they could have. The taxi driver spoke of these things during our drive. He had two children; if he had a third, the child's education would not be guaranteed. He would have to pay a fine, and he would no longer be eligible for government-subsidized housing. He and his wife stopped at two, and he seemed convinced that this was the best plan for the country.

The country did seem to be prospering. There was a lot of new construction and new areas under development. Of course, tourism and the free-port shopping added to the economy. I was happy to have seen another place and another way of life.

**DESTINATION: SRI LANKA**. The purposes of my trip were to help organize, and then take part in a governmental meeting in the capital, Colombo. I would be working with the Sri Lanka AVS (SLAVS) organization in Kandy. There I was to help conduct a training meeting for the professionals who would later serve as the leaders of a counseling program. It was a heavy assignment.

I was met at the airport by Mr. Dessanayaka, Director of SLAVS, who was dressed in the national white garb of Sri Lanka. With him was Mr. Kunaratna. We started immediately for the three-hour drive to Kandy, an old city in the center of the country. Kandy was once the headquarters of the Kingdom. It boasted the famous Temple of the Tooth Relic of the Buddha. The SLAVS headquarters were in that city and it would be where I would be working. During the trip, Mr. Dessanayaka informed me that I was to be the keynote speaker at the big meeting that would be attended by most of the ministers of health and social programs for the country.

The ride was a shock after all the orderliness of Singapore. Because it was already dark, it was even more frightening. As we raced over narrow roads, we had to dodge people, cattle, goats, and dogs. The sacred cows really do have the right of way and are not the least bit intimidated by vehicles. To make matters worse, we seemed to be driving on the left side of the road for no apparent reason. When a car approached from the opposite direction, also driving on his left, each driver had to make a sudden swing to the right. We had a lot of close calls, but my traveling companions seemed to think everything was fine.

About midnight, I checked into the Queens Hotel. It was formerly the Governor's Mansion, but in 1895 had been converted into a fifty-four room hotel overlooking Lake Kandy. It was only a short walk from the Temple of the Tooth, founded in 1595. I felt surrounded by history.

My room, with wonderfully effective ceiling fans, was sparsely furnished and it featured twin beds with the hardest mattresses I ever felt. They were about two inches thick and they rested on a solid wooden platform. Early the next morning, I woke to a horrible screeching racket that turned out to be thousands of crows. When I looked out the window, I saw that all the trees were covered with fluttering wings. This migration was a ritual that occurred every morning and every night from five to seven o'clock. I never learned where the birds went or where they came from.

After my first week of work, I had a three-hour treat on Sunday when I was taken on a trip to see some of the local attractions. I accompanied two young staff workers who took me to the museum of archeology and then to the elephant baths. In a river, there were mahouts scrubbing their elephants with long handled brushes. They communicated with the working elephants in the Sinhalese language, and it was fascinating to see how well the animals followed instructions. Suddenly, one elephant sprayed me with river water. I suspected the elephant had been taught to do this and had been instructed to do it for the fun of all the mahouts, who were laughing at my shocked reaction. While the heat of the bright sun was drying my clothing, we drove to see a new dam under construction. This dam will divert the river and submerge entire villages in order to provide a more adequate water supply for much of the country.

From the dam, we went to see a cave temple, the walls of which were covered with beautiful frescoes in colors as bright as the day they were painted, in spite of the fact that they were hundreds of years old. In the cave was a huge recumbent Buddha carved from a solid piece of wood. The monk who escorted us was dressed in his traditional garb: he had a shaved head and wore a saffron yellow robe. He had a very stern expression on his face but in fact was most gentle and kind. He wanted me to feel the weight of the centuries-old key to the heavy door, and to point out the most impressive frescoes so I might photograph them.

That ended the sightseeing, but before collapsing on that slab of a bed, I worked until about two o'clock in the morning, preparing my keynote address.

During the next few days, I visited clinics and health centers, and traveled to a district health center some distance from Kandy. I met with public health nurses and rural health inspectors. At the hospital, I asked to see the operating room. To my dismay, it was almost entirely empty. It was just a room with a cement floor, an operating table in the center, and two or three small instrument tables along the wall. There were no emergency supplies, no general anesthesia capability, and no drugs for an emergency. I asked how they would handle a problem such as a woman experiencing a respiratory problem due to the medication they were using for sedation. The head nurse replied that they would give mouth-to-mouth resuscitation – and chest compression, if necessary. But they did not expect problems because in the two years since the doctor had finished medical school, it had not happened. It made me appreciate the hospitals in the developed world.

The next day was May Day, marked as in much of the rest of the world by political speeches and rallies. We left in the morning for our trip to Colombo, where the governmental meeting was to be held. Along the way, we passed through one village where yellow banners were strung across the roads and from lamp posts and windows. Other villages had banners representing the various political colors (blue for the current government) but the yellow was not a political color. I learned that in that one village, a monk had died, and in the Buddhist tradition, they mourned his passing in this way.

In Colombo, I checked into the Galle Face Hotel, built in 1864 on the shore of the Indian Ocean. To the side, it overlooked a large plaza where political rallies were being held. From the window of my room, I could hear the bands, watch the parades, and hear the political speeches being broadcast over the loudspeakers.

The Galle Face Hotel was still functioning as it did in the days of the former British Colonial rule. When I arrived, I looked for a check-in counter but there was none. There was instead a lovely large living room full of comfortable chairs. Then I spotted a magnificently carved table with a sign on it reading "Reception". And there sat the person who took my name and arranged for my luggage to be taken to my room.

Throughout the hotel people were standing around waiting to serve. The great veranda seemed a tempting place to enjoy High Tea in the afternoon while overlooking the palm-fringed sandy beach. One could relax and listen to the waves lapping the shore while the waiters in their white sarongs and bare feet padded around, ready to bring food or drink.

Later in the afternoon, I visited with counselors at a Catholic social agency to discuss the possibility of their assisting in the project we were planning – to teach counseling skills for family planning. Although they could only teach about periodic abstinence (the rhythm method), they agreed they could teach the skills necessary for counseling. I thought this accord I reached was a real step forward.

Finally: the big day of the meeting with all the government officials. The meeting took place in the Bandaranaike Memorial International Conference Hall, a spectacular marble structure built by the Chinese government as a gift to Sri Lanka. The sparkling white marble façade of the octagonal building was breathtaking. Tall columns all around the building add to the aesthetic appeal of the building, as did the bubbling fountains in the surrounding plaza. Inside the building, we were directed toward one of the spacious conference rooms that had been set up for our meeting.

At the front of the room, near the podium, there was a large oil lamp-stand that would allow each dignitary to light one section. The tradition of opening a meeting with a ceremonial lighting of this oil lamp, called a *Magul Bera,* stems from the desire to honor the Buddha, regarded as the dispeller of the darkness of ignorance. Because the purpose of the meeting was to embark on a new training program for counselors in the family planning program of the country, it seemed very appropriate to me. I was so proud to be a part of the ceremony and to take part in lighting the lamp.

In preparation for the meeting, Mr. Dessanayaka had suggested that when I was introduced as the speaker, I should use the symbolic *namaste* greeting. He showed me how to press my hands together, palms touching and fingers pointed upwards, in front of my chest, in a non-contact form of salutation. I followed his advice and noticed by the reactions of the audience that the gesture had been noticed and appreciated. After the program concluded, I had as many comments about that gesture as I did about the contents of my presentation.

The entire meeting went well. I was able to answer many of the questions posed by the audience. I think one of the significant changes was the concept that individuals were being empowered to make their own medical decision instead of meekly following a suggestion or advice from someone else. At the end of the day, we took the three-hour drive back to Kandy.

The next morning we had a bit of a break in the schedule. The two young ladies who had taken me on the Sunday sightseeing trip decided that I should go shopping for a sari. They insisted that I be able to wear the sari to the course I was to begin the next day. Not only did we have to buy the material for the sari, the blouse and the slip, but find a tailor. I anticipated that finding a pair of suitable sandals would be impossible because my Dutch feet were so much larger than the dainty Sri Lankan's.

At a store stacked high with bolts of many varieties of colorful and beautifully-designed fabrics, I selected a sheer light blue cloth with small black flowers. Sari fabric is printed with borders that add to the attractiveness of the finished dress. We would need a six-yard length for the dress, plus some plain white cotton for a simple half slip. We managed to find a plain blue fabric for the blouse that would match the sari cloth. Surprisingly we even found a pair of gold toe-strap sandals that were my size. I spent a total cost of five hundred rupees, about twenty dollars. Next, we set off to find a seamstress. The ladies knew of a sewing instructor at the YWCA. When we inquired about having a dress made quickly, she suggested one of her favorite students, who was deaf and mute. The girl was willing to make my outfit for six dollars. Big spender that I am, I gave her a two dollar tip when we picked up the finished sari an hour later.

*My first sari.*

Early the next day, my two fashion advisers came to help me dress. The slip was a one-size-fits-all garment. The waist had a folded hem enclosing a cord to tighten the belt. The blouse was sleeveless, with a scoop neckline. The bottom just covered my ribcage. Adjusting the folds of the sari was the most difficult part. First, one end of the length of the fabric was wound around me, starting at my front. On the second time around, we made a series of pleats in the front. To keep them secure we used a large safety pin. The pinned cluster was then tucked into the tight belt of the slip. After the final wrap, the rest of the length was draped over my shoulder to serve as the scarf and to hide my flesh a bit between the blouse and the skirt portions. I silently prayed that I would not trip as I walked or climbed stairs.

At the training course for the counseling resource people the next day, I got a flavor of the socially acceptable separation of the sexes that exists in

Sri Lanka. There was a two-hour lunch break so that the private practitioners could tend to their private patients, thus supplementing their government salaries. Those of us who remained were treated to video tapes. The men went off into one room to watch a porno film. A while later, they invited the ladies in, but by then they had switched the film to "My Fair Lady", apparently hoping that we would think they had been watching that film all the while. We had time to watch a forty-five minute segment before the meeting resumed.

The following day, I had another taste of the sexism. One of the SLAVS board members had a party and I had been invited. I wore my new sari for the occasion. The host greeted me and then said that in Sri Lanka, the women and men do not mix at social affairs. According to him, no matter how the men might try, the women preferred to be with other women. With that announcement, I was escorted into the "Ladies Room", where punch was being served. The men stayed in another room and were served alcoholic beverages. As new couples arrived, the ladies joined us, and I was introduced to them. I never did meet any of the male guests. Talk among the ladies centered on admiring each other's saris and news about their children. About ninety minutes after the party started, people began getting up to leave as though on cue, and I realized that the party had ended.

During the week I was also exposed for the first time to a formal luncheon where everyone ate curry dishes with their hand. This is quite a sight for a westerner, but I guessed I would get used to seeing people mix and pinch their rice, fish, vegetables and meat together, and push balls of it into their mouths. Maybe I will some day try it, but for this first time, I was thankful for the spoon someone offered me.

Packing to leave Kandy to spend one last night in Colombo before flying home, I was a bit sad to be leaving. I had really enjoyed the people and the assignment. I had been in Sri Lanka for two full weeks, working with people who were most gracious, kind, and pleasant to work with. All had gone out of their way to make my stay interesting. Sri Lanka is a beautiful country, and I was sorry for the turmoil that existed between the Tamils and the Sinhalese. Unfortunately, many of the educated Tamils felt forced to leave the country. Because of some Tamil terrorists in the north, Sinhalese all over the country had been retaliating by burning homes of Tamils. One evening, I was invited to dinner at the home of a Tamil doctor who was preparing to take his family out of the country to flee to a strange land for the safety of his family. It seemed a shame that the country was losing some of its most talented people.

I had mixed feelings about leaving, eager to return home, yet having to say goodbye to my new friends. I remembered similar feeling when I had worked in Guatemala the previous year. When I've been thoroughly involved in a country, working with the local people toward a common goal, I cannot help but feel like a part of it. I'll always feel a connection with Sri Lanka.

On the way to Colombo, we experienced monsoon rains for the second time on this trip. It was a very heavy downpour but it didn't last very long. The road was now familiar to me, this being the fourth time I made the three-hour journey. Along the way were more of the familiar sights. I saw an alligator slowly crawling out of a river, elephants carrying their heavy loads or lying down being bathed by their owners in a river at the end of a day's work. I have seen men clothed only in a loin cloth working in the rice paddies. I've seen oxen plowing the rice fields and bullocks pulling loaded carts. I've seen the poor people and the beggars.

During this last ride I learned that in the whole land, there were only 117 beggars, fifty-six of whom were under age twelve. Mr. Dessanayaka, with whom I had been working, had made it his own personal project to try to find homes for these beggar children, using his own money and working on his own time. He had been trying to establish a boarding school because a day facility would only mean the children would be turned out on the streets every afternoon. He was willing to house as many as thirty-six children himself if he could raise some money to help with expenses. Already he had six orphan children in his home, cared for by a housekeeper. Every morning, "Uncle", as they called him, got up early to go over their homework with them, and to be sure they were ready for school. Many evenings also were spent tutoring the children. I met the children just before we set out for the drive this day. They were charming kids who apparently were healthy and happy to have some joy in their lives.

*Mr. Dessanayaka's orphans.*

I spent my last night in Colombo at the Taj Samudra Hotel, once a historic men's club – a place where men could get away from women to play billiards, cards, or whatever men did together in those days. The beach was visible across the way, as was the Galle Face Hotel where I had stayed earlier. I had a luxurious room for my final night. I slept, thinking of the next stop: India!

**RETURNING HOME VIA INDIA**: Well, I got to Delhi, but it was not by early evening as was scheduled. It was after midnight, and quite an experience. Bombay airports are difficult. I flew from Colombo to the International Airport in Bombay. From there I had to travel to the National Airport to make the connection to Delhi. There was a delay of about four hours in the crowded airport where the floors were covered with reclining bodies - people sleeping or resting. There was a general state of confusion due to the scheduling problems. I was hot, exhausted, dirty and sweaty when I finally boarded the plane to Delhi. I jumped into the shower as soon as possible after I had checked into the Oberoi Hotel.

The night was short. I got up at five in the morning so that I could get a train to Agra scheduled to leave at seven o'clock. Called the Taj Express, it makes daily trips, arriving in Agra at eleven o'clock, and returning in the evening, departing at seven to arrive back in Delhi at eleven. While on the train, I bought a tour ticket for a day's outing that would bring the passengers back to the train in time for the return trip. The tour included all the places I wanted to see, the ancient deserted city of the king as well as the Red Fort, where Shah Jahan lived. When his favorite wife, Queen Mumtaz Mahal, died in 1631 as she was giving birth to their fourteenth child, the heartbroken Shah had the tomb built for her within eyesight of the Fort. The tour would end at the Taj Mahal.

It was quite an exciting day, but it was also very hot and dry: over 100°F. I was never so thirsty in my life, but it is not every day one gets a chance to see the Taj Mahal, one of the Seven Wonders of the World.

I had an interesting experience at the railroad when I was waiting to buy the ticket. An Indian businessman, standing ahead of me in the ticket line, offered to buy my ticket for me, saying it would be easier for him because he made this trip regularly for his business and knew the routine. He did not want to accept money from me when I offered it, saying we could settle it later. I was cautious, but accepted his help. He bought first class tickets and knew exactly which train and which car to board. I appreciated having his help as I realized I would have experienced a lot of confusion without him with all the herds of people coming and going, and resting bodies strewn all about the ground. Eventually, he accepted my money to pay for the ticket. I assumed his delay was a form of "machismo", not wanting to be seen accepting money from a woman.

Along the way between Delhi and Agra, I had a chance to see quite a bit of the countryside, many tent villages and shanty towns. A common sight was to see people bathing or collecting water at whatever common water source there was. Frequently, it was only one pump or well that would serve an entire village, resulting in long lines of people waiting their turn. In one spot, an overhead water pipe ran parallel to the train track for some distance. Along its length there were either leaks or faucets, and everywhere water was leaking out, people were showering. It was also common to see people squatting in the fields and along the railroad tracks, using the open fields to relieve themselves.

At one location I saw a tree full of vultures; at another, I saw a field full of eagles. According to my traveling companion, the birds migrate from as far away as Siberia to spend time in the warm weather of India. There were flying birds of bright and beautiful colors – almost neon blues and greens. I also saw a herd of camels and many elephants.

When we arrived at Agra, my new friend urged me to go quickly to the tour bus, offering to purchase our return tickets immediately so that we would not have to stand in line before boarding that evening. We would meet fifteen minutes before the scheduled departure. Once again, he did not want the money in advance. I figured I had nothing to lose. If he did not show up, I would still have time to get my own ticket. But he did appear at the station; he got us settled on the train and provided pleasant conversation during the four-hour return trip as he had in the morning, explaining many sights along the way.

India offered such an array of sights. Ladies were wearing the *salwar kameez* (narrow-legged pants with a long tunic top and a scarf) unlike the saris I had gotten accustomed to in Sri Lanka. Many of the men were wearing turbans. The Taj Mahal was a breath-taking sight, perfect in its symmetry, and so restful. I thought *"If only I could get some cool water, it would be perfect!"* In spite of my dehydration, it was so exciting to be in a place I never had dreamed I would see.

I was wearing stockings, as I had always done. I was also wearing high-heeled backless shoes that were very comfortable for me because they had a solid wooden sole and heel. I had learned in Holland that cobblestone or rocky roads were much easier if the feet are protected by a layer of wood. A few times in Sri Lanka, as well as in India, I had noticed people staring at my legs and then talking to each other or giggling. I had assumed they were amused by the high heels in these places where everyone wore sandals. On the train that evening, I asked my companion what he thought had caused the reaction. He immediately said it was the stockings that marked me as different. He said that porno films were fairly common in India, and they frequently featured women wearing stockings. Because stockings were not worn by Indian ladies, hosiery has been associated with whores and porno stars. I made a vow to myself to buy sandals and go bare-legged next time.

At eleven o'clock, we pulled into the Delhi train station. It had been a very full day, both exciting and very uncomfortable. I had already checked out of the hotel that morning and checked my luggage for the day. I now had to pick up my baggage and proceed to the airport for a three o'clock departure. Before I left the hotel, I washed up as best as I could in the ladies room of the hotel, using paper towels. I changed into fresh clothes. What I really needed was a bath and a night's sleep, but could only get a snack and a cold drink in the coffee shop.

The plane was late, so I had some hours to sit in the un-air-conditioned airport. It was about five in the morning before we left Delhi. The first stop was Karachi, Pakistan, where starter trouble in our plane caused another two-hour delay. This resulted in the New York passengers having to be re-routed through London, where there would be another six hours of waiting. That would make a total of twenty eight hours of travel from Delhi to New York.

During these many hours alone, I had to face the fact that I was returning to continue life without our daughter. We had not even had an opportunity to decide what to do about her ashes. I thought about the custom of funerals in New Orleans where the mourners sing the funereal dirges while slowly accompanying the casket to the cemetery. There they say their last farewells. After the burial, as they return to their lives, the musicians pick up the pace of songs. Each song gets more cheerful. The entire practice demonstrates that death is a natural part of every life and that the living must go on. Grief is left at the cemetery. Life continues for the living survivors. The responsibilities of this assignment for me, with all the new experiences I confronted, had totally occupied my mind. The trip had probably been beneficial to me and helpful to my adjustment.

It was now almost three weeks since I had left home. I was returning feeling a bit proud of myself for having made the trip around the world without any serious mishaps, seeing new and exciting things, and meeting a wonderful variety of friendly people. I also had the satisfaction of feeling that perhaps I made a difference in Sri Lanka.

# CHAPTER 7: BRAZIL, 1984

A conference pertaining to voluntary sterilization was to be held in Rio de Janeiro, and I was sent as a representative of the Medical Division of AVS. Representatives of all the countries in Latin America had been invited to participate. It was a trip I looked forward to, in spite of the strong warnings we had been given about the dangers of Rio.

The wealthy people of Rio, including travelers to Brazil, were so far removed from the very poor of the country that crime in the streets was at an all-time high. In fact, by the time we departed from the country, several of the participants had been robbed. At the hotel, the desk clerks would remind us to remove our watch, rings, or any other valuables, and place them in the safe. We were warned that if a robber wanted our rings, he would not hesitate to cut off our fingers to get them. Similarly, they would kill a victim who resisted.

The beaches of Rio (such as Copacabana and Ipanema) have always been known for their beautifully decorated tiled sidewalks. Each section had its own distinctive design. On the beaches were the most trim and athletic bodies I have ever seen. It seemed to me that the Carioca of Rio (defined as someone who came and stayed) spent all their free time on the beach, sun- bathing, exercising, swimming, or playing ball. These bathing beauties, male and female, golden tan, were everywhere. Even on lunch hours, workers from the near-by businesses got into their brief swim suits and went to the beach. Definitely a feast for anyone's eyes!

One night, a few of us went into town to a restaurant that featured churrasco (meats roasted over open fires), a typical staple of the gauchos and cowboys of the southern part of the country. Each waiter came around with pieces of meat on a long skewer, cutting off slices for the customers. As soon as one waiter had passed, another would offer different cut of meat. Some waiters had a series of chicken pieces on their skewers, or many links of sausage. This was no place for vegetarians.

The homes of the poor were frequently not homes at all, but boxes under bridges or tucked into ledges of the mountainside. Some seemed to be caves, dug into sides of the hills. Where there were structures, they looked like piles of shanties, row upon row, on the hillsides. How one could even climb up or down between them was difficult to understand. This part of Rio does not appear in the photo books sold to visitors. Nor are there post cards of this national shame.

On a free day, some of us took a public bus to Petropolis. This was an old city that still had cobblestone streets, old buildings, horse drawn carriages, and a beautiful garden to visit. Getting out of the modern Rio, and seeing a bit of Brazilian history was a pleasant change.

On another day, we had time to take a tour of the harbor area to ride the cable car up to the top of Sugar Loaf and to visit the mountain that has the large figure of Christ called *Corcovado*. From each of these high spots, there was a broad view of the city of Rio de Janeiro.

No trip to Brazil would be complete without seeing the Mulatto Girls in the Oba-Oba Night Club. Unlike people in most other countries, Brazilians have a great pride in the beautiful tan mulatto women, and rightly so, as everyone was gorgeous. For part of the show, the girls wore the elaborate costumes of the famous Samba dancers, with enormous headdresses, feathers, and other lavish decorations that are also standard in the Carnivale (Mardi Gras) parades.

Brazil is the major source for many of the world's semi-precious gems. The H. Stern Jewelers encouraged tours of their gem-finishing and jewelry-making shops. It was hard to leave without making at least one purchase. I have two lengths of multi-stringed, light and darker amethyst beads as my souvenir.

We had an opportunity to enjoy the most typical dish of Brazilian cooking, called *feijoada*. It consisted of black beans with chunks of pork. The hotel where we stayed featured it once a week and I enjoyed it. The various cuts of pork were all in separate pots. For example, one pot had well-cooked chunks of pork roast, another had bacon, and another had ribs. Others had snouts, ears, tails, sausage, crisp rind, or any other conceivable part of the pig. A powdery cassava meal was served to sprinkle over the meat and beans. The feast seemed to call for a cold beer, followed by strong Brazilian coffee.

I made a brief visit to a street market one day. There I had my only experience with theft. I found a woman with her hand in my shoulder bag. Fortunately, I was able to grab the bag and wrest it from the woman before she knew what happened. My purchase at the fair included a pair of light aqua-marine earrings, a small square table cloth, and a vase that looked like stained glass, creatively made from a recycled bottle. They have served as reminders of a very pleasant trip to Brazil.

*Side trip to Iguazu Falls.*

# CHAPTER 8: SIERRA LEONE, NOV, 1984

Anticipating a journey to a new part of the world has always been exciting to me, but perhaps a visit to "black" Africa, south of the Sahara, held a particular mystery for me. It was difficult to imagine the largest continent being the least developed, and to consider the vast problems posed by the lack of progress, especially in the area of public health services.

The purpose of my visit was to participate in a sub-Saharan Conference on Reproductive Health, the first attempt to bring the various countries of Africa together to discuss their reproductive health plans. Our host country, Sierra Leone, was using their motto: "Health for all by the year 2000". I thought it would be interesting to return in sixteen years to see what changes might have occurred.

The airport for Freetown lies across a sea, necessitating quite a journey to get to the capital city. Our plane arrived at Lungi Airport about six in the morning, and it was the beginning of a fascinating week. Currency control was quite rigid. All money and traveler's checks had to be registered upon entry; subsequent balances and receipts were to be cross-checked upon departure. As I began to write these notes a few days into the trip, I realized that I was already in trouble. I didn't have receipts for some purchases. I was given a gift of cloth that would look like another purchase, and I had exchanged some dollars on the black market, so I didn't have a stamp on my currency register. Departure could be more troublesome than arrival.

A vehicle had been hired to transport conference attendees to the Bintumani Hotel. Tightly fitted into a dilapidated van, we proceeded over dirt roads to the ferry landing, a ride of about thirty minutes. Fortunately, a ferry was waiting. I had already heard stories about waiting as long as five hours for a ferry. The ride took about forty-five minutes, and was actually quite pleasant, with cool, early morning breezes. Some people on the ferry were taking produce to Freetown to sell. Women and children had boarded the boat with us carrying huge baskets or enameled pans of cooked fish on their heads. There was another period of forty-five minutes through the central portion of Freetown to reach the beach and resort area where the three tourist hotels and the conference center were located.

It was between nine and ten o'clock in the morning as we drove through mid-town. The squalor was depressing. There were only dirt roads for the most part, but even where there were paved roads in the commercial section, open sewer trenches lined the streets. There were troughs extending from buildings that fed more waste water into the main sewer line. It was not uncommon to see men urinating into them, or to see children squatting over them. Water supply pipes were located adjacent to the sewer line so spilled water flowed into the sewer system. Needless to say, tap water in Sierra Leone was not potable. Bottles of spring water were available for purchase. A quart bottle cost six Leones, (the local currency) which was the equivalent of two and a half dollars. In the heat of Sierra Leone, it would have been impossible for us to survive without bottled water.

On Sunday morning, petty traders lined the streets, and I found it was not hard to understand the system. Most people were selling little peppers or tomatoes of less than one inch diameter, green leaves of many varieties, cooked foods and fish. Items seem to be sold by the dozen or half dozen, according to the little piles. Greens were sold by the bundle. Rice and beans were measured by empty old food tins of about six ounce size. Fish were sold by the piece. There were no scales. I assume the petty traders had carried their products from the country to the city, on their heads, for this Sunday market. Perhaps the purchasers accepted these products because they were fresher than the goods available in the city market centers.

Eventually, the van headed down a beach road and soon arrived at the hotels, situated quite a distance from the city, enabling tourists to enjoy a seaside holiday without too many reminders of the poverty in the rest of the country. If it were not for an unusual circumstance, this is all I would have seen of Freetown and the surrounding area.

On the plane from London to Freetown, my seat companion was a man who had moved to Sierra Leone twenty years before with his bride. They were Lebanese, and saw Africa as a land of opportunity. He was an engineer involved in construction, and a businessman in Freetown, on his way back home after having brought his son to a community college in Chico, California. We talked from time to time on the plane, and he provided me with a better background of the people and the country than I had been able to glean from the country profiles I had read. He gave me his business card and offered to be of help and guidance to me in Freetown.

The day after arrival, we were free until mid-afternoon when a staff meeting was scheduled, and conference registration was to begin. AVS Medical Program Officer, Dr. Khairullah, and I decided to go downtown. While in the center of town, I checked the address of my traveling companion on the plane, Mr. Ahmed Beydoon, and it was only a block away, so we sought him out.

As soon as we entered his shop, he welcomed me like an old friend. He was happy to have a fellow Muslim, Dr. K, visit also. We were introduced to his wife and children, and served Turkish coffee in his office. They urged us to have dinner the following night with them in their home, and insisted on taking us on a tour of the area.

Mrs. Beydoon gave me the names of shops that sold locally made cloths and articles, and then said she would go with me. We set out, all four of us, to buy my usual souvenir: a tablecloth. Mr. Beydoon insisted on paying for it and also one for Dr. K. I was frankly embarrassed by all the hospitality, but Dr. K. said that in their countries (Arab speaking Syria, Lebanon, etc.) this was standard behavior and we would be obligated to return the hospitality should the Beydoon family come to New York. During the rest of our tour, Mr. Beydoon continued to do my purchasing and bargaining for me. He also exchanged Leones for US dollars on the black market for us at six to one instead of two and a half to one.

We drove to the top of a few mountains encircling Freetown; we saw the Kennedy Center and Fourah Bay College on one mountain, and a broadcasting tower on another. We even had a private escorted tour of the Parliament Building atop a third mountain. Of course, palms were crossed when necessary by Mr. Beydoon, who believed - and probably correctly so - that anything was possible if you had money to slip to someone.

Finally, Dr. K. and I said our goodbyes, promising to return for dinner the next day. We set off to wander through the marketplaces. In a way, the two market areas we visited were similar to what we had seen on Sunday morning, except that instead of just one row of stalls along the road, there were many rows. Also, these marketplaces offered raw fish, salted fish, raw meat and live fowl. And foul it was! Everything was fly-covered. The entire area stunk. Food to be sold was displayed on wooden tables. Tiny babies and small children of the saleswomen were lying either on the same table or sleeping or sitting below the tables, on the ground, sometimes on rags or straw, but other times on nothing but the earth. Needless to say, this was a learning experience - not a shopping expedition. The only thing I bought was a handful of small boxes of matches for two match-collecting grand-nephews.

Dinner the following evening was a real treat - an evening with friends. Because they knew that my son-in-law was Egyptian, they also invited the Egyptian Attaché for Cultural and Islamic Affairs. When I set off for West Africa, I certainly never expected to be spending an evening amidst Arabs. Mrs. Beydoon had obviously spent the day cooking. We had shish-kebabs, kebbe, chicken, stuffed vegetables (small squash, maybe), fruits, pita, hummus, tabuli, salad, and yoghurt. All great!

Throughout the evening, the electricity would shut off and Mr. Beydoon would go down to the ground floor to start up his generator. This happened frequently in Freetown, even in the hotel. Electric supply had been very short for the last three or four years and there were no plans for improvement. Mr. Beydoon said that a German team had been summoned to fix all the electrical systems a year or so ago. When they had done so, the local people in charge of the municipal supply were told to limit the drain on the system very carefully because there were more consumers tied into the system than could be handled. A system of alternating supply was recommended so that current could be equally distributed. However, people bribed the workers to turn on the power in their area, even in "off hours", and the workers obliged. It was only a matter of days before the entire system was broken again.

It was really not surprising, but it was depressing, to learn that in spite of teaming population problems, the attendees all seemed to hold such pro-natalist views. "It's our culture to have many children." "We must have large families because some children will die before adulthood." "African men will never accept family planning as their responsibility." "African men desert wives who are sterile." "No one would marry a sterile woman." "If a woman cannot have children, and she has no husband, she will have to fend for herself with no hope of a partner." "I would not consider giving any birth control information to anyone under age twenty-four." "A woman under thirty-five cannot have her tubes tied." "Only after seven children do we counsel women about sterilization."

On the final day of the conference, site visits were arranged for those who wanted to visit either a district government clinic or the Princess Christian Maternity Center. I chose the latter because it was the best facility in the country. It had a section equipped to provide voluntary female sterilization, supported by AVS, and it was the place where maternity patients with serious problems were referred from all over the country.

Goats were grazing in the grass. There were no screens, but I was not surprised at that, since I had not seen a screen in the city yet. It was no wonder malaria was so common. Cats wandered in the yard and climbed garbage containers. They were probably looking for placentas, which were thrown out in developing countries, providing a feast for the local felines. Sheets on beds and cribs were few and far between. Mattresses were stained. Babies were lying on, or wrapped in cloths that were apparently brought in by their mothers. Young women of perhaps fourteen years were nursing their babies, a common age for a first childbirth. One baby was pointed out as motherless. Her mother's uterus had ruptured during labor and by the time she had been transferred from the village to the Freetown hospital, she had lost a great deal of blood. Relatives were asked for blood, but according to the nurse who told me the story, "When we ask for blood, the family runs away". In spite of attempts to save her by removing the ruptured uterus, the young mother had died from severe blood loss.

I asked a nurse how the babies were identified. She said they used "sticky tape" with the mother's name on it, taped to the baby's arm or leg. She tried to demonstrate, but couldn't find an identified baby. "Oh well", she said, "the mothers feed and care for them, so they know which baby is theirs". I guess so. I reminded myself that we should not, in times and places like these, impose our own values on others.

The conference participants were treated to entertainment on three occasions. The first night, during the opening ceremony, the President of Sierra Leone declared the meeting officially opened and welcomed us to his country. We were then entertained by a performance of the National Dance Troupe. This was characterized not by melody but by the beat of drums, shaking of gourd rattles, franticly stepping dancers who seemed to be trying to outdo one another in wild activity, and masked, straw-covered "witch-doctor" dancers.

Two nights later, we were driven to a distant area on another beach where the government owned a facility for such occasions. We were served dinner and again entertained by the troupe. The following night, at our farewell dinner at the hotel, the troupe was again performing. Believe me, once would have been enough

On the last night, after the dance troupe had left and we had our farewell dinner, we were entertained by having a fashion show of African costumes - dressy, business-like, and leisure-wear. Then, the hit of the evening was a performance by "the international singing star, Bunny Mack". *(Who ever heard of Bunny Mack?)* Half the audience left before he arrived. When he finally came, he was dressed in a red jump suit with a broad white sash. A phonograph played his records while he pretended to sing. It was painfully obvious that the sounds were coming from the records.

The AVS staff, which had been over-worked all week, began to get slap-happy at this ridiculous performance and we kept wishing and waiting for the current to go off, as it periodically did. Sure enough, suddenly all was black and silent and Bunny Mack's "voice" stopped at the exact time the lights went out, proving to any possible naive persons there that it was all a farce! Our laughter was a bit loud, I'm afraid. When the power came on again, he picked up his act, but left shortly after. Thank goodness, because at last we were free! We celebrated with a late night swim in the hotel's pool. Unfortunately, about $275.00 in U.S. cash was taken from my wallet. I had not a penny left.

During the week I learned that what I had thought was a "Sunday" market along the streets was in fact an everyday occurrence. Even at night, some people stayed along the road with a small candle to light their goods.

The successful business class families (primarily Lebanese) had "house boys" to help with various chores and "house girls" to clean, do kitchen work, and help with children. For example, the Beydoon family had a boy who would arrive at eight in the morning and stay twelve hours, when he would return to his home. He was paid one hundred and twenty Leones a month, the equivalent of twenty-four dollars. They also had a house girl who cared for the two small children, aged five and seven, getting them breakfast, seeing that they were dressed and prepared for school, doing kitchen chores and cleaning during the day. She was just fourteen years old and had been doing this work since she came to live with the Beydoon family shortly after her ninth birthday. Mrs. Beydoon said that she was very small for her age, but could work very well, even then. The girl's family was given twenty Leones per month, eight dollars, for her services. The girl got nothing but food, shelter and clothing. Who thinks slavery has been abolished?

The last day in Sierra Leone was a long one - especially since we had partied so late the night before. We had gotten an early start for the journey to the hospital, returning to the hotel for an early lunch. I had persuaded the hotel to permit me to check out at five o'clock, so fortunately had a chance to nap for about two hours. My room had already been stripped of sheets, towels, and pillow cases, but the mattress did not look too bad compared to those in the hospital.

Soon I was awakened by a call from Dr. K. saying that Mr. Beydoon was at the hotel to say goodbye to us. We drank Turkish coffee, made by Dr. K. with the ever available equipment he carried with him. I really felt a friendship had been established, and once again, left a country knowing that there were wonderful people to whom I could return.

The old van was ready to take us to the airport at six o'clock. We stuffed ourselves in and started the long, slow trip to the commercial section of the city, past the landmark five-hundred year old cotton tree, and on through those narrow roads lined with petty merchants of food stuffs. We finally arrived at the ferry landing about an hour later.

While we were waiting for the ferry, I was talking to a small boy who was trying to sell me lifesaver-type candy. He was nine and in the fifth level at school, indicating to me that education begins at four years of age. He said he studied hard, attended regular school five days a week, and went to another school for more study on Saturday and Sunday. He was selling the candy to pay for the extra school. Saturdays were very busy because on that day, he had to wash all his clothes for the week. Evenings, he sold candy. He hoped to study hard so he could go to college some day in England or America. *What chance do these kids have?*

The ferry ride was quite pleasant with a full moon shining on the water. I bought five bananas with two Leones (eighty cents). I shared them with Dr. Marcus Filshie, from Nottingham, England. We decided that was a good move since there was no guarantee that we'd see food again until London.

I had been worrying about how I was going to get out of the country, having really messed up any chances of reconciling the Currency Control register with my loss of cash. Dr. K. lent me one hundred dollars. He had this extra from some of his "undeclared" money. But I was still shy of about two hundred and fifty dollars. When Dr. Hamid Rushwan, from the Sudan, heard about my problem, he gave me the required dollars, which he had not declared, so I could take it through the currency check point. Thanks to my colleagues, I got through.

By the time we got through the entire airport process, it was about ten in the evening, so we were in plenty time for the midnight plane. Marcus and I finished the bananas. I even had a chance to buy an African dress for my friend Vivian at the airport shop, which truthfully was just a cupboard with a few items.

An uneventful flight to London, a helicopter transfer from Gatwick to Heathrow airport, a two-hour relaxing wait in the Pan Am Clipper Club, a smooth flight to JFK, a helicopter to East 60th Street, and a cab to my apartment on 68th Street, marked the end of a thirty-one hour day of travel.

It was good to be home again, even if I had to leave for Mexico the next morning.

*Sierra Leone market.*

# CHAPTER 9: MEXICO, NOV, 1984

Juarez certainly did not look like all the other border towns I remembered visiting with my Mexican-American in-laws. Beyond the downtown area near the US-Mexico border bridge, this city could very easily have been imagined on the US side of the border. There were broad paved roads, a Denny's restaurant, hotels and motels and a few very gracious houses of Spanish design surrounded by intricate wrought iron fences. The general appearance gave me the feeling that the economy was perhaps not as depressed as the other border towns.

People in Juarez were more likely to speak English than further inland. They also celebrated US holidays such as Thanksgiving Day and Halloween. Christmas was more apt to be celebrated with gifts from Santa Claus on December 25 than on January 6 with the Procession of the Three Kings. Elsewhere in Mexico, to celebrate the day when the Magi are said to have arrived bearing gifts for the baby Jesus, children received gifts on that "twelfth day of Christmas", brought by the three kings.

The El Presidente hotel was the best Juarez had to offer. It was a sprawling structure, with rooms arranged in long rows. To get from room to room, it was necessary to walk through long verandas that were roofed and separated from the surrounding patios by arched stucco walls. It was an open-air design while yet being protected. The rooms, like the outside of the building, had exposed rough-hewn rafters, so the general appearance was of age and sturdiness. The rooms all had a sliding glass door leading to another patio. In spite of the fact that my glass door could not be locked, I felt no fear or worry. It reminded me of the hotel in Cairo where I had once stayed, where all the doors were left ajar for a bit of air to circulate. The lock was only a long hook and eye. I have felt less safe in some better secured places.

Dr. Sally Faith Dorfman was my traveling companion on this trip. I was to introduce her to our methods of conducting medical evaluations. She was also going to receive training in mini-lap so that she would better understand that surgical procedure. In order for her to be able to evaluate the skills of others, we needed her to have some experience with the performance of the surgical procedure. Sally was a county health officer in New York State, and as such, she did not have an opportunity to gain this surgical experience in our country.

Our additional goal was to evaluate facilities that AVS might use as training centers for the female procedures. This evaluation would include observation of surgical techniques, asepsis, staff attitudes, capacity of the facility, and qualifications of the possible trainers. During our first day at the clinic, we observed two surgical teams doing two procedures each. We also were privileged to see a Cesarean section. Surgical standards were at about the level of those in the United States.

The Family Planning Clinic of Juarez was a part of the health network called FEMAP, standing for *Federacion Mexicana de Asociaciones Privadas*. It was so much more than a clinic. They delivered twenty to twenty-five babies every day. They were fully equipped to perform major surgery, including hysterectomies and Cesarean sections. I found a wonderful sense of warmth and caring for the patients. To make them feel less frightened of the hospital setting, there were cheerful paintings and prints on the walls, curtains on the windows, and colorful linens on the beds. How nice to see a ward where every bed was decorated with flowers and butterflies printed on the sheets.

One tubal ligation was being performed on an American citizen from Silver City, NM. She had four children and could not afford a surgical procedure in the US. Through the Planned Parenthood associations of NM, and El Paso, TX, she made arrangements to have it done in Juarez, where the clinic offered all services without cost. She was delighted with her care and was very happy she had made the trip. The US should have been ashamed of their health care system when citizens in need felt they had to travel to a less developed country for service.

FEMAP was the brainchild of Mrs. Guadalupe De la Vega who, in the early 70s, was a witness to a woman attempting suicide in a public square. The woman's husband had abandoned her, pregnant with her tenth child. She had no income and had no contacts because the couple had recently migrated from a southern village to Juarez. The police arrived only to chastise her for being irresponsible and negligent. Mrs. De la Vega saw this as a desperate woman being judged by a community that was not offering to help. The primarily Catholic country was not supportive of birth control. Women's health care programs were unheard of. This woman had little control of her own body, but she was being punished for that lack of control.

Mrs. De la Vega, affectionately called 'Lupe', was the wife of a prominent and wealthy business man. She began a two room clinic in her magnificent home. She provided family planning and pre-natal care. She was joined by other women and began to obtain local funding. The program grew over the years to be a significant service and a model for the country. Assistance came from the Planned Parenthood Federation, and later funding came from AVS so they could add the surgical components to their services.

The Juarez outreach program was being operated largely by women who were concerned about the lack of maternal, child, and family planning care available to the poor people of Chihuahua State. The success of the program was due to outreach workers. A pyramidal system had developed. Reporting to Lupe were seventeen coordinators. Each coordinator had a network of *"promotoras"* working under her supervision. These promotoras were the community outreach workers who supplied the contraceptive supplies to the "users", arranged for free Pap tests, and referred women to the clinic for free pre-natal care or sterilization.

Sally and I had the privilege of joining Evangelina, a very active coordinator in the marginal, poorest sections around Juarez. Evangelina was a school teacher who taught from eight in the morning until one in the afternoon. For two hours before school started, and for many long hours after her teaching ended, she made her rounds. She visited her promotoras, making sure they had enough pills, condoms, lab test authorizations, etc. Her car was not in perfect condition. "This car refuses to go backward...just like me!" she explained.

In this forward-thinking vehicle we traveled to the dustiest sections I have ever seen. Breathing was difficult because everything was grey and dust-covered. Evangelina periodically instructed us, "Cross yourself!" because her glasses were dirty and the windshield was too coated with brick-making dust to see clearly. She stopped at the most unexpected places. Her promotoras (or *'promotoros'*, if they were men) were brick-makers, cigarette salesmen standing in the median of a road, gas station attendants, prostitutes, housewives, workers in machine shops, young mothers, and even an army lieutenant who serviced the military camp.

In addition to talking to the promotoras, she stopped pregnant women in the street to make sure they were getting prenatal care and to offer clinic services. She distributed contraceptives or offered tubal ligation information. She talked to young couples she spotted along the way to make sure they knew about birth control, and to give them supplies of the method they liked. She talked to older women and gave them lab slips for Pap smears. She signed up a new promotoro for the night shift in a gas station where she already had one on the day shift. On and on she went...a highly respected, much appreciated and dearly loved dynamo who chain smoked, talked loudly, and loved people.

One of the coordinators of the promotoras told us that she had a close relationship with the Roman Catholic Church. In the morning, before she set out on her rounds, she visited the local priest and asked for his blessing. He granted it daily, for the work she felt she "must do", but begged her not to ask him to add a vow to the wedding ceremonies he would perform, having the newly-weds promise to use family planning.

With FEMAP's Dr. Suarez serving as Sex Educator, we attended a class for sixth graders. They were shown a film on reproduction and then were asked to submit their questions confidentiality on a piece of paper. All questions were answered in a straightforward, but light manner. The children obviously felt at ease. Questions were of a broad range, including such as: "Where does the water come from when a woman is in labor?" The bag of water was explained. "If tubes are tied, can they be re-connected?" Surgical reversal was explained. "How does the foam work?" Barriers methods, their manner of use, and effectiveness were explained. "Why doesn't a baby choke in the bag of water?" Fetal circulation was explained. We left wishing US children had an equal opportunity.

Our next destination was Guadalajara, thought by many to be the most beautiful city in Mexico. It has been known as the City of Roses, and even in November, we found many flower merchants in the marketplace, selling big, beautiful displays and rose center-pieces. Carnations were also in abundance, all very artistically arranged.

Guadalajara was a delight of an old city, full of historic buildings. Construction of the cathedral had begun in 1561, and the Palace of Justice was originally the city's first convent, built in 1588. There were many lovely plazas, each decorated with at least one fountain that was both functioning and dramatically lighted.

We spent our first evening getting checked into the Hotel Mendoza, after having spent more than eight hours on the trip. We had had to fly north out of Juarez to Dallas, and to make a connection from there to go back south to Guadalajara. Upon arrival, there was another delay with the customs office officials at the airport. I had entered the country with an electro-surgery unit without having obtained a temporary permit to carry such an item with me. After much delay, reasoning, and requests for mercy - but no bribing (in spite of the official's frequent mention of a "tax"), he finally allowed my passage with a stern warning that the unit had to leave the country with me. He made a note on my passport to that effect.

The following day, we observed surgery and evaluated the teaching potential of the Civil Hospital. The building had 250 beds set aside just for gynecology. Even at that, there was a need to put two women in each bed. Our primary contact, Dr. Alfaro, said that on some heavy days, it was necessary to put three women in one bed. On those occasions, the two women on the outside had their heads at the head of the bed while the woman in the center had her head at the foot end. Nonetheless, the level of care was very high and no-one seemed to be having any pain or distress.

Later in the afternoon, while Dr. Alfaro was tending to some private patients, his daughter Lorena took us to the village of Tlaquepaque, which was a center for artisans of many kinds. There were hand-crafted glassware, trinkets, dolls, figurines, leather, serapes, onyx, jewelry, and clothing. In the streets, indigenous Indians dressed in native garb sold potato chips with hot sauce, fresh bread, roasted corn on the cob, and trinkets of many kinds. The women looked much like the indigenous people of Guatemala except their clothes were not as colorful. They wore layers of clothes, including an apron and a shawl, with babies in a sling on their backs. There was one difference from African mothers I saw who had their "back-babies" facing in the same direction as the mother, with a leg coming around each side of her waist. In Mexico, the babies were suspended in what appeared to be a cocoon in a sling across the mother's back. It looked like a more natural position to me.

We spent our second morning in the hospital. We studied their performance records, discussed complications they had experienced, and brain-stormed about what we might do for Mexico next. We were also invited to watch a few laparoscopies. In this procedure, the doctor operates through a lighted instrument through a tiny opening made near the navel. All was going well until suddenly all electrical current went out in the midst of an operation. Unbelievably, Dr. Alfaro continued to operate by shining the tiny bulb of a battery-powered laryngoscope onto the fibers of the laparoscope, thus sending a dim light into the abdominal cavity. There was enough light for him to identify the tubes and apply a band around a loop of each tube to seal it shut. I had a chance to observe the procedure through an extension on the scope. I was amazed at the surgeon's skill and vision, even without proper light.

Loss of electricity was often encountered in many of the sites where I was conducting medical visits. Because AVS was promoting the use of local anesthesia, the loss of power did not interfere with the client's respiration or pain management. I had often helped in surgery where small incisions were used to access the tubes, a procedure that was called mini-laparotomy, often shortened to "mini-lap". It was fairly simple to just hold a flash light over the incision, allowing the beam of light to shine into the abdominal cavity. This was the first time I had seen an emergency use of light for a laparoscopy, and I was so pleased to encounter the ingenuity of Dr. Alfaro.

In the afternoon, we had some free time to walk around the old Colonial center of Guadalajara. We went into the Cathedral. We visited the beautiful Kiosk donated by France, used for a band stand in the evenings, and we read the inscriptions on a monument built to the memory of the distinguished sons of Guadalajara. Walking towards the Plaza Tapatia, we entered the churches of San Augustine and San Maria de Garcia. We continued on to Degollado Theater, the Libertad market, and the Cananas Cultural Institute. This last building was once an orphanage, but later housed murals by the world-famous Jose Clamente Orozco, including the outstanding one entitled *"Man of Fire"*.

By five o'clock, we were ready for a bath, a rest, then dinner and a good night's sleep before moving on to Mexico City in the morning. The trip to Mexico City was the only leg of the trip on a non-American airline. It was more than an hour late but we eventually arrived in the capital. We decided to take third class accommodations on an airport bus as most locals did, instead of taking a taxi or airport limo as most tourists would have done.

After settling in, Sally and I ventured to Chapultepec Park, where many people were enjoying Saturday with their families. We climbed the "Grasshopper Hill" and I entered the castle, which now housed a museum, much of it containing more paintings by Orozco. When we returned to our hotel, we prepared for dinner at the restaurant *Fonda del Refugio* in the *Zona Rosa*. It was a charming restaurant with perhaps twelve tables on the ground floor, and a few more above. It was a pleasant way to be welcomed to Mexico City.

Sunday was an official day off from work so Sally contacted some acquaintances she wanted to visit. I was free to decide how I would spend the day and thought that the Floating Gardens of Xochimilco seemed most tempting. I approached a taxi driver who offered his services for the day for about twenty dollars. I decided to look for a better bargain and found a metered cab with a driver who knew no English, but who gave me a rate equivalent to three dollars to take me to the gardens. With my scanty Spanish skills, I thought we could communicate well enough. We started out on what turned into a forty-five minute trip, while I was more and more convinced I had misunderstood the fare. When we finally arrived, the meter registered 6,000 pesos, equivalent to about thirty dollars, but he really only wanted three. When he had no change for the 1,000 peso note, I told him to keep the change. He was happy and I still had a bargain. My return trip was more expensive: ten dollars, but by that time I had lost interest in shopping for a better price.

The area, sometimes called the Venice of Mexico, was once a lake that had been diverted to provide water to the capital. A series of canals in what were the deepest parts of the lake were left. The entire area seemed suitable to flower cultivation and tourism. I was eager to follow the example of the many people enjoying rides on gondolas. The boat ride itself would have been more interesting and enjoyable if I had not been alone. All the other boats had families seated around a picnic table, enjoying food and drinks. Children played and dragged their hands in the water. Mariachi bands, each in their own boat, would ride alongside to serenade anyone who would encourage them (for a fee, of course). Indian ladies in traditional garb made tortilla "sandwiches" on their boats. Some sold corn on the cob. Hot ears were taken out of steaming water, coated with mayonnaise, sprinkled with grated cheese, and enlivened with a few dashes of chili sauce. They were delicious. Many vendors sold flowers, serapes, and other souvenir items from their boats.

I bought a few items at the market at the boat landing and headed back to the hotel where I dumped my baggage, and took another cab to the Museum of Anthropology. Purely by luck, I was able to tag along on a tour being privately conducted by one of the Museum's English-speaking guides. She was moonlighting, and charging five dollars per person. For two and a half hours of interesting stories, it was a bargain.

In the evening, I decided to go to the Theater of Fine Arts for a performance of the *Ballet Folklorico*. I purchased a ticket for the last available seat. I remembered having seen a performance in NY in the early 50's. The official ballet had improved significantly since then. As I recalled my original viewing, the dancing was primarily a step-with-the-beat routine then. Since then it had become much more a historical presentation of the culture, history, and the people of Mexico.

Our first appointment the next day was at the US Embassy, where we learned of the terrible bomb-like gas explosion that had occurred at 5:40 that morning in San Juanico, a town just outside Mexico City. I had been awake shortly after that, and saw the orange sky. I thought it was just the light from the rising of the sun. Actually, the flames were so high, that the sky was orange for many miles around. Nearer to the explosion, windows shattered and the earth quaked. It would be quite a while before the full impact of the tragedy would be known, but already there were hundreds counted dead and thousands wounded.

I later learned that the San Juanico disaster had been caused by a massive series of explosions at a tank farm. It had consumed 11,000 cubic meters of gas, representing one third of Mexico City's entire liquid gas supply. The explosions devastated the town. It was estimated that 600 people were killed but the true number could not be verified because the heat was so intense that the corpses were reduced to ashes. Seven thousand persons were burned. This was one of the deadliest industrial disasters in world history.

Tuesday, November 20, was a National Holiday celebrating the beginning of the Mexican Revolution. Sally returned home to spend Thanksgiving with her family, leaving me to finish the assignment and write the reports. Because the clinics were celebrating, I had no appointments. Except for about two and a half hours of strolling in Chapultepec Park, I remained in the hotel doing the inevitable paperwork.

Wednesday was "vasectomy day" for me. I watched surgery at two sites, done by different doctors at opposite sides of the city. One doctor used the special equipment I had brought for him to test. He planned to use it for the rest of the week. When my work day was finished, I had dinner in a very beautiful restaurant, the Del Lago, overlooking a lake.

I think this was my first Thanksgiving Day without turkey and all the traditional festivities. The closest I got to it was purchasing paper mache vegetables the night before; symbols of the food preparations I would have been doing if I were home. Instead, a trip to the pyramids was possible, thanks to my having no medical visits scheduled and the American Embassy being closed for the holiday. I must admit, it was a very special experience - one I have wanted for thirty years. Perhaps it was fitting to spend a day, usually devoted to giving thanks to God, in an area where, according to Aztec mythology, the Gods of the Sun and Moon were created - the area called Teotihuacan.

The *Linea Gris* (Grey Line Bus Company of Mexico) conducts many tours, and this was one of their "regulars". Unfortunately, tour buses always manage to arrange at least two stops at shops that are supposed to be special (no-tax) discount houses but where the prices were about double what they would be in a market. I guess it could be considered the price one pays for the passage to a very special site for a very low fare. The trip was only seventeen dollars for the all-day tour.

The pyramids were not pointed as were those built in Egypt. In Mexico, the pyramids served as platforms or terraces on which the ancient Indians built their altars and temples to honor their Gods. Unlike Egypt, where the pyramids are tombs for deceased leaders, in Mexico, they were places of worship, and therefore more steeped in ancient history and mythology.

In the time available during the afternoon it was possible to explore the citadel where a voice would carry clearly in those days before amplification to the thousands of people who would gather for a meeting. Within the citadel was the pyramid of the god whose image is a feathered serpent. The message of this leading god of the Teotihuacanos and the Aztecs is that no matter how low we are, formed of the earth and dwelling in it, we too can rise like the feathered birds and ascend to the heavens. As I think back upon this, the message was not too different from the Calvinists' beliefs I was surrounded by in my youth.

The Pyramid of the Sun was a climb of about three hundred steps, but they were "high-risers", probably equivalent to the height of four hundred average stairs. A few, near the top, were very steep and it was more like climbing a ladder, but it was all worth the effort. As usual, when I reached a peak, whether it was the top of the dome of St. Peter's Cathedral in the Vatican, or atop the bell tower of an ancient church, or even to the top of the World Trade Center, I had found upon reaching the summit, an exhilarating sense of euphoria. Stairs seemed even better than elevators. (Maybe there's a hidden mountain-climber within me.)

After dinner in a local restaurant, where chicken mole substituted for turkey and dressing, the bus took us tourists back to the pyramids for the English version of their "Sound and Light Show". This was the first such performance I had ever seen and it was certainly impressive. Sitting on benches, wrapped in rented blankets, we tourists viewed the major pyramids, several minor pyramids, and the Road of the Dead. As various lights featured the gods represented by the pyramid built to his honor, a recorded voice spoke for the god. In such a way, they enacted the story of how men came together and decided it was necessary to have one God of the Day and one God of the Night. In order for that to happen, men would sacrifice themselves by throwing themselves into the fire. The first to sacrifice himself became the God of the Sun. The second became God of the Moon - not as powerful because his strength was secondary and dependant upon the Sun. And so the place was later named *"Teotihuacan"* by the Aztecs, the place where men became gods. No one knows who the *"Teotihuacanos"* really were because they had already disappeared by the time the Aztecs had arrived. All we know is from Aztec recordings of an earlier tribe.

Almost as exciting as the Pyramids was the next day's trip to the *Zocalo*, (the old city center) that is the main plaza of the city. It contained the Cathedral, the Palace, the National Pawn Shop, ancient archeological findings of the original Aztec city with its pyramids, about five museums and probably as many churches dating back hundreds of years. I could not believe there could be any one city so full of ancient history and culture. In the "digging site", only discovered about nine years earlier during the construction of a subway, there was even an original Chocmool, the reclining god who holds a bowl on his belly to receive human hearts of sacrificed men. The feeling one gets from such a site varies, I'm sure. I tried to imagine how I would have felt if I had witnessed Abraham completing the sacrifice of his son Isaac, as I stood before the altar on which Abraham had placed the body. It was awe-inspiring, to say the least.

In response to the San Juanico disaster, people had been bringing donations to the central plaza. Everywhere I could see, piles of clothing, bedding, toys, and furniture were growing. The citizens were doing all they could to assist the victims of the blast that had left so many families with nothing. Volunteers were helping to sort the donations and to help with the distribution. It was heart-warming to see that the donors of these items were clearly not wealthy individuals. They probably did not have many luxuries themselves but they were giving of their meager possessions to those who had even less.

All in all, this had been a fantastic journey. I felt that it was very beneficial for the work of AVS and for the future of family planning in Mexico. Because I am "Mexican-by-marriage" it was also good for my soul. I hoped all my children would some day be able to study their ancient heritage beyond the border towns they had already visited. Their Mexican background has been something they have been rightfully proud of, and an extended visit would, I'm sure, be a truly rewarding experience.

# CHAPTER 10: BANGLADESH, FEB. 8-20, 1985

Living in Bangladesh must be extremely difficult. Even getting there was a problem. After departure on the evening of the eighth, AVS Medical Director, Dr. Douglas Huber and I were to fly straight through to Bombay, India, arriving the morning of the tenth. Unexpectedly, there was a change of aircraft in Frankfort, but due to snow storms in England, there was a delay in linking up with next aircraft. Meanwhile, snow continued to fall in Germany, delaying take-off even longer. The result was that, after engine troubles necessitated further delays in Karachi, Pakistan, we arrived in Bombay three hours after our Bangladesh plane had left. There was no flight for three days. It seemed the best thing to do would be to hop back on the plane returning to Karachi in the hope of picking up another flight to Dhaka at one o'clock that day. We did...but there were no seats available when we got there, so were stranded until February twelfth.

Much of the time in Karachi was spent trying to arrange our flight to Bangladesh. But we did take a few walks and hired a taxi for a tour of the major points of interest, including a magnificent mosque. In the parks and on the beach, people were constantly being approached by men carrying a basket in one hand and leading an animal on a leash. I was surprised to find out that the basket contained a cobra and the animal on the leash was a mongoose. For a fee, the man would let them fight. I declined.

*Young snake charmer.*

Both Pakistan and Bangladesh were once part of India, but because people in those two separated areas were almost all Moslem, and the rest of India was Hindu, eventually they were separated and became East and West Pakistan. That didn't work out either, so East Pakistan became Bangladesh. I guess I expected that my brief exposure to Pakistan would have prepared me for Bangladesh, but I found the two countries to be quite different. In Pakistan, the general living standard seemed higher. Animal carts and small vehicles were commonly used. I saw no people pulling carts in Pakistan. In Bangladesh, after having been there for four days, I had not seen one animal used to pull carts. Instead, men pulled two-wheeled bamboo flat-bed carts. Transportation was most often provided by bicycle-powered rickshaws. Taxis for longer or faster trips were tiny three-wheeled vehicles called "baby-taxis". At hotels, a "limousine" could be hired for even short trips. They were not a "limo" as we Americans use the word. They were actually cars with a four or five person capacity.

*Clothes washing in Pakistan.*

To my surprise, I had learned in NY that we were booked into a five-star hotel in Dhaka, the capital city. I found the hotel to be on a par with other major hotel chains in major cities. But in the midst of the poverty in Bangladesh, there was something obscene about being there. From my window, gazing to my right, I overlooked two hotel pools and patios. To my left, with just a narrow buffer zone of trees and shrubs, I overlooked the homes of urban poor who did not even have drinking water from a common pipe. As I stood looking down, I realized that they could look up just as easily, and I wondered what they thought of the beautiful hotel.

During monsoons, the water table rises quite a few feet. The good result is that the overflowing Ganges River and its tributaries carry a great load of top soil with it, depositing the rich dirt in this delta area. The "top" soil is estimated to be about one hundred and forty feet deep. But the negative result is that the fields are totally submerged much of the time. Because of the fluctuating water level, houses are built upon *"baries"* or what the Dutch call *"terps"*. Men and boys work at earth-building. They chop soil in the fields with a broad-bladed adz, and carry the soil to form a mound. When the mound is big enough, huts can be built on it. In the rural areas, each bari is likely to have four or five homes of one extended family. In the urban areas, baries have been clustered together more closely, forming little neighborhoods. In wet seasons, people are quite stranded - especially the women who probably never get off their bari unless their husbands take them in a boat or raft to a neighboring bari. The men bring provisions to the bari by boat, and must use a boat if they are to get to a city job.

The combination of the effect of the isolating water-surrounded bari and the Moslem religion that does not permit women to travel alone, has necessitated special arrangements for women who need or want the services of family planning clinics. Much international attention has been paid to the fact that in Bangladesh, field workers have been paid a salary (or travel allowance) to escort women to the clinics for sterilization procedures. In fact, if the needy women were not accompanied by another woman, she could not leave her bari. If her husband were to accompany her, he would lose a day's pay. The arrangement is totally appropriate in Bangladesh, while it would be inappropriate in other cultures. But the critical international press, especially those supposedly protecting women from coercive sterilizations, have wreaked havoc with this situation.

Related to this is the fact that the clients who attended the AVS-sponsored clinic for a sterilization procedure, whether male or female, were given a new, clean garment to wear during the operation. For women in poor countries, a new garment (six yards of cloth for a sari) is a treat, but not one, I believe, a woman would "sell her reproductive life" for, as is implied by the critics of the program. In fact, where the clients are operated on in their own clothes, with no undressing or unnecessary exposure of the body that would be forbidden by Moslem codes, the new, clean garment is an aseptic aid, avoiding the client's own street-soiled clothes entering the operating room. Yet the critics say programs offering voluntary sterilization are coercing the clients by "bribing" them with a new garment.

Most homes on the baries have their own mat-shielded latrine. These shaky-looking shelters are generally on stilts, overhanging the side of the bari. As the water rises to reach the latrine level, it soon becomes full of bacteria. The people continue their daily practice of bathing in the river, which includes the ritual of washing their mouth as well. Cholera outbreaks begin usually on or about mid-September, just after water reaches latrine level and the incubation period for the bacteria has passed. Cholera gets back to the average level after the waters subside. The only hope is to treat the severe cholera patients. Unless modern water supply, sewers, and sanitary practices all are in place, Bangladesh will never control cholera - and this is not likely to happen.

*Mothers waiting for a minilap.*

Our work schedule was very busy. The AVS Asia office staff had planned days to begin at eight in the morning, and to end twelve or more hours later. We did not even have lunch breaks, but fortunately we were served tea with milk and sugar two or three times a day.

One exception to our schedule of long days was one when our first appointment was at two o'clock. I thought I'd finally have a chance to shop or visit "old Dhaka". But unfortunately, a *"hartal"* (a strike) was held. Hartals are political demonstrations. Dhaka University had been the seat of unrest, with the leaders pleading for student rights and a better educational system. During a recent demonstration, the police had shot a student, and now the students wanted revenge. By calling for a hartal, people were forced to stay home for safety, and the city literally closed down, thus providing a perceived support of the students who controlled the action. So, on my only free morning, I was confined to the hotel. By noon, traffic slowly picked up, and we got to our afternoon appointment in safety. In the weeks that followed, I learned that the situation got worse. Later, I learned that authorities had closed down all university campuses indefinitely.

Most days consisted of a series of appointments with every imaginable agency and organization, as well as some sessions with the Asia office staff. On or about the tenth day, we journeyed to Comilla, a district south of Dhaka, to review medical practices in that more rural area, and to investigate the quality of service. Our goal was to study the entire Bangladesh sterilization program, and then provide guidance and technical assistance to the government of Bangladesh so their services could be upgraded, and their staffs trained. Quite a task, I thought. I was being introduced to the programs, problems, and people during these two weeks, which was why Dr. Huber was with me. He had spent four years in Bangladesh, and was a good guide and teacher for me.

*Rural operating room.*

There is one sight that will remain in my memory forever. I saw it frequently on this trip into the southern area. There were no stones in this part of the country because of all the layers of top soil. Therefore, to make roads, they needed to make stones or gravel to mix with the cement. The first step was to make sun-dried bricks from the soil. Once the bricks had hardened, women were used to break the bricks into stones and gravel. They sat at the road-side in the hot sun, sometimes with babies at their side, breaking up the bricks with a hammer or mallet, and sorting the pieces into appropriate piles according to size. No men made gravel; this was "woman's work".

One thing I had to learn was to eat rice and curries with my hand. I remembered my amusement the previous year when I saw a table full of doctors and board members eating without utensils in Sri Lanka. By this time, I knew I could not go on being an outsider if I were to relate to people in the Indian sub-continent. So, among friends, at the home of our Asia office director, I had my first lesson. I still prefer utensils, but I've been told that once a person really gets accustomed to fingers mixing each portion together, the food never tastes as good with spoon or fork. We'll see!

I have always been pleased if I get to know someone special while I am traveling in another land. I have learned that there are fascinating, wonderful, courageous people everywhere...and many are women. In Italy, it was Maria Louisa Zardini. It Juarez, it was Guadelupe de la Vega and her "promotoras". In France, it was Anna Marie Dourlen-Rollier. They have all worked hard and long to fight Roman Catholic opposition to family planning, to bring reproductive health care to rural women, and to change restrictive laws that were making some birth control methods illegal.

In Bangladesh, much credit goes to Mrs. Khan. Many years ago, she began a small group called "Concerned Women". Two by two, these ladies would go into the baries and talk to women about their reproductive health and problems. These poor women had never been exposed to the idea that other women cared about their problems or their little children. Concerned Women had grown greatly. By the time of our visit, there were thousands of women working as bari visitors, bringing condoms, pills, and comfort to the under-privileged women of Bangladesh. Douglas Huber and I had dinner one evening with Dr. and Mrs. Khan. Hearing about her pioneering work was one of the highlights of the trip.

Toward the end of my second week, Dr. Huber left for NY, and I began to focus my attention on my next assignment in Nepal, studying my background papers to prepare for my responsibilities there. Two more weeks to go, and I'm already feeling a bit cut off from home.

PostScript:

I am proud to have a photo of myself taken with Maria Louisa Zardini, Guadelupe de la Vega, Anna Marie Dourlen Rollier and Pouru Bhiwandiwala. The person who took the photo thought that I had done an equivalent job in the US, making voluntary sterilization available.

# CHAPTER 11: NEPAL, FEBRUARY – MARCH 1985

Nepal is a fascinating country, and much of the fascination is due to the Himalayan mountain range that occupies the northern-most third of this rectangular country. South of Himalayas there is another strip of foot-hills, which Americans would call "mountains". Further south, in a strip beginning about a third of the way from the western border, there is a flat area called the *terai*, which reaches to the eastern border. That *terai* contains the most arable land, produces most of the vegetables, contains the small industrial city of Biratnagar, and is home to most of the people.

Kathmandu is the capital, and this city is nestled in a "valley" within the foothills of the Himalayas. This so-called valley is 4,500 feet above sea level. To get out of the valley, it was necessary for us to drive on many horse-shoe curves up and over the mountains until we could reach the flat *terai* where I was to be working for the next weeks. All the mountainsides were dug into steps for rice paddies; driving through them created in me a sense that they were really staircases to heaven.

The Himalayas have kept Nepal somewhat separate from the outside world. This isolation encouraged an exotic and individualistic culture in a spectacular setting. The isolation must have had a profound effect on the character and outlook of the people. Every occasion seems to be an excuse for people to gather. The Nepali people probably have more festivals than any other people. In October, there is one fifteen-day festival, soon followed by another important festival in November. Schools are closed for the joint events, and students are told to use the days between to study for the exams that would follow as soon as school reopened in mid-November. Then schools close again for the winter, to reopen in February. In reality, it's not just the schools, but the entire kingdom that literally shuts down for the October to November season.

During my visit, I heard about the Shivrati Festival, which had just finished the week before I arrived. For Hindu people, Lord Shiva was the greatest God - the God of creation. His symbol actually resembles an erect penis. On the anniversary of his birth (Shivrati) all the women go to the Swayambhunath Shrine dedicated to Lord Shiva. If they are unmarried, they pray for a husband. If they are married, they pray for the health and safety of their husbands. And, of course, if they are childless, they pray to the God

194

of Creation for a son (or sons). During the festival, the women eat only once a day, and must refrain from meat and spices.

The Holi festival occurred during my visit. Also called Fagu, this was the festival of color, celebrated with great gaiety. Holi is believed to herald the advent of the spring season; the colorful activities are symbolic of the colors that autumn brings. It is actually a week-long celebration that begins with the installation of an umbrella-shaped pole (called Chir) decorated at the top with pieces of cloths in different colors. The celebrations come to an end with the burning of the pole on the night of the March full moon. On that final day, when the entire kingdom had closed down, children were busy filling balloons with colored water (called Lolas). Bathed in various colors (predominantly vermillion, yellow, and black) the revelers sang Holi songs and toured the streets and lanes of Kathmandu, spreading colored powder and water on other people.

I decided to take advantage of the day off. It was my opportunity to see Mount Everest. I made arrangements for a taxi to transport me from the hotel to the airport. From there, I took a one-hour flight along the Himalayan range, flying as close as fourteen miles from the snow-covered peaks. It was a spectacular sight. When I returned to my hotel, I went to the upper floor balcony where I could watch the antics of the people in the streets. I could enjoy the festivities while remaining uncolored by powder or dyed water. I enjoyed this day, one of my only two such free days in the entire month.

During the first week of my Nepal assignment, I was accompanied by Quasem Bhuyan, a program officer based in the AVS Dhaka office. Our first task was to tour about ten districts. The western-most was the city of Pokhara in the western foothills; the eastern-most was Sunsari, in the eastern terai. Except for Pokhara, which was to be our final stop before returning to Kathmandu, the entire trip was in the southern flat terai. There was one major west-to-east paved road, but all the village outposts were at least fifteen or twenty miles off the paved road. This meant that we needed to travel in a four-wheel powered Jeep, covering a total of about 1,400 miles, over a period of six days. We were fortunate to have with us Dr. Swaraj Rajbhandari, a lady doctor who would be our guide, but who would become my friend before the end of the trip.

The first night out of Kathmandu, we traveled to Birgunj, at the Indian border. Swaraj sent the hotel boy out to order a special treat that she described as little birds, a specialty of the area. I had mentally pictured them as Cornish hens, but when we went into the dining room of the hotel, the waiter brought a plate piled high with what appeared to be fried marble-sized balls. I soon learned that these balls were tiny unborn birds, fried in their entirety, served as an appetizer. We were to eat heads, necks and all. The idea was to eat each one in a bite or two, including bones, brains, and innards. I had trouble with the heads rolling around in my mouth. It took a lot of courage to chow down this feast.

*Toilet facilities in a restaurant.*

One of the side roads in the Bara district was particularly difficult. The worst part was a one-hour drive through the jungle, on dusty roads where rhinos were reported regularly. By "dusty", I really mean the road was made of thick dust that came up near to the height of the hubcaps. We kept the windows closed most of the time but even then, the dust crept in through the floor boards. The road was narrow, so when we met a bullock cart or truck, there was little room to get by. The distance we covered in that hour was about fourteen miles, an indication of how difficult the trip was. From that dust road (which would be impassable in the rainy season when it became thick slime), we continued over paths in fields, through a few small settlements, over some dry river beds, across a small wet river, finally getting to our destination.

We arrived at a rural school building that was being used as a temporary facility for female sterilization surgery. It was the crudest surgical facility I saw in the entire trip, yet the services appeared to meet standards. The women sat on the school benches waiting for their tubal ligations. They were screened by physical exam and had simple laboratory tests before going to the operating room. There were two tables in the operating room area so one patient could be gotten ready as the surgeon was finishing the previous one. After surgery, the women rested on floor mats for about two hours. They were then driven back to their villages in a Jeep.

The medical staff invited us to stay for tea, and tea was the one thing no one ever seemed to refuse. But they also served a platter of boiled eggs, and that really impressed me. These people, stationed here in this school building, were completely dependant upon locally grown food. That meant chickens, eggs, cauliflower, rice and lentils. They were sharing their limited provisions. These mobile teams deserve a lot of credit. They live and work without the luxury of running water; they sleep on school benches or on the floor; they dig their own latrine, and work long hours providing surgical contraception to people who would have no regular access to pills, IUDs, or even condoms. When all the patients in the area who have decided on sterilization have been served, the team moves on to set up in the next location.

*Nursing granny.*

*Rural recovery room.*

There were a full six days of such travel and of observing similar patient care and conditions in each location. Our last stop before returning to Kathmandu was in Pokhara, located a little west of the mid-point of this rectangular country. Travel to and from Pokhara was by a small, single engine plane flying out of a small airport. The pilot flew us between the mountains as we rose and descended. Even at full altitude, we just skimmed by the tops of the mountains. As spectacular as the flight along the Himalayas had been, this flight was more exciting to me. At one point, we passed so close to the side of a mountain, that if the window had been open, I think I could have grabbed leaves from the bushes growing on it.

Because of the mountain range, flying requires extremely experienced pilots. Even the International Airport in Kathmandu is a tricky one in which to land. I would not even think of flying in or out of the country on any other than a Nepal airline, because these pilots have the practice and experience I want for a better chance at surviving.

From Pokhara, if we went out onto the observation roof of the hotel early in the morning, we could see the Annapurna range of mountains peeking over the foothills. We also went for a peaceful boat ride in one of Pokhara's three lakes - a treat that makes Pokhara a honeymoon haven. There were quite a few trekkers in Pokhara setting off or returning from some of the most popular trails to the Annapurna. Tourists were also around, enjoying this beautiful, though primitive, mountain community.

Back in Kathmandu, I lost my traveling companions; Quasem had to return to Dhaka. Swaraj had to return to her normal routine, also. I had more independent work to do, offering technical assistance on quite a number of issues.

On Saturday, I was invited to a family picnic - the end of a six-day celebration. It was a typical arranged marriage - not a "love marriage" as some of the young people were beginning to wish for. The couple had seen each other only once, about a week before the wedding. Since neither of them had any grounds for objection, they were married. I was sure the family of the bride offered a sizable dowry in order to unite with the groom's family who owned a Thanka-painting school for Nepalese and Tibetan religious painters. The father of the groom was already planning to open another school for science students, because his new daughter-in-law, aged twenty-three, was about to get her Master of Science degree. The school would be for her to teach in and operate.

The picnic was held in a park heavily populated by spotted deer and playful monkeys. We arrived around noon and lunch was served soon after. Mats and blankets were put down in a large rectangular shape. Then a half sheet of newspaper was put on the ground in front of each person to serve as a place-mat. On it was heaped two handfuls of beaten fried rice, and that was surrounded by black-eyed peas, dal, and what I later learned was various mutton meats - probably mostly organ meat. A goat had been killed early that morning and a mutton stew was simmering most of the day, in preparation for dinner. When evening approached, we ate again. We had more of the dry beaten rice, more peas, plus the goat stew. Of course, we ate with our hands. At this meal, in addition to the newspaper placemats, we had "dishes" made from pieces of banana leaves, on which the meat stew was placed.

*Nepal bride and sister.*

I was particularly puzzled by the fact that no one seemed to need a bathroom all day. Even restricting liquids when I realized there was no "comfort station", my bladder was bursting at the seams by mid-afternoon. The year before, on my trip through India, I saw many people squatting in the fields. On this trip, on my travels to the rural districts there were times when I did the same. But a picnic ground didn't seem appropriate to me - and I guess the others felt the same.

*Picnic lunch.*

Once home, trying once again to adjust to the western world after a month in Bangladesh and Nepal, I think I've been very lucky. I traveled safely and without intestinal upset in spite of many new foods and less than sanitary cooking facilities.

# CHAPTER 12: THAILAND, AUG. 20 – 28, 1985

Unlike most of my trips, this assignment in Bangkok was more like a comfortable vacation. I stayed in a first class hotel and worked in an air-conditioned office with the gracious and efficient staff of Thai AVS.

My assignment was to provide technical assistance to TAVS as they embarked on a new initiative to institute counseling into their governmental and private family planning programs. It was necessary to define and clarify counseling concepts, to plan regional workshops for Thailand's policy-makers, to plan counseling training courses for hospital staff, to develop resource material in the form of exercises, tests, illustrations, and diagrams, and write a paper for their use in introducing counseling.

The work went so well that we were able to take the weekend off. The TAVS Director, Mr. Sributatham, took me with his wife Renoo and their daughters, Bam and Pook, to Pattaya Beach over Saturday night. This was a resort area about two hours drive from Bangkok. It was a quiet fishing village until the Vietnam War, when the US government began to send servicemen there for rest and relaxation. It seems that the city was able to supply lots of "recreation" in the form of beautiful Thai girls. As the news of an approaching ship came, thousands of girls headed for the beach to play with the *"falangs"*, their word for foreigners or US men. The town soon developed into a series of bars, hotels, prostitution centers and massage parlors. Also available were Thai boxing rings where elbows and feet were used along with fists. Gambling on cock fights was also a local sport.

On Saturday evening we went to a transvestite show, which was actually a song, dance, variety and comedy show rather than anything sexual. The auditorium was full of families, including many young children. Thai children were apparently exposed to the ways of the world at an early age and with a sense of humor. Escort services, twenty-four hour clinics for sexually transmitted diseases, massage parlors, homosexual and heterosexual meeting places all seemed to be taken in stride.

I thought quite a bit about the attitudes of the Thai people. Some people in the US have been a bit worried about the Thai practice of holding events such as a vasectomy festival. There have been critics of Thailand's holding such an event on the occasion of the King's birthday, when in a happy community spirit, hundreds of men line up for a vasectomy. But I found that this is well within the culture of Thailand. The same atmosphere pervades when they are trying to fill a blood bank. While I was in Bangkok, a festival in honor of the Queen was arranged for people to donate blood as a way of showing respect and honor. Even on market days, when the streets are filled curb-to-curb with stalls and vendors of all kinds, there is music playing and a happy spirit all around.

In training counselors, we try to establish the importance of being non-judgmental, not allowing the attitudes of the counselors to infringe upon the client. It seems the US should abide by the same code. We should not allow our attitudes, which may be far more artificial and more unnatural than those of other cultures, to infringe upon the happy, open, healthy attitudes of the Thais.

There is a flower that Arry Sriburatham said demonstrated the characteristics of the Thai people. It is of five long narrow petals; yellow at the center portions, gradually turning to red at the tips. The petals begin to twist and turn each in its own way as they shade from the yellow to the red. By the time the petal ends in the red tip, each one seems to be going in a different direction. Yet, no matter how crowded the flower is in a vase with others, no petal will ever touch another. Each has the freedom of movement and direction without infringing upon another. I had a bouquet for five days and found it accurately true.

Thailand is really a land of orchids of every size, color, and variety imaginable. Huge sprays and bouquets were everywhere. Street children sold them to occupants of cars stalled in the traffic, much as the single rose is peddled in NY City. Renoo bought one for me on the way to Pattaya and I enjoyed it for many days.

Unexpectedly, the day after I arrived in Bangkok, I saw more orchids than ever imaginable when I attended a Buddhist funeral service for the mother of the world-famous Dr. Mechai Viravaidya. The funeral was in a temple that was specially arranged for funeral services. Like a small city of temples, each one was a pavilion filled with rows of chairs. The coffin was at the front of the room on an elevated platform and it was completely bedecked with long sprays of purple and white orchids, sizes varying according to the height of each tier. On all the walls were rows of floral arrangements too, most of which were predominantly orchids. Some arrangements were delicately crafted, artistic, artificial flowers. I wondered about the need for artificial flowers in this fertile land until I learned that for funerals of well-to-do persons, the services continued for extended periods of up to a hundred days.

The service itself was a new experience for me. As we approached the pavilion, I noticed that it was perhaps the largest of all the nearby pavilions, and even so, extra rows of chairs had been added in the back, under additional canopies. The family, dressed in black, was standing together greeting the visitors. Although I had long known the name and work of Mechai in family planning, this was our first meeting. I was impressed with his manner. Even though his mother had suddenly died in her sleep the previous day, he was calmly performing the duties of the eldest son. He asked me if I had ever attended a Buddhist funeral service before, and when I replied that I had not, he said he thought it would be an interesting experience for me and thanked me for coming. We entered the pavilion and sat down. Everyone was dressed in either black or white, which I had suspected was the custom. Fortunately I had brought a white dress and had worn it.

We were soon served cold drinks. A bit later, the monks arrived. Four of them conducted the actual service, but there were others sitting in attendance. The four began to chant the first of five invocations. They were about the five major prohibitions of the Buddha: Thou shall not lie, steal, kill, commit adultery, or become intoxicated. During the chant, which took perhaps five to ten minutes, the monks, dressed in their saffron-yellow robes, sat cross legged along the right wall, holding in front of them a vertical stick with a large oval disk in front of their face. I learned that the disk was to help prevent their distraction from their prayers.

After a pause of ten minutes, they began the second invocation. No one seemed to know what any of these Sanskrit chants meant. Between the third and fourth session, we were served coffee or tea and three little sweets that looked like petite fours, but were light and delicately flavored. After the fifth and final invocation, baskets of gifts were presented to each monk. In each basket there was also a gift of money. This service continues every evening until the cremation - a rather expensive obligation. Buddhists may also repeat such a service on the anniversary of the death.

In Nepal, on an earlier trip to that country, I learned that Hindus have a similar practice of multiple funeral services. During the first year after someone's death, the eldest son must conduct a total of eighteen such services, each including housing, feeding, and giving gifts to attendees. It is one reason a future daughter-in-law gives serious thought about marrying the eldest son of a family, and why having a son is so important.

For me, coming to Thailand was a trip to the most important center of surgical birth control. It was at Ramathibodi Hospital in 1970 that a laparoscopy service was first begun, and where they soon initiated local anesthesia to perform it. By the time AVS had begun its international work in 1973, Ramathibodi, under the direction of Doctors Vitoon and Kamhaeng, had begun mini-laparotomies. It was in Thailand, also, that Dr Arunee first taught midwives to do mini-laps and where operating room nurses were first taught to do postpartum mini-laps. Here, too, was where paramedics and nurses were first permitted to learn and perform vasectomy. Over the years, I have been with all these superstars in other countries, but it was a high point in my career to see them all on their own turf.

Two nights before I left, TAVS arranged a dinner for me and presented me with a Thai commemorative plate "In Remembrance of Your Visit to Thailand, August 20-27, 1985". I felt much honored to be here and thought it would have been more appropriate had I bestowed honors on these important people.

The night before I left, I found myself in an unusual position. My work was finished and even my written report was done. The hotel was putting on a Thai dance performance in their Seafood Restaurant. So, while I dined in style on raw oysters, followed by lobster flamed in Pernod and brandy, I watched the traditional costumed dance performance and listened to original Thai music. The vocal part was very off-key, but I think it was meant to be. The xylophones were of two types - one of teak wood, sounding very full but mellow, and the other of bamboo, with a hollow tone. Other bells, cymbals, and flute-like instruments were part of the orchestra.

The dancers, for the most part, wore tall, pointed jeweled headdresses. Most of the dances were stories from Ramayana (Hindu) or Ramakien (Buddhist) mythology. They dealt with Lord Rama, one of the reincarnations of Buddha. I remembered that earlier that year I had been in Janakpur, Nepal, which was the location of the marriage of Rama and Sita. Some of the stories were about this couple, including the one in which the monkey God, Hanuman, saves Sita from being kidnapped. Hanuman, along with Ganesh, the elephant God, is still highly revered in Nepal. When I was there, I saw many temples and statues in their honor.

I have pledged that the next time my work takes me to Bangkok, I will bring lots of money and everyone's measurements. Thai silk is fabulous. It is iridescent and seems to be alive. It's a wonderful place to have silk clothes made to order.

My trip had come to an end. I was to travel directly to Nepal, where the monsoon rains would be at a heavier level; where the inner-spring mattress I had enjoyed in Thailand would be replaced by two inch foam; where air-conditioning would be replaced by a fan; where contagious meningitis would be more a risk than sexually transmitted diseases, but where a hotel room would cost seventeen dollars, as compared to Bangkok's forty-five.

# CHAPTER 13: RETURN TO NEPAL, AUG. – SEPT, 1985

Because this was my second trip within six months to this "roof of the world", I had not expected to experience many new things. However, I was pleasantly surprised.

My assignment was formidable. I was to help the Family Planning Association of Nepal (FPAN) to organize a three day workshop for policy-makers, on levels as high as the Queen. Also, I was to help them plan a six-day course for training of trainers, to train sterilization counselors and to provide technical assistance for Nepal's new counseling endeavors.

To my surprise, when I arrived at the FPAN office on Thursday morning, ready to begin, I learned that they had scheduled the six-day course, starting Sunday morning, and that I was the principle presenter and in charge of arranging the entire program. Further, the country was celebrating two of their many festivals on Friday and Saturday, so all the work had to be done by the close of day.

I spent most of the day arranging the week's schedule and then planning the tests, exercises, diagrams, illustrations, etc., that needed to be duplicated for the participants. On Friday and Saturday, I sat in my dimly-lit room and planned my presentations. Sunday, I was on stage and feeling a bit uneasy. But all went well. The sixteen participants got more and more excited every day. It was obvious that they were not only enjoying it completely, but they were thrilled with their increase of knowledge and were proud to be part of a new movement for Nepal.

I must confess that by Wednesday afternoon, I realized I was enjoying the position I was in. I had always told myself that I was not a teacher - not a leader. But I realized that the participants were at the point where they would do what I subtly directed them toward. Furthermore, they showed their enthusiastic support for ideas I had planted. What a powerful and awesome position to be in.

My fellow traveler was again Quasem Bhuyan from our Dhaka, Bangladesh office for Asia projects. This time, unlike our previous trip to Nepal a few months before, we were able to spend a few evenings in the old central part of Kathmandu. We searched out the "bead bazaar" in one of the ancient sections, and I bought a few sets of beads, made to order. Most of the time, we just wandered, with Quasem occasionally stopping to buy gems like golden topaz and moonstones.

The old city was not what I would call "map-able". It was full of little clusters of shops or stalls with a path between. Only some of these paths were wide enough to be considered a rickshaw road. Other "real" streets were wide enough for a car.

Temples! They were everywhere. Nepal is the only Hindu Kingdom, and signs of both the religion and the royalty were always in sight. The entire front page of the daily paper consisted of reports of every move made by the royal family. Hindu Gods are not only in the temples, but in little crèches in the strangest places. Many were below street level, in roads, or curbs. They were once alongside the road, I was told, but the city literally grew up around them.

Some of the squares in the old section of the city had at least five or six temples all together, with cars, rickshaws, and people filling every vacant space. One temple was made from the wood of a single tree. Others were on elevated steps, reminding me of a small Mexican pyramid.

Of the two holidays I encountered on this trip, one was the day Hindus get their new thread placed around their wrist by a monk. The string around the wrist was what I thought to be similar to a good luck charm. Traditionally, the thread is yellow, but I have seen all shades from white, grey or tan to pink or orange. Some people also have the monk tie a heavy thread across the chest, with it resting on the left shoulder and tied below the right arm.

*Boy dressed as cow.*

The second holiday was the day the people parade through town in a musical procession, leading a decorated cow. The rationale for the cow parade is based on the Hindu belief that only a cow can open the gates of heaven. Playing music and singing songs about dear ones who have died within the past year is supposed to encourage the cow to open the gates so all those souls that have been patiently waiting can finally enter. Of course, not every family could afford a cow. In fact, very few could. Instead, they used small boys, of whom there was no shortage, to head the procession, dressed in costumes to look like cows. The most fascinating experience was seeing the Kumari - the living goddess. The Kumari at the time of my visit was six years old, having been installed when she was just four. Her name was Rashmila Shakya, and as every Kumari, she had been chosen by astrologers and had come from the same caste as the Buddha himself, a clan of silver and goldsmiths.

The Kumari is believed to be carrying the spirit of the mature mother-goddess, Taleju. After rigorous tests and examinations, including being observed for serenity and fearlessness, and assurance that her horoscope is well matched to that of the King, she must be purified so that she can be the unblemished vessel for Taleju. She will hold the position as long as she has no bleeding. This means whether it comes from a minor cut or scratch, internal hemorrhage, surgery, or menstruation.

I had the opportunity to discuss the Kumari's life style in a brief conversation with the man who was in charge of the compound in which she was living. When she was not being worshipped by people of all levels, including the King who came regularly to pay homage to her, she was allowed to play with the keeper's children like any other little six-year old girl. When she must step down, she would be permitted to pursue an education and try to live a normal life. But how can a goddess make such an adjustment? Since 1978, no Kumari has gone on to be married or have children. Rashmila Shakya published an autobiography entitled *From Goddess to Mortal*. It describes her transition.

Nepal is a country full of mysteries for me, but I am drawn to it like no other culture.

*Accommodations:*

*For the dead...*

*...and for the living.*

# CHAPTER 14: INDIAN AIRPORTS, AUG – SEPT, 1985

India was, for me, a difficult country in which to travel, but my experience, other than my one day in Agra, was limited to the airports of Delhi, Bombay, and Calcutta. During the many years I worked in the Indian subcontinent, travel connections had to be in one or two of these airports.

On the trip I made in late summer of 1985, I needed to visit our Asian office in Bangladesh before and after my assignments in Thailand and Nepal. I was to change planes in Bombay for a Bangladesh airline to Dhaka. Unfortunately, the Pan Am flight from NY got a late start, so my transfer time in Bombay was severely cut short. To make matters worse, my luggage was the last coming off the plane. By the time I found the check-in counter, there was less than an hour until the time of takeoff.

On that occasion, I was sent on all kinds of wild goose chases, looking for the Bangladesh counter. After climbing up and down stairs, by now exhausted, sweating like a pig in early morning heat, and panting for breath, I finally learned that the counter had been closed early due to security reasons. In spite of the fact that the plane was still boarding, and there was still forty-five minutes before departure time, there was no chance I would be able to board that plane.

It seemed to me that the best thing for me to do would be to go to Calcutta and then try to connect with a later flight to Dhaka. That way, I could still arrive at my destination on the same day. Well, that was not so easy. First, I had to make my way from the international airport, where I had arrived from New York, to the domestic airport that handled the flights within India. That meant that the international departure tax I had already paid had been wasted, and I would have to buy domestic departure tax stamps. Then, I needed rupees to pay for bus transportation to the other airport. By this time, I was feeling so miserable that a taxi would not have made me feel any better. Besides, the bus driver had to follow a designated route and I wasn't sure where a taxi driver might take me.

I finally got to Calcutta and managed to get another flight to Dhaka. I even tried to be philosophical about it, saying to myself that it was a good experience because my return trip was scheduled with the same transfers from Dhaka to Calcutta to Bombay.

I think it was the crowds of people in the airports that upset me most.

People were lined up at all doors, roped off areas, observation points, and streets. It was almost impossible to plow through. Manners seemed to be unknown; at least there seemed to be no thought of letting someone else proceed. I guessed that every day was a series of needs to push for existence.

Individually, I found Indian people quite pleasant to be with. The women were usually curious, gentle people who seemed eager for a glimpse of life outside their own constraining situations. The men have been gracious and friendly. At times, their manner seemed a bit gruff and direct, but they were all very interesting and intelligent.

By the time I was returning to the states, I felt I had gotten accustomed to the Indian sub-continent. I could, by then, sit in a public place and read a book during a long wait, unbothered by the hordes of people who were standing around staring at me.

I was making notes about my trip while waiting for the Pan Am flight from Bombay to New York. I had been plane hopping since noon that day and in about one and a half hours I would be boarding the plane for the final leg of the journey. The flight was scheduled to depart at five o'clock in the morning. I had been standing in lines, going through various check-points, and waiting since midnight. India was always interesting, even if not efficient.

Postscript

I enjoyed going back to India in 1988 when I had an opportunity to see the changed, new Indira Gandhi International Airport in New Delhi. Gone was the old concrete slab structure with its peeling plaster, bare light bulbs hanging from the ceiling, the loose wires, the solitary immigration official and the endless line of passengers. Gone was the old two-hole ladies room with neither running water nor paper. In its place was a new terminal, much like those in other big cities. It would be difficult to know where you were without the signs. The new building was air-conditioned and the officials seemed to have been briefed on efficiency.

The only thing that still clearly identified it as the Delhi airport were the hordes of waiting passengers sleeping on the sidewalks outside the terminal and on the floors inside, making it difficult to pass.

# CHAPTER 15: HONDURAS, EL SALVADOR, MAY – JUNE, 1986

**HONDURAS**. I began these notes when I had just returned from having spent five days visiting service sites in various cities and villages of Honduras, averaging about six hours a day in a crowded, uncomfortable jeep. Travel was difficult, necessitating driving over and around mountains, hugging the road when there were sheer drop-offs while praying that there were no on-coming cars, and even, on two occasions, crossing a river where there was no bridge.

On this trip, I was serving as team leader to work with a doctor and a program person, Ana Klenicki. We were to review both medical and voluntarism issues in programs being funded by the US Agency for International Development. We were accompanied by the medical supervisor from the Honduran National Family Planning Organization, who also served as the driver of the jeep. For four of the five days we also had a doctor from Agency with us, which necessitated three people in the back seat.

I found Honduras to be quite mountainous, and except for the cities, not heavily populated. Fires in the mountains were a common sight every day for various reasons. Some were the result of careless smokers, but others were started by angry workers retaliating against their landlords. Another explanation for the fires was a myth that had been passed down for many generations, that burning was essential before new crops could be planted. Regardless of the reason, every fire resulted in more eroded land, so the mountains do not have the healthy green look of Guatemala and Mexico.

The vision of Honduras that I will always remember most fondly is the sight of small homes with orange tiled roofs surrounded by acacia trees abloom with red-orange flowers. These trees were a ubiquitous part of the landscape. Their leaves and shape were somewhat like the mimosas in our country. They looked to me like a green pedestal table over which someone had thrown a red mantle.

Street vendors were an important part of the scene, also. There were no stores or market stalls. Generally, there was some collection of up-right posts with tree branches or a cloth tied above for shade. Often, the vendor was just a child standing in the sun at the side of the road, holding up his or her arm with whatever was for sale: a dozen eggs in a bag, a sack of little fruits, fudge wrapped in leaves, a parrot on a perch, an armadillo on a leash, baskets, bird cages, and of course, the always plentiful bananas and pineapples.

I found that the people were peaceful, gentle, gracious, and friendly. Even extreme poverty didn't seem to have made them bitter. Instead, many believe that people who were wealthy, such as land owners and cattlemen, must have made a pact with the devil, selling their souls in exchange for wealth. Because vast sections of Honduras, especially in the flatter northern part closer to the Atlantic Ocean, are still owned by American fruit companies, there may be some truth to that. It seems the banana and pineapple growers were once so powerful, they even controlled elections.

Honduras has had some national leaders who were not so nice. Our driver said he remembered when he was about six years old, people were afraid to be on the streets if the president was known to be traveling in the country. If accused of raising dust on the unpaved road he was using, one's life was in danger.

There was not much sign of danger during our visit. Soldiers were stationed at intervals, but that had become such a common occurrence in most of the world where I traveled that I accepted it as the norm. We were only stopped by the military once, and that was only a brief check of our identification. We passed only one military base of any size. Of course, we avoided going into the hills where the "Contras", or guerrillas, were in hiding.

The family planning program, especially the surgical contraception services, could not exist if it were not for the dedicated "*promotoras*". These women provide an entire array of services. They provide the initial information and sometimes help convince a hesitant husband to consent to his wife's surgery. They transport the clients to the service site, whether it is a clinic or hospital. They assist in filling out all the forms and wait during the procedure so they can help bring the client back to her home. On some occasions, they provide child care while the mother is in surgery. This was especially helpful in postpartum cases, where a day-old infant needed to be tended.

The client's experience was not one of ease. The common practice was to have the woman arrive at six in the morning so she would be ready for the doctor to operate at seven-thirty or eight. That usually meant a very early departure from home. One woman I met had ridden twenty-eight kilometers on horseback to her aunt's home where she left the horse. From there, she traveled by bus to the hospital, and planned to return the same way after surgery.

I cannot imagine American women being so willing to put up with such discomfort. Even in the maternity ward, I met women, including one who was only thirteen years old, going home with their babies the day after delivery. They carried their babies and a small bundle of possessions, walking as straight as though they had just had a vacation. I remembered the many complaints by American maternity patients complaining about sore bottoms, and not being able to walk for many days after delivery.

On our last work day, in the small city of "El Progresso", we were treated to lunch at the home of Dr. Panchame' who was in charge of the local clinic that served as a small hospital. While there, we admired their beautiful hand-carved mahogany doors and furniture panels, and we heard an interesting story. There was once a convent in the area where the nuns taught the novices the art of wood carving. Most of the work was shipped to Germany for sale. Eventually, the convent gave up the craft and a local man bought the wood-working tools. Since then, that man had continued a wood carving school and craft shop. We were escorted to the shop by Dr Panchame' and his wife, who bought me a hand-carved jewelry box as a souvenir.

Nearing the end of our trip, while necessarily spending time reflecting on the activities of the past two weeks in order to prepare our report, I realized that we had covered a lot of ground, literally as well as figuratively. Our report contained information about practices we had not previously known about, recommendations for changes, and suggestions for new directions. It would be very rewarding to learn some day that improvements came about as a result of our work. I optimistically think they will.

I also realized that, once again, I've been put into a new situation to live and work with new people to achieve their goal. As engrossed in the work as I have been at such times, thoughts of family and loved ones creep in. Sometimes, like one day this week while suffering heat prostration, I wonder what I'm doing here. Then I remember that since I was a young teen, my intention was to leave the world a little better off for my having been here. I hope I succeed.

**EL SALVADOR:** After an unexpectedly very brief trip that did not allow me to go beyond the city limits of the capital, San Salvador, I was forced to leave the country.

On Saturday, June 7th, my partner, Ana Klenicki, and I left Tegucigalpa, Honduras, for San Salvador. As is common in much of the developing world, the flight was delayed about four hours. The reason was that a local political leader in Belize had arrived at their airport. For security reasons, all other aircraft were grounded, including our plane, which was on route with a stop-over in Belize. There was a resultant delay of four hours. We were fortunate. Another flight was cancelled completely because a political leader in San Salvador wanted to charter the airline's plane. Those unfortunate passengers had to find overnight hotel accommodations with vague hopes of leaving the next morning. We took advantage of the extra time we had in Honduras to return to central Tegucigalpa and enjoy a refreshing lunch featuring palmetto salad (hearts of palm).

By the time we reached San Salvador and got settled in our hotel, it was evening and too late even for the Sheraton's swimming pool to tempt us. The entire day had been spent getting from one city to another; our twenty-five minute flight had taken all day. The actual time needed to drive the distance would have been only about three hours. Unfortunately, terrorist activities along the road had precluded that possibility. The terrorists, needing money for guns and ammunition, were regularly resorting to stealing, hijacking, or holding someone for ransom.

Finding no instructions or messages from the US Embassy for us at the hotel, we spent part of our free Sunday going to the *Mercado Cuartel* (the main market), in the oldest section of the capital, San Salvador. We hired a taxi to drive on a tour of the section of the city having the oldest historic buildings and then asked the driver to accompany us, for safety, into the mercado. The best products of the country included colorful high grade cotton towels, fabric called *"manta"*, a very durable and wrinkle-resistant cotton cloth, and brightly painted wooden plaques with scenes of buildings, animals, or birds. Of course, I bought samples of all three specialties.

The shopping, touring, swimming and relaxing around the pool were very special treats for these two travelers who had endured a rather rigorous two weeks in Honduras. We topped it off with a good dinner in the Sheraton's main restaurant, with only one other table occupied. El Salvador did not attract tourists in this troublesome time. Complete filet mignon dinner from a cocktail to coffee cost about ten dollars.

The first order of business on Monday morning was our briefing session at the US Embassy, office of the Agency for International Development. There we received the news that due to security risks associated with escalated terrorist activities, only one person was permitted under USAID auspices at one time, and my partner had been arbitrarily selected. The choice was unfortunate because I was the person who could conduct the medical visits that were a critical aspect of the assignment. Phone calls to the AVS office in N.Y. and attempts to have the embassy make an exception to their policy all failed. It was finally decided that we both would have to leave on the first flight Tuesday morning.

So it would not be a totally wasted trip, I did get to visit one clinic in San Salvador. AID gave us the security rules. We could visit only the San Salvador service site, travel only by taxi or clinic vehicle, and eat only in our hotel. Downtown walks were off-limits, as was the entertainment center called the *Zona Rosa*, where six Americans had recently been shot. Absolutely forbidden was any bar - or even a restaurant that had a bar. So while AID took our plane tickets to change our reservations, we were driven to and from the clinic, after which Ana returned to the family planning association office to clear up some budgetary business, and I was free to return to the hotel to pack.

The taxi driver was not difficult to convince that a bit of a detour to the *mercado* would not be unreasonable. There, I was able to buy some more blouses before returning to the hotel. For his *bocca cerrada* (closed mouth), I rewarded him with ten Colones, the equivalent of about two dollars, so we were both happy.

Being driven to the airport early the next morning in the Embassy's bullet-proof van, I thought about the irony I found in this country. It was so peaceful in nature, with beautiful flowers, majestic mountains, colorful singing birds, and gracious people. Yet, it was so full of inner turmoil, causing a seething violence that could erupt any moment like the nearby mountains that were really active volcanoes.

*Roadside vendors.*

213

# CHAPTER 16: GUATEMALA, JULY, 1986

This assignment was supposed to follow immediately after our trip to El Salvador, but because we were hurriedly escorted from the country, we had no choice but to return to the office until we were due in Guatemala.

I looked forward to this return trip where I had first been introduced to the kind of work I would be doing on medical site visits three years earlier. This time I did not have to be driven in an armored car, accompanied by a guard with a machine gun when I visited the offices of USAID at the embassy. There were no tanks on the roads. There was no trouble getting clearance to travel throughout the country, although our itinerary still had to be approved. We were only warned to beware of terrorists and robbers who might hold us up in the countryside. In short, our security orders said we should be as cautious as we would be in New York City.

The work team this trip was made up of Ana Klenicki, who was with me in Honduras and El Salvador, and by Dr. Anibal Castenega, a laparoscopist from Medellin, Colombia.

After a few days working in Guatemala City, we set out for our first week on the road. First stop: Retalhulen, from where we will travel to nearby cities, using the Posada del Don Jose as our home for two days. We arrived in the dreary-looking village after dark, and entered the lobby expecting the worst, but found a lovely patio and dining room inside.

A couple rounds of Venado, the local rum, and a grilled steak dinner cost me about four dollars. My single room was not luxurious but cost less than the dinner. Besides, it had air-conditioning, which I did not have at home.

Retalhulen was big enough to have at least two *funerales*. Even smaller villages must have one and they were all very visible, unlike in our country where the average person never sees a selection of coffins until after a family member has died. In these countries, where death was a part of life, the coffin stores were on a main street, showing their stock to all who pass by. As often as I saw them, I was still distressed by all the children's coffins in varying sizes, painted white. In really poor areas they were pre-decorated with plastic flowers, presumably because the family might not be able to afford fresh ones.

I am also constantly amazed at the distances people walk in many countries, and that was very obvious on this journey. We commonly passed by peasants walking along a highway with bundles on their backs or baskets on their heads, and when we returned hours later, these same people were still walking in the same direction we had seen them doing earlier, still carrying their bundles on their heads.

The names of the cities show the cultural heritage. On this visit, we were visiting Mazatenango, Quetzaltenango, Sololá, Panajachel, Chichicastenango, Zacapa, and Antigua. Most of the travel, with the exception of a two-day trip to Puerto Barrios on the Atlantic Coast, took place in the *"alto plano"*, the high ground in a belt of thirty-three volcanoes. There was a lot of travel up and down mountainous roads with horse-shoe curves.

When I entered the clinic waiting room in Quetzaltenango, I was surprised to hear a "good morning" along with many *"Buenos Dias"*. One of the patients waiting for surgery was originally from southern Illinois. She came to work in Guatemala twenty years ago, later marrying local man and having five children. She was extremely nervous, never having surgery before. She was unaccompanied because her husband was working in another location.

*After surgery.*

After talking for a while, I offered to stay with her throughout the procedure. She was so relieved; she told everyone that I had been sent by God. I stayed with her until she recuperated from the sedation, when it was time for us to move on.

Puerto Barrios was a port city with a lot of Cuban influence. It was hot, dry and dreary, and lacked the color of the cities more heavily populated by indigenous Indians in their traditional garb. Nearby was Livingston, which had a reputation for being a beautiful area reachable only by ferry. Unfortunately, we could not fit a side trip there but were able to hire a motor boat to take us to an old restored castle dating back to the sixteenth century. The brief *Rio Dulce* ride was a pleasant diversion, as was *Castillo de San Philipe*.

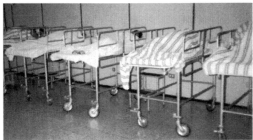

*Recovery room.*

We were able to make one other side trip to Quirigua to see ruins of a Mayan settlement. After walking through a large park-like area with tall monoliths *(stellas)* erected by the Mayans, we came to the remnants of the temple area. The pyramidal structures were not as well preserved as the ones further north in Tikal, but I was glad to have seen the magnificently carved monuments of Quirigua, at least.

As these journeys in Central America drew to an end, an increasing amount of time was spent organizing notes, discussing ideas, and gathering information in preparation for the final report. We would have to share our findings and recommendations with people at USAID and the family planning program of Guatemala before we left the country.

It was sometimes a challenge to present such a report in a constructive way, allowing local providers to "save face" while identifying practices that were sub-standard. These last three countries had been especially difficult because I had to juggle with the input from my two colleagues while serving as the team leader having ultimate responsibility.

*Five-year-old babysitting while mother has her tubes tied.*

# CHAPTER 17: SINGAPORE, OCT, 1986

I was back again in this country where the good of the society definitely took precedence over individual freedoms. In an effort to achieve a no-litter society, chewing gum had been outlawed. On the roofs of trucks, there were lights that blinked when the speed limit was exceeded, thus beckoning the traffic police. No one would think of considering more than the regulated four persons to a taxi. As clean and orderly as Singapore is, I felt a bit of discomfort with such regimented living.

The purpose of this trip was to take part in a workshop involving experts from all parts of the globe. Our goal was to expand and update a manual about ensuring a high quality of surgical services in our programs, much of it drafted earlier by me. My heavy travel schedule required that my flights in and out of Singapore had to be without layovers, with each trip involving about thirty hours in flight each way.

The only bit of "free" time was the day of my arrival in Singapore on October 20th. I could not have been more fortunate. That day marked the celebration of the Thimithi Festival, held to honor the purity of the Goddess Droba-Devi. The Hindu story that originated this festival tells of the prince, Arjuna, who vanquished the father of Droba-Devi and took her to his home as booty. Arjuna's mother decided that the loot would be shared among his four brothers and that she had to spend a year at each brother's house. Droba-Devi carried out the order, but at the end of each year, she walked on burning embers to prove her purity. Hindus believed that those pure in mind and soul would not be harmed by fire.

Devotees pray to the Goddess for aid. Those whose wishes have been granted are then obligated to pay their debt by literally walking on the burning embers. Prior to the ceremony, they cleanse their minds by prayer and fasting. Just before they walk across the pit, about seven yards distance, they take a ritual bath and receive lashes of penance from whip-wielding priests.

I had no intention of missing an opportunity to witness this event, so at mid-afternoon I started out by taxi for the Sri Miriamman Temple in the heart of Chinatown. Due to the crowds near the area, I decided to walk the last two blocks to the Temple, arriving before four o'clock. The temple area was packed solidly with people, only about ten of whom were not Indian.

To get a spot from where I could see the fire pit seemed impossible, but I finally found myself in the perfect location, about fifty feet from the pit, in good view of a television monitor, set in an area where the wives of the devotees could watch. The area was thick with incense. Music was playing loudly. I was near a sacrifice altar, where I discovered later, the devotees would offer their amulets, clusters of leaves and limes after having crossed the coals.

Two hours later, the pitch of excitement rose, and the raked coals seemed to have reached the proper stage. The intensity of the drums and cymbals increased. A young woman about three feet away from me raised her clenched hands and arms in the air and began to sway with the music. Almost instantly, she doubled the speed and I realized she was going into a trance. Suddenly, the woman next to me started the same behavior. People nearby supported her so she would not get hurt while in the trace. Her eyes were glassy, staring at nothing; her tongue protruding. Faster and wilder, she bounced about until she collapsed.

This was about when the first of the priests and worshippers started across the coals, with much shouting and encouragement from the crowd. A constant procession walked that evening, some running, some more casually walking. Each carried something to place at the altar: a lime on a stick, a bundle of green leaves, or a combination. Every devotee was wearing a yellow amulet tied with string around their wrist. These were offered at the altar where I was standing. I found myself in the midst of devotees, wearing soaking yellow garments and liberally sprinkled or streaked with yellow powder. Meanwhile, people continued to go into trances all around me.

Suddenly, a man appeared, carrying a sponge from which stuck many skewers and hooks. People lined up to have them inserted - a practice that is also widespread at another festival, Thaipusam. This is meant to demonstrate a man's capacity to endure suffering by exercising mind over matter. Most of the people just had a skewer put into the flesh of the forehead, but one man stole the show. He also had a long skewer inserted into his left cheek, through his protruding tongue, and out his right cheek. Another was vertically placed through the lips and tongue tip. After the application, which took place less than a yard away from me, he went into the temple to pray. Thirty minutes later he returned for removal. Amazingly, he did not seem to feel pain, and no blood was shed.

At about seven o'clock, I decided to leave. When I got to the street, there was still a block-long procession of devotees waiting to fulfill their vows. All the devotees, I learned later, had started their procession about two to three miles away, at another temple in the Indian section of town, probably about the time I had arrived at Miriamman Temple. By this time, the streets were incredibly crowded. It was impossible to direct my steps. I just picked up one foot after another and moved in the direction of the strongest push. It took almost an hour to get to a clearer spot, to locate a taxi stand, and return to the hotel for an immediate shower.

What an incredible thrill to be in the midst of such a celebration; to experience the sights, smells, sounds and sensations of such an occasion!

# CHAPTER 18: KENYA, OCT 30 – NOV 23, 1986

The trip from New York to Nairobi was long, but quite an easy journey because it didn't require any changing of aircraft. There was a chance to stretch our legs at the door of the plane in Dakar, Senegal, and Lagos, Nigeria. When the plane was getting cleaned up at the Monrovia airport in Liberia, we could get off the plane for an hour. My traveling companion, Lynn Bakamjian, and I left on a Thursday night flight. After take-off, we were served drinks and then dinner. By the time the movie was beginning, we were both ready to catch some sleep as best we could. After having worked the full day, we were tired.

We continued flying east, going through a short night, a short day, and into the next night, arriving in Nairobi after midnight Saturday morning. The airport was active. We changed currency for taxi fare and tips, and got through customs before we were crowded in by eager taxi drivers, all clamoring for our luggage. Finally, one succeeded in getting us to his cab, and away we went.

At the hotel, we found a message from Nancy, another NY staff person who had arrived a few days before, and Joseph Dwyer, our African Regional Office Director, stationed in Nairobi. They had planned our first day and would pick us up at noon. Sleep came quickly - but so did the sound of the alarm on my clock. According to my anti-jet-lag theory, I refused to sleep in the day time – so no matter how few hours I had slept, I had set it for an early hour.

Our first lunch was a meal typical in central Kenya. It consisted of irio, which is made from cooked maize, dried beans, potatoes and kale, all mashed together. It was served with a beef stew and I thought it was delicious. After lunch, Joe treated us to an introductory drive to a game reserve near the city. As we followed miles of dirt roads, we met ostrich, zebras, giraffes, wart hogs, buffalo, and lots of antelope-like animals - all in different varieties and sizes. We didn't spot any lions and the hippopotamus pools were unoccupied.

The next day, we met the three Kenyan members of our teams. Lynn, Nancy and I would each be paired with a Kenyan, and each team would cover a separate area of the country. With Sellah Nakhisa, the nursing coordinator for the Protestant Churches Medical Association, I would be working in areas northwest of Nairobi. Because my team would be traveling the greatest distances, we would not return to Nairobi until November 18, giving us sixteen full days in the "bush".

One of my first surprises in Kenya was the pleasant climate. Even though the equator passes through it near the cities we were traveling through, there was usually a cool breeze. Even at noon, it was not uncomfortable. Another surprise was the gentle, quiet nature of Kenyans. Remembering stories of Masai warriors, Mau Mau uprisings, and the vicious war for independence, I had been prepared for more boisterous people.

The life style I encountered in the Kenyan country-side was no surprise to me, having by then worked for a few years in underdeveloped areas of the world. I had come to believe that most of the earth's people lived in huts, most women were clothed in just a rectangular piece of fabric, most people were barefoot or in thongs, most burdens were carried on the top of a woman's head, most diets were limited, and clean water was scarce.

The villages we visited were just poorer, smaller versions of the cities. The center streets of the larger cities, such as Nakuru and Eldoret, were not much more than a block or two of stores, each just a small room with a counter, and some shelves of stock. Stock was limited to necessities. There would usually be a store for drugs and health supplies, one for housekeeping essentials such as soap, buckets, plastic containers, and brooms. Another might sell kitchen utensils, especially stainless steel teapots, creamers and sugar bowls. The larger cities would have a hardware store and maybe even a shoe repair shop. There might be a stationery or book store where customers could buy paper by the sheet, or individual envelopes. Gift shops, souvenir stores or jewelry shops were absent in Kenya – at least outside of Nairobi or Mombasa. I found one small shop in Kitali owned by an Indian, as were most businesses, which had some beads, ivory articles and some rather poor quality custom jewelry.

*Eldoret market.*

One day, we traveled to the northern-most village in our assigned area: Kapsowar, in the Cherangani Hills. It was such a beautiful setting for the small hospital there, run by medical missionaries associated with the African Inland Mission. Situated atop one hill, shaded by trees, we could look across beautiful landscapes to other hills around. The air was fresh and clean, and many of the patients were lying or sitting on the grass, enjoying the sun and fresh air. How much nicer than a crowded hospital ward.

Leaving Kapsowar, we spotted a lady at a bus stop, dressed in the traditional garb of the Turkana tribe who occupy an area north of that city, near Lake Turkana. She was wearing a black wrap, lots of strings of beads, many earrings, and a stud in her lower lip. She agreed to pose for a photo for me, encouraged by her husband who wanted some money for a soda.

*Turkana lady.*

Continuing in our task of visiting our third of all the family planning sites, and investigating some potential sites, we headed further west, getting closer and closer to the Ugandan border. There, traveling north to south, following the Uganda border, we spent a few days in the most rural and underdeveloped sections of Western Kenya.

The dietary habits had changed soon after leaving Nairobi in the central province. Instead of irio, the main staple in the west is ugali, a thick, putty-like white lump of cooked grain, resembling farina. Also not available, except in hotel restaurants, were eating utensils. The way to eat in western Kenya is to pick up a lump of ugali and mold it into a cylinder in the palm of the right hand. Then, using the thumb and one or two fingers, pick up other food items, whether stew, a whole fish, a piece of chicken or cooked greens. When a bite-sized piece is picked up, it's put into the mouth, followed by a bite of the palmed cylinder.

I was introduced to another interesting eating habit. People in the western area eat ants. We found many family groups sitting around their ant-hills eating white-winged live ants as they crawled out their nests and fell into a trap prepared to catch them. Usually, they were eaten raw and alive, although they were sometimes fried or roasted. These white ants were caught seasonally during the day. Although I was glad to see them during their season, I had no desire to try one. I learned that they also harvested a darker colored, larger ant that crawled out of large ant hills during the night.

Sellah was originally from western Kenya. When she was a little girl, she had been taught to help her family by gathering the ants. She remembered trying to eat a live white ant for the first time. It crawled around in her mouth, until she threw up. Then she killed one and yellow stuff came out. She decided then and there she would not try another - dead or alive.

The women of western Kenya had a peculiar manner of smoking. After they lit the cigarette, they inserted the burning end into their mouth. It apparently was prompted by a wish to protect their infants from a burn. We stopped along the road to talk to two elderly smokers. One proudly offered to show us how she smoked and to have her photo taken. The other explained that because she had lost her teeth, she has had to smoke like a man to keep from burning her tongue.

*Luya lady smokers.*

One night, while staying in the border town of Busia, we decided to see if we could walk into Uganda for a "look-see". We were granted permission by both the Kenya and Uganda border patrols, so we passed through, having been warned by the Uganda guard not to buy more than one object each. Ugandans enter Kenya for food products and Kenyan shillings. Kenyans like to buy the higher quality cloth and less expensive radios in Uganda.

I became a main attraction for little children soon after starting our walk down the main street. I had a group around me all laughing and trying to have me touch them or shake their hands. Some even ran up, stroked my bare leg and ran off. Such a curiosity about white skin!

Sellah and I each bought a piece of cloth. John, our driver, bought a shirt. When we tried to leave Uganda, the border guards had changed and they tried to prevent us from leaving with our purchases. They said we had to go back to the police station for authorization. Believing this was just a ploy for a bribe, I said we'd be happy to go to the police, and asked directions. At that point, they let us go.

Sellah Nakhisa was a woman of many talents, and I was happy to be working with this dynamic but soft-spoken lady. In 1979, she had been the first government-employed health educator who took an interest in encouraging breast feeding of infants. In her community nursing work, she had noticed that the preponderance of infants who developed gastro-intestinal disorders had been fed infant formula with a bottle. The large American companies, like Nestle, had been giving samples and doing some hard-sell advertising, so Kenyan women thought that bottle feeding was better. It had become a status symbol. When Sellah recognized the cause and effect, she decided to "stamp out bottle feeding", to put it in her own words. She worked with a small group of volunteers who formed a breast-feeding support organization, called B.I.G.

By 1983, the government had a policy not to allow bottle feeding in any of the hospitals or maternity clinics. Babies were taken off bottles and if the mother had no milk, they were fed by a cup. Even as we traveled together on this assignment, she was recognized all over as the "Breast-Feeding Lady", and asked about the project.

One day, when we visited Kitale, we found street vendors selling household goods on the sidewalk. Three of them had a couple baby bottles for sale. Sellah gave each of them a lecture about the government policy. She told them that not only were they disobeying the policy, but they were contributing to the death of infants.

Sellah has since decided to "stamp out" spousal consent for tubal ligation. She encountered many women being denied the procedure because the husbands refused to take part, or because they wanted the wife to continue producing children. Meanwhile, the husband took no responsibility for child care. Additionally, in the polygamist society that exists in much of Kenya, a man has more than one wife producing children. As an "equal opportunity" woman, she was as upset as I was a few days earlier when a man was turned down for a vasectomy because he lacked his wife's consent. Spousal consent requirements in Kenya worked both ways, but we did find a few places where the service was provided in the absence of a partner's participation.

One woman in a child-health clinic had an infant on her lap (her tenth child) while she listened to a lecture on family planning methods. When the nurse got to tubal ligation, this mother got very interested. When told about the need for husband's consent, she got very forceful and said "Look at me! I have a baby every year and he wants me to have more. I have nothing else. I look older than my years. My milk is drying up so I can hardly feed this baby. I want the operation and I'll sign my own consent!" The other mothers in the room all supported her and by the time we left the clinic, arrangements had been made for her to have the tubal ligation the following week - with or without her husband.

The day Sellah was trying to stamp out the bottle sellers in Kitale, we had another interesting encounter. While having tea and samosas for lunch in the ancient New Kitale Hotel, Sellah introduced me to Mr. Masinde Muliro, a Member of Parliament. He was the owner of the hotel, so could often be found in the lobby. Sellah was a friend of one of his wives, so felt free to visit with him. I was glad to meet him because he was one of the very active fighters for independence, along with Jomo Kenyatta. As soon as Sellah explained what we were doing, he turned to me and angrily said that the US was doing harm in encouraging family planning when Kenya needed more people. He felt US aid should be directed toward economic and industrial development. I was a bit surprised at his verbal attack in spite of the fact that I had been warned that he was not always in step with the rest of the Parliament, and that he was very outspoken.

The Kenyan government had taken a very active role in promoting family planning. Posters and signs were quite openly encouraging smaller families, and health workers have had special training to be able to address the needs of the people. So far, the birth rate had been lowered but large families were still the norm. Polygamy was widespread, especially among the tribes in western Kenya. Sellah's father-in-law had thirty wives who produced forty sons and uncounted daughters. By the time a woman got her tubes tied, she had already had seven or more children.

In a country like this, where people really live off their own land, they need land to grow their crops and to graze their milk-producing animals. If they had six sons, it would be expected that the land would eventually be divided six ways. But if each son were to have six children, those children would not have enough room for their crops and cattle. The shortage of land had gotten critical in some areas. Some plans have been made by the government to resettle families to the more remote, less populated areas, such as western Kenya. There, the high birth rate has been off-set by the high infant mortality rate (more than two hundred out of one thousand infants were dying), high malaria death rates, and inadequate health care.

Women of Kenya seemed to me to be developing strength in spite of the fact that they still were second-class citizens, with fewer rights and less respect than men. As an indication of the wife's status, in western Kenya, Sellah pointed out that the form of address for a wife is *"Omuteshi....."* followed by the surname of husband. Translated, it literally means "the cook of Mr. ..." Similarly, if someone wanted to know where a woman was living since her marriage, the question would be "Where are you cooking?"

Not long ago, girls were still being kidnapped by unknown suitors to be taken in marriage against their will. The would-be husband may have heard about an eligible girl from a go-between, or he may have admired her from a distance. In either case, the kidnapping was done with friends, so when the bride was captured, perhaps on her way home from the market, she wouldn't know which one of the group was to be her husband. Her shouts were ignored because people would know she was just going to be married. She would be taken to the *"isamba"* (bachelor hut) of the would-be husband. If she were successful in fighting off the sexual advances until her family rescued her, there would be no marriage. However, if the sex act had taken place, there would be no undoing of the situation because no one else would have her in a "damaged" condition.

Approaching the end of this "safari", I was very grateful for having had such good companionship for the past two weeks. Sellah, John, and I had lots of time while driving to share stories, traditions, and feelings - something to be treasured in a work relationship. On the other hand, there were many lonely hours after we checked into our hotel for the night and had our dinner.

I reached the end of the trip with a feeling of real accomplishment. I think the entire team of six did a fine job of addressing Kenya's situation, dealing with both the positive and the negative sides. We were able to make some reasonable recommendations for solving problems and improving the quality of family planning services being provided.

Personally, I was proud to have been able to help the Kenyan medical authorities develop a system for client record forms, which if adopted by the government, should improve medical supervision and ensure safe medical practices. I looked forward to returning in six months to follow up.

*Hand-operated wheelchair*

*Man-power*

# CHAPTER 19: NIGERIA, FEB 15 – MAR 5, 1987

This trip started off beautifully with a helicopter ride from Manhattan to JFK airport. The moon was just a sliver less than full, and the air was clear. All the tiny lights of the cities and highways really resembled strings of diamonds. An extra advantage of using the helicopter, besides avoiding the drive, was the easier handling of baggage. After only a five minute taxi ride from my apartment to helipad on East 60th Street, my luggage was checked through to Frankfort, completely eliminating the long lines at the airport.

Packing in the winter for a trip to equatorial Africa posed a bit of a problem. I settled on slacks, a blouse, a heavy cuddly red sweater, and a raincoat. The sweater was a blessing on the plane, but even with the raincoat, I was quite chilled in Frankfurt. I kept reminding myself how warm I'd be the next day.

I was able to take a Frankfurt city tour in the free hours I had until the next plane would take me to Lagos. Not many buildings survived the Second World War, but the city had attempted to repair all that were possible. In the town square were replicas of the buildings that had been there before the war. Although they were only seven or eight years old, it was quite possible to get the flavor of what the area looked like when it was thriving. It was easy to imagine townsfolk filling the large plaza, listening to speakers from the balcony of the city hall, perhaps bands playing and people dancing on the cobblestones.

Lagos, as all of Nigeria, did not have a good reputation among foreign visitors, so I was prepared for a difficult entry. Actually, it was rather smooth, made a bit nicer by the fact that I was met by a US Embassy staff person and a driver. I found the airport and customs procedures to be better organized than Sierra Leone, to have fewer checks and rechecks than Nepal, and to be far less crowded than Egypt or India.

As I saw some of the city on my way to the Eko Holiday Inn, it appeared quite well developed, with super highways and skyscrapers. Although there were many slum areas along the way, it appeared to be the most modern city I had yet seen in Africa south of the Sahara.

The rural areas appeared to be similar to rural areas in much of the developing world. Every structure was the color of the earth, understandable because roads and buildings were constructed of cement and stone. Everything else, such as laundry hanging out to dry, seemed to pick up the color of the dust.

Large buses went from major cities across state borders to other major cities. Within the states, the only local bus service was by Volkswagen vans. I was entertained by the unending variety of slogans printed on the side panels or rear windows. They expressed religious beliefs, virtues, plans, political philosophies and queries. For example: "The Lord is my Shepherd", "Jesus Saves", "Honesty", "Haji Tomorrow", "The Young Shall Grow", "Have Mercy, O Lord", and the mysterious "It Pains You Why".

Nigeria in 1987 was a union of nineteen states divided into tribal areas as well. Three major tribes were somewhat divided by the Y-shaped Niger and Benue rivers. The Yoruba occupied the south-western section, the Hausa occupied the north and were mostly influenced by the Muslim/Arab world near them, and the Ibo were in the south-eastern third.

Clothing varied in the three sections, also. The Yoruba women wore a blouse, wrapped skirt, shawl and headdress all made of matching, printed fabric. The Ibo women wore silk or satin headdresses, lace blouses and a double skirt wrap. The bottom layer would be ankle length, and the top wrap above the knee level. The Hausa wore Arab style clothing and head shawls more suitable for the drier desert land where they lived.

Facial scars were very common on both men and women. I had always assumed these scars were made at a coming of age ceremony so was surprised to learn that the surface wounds were made very early in life - probably by the time of the naming ceremony. I think they may be tribal markings. Some scars were a series of horizontal lines; others were diagonal. Some were smaller and vertical, almost like tear drops. And, of course, some fancy ones were a combination.

The Nigerian diet was very similar to that of western Kenya, where I had learned to eat the thick white *ugali* cereal with vegetables. Ugali is made from corn flour. In Nigeria the people prefer to make their comparable staple food, called *fufu* or *garri* from either white cooked yams or cassava root pounded into hot water. The vegetable dish was soupier and more difficult to pick up with the small ball of fufu held in the right hand. The right hand is the eating or "clean" hand; the left is used for toileting and is considered improper for handling food.

Also, I was instructed to swallow the mixture without chewing it first. I learned that they did not want digestion to begin in the mouth, so even little children were corrected if they tried to chew it. One night, while we were out eating in a local country restaurant, I was instructed, "Just let it go plunk where it will keep you full longer". That was when I realized the rationale for their not chewing fufu.

While in the Ibo region, I experienced a cola nut ceremony. People in all of Nigeria chew cola nuts, but it was a very formal process in the eastern area. Upon receiving guests, a host would offer a plate of cola nuts. He would first hand the plate to the nearest male, who would then admire them and, without touching, pass the plate to the next man. Women were absolutely excluded from the process, but were permitted in the room. When the plate reached the host again, he would take notice of the number of nuts. If there were more nuts than men, he would ask the guest(s) of honor to "take one for the pocket". This was so that the guest could take it home and tell about his visit. Finally, the host would cut up the remaining nuts lengthwise. If necessary to create extra pieces, he may also cut them horizontally. The pieces on the plate are then passed around again. This time, the women would be included. I found the nut to have a bitter, alum-like taste, and because it was already late afternoon, I didn't eat it all, concerned about the stimulant effect it might have.

The people in the rural areas were very well mannered, carrying on many of the traditions of their culture. For example, statements made to women almost always ended with "Ma", such as "Thank you Ma", etc. It was a shortened version of Mama or Madam. Also, it was considered impolite not to either offer or accept food or drink. At times we spent more than one hour of our visit, after work was done, just waiting to receive the host's food that had not yet arrived. At one site, the food was quite strange. I quietly said the "missionary's prayer" (Lord, I'll put it down; please keep it down.)

*Nigerian mother.*

One day, in Imo state, in the eastern region, we went hunting for a local treat: fresh palm wine. We were guided by our traveling companion in that region, a nurse named Veronica. She told us that at sun-up and again when the sun went down, men would climb the palm trees to tap them for wine. The best wine is said to be the wine that never reached the ground. On our morning try (before work, on our way to a hospital) we found some from that morning's tapping. Later, when we were sampling it, we learned it had fermented rapidly and had probably been mixed with water and wine left-over from the night before. We ditched it. That night, we made a special trip to pick up a local guide to take us to a tapper's compound where we bought the real thing. Unfortunately, the man had already reached the ground when we found him, but the wine was sweet and unadulterated. We had dinner in a small local restaurant: gari (the white cooked staple), vegetables and stock fish (dried cod cooked with a mixture of greens). We brought in our own wine. It was a tasty combination, and I was allowed to chew the fish.

The educational system in Nigeria left quite a bit to be desired. One day, when I was at the Lagos University Teaching Hospital, I noticed a list of quotations on a blackboard. The professor told me they were statements made by students who had about one year to go before finishing medical school. They included: "A uterus that is not pregnant is said to have preganted *(sic)* itself"; "To detect ovulation, look for the ovum on the pad the woman uses"; "After ovulation, the cells develop wings"; and "Are scrotum in testes?" The professor felt that the secondary school level was not properly preparing these students for higher education and kept examples on the board to demonstrate the problem. I was left worrying about what kind of doctors these people would soon become.

Many of the tubal ligations that were provided in AVS programs were performed by medical officers. They had a basic medical education but then became specialists in a specific procedure. Some were trained to do very delicate eye surgery. Others learned general surgery. Some became specialists in doing a tubal ligation. By concentrating on a specific procedure, these medical officers achieved a high degree of talent.

One of my responsibilities while I was Deputy Medical Director was to collect reports of all complications following male or female sterilization. Both the Medical Director and I each conducted medical evaluation visits to our programs to assess quality of care, determine who needed further training, and to consult with the surgeons about how we could reduce the numbers of complications they were experiencing. Constant monitoring of these reports, along with the site visits helped to keep the mortality rates low. The surgeons in our programs were probably among the best trained medics in the land.

School children were all taught English, but in the "real world" outside of school, the language was a pidgin English, and very difficult for outsiders to understand. I found two examples of written pidgin in newspaper cartoons. The first cartoon showed a woman on her hands and knees, on the floor, with her husband sitting "horseback" on her. He says, "All the money I take for buy beetle you don take am chop, buy dress, perm hair. Na you go carry me to work today". (You spent the money I saved to buy a Volkswagen, so now I'll ride on you to work.) The second showed a wife talking to her husband, and she's holding a pot. She says "Pot don empty!" He replies, "Make I jump inside?" (What do you want me to do about it - jump in it so it won't be empty?)

This was one of the seemingly longest and most lonesome trips I've made yet. Even though I was accompanied by Dr. Ade Adetunji, our program manager for Nigeria, there were hours of driving with only occasional spurts of conversation. Many afternoons, we finished our work by mid-afternoon, and I was deposited in a hotel room with no place to go until dinner that evening. Quiet dinners with Ade were accompanied by a tall bottle of beer, which I prayed would make me sleepy enough to shorten the night. Because there was some degree of air conditioning in the room, and I would have been a stranger wandering around a village in the sun, I spent my free time in my room, wrote reports, and read. At six in the morning we would begin another day - and so it went. Actually, I was pleased when our days included long driving trips so there were fewer hours of seclusion. My biggest regret was not having carried some decent reading material. I was forced to pick up whatever was available each time I returned to the Lagos hotel, where there was a small shop.

I had heard quite a bit about the police checks in Nigeria long before my trip. In fact, that kind of behavior was the reason that AID offered to have someone escort me in and out of the country. We had frequent experiences on the roads with the checkpoints. One was especially memorable. We were in the eastern rural part of Nigeria and were carrying two anesthesia machines in the car trunk, as well as our luggage. When we were stopped by a particularly inquisitive police guard, he demanded that we open the boxes and show him the components of the anesthesia machines.

While Ade was trying to explain the mechanism, I decided to produce a "To whom it may concern" letter from the United States Agency for International Development (USAID), explaining that I was representing the US government, donating medical equipment to Nigeria. I handed the letter to the policeman through the car window. He took it and held it as though he were reading it. Suddenly, he pointed the machine gun directly at my face and proceeded to scold me for having handed the paper to him with my left hand. He considered it a gross insult, obviously. I would have liked to have told him that in the USA, we hold our bread in our left hand and wipe our bottoms with our right hand, but such courage is hard to come by when looking into the barrel of a machine gun. So I apologized. We were finally released.

Political tension was ever present in Nigeria. Ibrahim Babangida overthrew Buhari's regime in 1985, promising to bring an end to human rights abuses and to hand over power to a civilian government in five years. However, during his years in office, until 1993, the abuses continued and there were many political assassinations. During one of my visits, over a dozen government officials were lined up in a court yard and shot in their heads. I was always on alert to follow the Nigerian news those years and I confess to missing knowing what is going on now. Our newspapers do not cover what really is happening in the world. I was far better engaged in those years because any shift could affect our safety.

On February 28, I attended a Fourth of July picnic at the home of the U.S. Ambassador to Nigeria. As he explained in his address, the actual holiday date in Nigeria falls in the rainy season, so they have followed the U.S. pattern of switching holidays from the actual dates to convenient dates. Thus, Fourth of July was celebrated in February.

I went to the picnic with Joyce Holfeld, a former AVS employee now working in West Africa. I had met her accidentally at the AID office the day before. We ate hot dogs, drank beer, listened to American music, and watched entertainment provided by school children from the US International School. But the best moment was the lowering of the flag after hearing the National Anthem sung. I doubt there were many dry eyes. I know Joyce's and mine were not. No matter how I complain about the song, I admit it sounds awfully good when you are half way around the world and three weeks out of touch with those you love.

This trip was too long for my comfort. I was unable to make a single phone contact no matter how often I tried. People in Nigeria actually waited more than ten years to get a phone installed, so I guess I could not reasonably have expected much better, but it was frustrating never-the-less. The significance of what we accomplished helped, but I was very excited about the idea of leaving. I got to the airport by 8:30 in the morning for an 11:35 flight on March 4th. Two "expediters" from AID helped me through the process, but then I had two and a half hours of sweating before we boarded. I hadn't realized before how happy I would be to get on a plane, but there was something very reassuring about the familiar atmosphere of the intercontinental jet. The first thing I did was to drink three glasses of water direct from a faucet. It was a treat.

Stopping overnight in Zurich gave me a bit of culture shock. There were no men fighting over who was going to carry my bags; there was no confusion at the passport desk or customs; I didn't have to pay more than a day's hotel charge as a deposit. In fact, I could pay it all when I checked out. In my room, the air-conditioning was both working and quiet; there were soap and clean towels in the bathroom - even shampoo, shower cap and bath foam. The toilet flushed and there was a seat on it - and it wasn't even cracked. The bed was comfortable and there was a carpet on the floor. Best of all, there was a reading light next to the bed. Such luxury! I could easily get spoiled if all my travel accommodations were like this.

# CHAPTER 20: RETURN TO KENYA, APRIL 9 – MAY 7, 1987

I decided to schedule a weekend vacation before starting my three and a half week assignment. While plans for this trip were developing, I had learned that my British friends Penny and Pete McQuilkin would also be on route through Africa at the same time. They were the owners of Femcare, the company that made and distributed the Filshie Clips for female sterilization. We planned a joint safari to the Masai Mara game reserve. Within hours of my arrival, I had a weekend bag packed, had showered and changed clothes in their hotel room. I stashed my extra luggage, and we left for the tiny Wilson Airport, where a DC-3 carried about twenty passengers to a grassy landing strip in the Mara.

We were met by Land Rover vehicles, one of which was assigned to us and another couple. Our driver, a former Masai warrior, would be with us until we would leave, protecting us, if necessary, with a club he kept in the vehicle.

Before checking in, we began our first game drive. Thompson gazelles, impala, topi, buffalo, elephants, giraffes, and baboons were plentiful, but I had seen these before and was particularly eager to see the large cats. Our first great treat was to find a cheetah feasting on a Thompson gazelle. We drove right up to him and were able to watch and photograph him from a distance of about seven feet. Unfortunately, my film was later damaged so my prized shots were lost. Fortunately, Pete was taking video pictures and I eventually got a copy.

The second day we found a young leopard stalking in the grass. We stopped to watch. He was heading for a tree in which sat another half-hidden leopard. Our driver, David, explained that the stalking leopard was one of two cubs born in that area two and a half years earlier. From his actions, David deduced that the hidden leopard must be the mother. If it were his sister, he would have been more aggressive; if it had been an adult male, he would not attempt to steal the meal being devoured in the tree. But it was natural that a young male cub would take food from his mother, having given her a chance to eat some first.

Slowly, the cub approached the tree. Then suddenly he climbed up, grabbed what was left of an impala, and dropped to the ground. He carried the meat a short distance away and began his dinner while mama finished crunching some bones. She then began to lick her paws and clean her face just as a house cat would do. After cleaning up, she slowly descended the tree and walked away. The cub then picked up the meat and climbed the tree to finish his meal. Leopards, unlike the other cats, are not willing to share their catch with the family, and they prefer to eat in a tree where other animals are not as likely to find them.

We saw a number of lion families. Some groups were just females and cubs; others were couples or a male with two or more females. All were beautiful. One group had just filled up on a topi, the remains of which would feed a hyena or jackal before the vultures cleaned the bones.

Although it was sad to think of these graceful deer-like animals being killed, the natural way of life in the game reserves is so much better than seeing animals artificially fed in a zoo. The ugly wart-hog could not escape the lion either. We saw a lioness dragging her strangled kill with its skin still intact. We didn't know if she was just looking for a shady spot to eat, if she was taking the wart-hog away from other animals, or if she was bringing it to share with her mate. But she was certainly working hard. Every fifty feet or so, she stopped, dropped the neck, panted and rested a while, picked it up again and continued to drag the load that was probably a third or half her body weight.

We stayed at Governor's Camp in tents that each had an adjacent bathroom tent. We had a gas lamp lit in the bathroom each night, and one more that could be brought in from the "front porch". In the morning, the "tent boy" would relight the porch lamp, unzip the tent (calling first to wake us up) and bring in a tray of coffee or tea and a roll. Half an hour later we assembled at the vehicles to see the animals as the sun rose.

One night I was awakened by a loud chomping sound outside my tent window. I looked out to find a hippo grazing in the grass not six feet from me. We also heard lions and hyenas in the night, and frequently saw a local elephant, named "Taka-Taka". This elephant liked to steal food from the kitchen and regularly had to be chased away by the Masai guards with their clubs or spears.

As an extra treat, Penny, Pete and I signed up for an early balloon safari. As the sun rose, we were lifted up to float for two hours, landing near the Tanzanian border. We crouched and hung on to handles in the basket walls as we were about to touch ground. Upon impact, the basket tipped on its side, and we tumbled out. The crew then cooked breakfast while we sipped Champaign in the grass in an area marked off with pointed spears stuck in the ground to keep away the birds looking for an easy breakfast.

My first week of work took me west of Nairobi to the cities of Naivasha, Nakuru, Eldoret, and Kakamega, all where I had been in

November. This time we also visited Kisii, the most heavily populated area in all of Kenya. To get there, we drove through Kericho in the area where tea was the major crop. There were miles and miles of tea estates, each of them with a little "village" of housing units for the workers, who probably never left the estate.

We returned to Nairobi just before the four-day Easter holiday. I worked on reports and began the investigation of a death that had just occurred in one of our programs in a Nairobi hospital. Completion of this death investigation, conduction of a medical site visit, and recertification of the surgeon was now be added to my other assignments while in Kenya. I was glad I had scheduled the last two days rather lightly, so this extra work will not prolong my already lengthy trip.

Early Saturday morning, I was again at Wilson airport with my weekend bag, ready to take off for Amboseli game reserve, at the foot of Mount Kilimanjaro. The mountain, situated in Tanzania, just over the Kenyan border, has an interesting history. The countries of Kenya, Tanzania, and Uganda were all called East Africa and were controlled by the United Kingdom. Queen Victoria gave Mount Kilimanjaro as a birthday gift to her cousin, the ruler of Germany, because he loved mountains. As a result, that area (now Tanzania) was later governed by Germany. After the Second World War, the area was returned to Britain.

We took off in a six-seat Cessna, and I was the only passenger. The trip was about thirty-five minutes. As we were approaching, I had a wonderful view of the snow-covered Mount Kilimanjaro to welcome me to Amboseli before the clouds rolled in.

My reservations had gotten mixed up. I was informed that my trip arrangements did not include a game drive. I decided to arrange for a private driver, an elderly man who had worked in Amboseli for fifteen years. He had a dirty but sturdy Land Rover in which he could cross the areas where roads were inaccessible to the prettier vans used by others. He was also willing to disobey the rules about staying on the roads. Because of this, I got to see more animals on my one drive than most visitors see in four.

He found two rhino for me, still at quite a distance, but visible through my zoom lens. He found hippos wading, also not very near, but visible. He drove off the road so I could see a beautiful lion about twenty feet from us. He intentionally drove into a field in the path of an approaching herd of elephants, so that the herd had to split to walk around us. He pointed out and named various birds and clapped his hands so I could try to photograph their wings as they responded.

In the afternoon, a group of four Americans invited me to go with them in their van. Although we did finally see two cheetahs quite a distance away, the ride was anti-climactic. I decided not to try to arrange any more rides and just enjoy my quiet Easter Sunday resting in the camp, reading, thinking, and taking a swim in a pool on the campgrounds. It was a different Easter than all my others – in Africa, alone with no one to talk to, instead of being with family.

I crossed the Equator a number of times on this trip. One crossing was near the town of Timbaroa, at about sunset. We were high in the mountains at an elevation of over nine thousand feet, and it was very chilly. It was also a beautiful view looking down from mountains covered with fir trees, across potato fields, under lovely pink clouds.

Another crossing was at just before dawn in the town of Nanjuki, on our way to the Samburo game reserve. We huddled in the crowded vehicle, trying to stay warm, but not succeeding. I don't know the altitude, but I suspect it was about seven thousand feet. The town was on the slope of Mount Kenya, which is over seventeen thousand feet high. How strange that in Kenya, the coldest spots are at the Equator. The further away from the equator (whether north to the arid Savannah or south to the humid coast) the hotter it gets.

About two weeks of my month-long trip were spent in Nyeri, attending a training course for doctor/nurse teams. I left Amboseli on a Monday morning in a four-seat plane, having my last sight of Mount Kilimanjaro, Africa's highest peak, and was then driven from Nairobi to Nyeri in the afternoon, to arrive within sight of Mount Kenya, Africa's second highest peak.

During the two weeks of the course, I had a side trip to visit hospitals - all situated around Mount Kenya. It gave me an opportunity to see the snow-covered peaks from all sides as we drove entirely around the mountain in two and a half days.

*Accommodations in Nyeri.*

Chogoria Hospital was one site I visited. It had been started by the father of Dr. Jeoffrey Irvine, who was a man of great foresight. Jeoffrey, now about 60 years of age, followed in his father's foot-steps, expanding the hospital to become the hub of a community health outreach program.

The hospital now had about twenty-five dispensaries and clinics affiliated with it and over three hundred community outreach workers offering health services, including family planning. The Irvine family, originally from Scotland, became Kenyan citizens when Kenya became independent. In fact, Jeoffrey was born in Kenya. These two doctors, father and son, have really contributed to the country they called their own.

How different that was from another hospital I visited. When I was met by the administrator of the Nanyuki Cottage Hospital, I felt I had taken a step back in history. It was once the English settler's small hospital where care could be obtained if not serious enough to be transferred to a larger hospital. The administrator proudly showed me around, including a tour of the two-bed maternity suite, and the labor room, which contained a white-painted metal bed. She proudly declared that she had delivered her four children on that same bed. To make ends meet, they have begun a geriatric unit, caring for senile and weak old white "settlers" in the old style, including afternoon "tea and crumpets". The only sign that we were in Africa was the sight of three black nurses catering to the old white folk. I wondered how they would survive after the old folk die, and there would be no more pension money to support the hospital.

I received very little international news while I was in Kenya. Actually, in the four weeks, there were only three headline stories - none of which were concluded while I was still on my journey.

The first story dealt with Omweri, a python snake. Omweri was the "wife" of another python and the couple had played a very important role in the legends of western Kenya for the last fifty years. The snakes had been known to appear when important people died. They also were responsible for bringing on the rains. Shortly before I arrived, there had been a fire in western Kenya, and Omweri was severely burned. A specialist from the Nairobi snake park was called, and Omweri was picked up and admitted to the intensive care unit. The Luo tribe, who live in western Kenya, got very upset. They felt that the veterinarian should have treated the snake in "Luo-land" rather than in Nairobi. They started a civil lawsuit, selecting a lawyer to defend Omweri's rights. Another lawyer was appointed to protect the rights of the "husband" who had been denied her companionship while Omweri was hospitalized. By the time I left Kenya, the suit had not been settled; Omweri was on a normal diet, she had been taken off the critical list, and rains had begun to fall in Luo-land. Of course, the Kenya rainy season had also begun, so who was I to judge whether the snake was responsible.

The second big story had to do with the death of Mr. Otiende, a well-known criminal lawyer and a member of the Luo tribe. According to Luo customs, the place of a person's burial was determined at birth. All Luos are buried in their ancestral "home". But, according to Mrs. Otiende, her husband wished to be buried on the grounds of the home he had built in the Ngong Hills outside Nairobi. This caused the biggest battle ever fought for women's rights in Kenya. According to tradition, the wife's role was to weep and wail at the funeral while the male family members made all the arrangements.

Attached to this traditional practice is the fact that the Luo widow is later "looked after" by brothers-in-law. She could select one to be her provider - which would include his providing her with children if she was young enough. If she did not wish to stay with the family, she would have to leave without her children and without any goods, because they were all considered to be properties of the husband's clan. Once she had married, she would not be welcomed in her father's home either, so the choice would not be broad. A few women decide to leave their children - but this does not happen often. Mrs. Otiende, a respected pediatrician and non-Luo, was willing to challenge the traditional custom, and when I left, the court battle still had not been resolved. Meanwhile, Mr. Otiende's body had been re-embalmed for further preservation, having already lain in the mortuary over one hundred and forty days.

The third big story was that of a man and his lady friend who were surprised by muggers on a dark lonely road. The woman was not hurt, though she claimed they attempted to rape and strangle her, and that in that struggle, she had lost her panties. The man, however, had been fatally mutilated and his head badly smashed. Both their spouses were away at the time, and everyone believed the two had been having an affair and got caught in the grass. Every day, Kenyans would buy up the local papers that carried word-for-word reports of all the claims, details, and questioning of this court case. Sympathy was generally with the widow, a cardiologist, and with her children who were hearing very nasty things about their father. Regardless of what the court might eventually decide, the pair had already been judged guilty by everyone.

Although this was a long trip, it was a comfortable one. Hotel accommodations were good, and I met and worked with interesting people. These four weeks, in addition to the three weeks I spent there five months earlier, have given me the opportunity to visit most of the major areas of populated Kenya, excluding the coast and sparsely populated northern districts. I've seen Masai warriors, Samburo dancers, and lots of animals. I have the pleasure of knowing that the work I did was both needed and appreciated. I may have made a significant contribution to the safety of anesthesia practices in Kenya (only time will tell), and I've already been requested to return early in 1988.

# CHAPTER 21: COLOMBIA, MAY 24 – JUNE 5, 1987

In many ways, this trip was easier and more pleasant than most, in that I was traveling with staff members of our regional office, and I was able to meet with so many old friends. It was so much nicer than being alone or with people unknown to me.

On the other hand, I had become a bit spoiled, accustomed to traveling in Africa where English was spoken. Here, in South America, I once again had to become "tuned in" to Spanish. It was one thing to speak Spanish in a language class a few times a week, and another thing to hear nothing but Spanish - and have to speak nothing but Spanish. Off duty, at least, I had brief English conversations when I was with staff or friends.

One purpose of my visit was to participate in a vasectomy workshop for Latin America. Many of my former contacts, all doctors from South America and the Caribbean, were there. It was a pleasure to see them again. My second task was to make medical site visits to five cities where I was to teach both AVSC regional medical staff and consultants how AVS carried out medical assessment of programs. This would take me outside the city of Bogotá, to Medellin, Santa Marta, Barranquilla and Cartagena. Each city was different, and each was interesting.

Bogotá was huge. It was also at a high altitude and as a result, it was easy to get out of breath when climbing stairs or working hard. The weather was cool, and evenings required a wrap or warmer clothing. Medellin was in a valley north of Bogotá. It took only thirty minutes to fly there; but driving would have required a very difficult twelve hour trip. The other three cities were all on the Caribbean Sea, northeast of Panama. The weather there was much warmer - hot, in fact. The economic level was much lower, generally, and people seemed to have a very lazy *"manana"* style - so typical in hot climates. Of all, I enjoyed Medellin the best. The standard of living was high, the weather warm in the day and cool at night and the people more "European" or sophisticated than elsewhere. The level of medical care I observed was high, so my job was easier. The restaurants were great and our hosts were gracious.

Among the coastal cities, I found Cartagena to be the most interesting. It consisted of a group of islands, the oldest of which was the original walled city. Streets were narrow, and there were overhanging balconies in the old city. We took a horse and buggy ride one night from our hotel, through the old streets, to a fish restaurant near the harbor. It took two hours and felt like a trip back into history.

During this trip I thought a lot about how fortunate I was to have been able to travel as much as I have. Although I had always wanted to, I never thought I would ever get to see the things I have. I have visited the pyramids in both Egypt and Mexico, Roman ruins in Italy and Tunisia, Greek temples in Sicily as well as Greece, and ancient oriental temples in Korea, Thailand, and Indonesia. I've participated in a Buddhist funeral, visited Hindu shrines, and been in countless Catholic Cathedrals. I have seen the location of Columbus' arrival in the new world. I've enjoyed tropical colorful birds, wild animals, and climates of all kind. I've eaten strange foods including tiny birds in Nepal and crocodile, zebra, gazelle, and gnu in Africa. I've lived in elaborate hotels and in grass-covered huts. I've seen jails used during the Spanish inquisition, and seen the sites of so many historic events. I've known the excitement of having the first view of the Taj Mahal and struggled alone through the city of Bombay.

I have spent hours of solitude in hotels and planes and I have had other times when I wished for a minute to myself. I've struggled with many languages, cultures, dances and drinks. I've done the meringue in the Dominican Republic and a native dance in Kenya (both of which I would have rather watched instead). I've been to some museums, but most of what I've learned has been from the people directly. My assignments really do not include time for museums or galleries.

Throughout my travels, I have felt most in touch with my loved ones back home at night when I've been able to look at the stars and see the same moon they are able to see. It's as though the sky were a mirror, and by reflection, I could connect with them. During the day, I was in another world, with no common horizon, and that's when I felt most distant.

Some of my favorite memories include the flight along the Himalayan Mountains that seemed close enough to reach out to touch Mount Everest, listening to the wild animals while sleeping in a Kenyan animal reserve, waking up to find a hippo just outside my tent, traveling in the distant terai region of Nepal through hours of either dust or jungle, visiting a little known and hidden shrine of a reclining Buddha in a cave in central Sri Lanka on my first trip around the world. Then, when the plane is on its way to New York and home, I feel the eagerness, along with some anxiety, to learn about what had happened to my family while I was away.

While on an assignment, I have become quite aware that children in the developing world do not have toys. It became more obvious when I saw the first toy in Kenya a month before, after years of having seen none. A young boy was pulling a "car" made from a box that had packaged a tube of tooth paste, with four soda bottle caps for wheels. There had been no attempt to cover up the writing on the label, but it was clear that the boy did not see the "graffiti" as he proudly pulled his toy along the street.

My shopping for trinkets had decreased over recent years also, replaced by photos and notes. If I saw something that I knew would be of interest to a family member, I might indulge. I looked for small wall plaques for my growing collection or for a sample piece of locally woven cloth that I might use as a table cover. My age is given away by the fact that I still looked for charms for yet another charm bracelet.

Most rewarding was the fact that when I returned from a trip, I still felt I had done something new - often something that I was uniquely able to do for our organization - and that maybe services would be of a higher quality after my visit.

*View of Bogotá from my hotel window.*

# CHAPTER 22: VENEZUELA TO NIGERIA, OCT 3 – 28, 1987

This was a month of contrasts in spite of a few similarities. I went directly from an assignment in Venezuela to one in Nigeria. Both assignments involved a conference. Both involved working with friends and other AVS staff, so there were not the lonely hours I had gotten accustomed to on my overseas trips. Both included social evenings, a conference banquet, and receptions. Both were in warm climates. But that was where the similarity ended.

In Caracas for AVS' International Conference, we stayed at the Hilton, where everything was neat and clean. Everything worked as it was supposed to; the shower had hot water, and the bed was comfortably firm with soft pillows.

In Lagos, we stayed at a Hilton Hotel, too, but it was not a part of the international hotel chain - just a copy of the name. There were tissue holders, but no tissues; a small cake of soap, cold water with a hand-held nozzle for the tub, but no shower curtain. There was a total of sixty watts of light in the room - and that was up near the ceiling, making any reading or writing at night impractical. In all the cities I visited, Jos, Makurdi and Enugu, as well as Lagos, the rooms were similar, with lumpy bedding in a hard wooden box frame. Since most of my trips involved similar accommodations, I expected no better.

Another difference was that in Caracas new material about all methods of contraception was presented. I had an opportunity to update my own knowledge. In Jos, where the Nigerian Conference on Quality Assurance was held, I was a resource person, there to help upgrade others.

Caracas was a city with many tourists with many attractions related to shopping. Nigeria was not associated with tourism and there were very limited shopping opportunities. I was not tempted to seek out any shops in Caracas, while I did seek out traders in the market area of Jos, Nigeria. The local crafts and traditional arts of developing countries are much more attractive to me than bargain shopping in fancy boutiques. I was able to find another "Cross of Agadez" to add to my collection. I had learned that these silver-nickel pendants originated with the Tuaregs in Saharan Africa.

There were over twenty styles, each representing a major Tuareg city. Elder fathers would pass his crosses to his sons so they would always know the area of their origin. Like totems used in other cultures, being able to identify the heritage of a stranger could either help form a bond or prevent a person from unknowingly marrying a cousin. These crosses were not easy to find so I was always pleased to seek out a trader's stall.

Just before I left for Africa, I received newspaper clippings from AVS Nigeria representative, Dr. Ade Adetunji, describing problems with air travel at that time. One clipping blamed delayed air traffic on a fuel shortage. In Lagos, the largest city, there was no fuel at the national airport although there was some available for international travel. Domestic flights could have been temporarily moved to the international depot except that pilots were reluctant to do that because of the distance between the terminals. The newspaper said "that is why they don't have fuel". The result was massive chaos at the airports. Snack bars ran out of food and drinks, and passengers who were stranded got more hungry and thirsty as they got more tired.

Although the shortage of fuel was blamed in the newspaper article, I learned that a shortage of planes added to the problem. Nigeria had four or five airbuses for in-country travel. While I was in the county, three were out of action because of crashes and breakdowns.

Another article told about practices at the airport when a plane finally became available. The crew would ask for a show of hands for those desiring to go to each city; the plane would be sent off to the most popular destination.

One problem I encountered was with a flight scheduled for a late morning departure. By evening, we passengers were still in a row on the tarmac with our luggage. An engineer told us "It's a tire we are preparing to change. I'm not sure if it will go today". So much for spare parts.

As a result, when I was planning my return home from Nigeria, I chose to hire a car and driver to take me on a seven hour, hot drive from Enugu to Lagos rather than to risk a one-hour flight fiasco. It was not the first time, nor would it be the last time I had to risk putting myself in a stranger's vehicle for hours or for days. As it turned out, it was a safe and uneventful drive, even picking up a hitch-hiking soldier along the way. I arrived in Lagos about mid-afternoon and relaxed at the air-conditioned Sheraton Hotel Lounge until time to go to the airport for a midnight departure.

Once on board the Alitalia flight to Rome, I stripped down and washed up in the tiny bathroom on the plane, donned a complete set of clean clothes, and settled in for a 40 hour trip back to the USA.

# CHAPTER 23: NEPAL ONCE MORE, MARCH 1988

This was my third trip to the little Kingdom of Nepal, and because my itinerary was taking me over familiar ground, I did not plan to take any notes. However, after being home for a week, I realized there were some thoughts and impressions I wanted to remember.

My favorite memory of Nepal is the playfulness of the children. The Nepalese people allowed their children to play - even encouraged it. I've often been saddened by seeing little, drab, three-year-old girls in Central America, scrubbing pots at the side of the road, or carrying water jugs or bundles on their heads in Africa. In Nepal, there were happy children playing everywhere. Their joy was obvious. They jumped rope, played with stone "marbles", wrestled, ran around, played soccer or threw balls, and pulled boxes on ropes.

Maybe the Nepalese culture, with its countless festival days and holiday-making is tied to the fun-loving, happy childhood there. Whatever the cause, it was refreshing. Even the six-year-old boy learning to string beads alongside his father and grandfather in the narrow dark stalls of the bead bazaar was allowed to take breaks, play a bit, and come back to work without being called.

Another thought that kept occurring to me is how fortunate I've been to see so many architectural sites before the renovations were begun. While in Nepal, I learned that parts of India's Taj Mahal were now in scaffolding, the preservation work having begun. Also, I read that the Nepalese government was beginning to be concerned about the old, beautifully carved wooden balconies, windows, and doors in the Kathmandu valley. Plans for reconstruction or supportive work are underway.

If I am fortunate enough to return to Nepal, I would not be surprised if renovations had begun, and the Temple Squares of Kathmandu, Patan, and Bhaktapur were full of bamboo scaffolds and workmen. I'm delighted that these structures will be saved, but so grateful that I saw them in their original form.

I've seen Rome before renovation. I've seen the wall of martyrs in Geneva before, then during repair. I've seen the mosaics of Carthage in their natural environment, some of which have now been taken up for display in the New York Museum of Natural History. I saw the treasures of

King Tut in Cairo's museum long before some of them were on the U.S. museum tour in more unnatural (though better lighted) show cases. I've been able to climb on pyramids in Mexico and Egypt, and see the Sphinx, which will probably soon be covered in scaffolds.

The final thought I want to remember is about art. I've always felt that people have an inner need for beauty and artistic expression. This inner need is even more obvious in poor countries and in primitive cultures where there is no chance for formal study of art, no art galleries, no time or money for non-essentials. The fact that art is essential is shown in many ways. Certainly, the wood craftsmen in Kathmandu expressed it openly.

But even in the rural areas, people tried to add richness to their lives by decorating their possessions, satisfying their need for beauty. The poor rural women, who had no other clothes to wear except one six-foot length of fabric to wrap as a sari, and who lacked material, patterns, thread or scissors to construct a blouse to wear with it, have their upper arms tattooed to take the place of the garment.

I noticed this craving for beauty in the hilly sections of Nepal where the houses had painted borders around windows and doors. I noticed that in the hot terai districts, where the homes were constructed with cow dung, the exterior walls were embellished with painted designs. I also noticed crude or primitive paintings of animals or flowers on the homes in rural villages.

*Decorated rural homes.*

In the Indian sub-continent, the need for art and beauty is also expressed in bangles, beads, metallic threads in shawls, silk saris, color-splashed animals, shrines smeared with blaring vermillion powder, gods glittering in silver and gold foil. Pottery, masks, religious articles, and the Thanka paintings are further evidence.

Except for a few crafts (carpet weaving, Thanka painting, wood carving and metal work or pottery), I don't believe there was any formal art education. These craftsmen were motivated by the commercial nature of their work. People in these countries were totally occupied with economic survival and provision of basic human needs. My hope was that as they progress in development, people will have more opportunities to express artistic creativeness in more ways and that they begin to support artists and galleries. Meanwhile, the traveler will find art everywhere if he or she has an eye for it.

*Hindu holy man.*

# CHAPTER 24: TURKEY, ATHENS, TUNISIA, OSTIA ANTICA, 1988

Unlike my usual notes, these were being started at the JFK airport on my way to my next assignment. As I sat in the Clipper Club at the Pan Am terminal, I was having my first free moments to think about my last trip, which ended only five days earlier. Actually, these two hours of pre-boarding time have been the only hours I've had to just sit and reflect.

Before the departure for Turkey, I had three days of headaches. Coincidentally, I was going through a series of tests and examinations at Cornell/NY Presbyterian Hospital's Cardio-Hypertension Center. Their assessment of the headaches was that they were unrelated to heart or blood pressure. When asked if I was under stress, I said, "No". Later, I thought about that question and had to admit I was under a great deal of stress. My thirty-two year old son was suffering the last stages of his HIV/AIDS disease, and that was a constant source of concern. I remembered the recent pattern of the headache's disappearance before my departure for an overseas assignment, and the onset of intestinal problems as soon as I returned to the USA. These symptoms had continued until today, when I'm again leaving. Maybe there is less stress working overseas, where I get totally engrossed in a single job.

Upon reflection, the Turkey-Tunisia assignment was one of the most varied trips I've made, and it involved many historic places. On the route from Turkey to Tunisia, the schedule permitted a layover in Athens. Arrival in Tunisia preceded my work assignment by two days, and that permitted a mini-vacation in Hammamet, on the Mediterranean coast of Tunisia. The return flight permitted a layover in Rome, which enabled a side trip to Ostia Antica.

**TURKEY:** I must confess that I had not understood the significance of Turkey in New Testament history until preparing for this assignment to look at the medical quality of services recently legalized in this country. When I was taught about Paul of Tarsus, I had no awareness that Tarsus was in Turkey. I had not known that the capital of Turkey, Ankara, was once called Galatia, and the county's people addressed in Paul's Epistle to the Galatians were citizens of present day Ankara. So I was increasingly excited by the idea of making a trip "in the steps of Paul".

Upon arrival in Ankara, via Istanbul, I immediately made arrangements for a driver and a guide to take me to the Goreme Valley. This was such an exciting piece of land. It included underground cities where Christians hid during the Roman persecutions in the early years of the current era. It included many cave cities that had churches where the early Christians (including Paul) worshipped, notably the cave churches in the area near Zelme.

*Cave churches.*

*Cave dwellings.*

The largest underground city was eight floors deep, with a church on the seventh level. What impressed me was the architectural ability of the builders. The many rooms on every level were ventilated by four air shafts dug to a depth where water was available, so the air shafts also provided water. Thinking of how these rooms had to be dug out and the rubble brought up and away, it made me wonder how the plan was ever devised, how many people were employed, and how long it must have taken.

The corridors were low and narrow, and had two safety features. There were traps in the floor through which unknowing Romans would likely fall, and disc-like stones that could be rolled into the corridor to prevent further advancement by pursuers. When not in use, these stones were stored by rolling them into a slot on the side wall.

The above ground caves were used for housing until about 1957, when the government felt that too many rock faces had collapsed, and living in the caves had become too dangerous. Most of the people moved to small houses in new villages that sprang up in the area. Reluctant to give up their caves, most were sealed up, leaving small openings for pigeons to get in and out, and one opening large enough for the owner to get in to remove the pigeon droppings to be taken to a garden for fertilizer.

The city of Ankara had some historic locations, including Roman baths that have been excavated, a citadel high on a hill, and an ancient mosque, mostly underground except for the domes. But most of the city seems to be a memorial to Ataturk, the leader in Turkey's struggle for independence.

Istanbul was an architectural treat, but so different from the Goreme Valley. The huge domes of the Hagia Sophia and the Blue Mosque were an incredible sight. The perfect proportions and relationships between the major domes, the smaller domes and half domes gave me a very peaceful feeling - a feeling similar to that experienced when I saw the perfect symmetry of the Taj Mahal.

How fortunate I was to have been able to stay in a renovated block of old homes between the Hagia Sophia and the Topkapi Palace. It really added to the historic significance of Istanbul to walk down the cobblestone street, eat dinner in what was once a cistern that supplied the water to the area, and to look out of the bedroom window at the minaret of the Hagia Sophia just across the street.

The delicious food, economical prices, the bright, energetic, enthusiastic people I worked with, a country full of history, all made the week in Turkey one I'll not forget.

**ATHENS:** To me, the significance of Athens was the Parthenon or the Acropolis - not the city of Athens itself. This trip allowed me to fulfill my desire to climb the Acropolis and wander among the various temples around the Parthenon. Staying in a small hotel at the bottom of the hill made it possible to do this without having to encounter modern Athens.

My first interest in the buildings on the Acropolis dates back to a brief stop-over visit I made to the British Museum on the way home from Tunisia and Egypt about ten year earlier. In the British Museum, I had seen the Elgin Marbles, figures and bar reliefs taken from the Acropolis by Lord Elgin. I was so impressed by the feeling of lightness of the marbles statues, as if they could float into the air, that I decided I really had to see more in their original location.

The Caryatids, the female figures serving as the columns of one of the temples, are all indoors now for preservation. There are copies outside instead. Besides the one in the British Museum, there are five in the museum on the Acropolis. Once again, I got the sense of lightness created by the sculptors in spite of the heavy marble.

Seeing the Parthenon was not as exciting as I had expected - probably for two reasons. I had seen an exact replica of the original building (before any destruction) in Nashville, Tennessee, and was disappointed in the amount of "incompletion" of the Parthenon due to crumbling and deterioration. There really was not enough left of the pediments to give a viewer a real sense of what it once was. Similarly, the interior walls have fallen, and there was nothing left to indicate where the great statue of Diana once stood. The second reason was that I had, by now, seen so many Greek temples in Sicily, especially the temple at Segesta, which were in much better condition. Never-the-less, I was satisfied that I finally saw the

Acropolis, and that there was still something left that air pollution had not totally destroyed.

**TUNISIA:** Having gone to Tunisia in one of my earliest trips abroad, this segment of the trip was not one of the highlights for me. The treat was really to have enough time before my scheduled meeting to go to a Mediterranean hotel in Hammamet. Staff from our Tunisia regional office left instructions about how to get to Hammamet by public bus. So although I arrived late in the day from Athens, I was up early and off to the bus station. Traveling by local transport is not always the most comfortable but it is always interesting. Difficulty is worse when it's a new experience and you don't know how long the trip will be, what you'll have to arrange when you reach the city, how to get to your hotel, and when buying tickets at the bus station requires knowledge of French or Arabic.

In brief, I enjoyed the mini-trip, enjoying a day and a half in a lovely atmosphere on the sea, complete with topless sunbathing, before I had to return to Tunis and report for work at our North Africa/Middle-East Regional Office.

**OSTIA ANTICA:** Some years ago, I had read a book, the title of which I regret I forgot. It described Ostia Antica as an excavated city where some treasure or message had been hidden among the ruins, and which the heroine finally found. It stimulated my interest, but in past trips to Rome, my time had been fully occupied seeing the traditional sights of that great city.

This time, when I realized that there would be a half day free on an overnight stay in Rome on the way home, I was determined that it was time for me to go to Ostia Antica. Remembering that the heroine took a metro train from Rome, I got directions from the metro station master at the Coliseum station. It only required one change at Pyramides, to get the train to the Lido, getting off at Ostia Antica. From there, it was a brief walk to the excavations.

Unlike Pompeii, which was only a summer resort for wealthy Romans, Ostia Antica was a flourishing city on the river, making it a major center for traders and craftsmen in the century or two before Christ. By the year two thousand, it had reached its peak and in subsequent years, as trade shifted, the city became less important. As time passed, and the buildings were unoccupied, builders took bricks, marble columns and decorative statues for use elsewhere.

Eventually, Italy decided to stop the pilferage, but only after Julian II took a great deal of material to construct a castle near by. In the early 20th century, excavations and repairs began, and these efforts continued actively until about 1936. Since then, it has been maintained, but has not become a major attraction as well known as Pompeii. Once again, I had the thrill of getting to a historic spot before hundreds of other tourists. During the entire afternoon at Ostia Antica, only a dozen or so others were there. It was so much better than the crowds to be contended with when a museum decides to borrow parts of a building, such as the mosaic floors, to put on display in major cities throughout the world.

Walking on the streets of this very old city, excavated down to floors and streets of the second century, I had much the same feeling that I had when I first walked in the Roman Forum. The only differences were that I did not have the sense of sharing the cobblestones with well-known persons, such as Julius Caesar, as I did in Rome. But I had a sense of sharing a life style of the middle class citizens of long ago.

*Ruins of Ostia Antica.*

The theater was pretty much intact, with its semi-circular rows of seats carved into a natural "bowl" at the stage; but extending upward quite high by man-made elevations of the structure. Among all the buildings, this was in the best condition. While I was there, workmen were setting up lights so the stage could be used for summer productions.

The Forum in Ostia Antica had clear evidence of the magnificence of the Assembly Hall at one end, and of what must have been a beautiful street of important buildings for the religious and political life of the time. Some of the homes and all of the public bath houses had wonderfully preserved mosaic floors - still in excellent condition considering the fact that they had been out in the open, free for people to not only look at but to walk upon for 1700 years.

Most impressive were the Baths of the Athletes. This section was the furthest from the entrance; and I suspect most visitors never walk to the end of this large city. There, the mosaics were in the best condition. They were black and white illustrations of men in athletic poses - so life-like and clear. I couldn't help but wonder if future generations would be impressed if they excavated a Jack LaLanne gymnasium.

*Mosaic floors.*

As I think back on the entire experience, I believe that what impressed me most about Ostia Antica were the "modern" features I found there. For example, some of the buildings were apartment houses - which I hadn't realized had existed at that time. Another surprise was the public toilet room built with twenty seats in a large room off the main street. What most amazed me about the toilet room was not the sewer system so much as the revolving doors that were there to provide the users some privacy as people entered from the street.

*Public toilets.*

So much for this very "historic" trip. Now, I was off to "modern" Kenya, where there would be no theaters, no revolving doors and no topless sunbathing.

# CHAPTER 25: KENYA CINEMATOGRAPHY, JULY 1 – 15, 1988

The interesting part of this trip was not the places I went to, or the people I met, or the cultures I encountered, because I had been to this country a few times before. Most of the people I met on this trip I already knew, and I was already familiar with the cultures and life styles of the Kenyan people. My assignment was the new challenge. I was to oversee the production of surgical training films. As the Deputy Director of the Medical Division of AVS, I was the person selected to supervise all the medical and surgical components of the films. It was critical that a film to be used to train new providers of service had to be without flaws.

One technique used in the instructional films was mini-laparotomy surgery done within hours of a delivery, in the immediate post-partum period. The incision for that procedure was just under the rim of the new mother's umbilicus. The other procedure was called an "interval sterilization, which is in the interval time not associated with a recent birth. That incision was at we called "the bikini line", low on the abdomen. The films would be used to train both surgeons and operating room nurses. They would also include a section to help train new staff in counseling techniques.

*Cinematography.*

This really was an exercise in team work. There was a film crew of four men - the cinematographer, the lighting man, the sound man, and the general helper. The production crew consisted of three women - the film contractor, the editor, and I. In addition, we worked with four operating surgeons, many, many nurses and counselors, and a few consultants who were to be interviewed on specific topics.

In previous visits to Kenya, I had the pleasure of working with a doctor who had excellent surgical skills and operated regularly. He was extremely gentle, and seemed to have magic fingers that could identify the tubes and ligate them with no discomfort for the woman who was wide awake during the surgery.

AVS had an office and staff in Nairobi for the East African programs it supported. The medical staff doctor was to take a leading role in the film's production. Unfortunately, that doctor spent most of his time overseeing program issues and not doing any surgery. With the help of the film editor, we were able to feature the staff person in the distant or broad scenes, but when the film showed the surgical details, the gloved fingers of the surgeon were those of the expert.

While the rest of the crew was working with the counselors on non-medical matters, I had one night free so I spent it in "The Ark", which is a shelter in the midst of an animal reserve. On earlier trips, I had gone on game drives, but had not had an opportunity to watch animals for extended periods of time. The driver and other passengers were always ready to move on after a brief stop, in search of another variety of animals.

The Ark was built at a natural "salt lick", a watering area with salty dirt. All night long, I was able to watch the animals come to the water's edge. I observed the nocturnal animals that are not out in the day. I did not get to see a rhino or a bongo, as I had hoped I would, but I did see a genet cat, a white tailed mongoose, and a giant forest hog. These were all new to me. In addition, I saw the usual variety of deer-like animals, elephants, and others.

I'm looking forward to coming back to Kenya in three weeks for my next assignment.

# CHAPTER 26: PERU, ECUADOR, COLOMBIA, FEB 21 – MAR 12, 1989

Planning itineraries for trips to some parts of the world is an exercise that can, at best, produce drafts. The day before my departure, I thought I had a final plan. It would have me visit Peru first in the hope that a doctor's strike in Ecuador would end before I would go to that country. My final stop would be Colombia. Upon arrival in Lima, I learned that all the in-county travel had been rearranged, there was no indication that the strike in Ecuador would end, and the US Embassy in Washington had not yet cleared me for Colombia.

My first appointment was to go with my traveling companion, Dr. Alcides Estrada, to the AID office at the Embassy in Lima for our security briefing. We learned about recent activities of the Peruvian terrorists. In brief, there were two leftist groups. One was called "Shining Path" and was led by students of Mao. The other was the "Revolutionary Movement", with heavy USSR and Cuban influence. Shining Path had been opposing capitalism, and their activities involved attacks on industry, technology and capitalistic ventures such as hotels and restaurants. I had a taste of their activity the night I arrived; they bombed an electrical power tower, causing a city-wide black-out. The Revolutionary Movement was involved in drug traffic, so they were attacking their opponents, primarily the government of Peru and US organizations, including the US Embassy.

A third terrorist group represented the political far right. They were attacking anyone that was not in support of the government of Peru. That meant that they attacked both the Shining Path and the Revolutionary Movement. Consequently, we were given a long list of places that were off limits. We were instructed about how we were to act, and given stern warnings about avoiding crime in the streets, an increasing problem because of drugs and the poor economy. With all this, the officer welcomed us to Peru!

When we left the USAID office, we proceeded to the local family planning organization, where we spent the remainder of the day observing services. The next day, we made a day trip to Chiclayo, in the north, to see surgical services there. Fifteen women had been scheduled for tubal ligations, but only seven were done while we were there. Electricity suddenly was lost in the area. The last two operations we observed were done by flashlight. The doctors told the waiting women that they could stay and wait for the electricity, because they themselves were willing to begin to operate even if it were late that night. Nice attitude.

The third day called for an early flight to Cusco. As the day before, this meant getting up well before dawn. We flew southeast from Lima and saw snow-covered mountains peeking through the heavy cloud cover. We were met by Carol Plaza, who took us to our hotel and ordered *mate de coca* for us. Mate is a cocaine tea that helps with altitude adjustment. She insisted we rest until noon, when she and her husband would take us for a light lunch and a tour of his partially constructed small hospital. We followed her advice, had more mate with soup for lunch, and spent a quiet evening in the hotel. The treatment apparently worked well.

The Plaza family, Reinhard and Carol, had been in Cusco about five years, and their dedication to providing health care to the poor people of the area was a joy to see. We had the pleasure of observing two procedures of female sterilization done with only local anesthesia and a preoperative dose of Valium. His skill and manner with the women were excellent, and truly showed they cared about their clients. It will be a pleasure to be able to assist them and help their work.

Cusco is the nearest city to the archeological site of Machu Picchu, atop a nearby mountain. To reach it, we would have to go down from the very high Cusco, through the Valley of the Incas, and then up another mountain. We planned to do this while we were in the area, by a combination of bus and train transportation.

In addition to the thrill of finally seeing this mysterious place high in the Andes, three things have remained in my memory. First, as the train was on the approach to Machu Picchu and about to cross over a little bridge, we were startled by the sound of a loud "fire-cracker". We were sure it was a bomb. It turned out to have been a warning signal set by an advance two-man car riding the tracks. They had discovered some damage to the track. Apparently, farmers on strike (or possibly the Revolutionary Movement) had attempted to derail the train. The conductor was able to get the train over the bridge with very slow progress. The track was repaired before we returned in the afternoon.

The second memorable moment, similar to the first, was during the bus portion of the ride back to Cusco. The road had been strewn with rocks for many miles - again to delay transportation. At times it was necessary for drivers to clear a path in order to progress. At one point, I saw men and boys gathering cobble-stones from a field, and loading them into a pick-up truck, apparently getting ready to dump another load on the road.

The third memory is of the most spectacular rainbows I have ever seen.

The first was while we were returning to Cusco on the bus, after a brief rain shower. It shone vividly in an entire bow from horizon to horizon in the brightest colors imaginable. A few days later, we observed a rainbow of another sort, while at Quito in Ecuador. There, about mid-day, while sun-bathing at the hotel pool, we looked up to see a complete circle of a rainbow around the sun that was somewhat covered by clouds. I hadn't known such a sight was possible.

We seem to have closely avoided a number of events that could have been quite dangerous. Every night while in Lima, there had been bombings near us. Days later, as we flew to Quito, Ecuador, we barely missed an earthquake that occurred just south of that city. Just after our departure from Quito in a heavy rain, there was a tornado in that city. Dengue fever and a contaminated water supply forced us to avoid raw salads, to use mosquito repellent and drink only bottled water in Guayaquil.

A friend of Alcides was the victim of a shooting Bogota, Colombia. Alcides held hopes that this man might someday become the President of Colombia - if he survived his three bullet wounds. A strike at Eastern Airlines threatened to prevent my leaving Colombia.

Two previous concerns, however, were resolved. The doctors' strike in Ecuador was terminated just before we were due to go there, and I was approved for my trip to Colombia - unless the activities surrounding the funerals of Bogota's victims caused more concern to the US Embassy.

Once in Ecuador, a side trip to Machala, south of Guayaquil, turned out to be quite an adventure. We left at noon, having spent the morning in surgery. It should have been a two and a half-hour trip but it took an extra forty-five minutes to make an eighteen-mile detour because a bridge had been washed away. The detour took us over bad roads, mostly through banana fields and through one very poor village probably inhabited by banana workers. Machala boasted that it was the banana capital of the world.

We were able to visit a family planning clinic and visit another site where I could observe sterilizations being done. We were able to complete our business, and leave again by about six o'clock that afternoon. As we approached the detour, we realized that the traffic was going to be a lot worse than on our way to the city. To make matters worse, we experienced a heavy down-pour. In no time at all, vehicles were getting bogged down, sliding around, and tipping over. We would advance a few feet and have to wait twenty minutes before we could proceed.

One vehicle at a time had to be helped out of its jam. The local men and boys saw it as a social event as well as a way to earn a few *sucres*, the local currency. They would jockey vehicles around, directing traffic so that jams could be broken up. They shoveled dirt so pools of water could flow from the road. They pushed vehicles that were stuck, and generally tried to be helpful. If this had happened in Peru, we would have had the extra fear of thieves, but this rural part of Ecuador did not pose that additional problem. It took about four hours to get through the difficult area that was probably only about six miles in length. The rest of the way was bad, but manageable, in spite of water-flooded roads, pot-holes camouflaged by the water, and continued rain. We got back about midnight.

One of the problems with traveling to so many places - especially when they are almost all in the Equatorial zones - is that I have reminders of scenes and cannot remember where they were. On the trip to Machala, I saw many houses on stilts, with little bridges from the road to the door. I remembered having lunch at such a place in another country where the scenery, wetlands, and poverty were much the same. It haunted me, but I could not remember where it had been. Then I remembered that the lady in back of the eating area was making tortillas, so it must have been in Honduras or Guatemala. I remembered driving through a banana plantation before, too, and we stopped at a historical spot where there were monoliths - memories of an ancient people who lived there. Where was it?

The greatest visual thrill on this trip was on one of the flights between Guayaquil and Quito in Ecuador. We flew, in perfect weather, over desert and then mountainous areas. The colors of the mountains were crying to be reproduced on canvas. Some hills varied in shades of ochre; some were purple; some seemed to have been sprinkled with green powder, and the shadows were deep blue. One snow-capped mountain peeked above a few clouds.

As we were approaching Quito, the pilot announced he was going to show us Cotopaxi, an extinct volcano, the second highest in Ecuador. His announcement was no preparation for what happened next. Suddenly, I looked out my window and we were flying next to snow! The plane slowly descended with its wing tip almost in the snow of the volcano. Continuing to circle entirely around the mountain, the plane gradually rose higher so we could look down into the crater. After a turn and a half, we straightened out and headed for the Quito airport. The passengers applauded in appreciation. My regret was that both my cameras were in my checked baggage. Although we flew over the same area two more times, with my cameras in hand, the pilots did not treat us to that thrill again.

In both Peru and Ecuador, there were many indigenous people seen in the cities, selling hand crafted articles, knitted sweaters, old beads or ancient shawl buckles. Others were simply asking for contributions. As in so much of the world, the children are brought into this "industry". Tiny children appeared to be alone, begging, but actually their mothers were around keeping an eye on them. One little boy, not yet three, I'm sure, had a box of Chiclets in his hand, which he rattled as he said "Please buy Chiclets". When I didn't, he begged "Please, buy my Chiclets or my mother will beat me". I thought it unlikely, but an effective approach. He spoke only Spanish, so his pleas were perhaps not understood by the tourists most likely to respond. Later, I learned that, indeed, some mothers sometimes did beat the children if they failed to bring in money. Childhood is no fun in these poor countries.

On the eve of my departure from Bogota to NY, I reflected that this trip was different from most in that there were many very pleasant meals shared with the local people. Much of this was because of Alcides and his long friendship with the people we were working with. But another factor, I think, was that the cities we visited were urban, and had good restaurants. Of course, there was also the fact that the people in this part of the world are gracious and cordial.

In Lima, we had dinner at a Chifa-(Chinese)-Peruvian restaurant with Dr. Cesar Guzman. We had lunch with Dr. Miguel Ramos and some of his associates. We had wonderful *escobiche* (marinated raw fish and seafood) in a side-walk cafe called Puerto Viejo. Another night we had a lovely evening with Dr. and Mrs. Alfredo Larranago, eating in the Rosa Nautica Restaurant on the beach. In Cusco, we had lunch in a typical Peruvian restaurant just outside the city. That night we took our hosts, Dr. and Mrs. Plaza, to a rather classy restaurant just off the central plaza. After dinner, we strolled through the old part of the city to see the old Incan walls upon which newer buildings rest.

While in Ecuador, Alcides and I ate in the formal restaurant in Quito hotel where we were staying; and got "white glove" treatment. Then in Guayaquil, we were invited to the home of Dr. and Mrs. Luis Torres for a home-cooked gourmet dinner prepared by Mrs. Torres herself. In Bogota, Alcides took me and Fernando Gomez (our Regional Office's Director) and his wife and daughter to a well-known restaurant in the northern residential part of the city. The next day Fernando took Alcides and me to a restaurant, Casa Viejo, in downtown Bogota. The atmosphere in the "old house" and the traditional food served was a great send-off.

Thinking about these past three weeks, I am especially pleased that I was able to get along in Spanish as well as I did. It had been over three years since I dropped out of my language studies at the United Nations. That was due to my heavy travel schedule to places in Asia and Africa, where my developing Spanish skills could not be used. I was surprised that I remembered as much as I did. I also regret that I hadn't brushed up on some grammar rules before the trip. As I concluded the journey, I promised myself to continue Spanish study in the hope of more fluency before my next assignment.

# CHAPTER 27: PARIS TO MALI, AUGUST, 1989

**PARIS:** I had anticipated my brief stopover in Paris so eagerly, but upon reflection, it was not much of a highlight in my life. I was on my way to West Africa, where I expected the usual travel complications, but I thought Paris would be problem-free. Looking back, I had as much need to shift plans and manage strange situations there as I did in the underdeveloped countries.

I arrived at the Paris airport in a cluttered mass of people who were all trying to get through the one-person counter for passport control. Hot and tired, I got to my hotel room, rented for the day only, realizing that I had very little time left to see something of the grand city.

I asked for directions in English, not knowing any French. I was directed to a train stop, where the ticket agent advised I go to the *Gare de Nord* (North Station). I had to wait almost an hour for the next train, only to find, when I arrived at North Station, I saw nothing I recognized from Paris post cards.

I was next directed to the Metro and told to get off at the Louvre. I then walked quickly about a mile to the address of the tour company I was looking for, only to find that the last city tour bus had left at three o'clock, while I was buying my train ticket. Trying to be philosophical, I bought a metro map and studied it while enjoying a refreshing beer in one of the typical Parisian sidewalk cafes.

I decided to take the metro to the Arch de Triumph. I walked around it briefly while locating the bus stop that I needed to get back to the airport hotel. The bus gave me just enough time for a quick shower, change of clothes, and repacking a bit for my next overnight flight to Bamako. More of Paris will have to wait.

**MALI:** I read the book, *"Segu"* in preparation for my trip to Mali. It described life in this important Malian empire about one hundred twenty-five years before, when the Arabs from the north and the slave traders from the west were encroaching upon West Africa. Segu was the center of much of that activity, so I was especially pleased to find that my in-country travel would include a trip to that city. I enjoyed the opportunity to see the ancient red, soft-looking buildings made from some mixture of soil, clay, and straw. They looked as if I could leave a hand-print if I pushed against

260

the wall. I felt as much a part of ancient history as I've felt at the pyramids. I was glad I read the book.

Bamako, the capital of Mali, was where I was based for most of the first week. The purpose of my trip was to work with a local female surgeon, to train her to serve as a consultant for AVS. As a medical consultant, she would need to conduct site visits to assure quality of services. Training such potential medical consultants had become a fairly routine part of my international responsibility.

Dr. John Githiari, our Medical Officer based in the regional office in Nairobi, would be joining us on the field trips. We would be visiting various sites in Mali, conducting such evaluations, making recommendations, providing feedback to the local staff, and doing some on-site training, if it was found necessary. It was also an opportunity to show John what the AVS Medical Director expected of trainers, such as I had been, and what John might be called upon to do.

Because I arrived in Mali in the late morning, I had the rest of the afternoon to get adjusted to the local time zone before starting work the next morning. I wanted to visit the Bamako market - one of the largest in West Africa. I had met a Belgian man coming in from the airport who was also a new arrival in Bamako, so we decided to go to town together. It was definitely to my advantage because he spoke French, the local language.

The most interesting section of the market was the street where there were sellers of articles needed by the traditional healers. When a sick person went to the healer, he or she was told what ingredients to buy, and to bring them back to the healer who would make the appropriate medicine. I had seen many traditional healing "drug stores" in other countries, but this was the first time I encountered piles of monkey heads, with mouths open and teeth showing, seemingly laughing at me.

*Medicine market.*

"Hands" and "feet" of large apes were lying in rows. Heads of birds, chickens, ducks, and larger animals, perhaps goats, sheep, dogs, or small deer were in near-by piles. There were various hides and pieces of fur. Stacks of bones were quite well organized as in a modern pharmacy, with ribs on one pile, femurs on another, and fore-leg bones in yet another. I was especially curious about a pile of furry little sacks. I was told they contained testicles, but from what animal, I'll never know.

I had been prepared for a hot, dry, dusty environment. Much to my surprise, the rainy season had begun a bit ahead of schedule and the weather was quite pleasant. What I had thought would be entirely brown landscape, was in fact a blossoming, blooming green. I did not need the extra blouses I had packed for mid-day changes. The food was delicious - delicate sauces, well-seasoned fresh vegetables, wonderful French fries - all, I suspect, part of their French heritage.

The people were friendly. I felt safe in the country - even in the market place, which was overcrowded with people. As I looked around the hordes of people, I could not spot a single Caucasian anywhere.

While spending some after-hours time with my Kenyan colleague, John Githiari, I brought up the subject of the War for Independence in Kenya in the 50s. I had heard of it as the Mau Mau Uprising, but that was not a term used by black Kenyans. I was eager to hear the story from someone who had experienced it.

John told me his version of the struggle as seen from the eyes of a Kikuyu tribe boy. John had spent his early childhood years in a concentration camp, guarded by what he says were members of the Kalinjin tribe who were serving the British as "home-guards". John told me of having his father taken away first, and it would be many years until they were reunited. Next, his mother was taken from the camp because healthy women were used to dig holes, makes roads, and do other menial chores. That left John with his two small sisters. The older one managed to escape.

John, then about ten years old, was left to care for the younger one, about three years old. John prepared a hole under a section of the barbed-wire fence, camouflaging it with branches and leaves. One day, his mother came to the fence to visit. John had the little girl with him. He had hopes of helping the little girl escape, but there were guards watching the area while walking back and forth. On the first few rounds there was no opportunity in spite of the fact that John had a few other people with him to help the "cover-up". When the guard's back was finally turned, John pushed his sister under the fence. When the guard turned back, the girl was on her mother's lap. The guard did not notice the change. After a few more rounds of the guard, mother and daughter just walked away.

In the concentration camp, the prisoners were fed rice and gruel once a day. Everybody was hungry all the time. At one point, three days went by with no food. Then, the guards had one of the boys make tea, and by mistake, the ten or twelve-year-old boy put salt instead of sugar in the tea. The guard who tasted the tea shot the boy dead. The guards offered the tea to the people in the camp; after the three days of starvation and thirst, they were desperate enough to drink it. John still carried strong feelings against the Kalinjin tribe, of whom the President, Daniel Arap Moi, was a member.

I would have welcomed another trip to Mali, even in the hot dry season, but it never happened.

# CHAPTER 28: ETHIOPIA TO TANZANIA, AUG – SEPT, 1989

The site visit to Mali had just ended. I was to go from that country in West Africa to Kenya in East Africa. There, I would report my findings to the AVS regional office director and then proceed to Tanzania for a medical assessment visit. Following the Tanzania assignment, I would again return to the regional office before returning home.

The trip to Tanzania from Mali took a couple days. The first leg of the trip was an overnight flight to from Bamako to Addis Ababa in Ethiopia. The flight was on a plane owned by a Sudanese man, and the crew had been hired by him. He was on the flight, keeping an eye on his investment, even though he had leased the plane to Ethiopian Airlines.

The plane was certainly not up to standard. By the time we reached our first stop in Niamey, the capital of Niger, the plane had not one, but two flat tires and only one spare. They finally changed one tire, and after a couple of hours, managed to borrow another. But the borrowed tire was not full size, so the owner said the plane could only make one landing. That was good news - that meant we would not make a stop in Chad, but could fly directly to Addis Ababa.

Dr. John Githiari, the Medical Officer for AVS' East African office, had joined me for the work in Mali, and we were now proceeding to Kenya together. Because we had missed our connecting flight from Addis Ababa to Nairobi, Kenya, the airline put us up at the Ethiopian Hilton Hotel. It was an unexpected taste of luxury and a cheap treat.

I had always thought that the name Addis Ababa sounded exotic, so was pleased to have a day to enjoy the city. John and I decided to explore the market, reputed to be the biggest indoor market in Africa. It was expansive, to say the least. There were many buildings, each a small block square, and each containing rows of small shops. I decided against buying a gauzy white traditional dress, not quite seeing myself in a style like that, but did enjoy watching boys sitting outside the shops doing the needlework on them.

Returning to the Hilton was an adventure that required three taxis. Fortunately, we had gotten instructions earlier. Unlike the hotel taxis, which could be hired to go anywhere, the street taxis are limited to specific zones.

It was fun climbing into the little trucks through the back door, and squeezing into a spot on one of the two facing benches. The Ethiopians have a word for these vehicles, which translated, means that they force people to talk to each other. It was true. It was hard not to be friendly when knee to knee and eye to eye.

*Ethiopian embroidery.*

In Nairobi, Kenya, I dropped off the Mali reports at our Regional Office, picked up staff person, Grace Wambwa, a nurse who would be my partner for the Tanzania assignment, and flew from Nairobi to Dar-es-Salaam. The purpose of this trip was to be introduced to the Tanzanian sterilization program. I was to observe the quality of the surgical services, and to consider the possibility of using this country as a training site for female sterilization.

Grace and I flew from Dar-es-Salaam at the coast to the Kilimanjaro airport in the north. From there, it was a forty-five minute drive to Moshi, through Masai territory. Driving through the rural districts and seeing many Masai, I began thinking about books I had read about this tribe, common to both Tanzania and Kenya. In the fifties, I had read novels by Robert Ruark, "*Something of Value*" and "*Uhuru*". They were about what he white people called the Mau Mau uprising, but what black Kenyans called the War for Independence. The Masai played an important role, according to the books.

Grace said the Masai warriors were used as home-guards - as was appropriate for their warrior nature. Home guards were used to guard the black Africans being held in concentration camps under the leadership of the British. I mentioned to Grace that John Githiari had accused the Kalinjin tribe of serving as the guards.

Grace, who was from the Luya tribe, insisted that the Kikuyu themselves were split, with some serving with the British as home-guards, while others were in the revolutionary troops being led by Jomo Kenyatta.

She stated that the reason the Kikuyu could act as traitors was because they had been working in the homes of the British, where they were able to overhear plans that could be passed to the Kikuyu. Likewise, they could pick up plans from the revolutionary Kikuyu and report them to the British. Obviously, she had little respect for the Kikuyu, and felt that the Kalinjin, like the Luya, would be incapable of such behavior.

Grace's attitude toward other tribes was characteristic in Kenya. Add the fact that there were many tribes, and subdivision within tribes, all with different languages, dialects or accents, and it was easy to see why nationalizing Kenya continued to be difficult. Kenyatta said, and President Moi continued to say, that until all tribes think of themselves as Kenyans first, and tribes later, there can only be one political party. I think this will take more than my lifetime, and maybe that of the next generation.

I had just been in four countries that I had never been in before: Paris, France; Mali, West Africa; Addis Ababa, Ethiopia; and now had entered another: Tanzania in East Africa. I had gotten so used to dealing with new situations, new languages, new cultures, new foods, and new people to work with that I was thinking that travel obstacles were standard, unlike vacationers who would not tolerate them.

*Tanzania bus lines.*

For example, when we arrived in Moshi town, on the slopes of Mount Kilimanjaro, my first thought, after a rather grubby trip, was a nice hot shower. No water. It had been turned off for a few hours. *Well,* I thought, *at least I can have a drink of water from the pitcher in the room. No, that's empty. OK, I'll go downstairs for a cold beer.*

"We have no ice. Sorry." *Well, I've gotten used to that, too, so the thirsty, dirty traveler will enjoy a warm beer. Maybe I'll read my book while enjoying my treat. Whoops, there go the lights! OK, the evening is nice, so I'll just enjoy the darkening sky and watch for the moon and stars so I can remember that my loved ones on the other side of the world are seeing the same moon, and that way I'll feel closer.*

Suddenly, I heard the water trickling in the sink where I had purposefully left the faucet open so I could hear any returning water. Now, I thought happily, I can have my hot shower. No. There was only cold water, so I clenched my teeth and got under. I took two aspirins and went to bed.

It must be hard for people who only travel in the US, or in resorts or on cruise ships, to remember that even basic electrical power and water are luxuries for most of the world's peoples. I'm really glad I have had the opportunity to experience a bit of it, so I can retain the enthusiasm for the work I'm doing.

*Typical marketplace.*

Tanzania turned out to be very pleasant. The weather was perfect for me, though the local folks thought it was a bit cool, and my partner, Grace, had a sweater on her shoulders the entire week. The people of Tanzania were not only gracious, but very polite. Even their greetings are more than the typical Kenyan *"Jambo!"* or the Swahili *"Habari?"* which means "How are you?" They often used a special expression of respect for visitors or elders in one of their hundred-plus languages. I qualified on both counts, so was often greeted this way.

The country of Tanzania had probably the best structural system of government I had seen. Starting from the rural or village level, there was a party leader for every ten houses. Those leaders formed into groups of ten again, and choose a representative to be their leader. This continued up the line to the party chairman, who was the President. As in Kenya, there was only one political party.

The structure in Tanzania enabled people to get messages spread either up or down the line. We would be taking advantage of this system to get family planning messages out to the rural areas. As people on the lower tiers made increasing demands for surgical services, that message would be passed up to Ministry of Health levels. I couldn't help but wonder whether this regimented system might not have been the legacy of the Germans, who once ruled the area, then called German East Africa.

Food in Tanzania was much like that in Kenya – simple fare, mostly chicken or fish, not much in the way of seasonings or sauces, but good and inexpensive. We did treat ourselves to one fancy dinner at the Oyster Bay Hotel in the posh section of Dar-es-Salaam, on the Indian Ocean. Wonderful cool breezes, sounds of ocean waves, and a delicious fish dinner was our farewell to Dar the evening before we left the country.

While there, I found an excellent surgeon, Dr. Kapesa, who would be suitable as the chief trainer. Dr. Rukonge, the doctor in charge of the family planning organization (UMATI) was also a fine example of the kinds of trainers and program managers we like to work with. I will be returning to see a sample training program, and if it is of high quality, to begin to use this country as an African Regional training site. I looked forward to returning to Tanzania, probably in about six months.

It was time to return to Nairobi for a de-briefing meeting at the office. Nairobi had become a comfortable base for me. I knew the streets, shops, restaurants, hotels, and of course, our regional office and staff there. These two stopovers were especially pleasant because I had befriended a Norwegian missionary lady who had lived and worked in Zaire. She was staying at the same hotel I used in Nairobi, so we had a few meals together. On my last day in Kenya, I took her shopping so I could "show her the ropes", and introduce her to a few shop-keepers and vendors I had befriended over the last years. I rested in her room for a few hours after check out time, before heading for the airport to catch the midnight flight to Frankfort, on my way back to NY.

Dr. Kapesa                    Dr. Rukonge

# CHAPTER 29: RETURN TO THAILAND, NOV 24 – DEC 9, 1989

My work in Thailand was a comparatively small part of this journey. I had intentionally added vacation time to my schedule so that I could visit areas in Thailand that I would not be likely to see in the course of my work there.

I was in Bangkok to attend a three-day seminar that would be attended by the international experts in the Chinese-originated no-scalpel vasectomy technique. On the second day, December fourth, there was a King's Birthday Vasectomy Festival. Free vasectomies were provided to almost eight hundred men in the King's honor.

It was quite a sight to see: five large tents, each with six operating tables, staffed by a surgical team for every two tables. An assembly line? Yes, but everything went smoothly. The men were interviewed and had their questions or concerns answered before they signed the consent forms. At the next table, the men had a medical history taken and underwent a physical evaluation. They were then seated in lines to enter the tent that had an available table ready for the next client.

This festival provided an excellent opportunity to test the no-scalpel technique that AVS was advocating as an improved method of reaching the vas without cutting the skin tissue. It was associated with far less bleeding or bruising of the scrotal tissue, but no large-scale comparative study had been done before. Doctors in some tents were performing vasectomy by the traditional incision method. The other tents were staffed by doctors trained in the no-scalpel technique. Data was being collected and analysis of it would follow later.

While men were lining up awaiting their turn, there were group educational sessions being continuously offered. There were entertaining TV shows in the waiting room and music playing for the enjoyment of everybody celebrating the King's birthday. Snacks of juice and sandwiches were provided for the men after their vasectomy.

The outcome of this comparison of techniques is reported in the chapter, "Introducing No-scalpel Vasectomy". Another outcome was my creation and writing of the AVS manual titled *No-Scalpel Vasectomy. An*

*Illustrated Guide for Surgeons,* published in 1992.

After the festival, I took a tour with five other people, all strangers, with one guide. I had made the arrangements at a booth on the main street of Bangkok. I had no time for advance planning or a travel agent. My interest was in visiting the northern hill tribe villages in the area known as the "Golden Triangle".

After I had completed my work, I spent the first part of my vacation time with a hired car and driver, seeing the many fabulous temples and ancient stupas, called *wats* and *chedis* in Thai. I also visited the palace and had an opportunity to stroll through its gardens. And, as no trip to Bangkok is complete, in my opinion, until I visited a tailor to have a silk garment made, I did that also.

I began my notes about this trip in Chiang Mai, the northern city that had its claim to fame by being the location of the winter palace of the Royal Family. The Golden Triangle is the area where Thailand, Laos and Burma meet. This year, the name of Burma had just been changed to Myanmar.

The area is triangular due to two rivers converging. The largest river is the Mae Khong (Mekong); the smaller river that flows into it is the Ruak. This area was once the center of the opium trade, and the dealers could avoid arrest by crossing from one country to another, either by walking over a bridge between Thailand and Burma or using a boat to cross the Mae Khong into Laos.

The word "golden" refers to the use of gold as the exchange for the opium after Burma no longer used British pounds, and after Laos gave up the French francs. Unlike Burma and Laos, Thailand has never been under the control of another country, except for two short periods when Burma controlled the northern part.

On the way to the triangle, the tour group had visited Chieng Rai, a charming old city that was just beginning to attract tourists. A third hotel was under construction to accommodate the anticipated visitors. We stopped to walk around a bit and to buy some candy to take to the village children we hoped to see later.

We lunched at the side of the river, in the town of Mae Sai, very near the Burmese border. Here we could watch the narrow river boats and the rafts used for longer river trips. Those larger rafts had a toilet screen overhanging the side.

The bridge between Thailand and Burma was an immigration checkpoint, so while we could walk over to the Burmese side, setting foot down within that country, we could not cross the line. There was still a fair amount of trading taking place in this area, but Thailand had significantly reduced the opium trade. The primary trade was now for rubies and jade coming from Burma to Thailand. There were also handcrafts for sale. I suspected that there was still some opium changing hands but there was no evidence.

While in Chiang Mai, I visited quite a few handicraft factories. I watched lacquer-ware craftsmen and painters, wood carvers, silver and metal workers, umbrella and fan makers and painters, potters and jade carvers. All were interesting, but none compared to the weavers. I observed the process beginning with the simmering of the cocoons to unravel their silk threads, so fine they could hardly be seen. Many such threads are then made into one strand of silk fiber that is then dyed and woven. All this work is done by hand.

We left the tour minibus here and transferred to a river boat to the city of Chiang Sean, further south, where we once again boarded the bus that had driven to that city while we were aboard the watercraft. The boat was a low motorized craft with a front end that lifted up and out of the water. The propeller was on a long stick held by the navigator who sat in the back. We six tourists sat up front.

Before going south to Chiang Sean, the boat headed north on the Mae Khong, between Burma and Laos. At the farthest point northward, there was a large group of yellow-robed monks at the river's edge. They were in various stages of undress as they were going to take their afternoon baths in the river. I suspect the navigator intentionally took this route to treat the tourists to an unusual sight. The monks seemed oblivious to our boat. I can now report that Buddhist monks wear yellow underpants, and that they are not removed for bathing.

Temples were everywhere in Thailand and I thought they were spectacular. Many interiors were covered with gold leaf and small colored mirrors. Many were painted blue between the gold and mirrors, creating a very colorful and glimmering surface. The roofs of the temples had serpentine "wings" sculpted at the ends of the roof eaves. At the front and back peaks of the roof there would be a large curving ornament that resembled the beak of a bird, perhaps the Garuda god, half bird and half man.

*Spirit house.*

The shape and designs of the temples are replicated in the small "spirit houses" that are in the front yard of almost every building in Thailand. I rather liked the idea behind those little structures. The Thai people believe that when a building is constructed, whether a home, hotel or gas station, the construction disturbs the spirits who dwelt on that land. In compensation, a small house would be built for the spirits. Daily offerings, such as rice, flowers or fruit, were placed in the house. Some hung strings of flowers or ribbons from the pedestal that supported the house.

On our way to a new Meo village north of Chieng Mai, we visited the Maesa waterfalls and the Baan Chang elephant camp, where I accepted a ride through the woods on an elephant. It is at camps such as this one that the animals are trained to be working beasts of burden. Others are trained to entertain tourists.

The windowless homes of the Meo tribe were very small and primitive. The one we were invited to enter had a small fire in the center of the floor of the main room, which could not have been more than a hundred square feet. Near the fire was a pallet with blankets, the parent's bed. A small alcove off the main room had double-decked pallets for the children. The door frame was so low that we had to bend over to enter.

The Meo tribe, called Hmong in English, place a lot of significance in their house, the family, and the clan. The hearth is supposed to be a perpetual fire. When the family moves, they carry live embers to the next site. When a baby is born, the father buries the placenta in the floor of the house. They worship spirits, of which the spirit of the door is particularly important. They also believe in a local deity who rules the surrounding area. I learned about the spirit of the door only after our visit, and then surprised we had been allowed to enter.

Another village we visited was that of the Akha Tribe, called Eekaw in Thai. The Akha don't like the name Eekaw, which means "low slave". They are best recognized by the heavily ornamented peaked headdresses that look like helmets made with beaten silver, fur, beads, seeds and feathered tassels.

The Akha houses are on stilts and are divided into the men's and women's sections. There are no windows. Each house contains an altar for the family's ancestral spirits. Under the house are the animals, usually pigs and dogs who serve to guard the house as well as provide the meat for dinner. Yes, the Akha eat dogs. They also sacrifice all twin babies.

We were greeted graciously. The children were very polite as they lined up to receive pieces of candy we had brought. They thanked us respectfully with their hands pressed together, touching their nose. We were not invited inside a house.

The third village we visited was that of the Mien, called Yao by the Thais. These people originated in southern China where some still lived.

Others migrated to Vietnam, Laos and northern Thailand. This is the only hill tribe that has a written language. The Mien have adopted and preserved the Chinese script, so they possess written records and sacred texts. The other tribes have had to rely on oral records so have committed history and religion to memory.

The distinctive parts of the Mien dress are a black turban with a red ruff sewn on the collar and front edge of the woman's tunic. The children wear embroidered skull caps adorned with red woolen pom-poms.

The house that we entered was a "hotel". The family, headed by the widow of the former village chief, rented pallets on the floor to trekkers who needed overnight accommodation. Four trekkers were seated around a table in the main room, having a dinner prepared in the adjoining kitchen by the men in the family. In this tribe, the men share the house chores and child care with the women. Three of our small group were planning to stay that night, also, so the floor area would be wall-to -wall sleepers.

The Mien worship household and other spirits, along with Taoist deities adopted from the Chinese. This family was reportedly "Christian", but I noticed there was a corner of a large room that was still reserved for spirit worship. We were instructed by our tour leader not to walk into that part of the room, where there were religious wall hangings. I guessed it must be difficult for these new Christians to give up the spirits of their ancestors who have always dwelt in their home.

After the seminar and the Vasectomy Festival, I had an opportunity to go to Khon Kaen, a five-hour drive from Bangkok. I was escorted by a Thai family planning leader. The purpose was to visit a hospital and some clinics to learn more about the role of midwives in providing family planning. While we were there, we learned there was a Silk Fair going on, and managed a brief visit during our mid-day break.

We saw the most beautiful silk fabrics. Each weaving company was exhibiting the best examples of their work. There were weaving demonstrations as well as opportunities to buy fabric. Two types of weaving impressed me most. Mudmee weaving is a tie and dye method where tiny waterproof threads are woven across the fabric. After the cloth has been dyed, those threads are removed and replaced by threads of another color. The process is repeated many times, a seemingly endless work. I bought enough for a skirt. How could I not go home with a sample?

The other method that impressed me was one in which the cross threads were all pre-dyed. When the threads are woven, the weaver carefully lines up the colors with the previous thread. I could understand this more easily if the thread were dyed in one inch segments to create a simple check or stripe design. These threads were pre-dyed to produce beautiful floral pictures or intricate designs, not just once, which could be a random act, but repeated over and over for the length of the bolt of fabric. I saw the spools of this pre-dyed thread arriving at the weaver's table ready for the loom, so I believe it, but it will remain a mystery to me.

Although the Vasectomy Festival was an unusual event, I thought the visits with hill tribe people the most interesting part of this trip. Travel in all parts of Thailand has been a joy. Working with Thai doctors has always been a pleasant experience due to the good-spirited ambition of skilled, intelligent people. The combination of grace, beauty, talent, and charm is hard to beat.

*Fish markets.*

*Thai dancer.*

# CHAPTER 30: JAMAICA, FEB 6-9, 1990

I turned fifty-eight, alone, worried, sad, tired, and in another part of the world. It's not what we, as Americans, have come to expect in the way of celebrating significant days of our lives, or the end (or beginning) of another year. But spending important events, such as Easter and Mother's Day away from my family and friends had become fairly common for me these last ten years. A short work day today further enabled my reflective mood about life style, career, the future, and how this all relates to the closest people in my life, and to my relationships with them.

It was in this reflective mood that I began my brief Jamaica journey. I left New York at the end of an incredibly busy week, after a full day of work day on February sixth. I had no passport because it was in the Nigerian Embassy in the hope of getting a visa to go there next. I carried with me my birth certificate and marriage license, having been assured that would be enough.

The first checkpoint was at the airline counter. Because I had no passport, they needed a photo ID card. New Yorkers have their photos on their driver's license, but mine is still a New Jersey license without a photo. Nervously, I started systematically going through my travel and passport holder and the various compartments of my wallet, hoping I could find my old United Nations pass. One had been issued to me when I was studying Spanish there. Just when I had given up, I found it under my driver's and nursing licenses. It was approved by the supervisor and I got my boarding pass.

Upon arrival in Kingston, I used the U.N. pass once again for entry into Jamaica. The inspector paid no attention to my birth certificate or marriage license - or to the clearly marked expiration date of Dec, 1987 on my U.N. card. I hoped that the agents in Miami would allow me to re-enter the USA.

When I began to fly around the US in the 60s, the airports were similarly simple in appearance: concrete-block buildings with odors that seemed specific to the area. The Miami airport smelled musty, damp, and a bit like a locker room. Corpus Christi smelled like there was a pot of pinto beans cooking - and there probably was! I rather enjoyed the comfort of the likeness while at the same time enjoying the little differences. There was a raw oyster bar in New Orleans and a lobster store in Boston. The neon decorative lights were outstanding in Miami and Chicago. Then, all the US airports began to look alike. Most were re-carpeted in red, but purple was occasionally being seen. Food centers offered similar meals. Even NY installed a lobster stand! To a large extent, they have become all-of-a-kind.

When I started travelling internationally, I once again began to enjoy the local differences. No country could outdo Singapore for efficiency and order. Cairo and Delhi stood out as examples of the worse, but even they became quite efficient over time. The smaller countries, though, still kept their individual flavor to some extent. The similarity was that I would de-plane on the tarmac and walk in warm, humid air to the cement block building - like those we had in the US some thirty years ago. The customs and immigration systems were routinely slow and inefficient. Many papers needed stamping; there were mandatory reviews by other officials before I could get through.

Taxi service was routinely questionable in the developing world – perhaps in developed countries, too. *(Am I being hustled or is this really a taxi driver?)* So, I would look for a formal taxi stand, taking a chance if there were none. In between arrival and the taxi, of course, was always the currency exchange problem. Would a bank or money change office open? If not, how would I know the exchange rate? If I negotiate in dollars with the taxi, will I find later that I've been taken advantage of? It was a similar process with similar concerns everywhere.

Once in my taxi, typically, the car would make its way down a narrow plain road connecting the airport to the local road system. Tropical shrubs, trees and flowers would abound. There would be a clear sky with stars and moon visible because there were so few lights. I always seemed to arrive at night. There might be some small homes along the way. Vender stalls along the street were often lit with a candle or lantern, hoping to sell a soda or snack to a local resident. Finally, the hotel area would come into view. *Ah, I thought: I've arrived, ready to meet new people, work on new projects, and enter into the culture and environment for whatever time lies ahead.*

This trip to Jamaica was a short one - only two days. The primary activity was to take part in a workshop that would finalize the medical standards and guidelines for female sterilization services. I was very pleased to have the chance to work with Dr. Gary Stewart, AVS consultant for the Jamaica project. I had known his name and reputation for a long time and finally was getting as opportunity to know him as a person.

I met Dr. Hugh Wynter at the meeting. Born in 1933, one year after me, he was also celebrating his birthday that week. Dr. Wynter was an individual I had known about since the 60s. He had done much of his gynecological surgery through a scope inserted into the cul-de-sac of the vagina. With that approach to the pelvis, he avoided abdominal incisions for his patients. Among other gynecologists he was considered the "grand old man of culdoscopy". Culdoscopy was a precursor of laparoscopy.

It would be an honor for anyone interested in gynecology to work with Dr. Wynter. He helped promote family planning and reproductive services in Jamaica, resulting in a reduction of the county's infant death rate as well as its population growth. In 1988, he received the United Nations Population Award.

The weather was quite pleasant for February: warm but not hot, with cooler breezes after sundown. On February eighth, there was a full moon and I could only imagine how beautiful it would have been at the beach. But I was in New Kingston, walking to dinner at the Sea Witch restaurant, half a block from a Kentucky Fried Chicken Shop, in the commercial section of the city.

I found the people of Jamaica to be very warm and friendly. The medical people at the meeting appeared to be very knowledgeable and working toward a common goal, even though I had been told there was a power struggle going on between the Ministry of Health and the National Family Planning Board. But when they had been put in a room together to discuss medical issues, they worked as a team.

Workers at the hotel displayed the usual range of personalities. The bell-hop who carried my case to my room on the night I arrived was extremely friendly. He made courteous small talk on our way to my room. Then, when we were inside, he asked me for my name and told me his. This was followed by a firm handshake with a "Welcome to Jamaica!" greeting. He asked where I lived. His next question surprised me. He asked if I would take him to New York for a vacation! It was a charming and persistent request, but he backed down a bit when I told him I was married.

The other extreme was the taxi driver who took me to the airport. He asked if I'd like to sit up front with him or in the back seat. I choose the front, and it probably was a good choice. He spoke about equality of people in God's eyes and I suspected my choice of seat made him feel better about my attitudes. We chatted about conditions in Jamaica - the governmental system, the economy, and political leanings of the leaders. It was a pleasant ride with lots of religious commentary scattered throughout. He was a minister in a Pentecostal Church, driving taxis as an extra source of income.

What a time to live through! I just learned that Russia will have an election to choose a leader!

# CHAPTER 31: LIBERIA, FEB 19 – MAR 8, 1990

Monrovia welcomed me by cutting off all power supply while I was on a long taxi ride from the airport to the "Holiday Inn". I really had not noticed the decreasing light during the last part of the ride, being too occupied with the clear sky and bright stars. But when the driver pulled into a narrow, unlit road, and stopped in a dark section where I could hear people milling about across the street, I became a bit frightened. I wondered if I had been hi-jacked. If not, I would be disheartened to learn I had arrived at what would be my home for twelve days.

I followed the driver into a candle-lit lobby where I was informed that the current was off. Failing to find my reservation, we negotiated a room price. I was escorted to my room, three flights up, by a candle-holding staff as well as a luggage carrier. Hot and tired, I decided to freshen up a bit before going down again for dinner. No water! *Of course,* I thought to myself, *electricity was needed for the pump.* I should have known this. It was not the first time I have lacked power in my hotel. That meant no telephone either.

I went down the three flights with the little candle the bell-hop had left with me. I spoke to the clerk, "Sir, Is it possible to get some water?"

"Sorry, we have no power."

"But do you have a small supply you can give to me? Perhaps a bottle?"

"No, Ma'am. We have no bottles."

"Is there a restaurant in this hotel where I might buy a bottle"?

"Yes, Ma'am. Maybe they have a bottle."

"Can you please tell me where this restaurant is?"

"On the top floor. Number five"

"Are they open at this hour?"

"They are about to close now."

"Then I better hurry. Please call them to tell them to stay open until I get there."

"No power. No phone. Sorry."

I had no choice but to rush up the five flights of stairs with my candle and was fortunate enough to be able to purchase one plastic bottle of water before they closed and locked the door for the night. I took a slow breath and began my descent to the third floor, to my room.

That one bottle of water took care of drinking, brushing my teeth, and "washing" until morning when power was restored. This pattern became routine the entire time that I was in Liberia. When I was in my room, I would leave the water faucet open just a little so that if the water were turned on, I would hear the trickle. At night, I would leave the light switch turned on, so if the sudden brightness awakened me I would get up quickly and take a cold shower. I could not risk waiting for the water to warm up. It might be turned off again any minute.

Liberia made it difficult for visitors to enter the country as well as for its citizens to leave. I had to get a certificate from my doctor stating I had no communicable disease. I also had to get a good conduct record from the police in NY City. The visa application process took two weeks, with four visits to the Liberian Embassy. I finally got a visa, good for multiple entries into the country for a period of twelve months.

To my surprise, when I got to the immigration desk at the Monrovia airport, they only granted me forty-eight hours in the country. They told me that I had to report within that time for an extension that could be granted at the headquarters in Monrovia.

This required me to find a quick photo shop so I could submit four more photos with my entry application. The US Agency for International Development person who was my contact was most helpful, and helped me obtain a stamp in my passport that would allow me thirty days.

My assignment was to help Dr. Patricia Devine prepare for a course she would soon be giving in mini-lap under local anesthesia. The task was well within my abilities. I prepared evaluation forms, pre-tests, and post-tests for the doctors and nurses who would attend. Dr. Devine was a dynamo, but with her heavy schedule of surgery, serving as Medical Director of the large JFK Hospital, and her private practice in the late afternoon, she deserved some help. I planned to stay for the first week of the training and then move on to Nigeria to do the same thing there.

I was not been tempted to go far from the hotel. The neighborhood was not attractive, and a short walk around to try to find postcards showed me stores and food shops that were not tempting. I went into two jewelry shops in search of a silver charm for my bracelet, but everything was gold. I thought that was interesting for such an underdeveloped country.

I strolled through a supermarket and bought a piece of imported Dutch Edam cheese imbedded with cumin seeds and a container of potato chips. This cost over eleven dollars. There were no fresh, locally-grown vegetables available. They only carried canned products from America. I learned that, because the Liberians considered their land as the one set aside by the US for the freed slaves, they felt entitled to live like they perceived folks do in the US. Apparently, that meant living on imported and processed foods from the US.

The cost of living was high. My dreary room cost seventy dollars – and that was a discount from the hundred it should have cost because it contained a double bed. This was a special consideration they made for USAID consultants. For breakfast, I ordered two eggs, a glass of watery Tang, and two tablespoons of Nescafe with hot water. It cost six-fifty, but to be fair, it included a piece of cold hard toast and one pat of butter.

On my free Saturday afternoon, after picking up some more imported Dutch cheeses, I went to visit my mother's second cousin, Clayton Pyche and his wife Mary. They had recently arrived from the Netherlands to serve as host and hostess for the Sudan Inland Mission's missionary guest house in Liberia. Although we had never met before, it was good to have a family visit so far away from home. We compared our knowledge of family history and promised to help prepare a family tree of the Haitsma family. Our grandmothers were sisters.

Clayton and I put on swim suits and enjoyed the ocean. Mary waded in with her skirt, which got quite wet. It was only the second or third time Clayton had ever been in the ocean. I think he felt chilly thinking about it being February. It didn't seem possible to swim this time of year. Nor did it seem possible that family members would meet for the first time as far away as Liberia.

Sunday was a very quiet and lonely day. My preparatory work was done, I had already read two of the three books I had carried with me. My Doctor-colleague, Ade Adetunji, had not yet arrived from Nigeria to audit the course.

Eating lunch in the hotel coffee shop, I met the reservation supervisor of the hotel. She knew I was in Liberia to work with Dr. Devine, and told me Patricia Devine was her doctor. She had had a tubal ligation performed by Dr. Devine at the JFK Hospital. Then I learned that she, Martha Hayes, had been the first Liberian woman to talk on TV about her experience. As I was the first to do that in the US, we had many notes to share about our common roles. Both of us had been given incorrect information before we proceeded to have our tubes tied. Both of us were pleased with the experience, having firmly decided not to have any more pregnancies. Both of us had friends who tried to discourage us from "going public" and we were both glad we did go public and would do it again.

Ade arrived Sunday evening, hot and tired from his flight from Nigeria, which first over-flew Liberia, went to Freetown in Sierra Leone and Conakry in Ghana before turning around and landing in Roberts Field, Liberia. This is about the equivalent of leaving NY, stopping in Pittsburgh, then Chicago, before landing in Philadelphia. Of course, there was no water in the hotel, so poor Ade could not shower.

Bright and early Monday morning we optimistically went to the hospital to start the course. To our dismay, the trainees had not arrived - nor had messages come to explain why. Patricia organized a "search and find" activity while Ade and I went to USAID so that Ade could arrange his visa extension. At this time, I learned that I would also need an "exit visa" to give me permission to leave on Friday. Thus, my passport was left in the hands of the USAID staff who would try to arrange this additional visa before my scheduled departure.

I could not help but wonder what would happen if one were to come in, get permission to stay for forty-eight hours, not go to apply for an extension, and then try to leave without an exit visa. Would one be forced to stay? Or would one be thrown out of the country? It was a tempting thought, but the other possibility (jail) brought me back to my senses.

Monday afternoon was now free - so we returned to the hotel, where after a week, I was beginning to feel a bit like a prisoner. No current. No water either. "OK", I thought, *"I'll just strip, lie down and hope for a breeze though the window."*

The situation was beginning to be oppressive. There been water and electricity only one night. I'd read all my books. I did my homework for the Spanish class I was taking at the United Nations. My battery-operated book light had "given up the ghost". The only light in the room, when the current was on, was yellow, and it shone on the foot of the bed - not good for reading. I was tired of going to bed without washing the dirt of the day from my body. My hair needed shampooing. *"How long could I go without flushing the toilet?"*

My short-wave radio provided a limited number of stations. I learned that there was a demonstration going on in Germany regarding the pros and cons of unification. The election in Nigeria had been held, with the president conceding that he lost. The situation in South Africa continued to be bad, but no details were given. All this came from Radio Moscow.

Lying around in this mood, however, I began to think about what it must be like for those people I could see from my window. They never had a working air conditioner, and probably felt the oppressiveness and limitations of this country's economic situation every day of their lives.

I watched the children playing in the "yard" - a dirt area scattered with garbage and building material scraps - and wondered if they would ever have the chance to know something better. I watched a mother plaiting the hair of her little girl, who was being held firmly by another woman. The child was screaming and trying to be set free, and I wondered, *"Why?*

Why, in all this poverty does a mother feel she must plait the hair of her child when she probably cannot even wash it? The struggle for beauty is always in us. And the trait of women to want to make order out of chaos seems to be international.

As I looked down from my window, and also from the third-floor balconies at the front and rear of this building, I also noticed the relative inactivity of the men. All weekend, they had been sitting around on benches while the women did the laundry, and washed and cleaned the kitchen pots, pans, dishes and utensils. The men played cards, lounged around, rested on porches, and listened to music while the women worked.

Because these women had to bend over the scrubbing board and bucket all weekend, I thought they probably had another job during the week. Perhaps they cleaned homes for others. Sunday was their only time to take care of their own family's needs. I hoped I was wrong, but doubted it.

The country was in a period of unrest. There had been opposition to the president, and about a month before I arrived, a grandson of the opposition group's leader was murdered. His head had been cut off and his body badly chopped. The newspapers described it as a "wrist-slashing and beheading".

Nimba County, in the northeast, was the center of guerilla warfare. People were escaping into The Ivory Coast, where on February 20th, the US airlifted rice and medical supplies so they could continue to shelter the Liberians. The Liberian government had been saying that "everything is under control" but other stories coming from the countryside denied this, saying many people were being killed daily.

Our trainees had arrived one day late due to the road situation and unrest. One of our trainee-doctors was from Nimba County. He had been doing extra duty, trying to treat the wounded. He told us that the situation was far from being under control.

For the doctor/nurse team from Nimba to return, they would have to start from Monrovia by noon to be able to cross twelve checkpoints on their way home. Making it more difficult was the road barrier that would go up at six o'clock every evening. At each checkpoint, soldiers inspected the travelers, even making men strip and women partially undress. Every container was gone through, and every corner of the vehicle was examined. The soldiers also demanded identification as proof of citizenship. Then, they demanded a fee from the travelers as an inspection charge!

The nurse from that area told me of her experience, which was probably not unusual. She produced an employment ID card. The soldier would not accept it, saying "I didn't employ you!" She then produced her official ID and the soldier demanded, "Defend it!" That would be like US citizens trying to prove that their passport and the photo on it is really theirs. Of course, this was just a way to get more money.

One trip between Nimba and Monrovia could be quite expensive. The team stayed in Monrovia during the weekend between the two weeks of the course. This was because they would not be able to get through the checkpoints before the curfew on Friday evening.

I was a beneficiary of this team's inability to leave. The doctor was available in Monrovia on the day I was leaving, so he volunteered to drive me to the airport. The course would continue without me for the second week.

On my way to the airport, I stopped at the Sudan Inland Mission to say goodbye to Clayton and Mary, and to wish them well during their assignment there. I encouraged them to try African style food while they were in Liberia. I had found that, generally, the religious settlements in Africa segregate themselves to such a degree that they really do not experience the local lifestyle. While claiming to work "with" the people, they concentrate on setting up their own little enclave apart from the people.

I heard on the car radio that riots were occurring in The Ivory Coast, specifically in the capital of Abidjan, where I was heading to spend the night. The government had announced that to facilitate better education in the country, everyone would have to "tighten their belts". Government workers were going to suffer a salary cut, and people who worked in private industry would be taxed.

The people were rebelling, obviously. Molotov cocktails were being thrown, fires started, and mass movements were being staged all around Abidjan. However, when I arrived at about nine-thirty that night, all appeared quiet, at least overnight. I got to the airport before anything started up in the morning.

The World Monetary Fund people had told these countries to drop wages as a criterion for permission to engage in foreign exchange. The articles imported most often, liquor, high technology, cigarettes, perfumes, and such, were not the items that the common person needed. Under this new plan, the people would have less money to buy the family's necessities for living.

The condition seemed to be worsening in Africa. There was a Francophone Africa Summit Meeting planned for late 1991 or 1992. A Foreign Service political advisor I met in Abidjan predicted major uprisings would follow. Sad. Worrisome.

In spite of some of the miseries of this assignment, the actual work was one of the most rewarding experiences for me. I really felt that I've become quite capable at setting up doctor and nurse training programs, and in taking part in the actual surgical training. Imagine! I'm teaching doctors how to operate, how to train others, how to conduct medical supervision visits, and how to improve the quality of all aspects of their work. I still find all this hard to believe.

*Two doctor/nurse teams in training.*

# CHAPTER 32: RETURN TO NIGERIA, MAR 3 – 14. 1990

I used to think that Nigeria was the most difficult country in which to work, but after two weeks of working in Liberia, I could hardly wait to get to Lagos. I think the biggest problem I had was dealing with the attitude of people. Liberia had been the focus of the nineteenth century movement to identify a place where free blacks and former slaves could be returned to Africa. Over time, Liberians felt that America owed them something perpetually in return. As a result, they did not grow their own vegetables. They expected to eat American canned goods even though the climate was so conducive to farming. Surrounding countries were growing wonderful varieties of crops.

Many countries have donated medical supplies and equipment to Liberia. At the hospital where I was working with Dr. Levine, she showed me a large department where supplies, such as surgical instruments, were to be wrapped and sterilized in large autoclaves. The expensive equipment had been donated by a foreign country trying to help. However, in Liberia, the electrical system was so deficient that the autoclaves could not be operated properly. Nor were the local workers taught how to operate or repair the equipment. I saw all this equipment doing absolutely no good. In fact, if an autoclave is not running correctly, the result may be that the packages inside it do not become sterile, possibly adding to the infection rate for surgery. Furthermore, the autoclaves had gotten rusty and dirty over the years and were not much more than a waste of space.

I was pleased to reflect that in the AVS programs, appropriateness of the technology was always a factor in deciding what equipment to provide. When AVS donated laparoscopic equipment, for example, AVS made sure there was a component of the grant that handled repair and maintenance.

In countries where electrical supply was not reliable, AVS suggested or provided other methods. I thought back to my trips in Nepal, as a comparison. Even in the scarcely-populated, underdeveloped areas where there was no power, surgical instruments were boiled in a kettle over a wood stove. They were safer than the instruments coming out of a faulty autoclave in Liberia.

On my way to Nigeria, I had the pleasure of an overnight lay-over in a fine hotel in Abidjan, in the Ivory Coast. The room had a bidet, thanks to the French influence. How nice to have a really comfortable night after the past two hot weeks, and knowing what accommodations awaited me. I regretted that I could only enjoy it for seven hours because I soon had to return to the airport.

Lagos International airport had remarkably improved in orderliness since my last trip. They had eliminated the cumbersome currency declaration forms that were always a nuisance. The bank where I exchanged three hundred dollars' worth of traveler's checks for a bag full of five Naira notes was fairly efficient, considering how long it takes to count all that money. I actually needed a separate tote bag to carry it all.

I was met by the office driver and Dr. Jack, a graduate student temporary working in the AVS Lagos office. They took me to the Lagos Hilton ("Heaven Away From Heaven" is their slogan), and I was on my own. As in the case of the "Holiday Inn" in Liberia, this "Hilton" had no connection to the international chain. Nor did it have the amenities.

I spent the rest of the day trying to call home. Finally, I got through to my mother and grand-daughter Sherean. I was relieved to learn that there were no critical problems. It was only in the past year that I ever tried to contact home by phone. Until then, the arrangement was that if anything happened to me, AVS would learn about it from the embassy in the country where I was working. AVS would then notify my family. On the other hand, I had told my family to notify AVS if there was an emergency at home while I was away. AVS would telex the embassy and they would try to find me in their country. Fortunately, that never occurred in all the years of my overseas work, although on a few occasions I returned home to find that a friend or family member had died in my absence.

The next day, I got myself to the national airport for a flight to Jos. That smaller airport was much the same as in the past. A common sight was men walking among the waiting travelers, clicking a small pair of scissors in their hands. The sound and sight of the scissors was an indication that the man wielding them was offering to cut the toenails of the passengers while they awaited the plane. It was the equivalent of seeing a shoe-shine boy in our country.

It was always difficult to understand the loudspeaker announcements about boarding. At the first crackle of the loudspeaker, people would start running to a plane, with the last ones sometimes not getting a seat. I ran along with them. Then we lined up in the sun until the boarding passes were slowly checked again before we were allowed to enter. The flight this time was pleasant and I enjoyed talking to my seat-mate, Nigeria's ambassador to Benin.

The weather in Jos is the best in the country because of the higher altitude in Plateau State. What a pleasant change from Lagos and Monrovia, Liberia. The jacaranda trees were in full bloom with their lovely lavender flowers reaching high above the shorter trees. The orange-red acacia trees, also called flame trees, provided the occasional bright contrast. Lots of other green trees filled in. In gardens, many flowers were blooming. Walls and trellises were covered with bougainvillea and some orange clusters. Of course, there was the ever-present color tan - the color of the dirt roads, walkways, cement buildings, and anyplace dust and dirt settled.

I had been enjoying the luxury of a small battery-operated cassette player on this trip. Although I only took six cassettes, they really helped make long, lonely hours a bit more pleasant. I had Strauss, Chopin, Nana Mouskouri, Tanita Tikaram, Ray Lynch, Mark Isham, William Ackerman and the entire London symphony orchestra with me. Since arriving, I've added Miriam Makebe and Nigeria's star, Fela, whose songs are all social and political criticisms. The hit I bought is "Overtake, Don Overtake, Overtake", referring to all the African countries where revolutionary groups were trying to overtake the seat of power.

The training course I came to both help conduct and assess ran from Monday to Friday. Each day I expected to hear from our Lagos officer about arrangements for Dr. Adekunle and me to go on site visits to Benue State, but no news. Adekunle was affiliated with the Ibadan University Hospital, and I was looking forward to doing medical visits with him. AVS Medical Director, Dr. Douglas Huber and I hoped we might be able to use him as a medical consultant in the future. Our trip would enable me to demonstrate what AVS expected in the way of a quality-assurance visit.

Meanwhile, I met some interesting people at the hotel. I had tea one afternoon with a pharmacologist heading the Nigerian Accreditation Commission for the schools of pharmacology. Besides talking about medicines and schools in Nigeria, he gave me some background on the government structure, plans to change from a military to a civilian government in 1992, and various struggles and tensions between the military and academia.

Another evening, I ate with a few ladies staying at the hotel. They were attending a conference on crime and the justice system of Nigeria. One was a university professor in Lagos, one a practicing lawyer, and the third a legal draftsman who wrote laws. It was a fascinating evening talking about women's roles, intermarriage between tribes, customs, and tribal differences in Nigeria. In exchange, I answered their questions about women in America. I realized how seldom I ever get to talk to women, and really appreciated this time of exchange.

I met a couple that was spending a weekend in Jos during a break in the husband's assignment in Zaria for the World Bank. Zaria lies in the north, dry, hot area of Nigeria; the climate of Jos was refreshing for them. This couple had once lived in Nigeria for six years. They had returned frequently to Africa over a thirty-year period. I was disappointed to learn how negative they were. It was hard for them to express something positive. They generally expressed their beliefs that back when foreigners were in control, things were better. Since Nigeria's independence, things had fallen apart, they said.

Saturday came and went with no word about our travel plans, so my partner and I began to make our own. I let Dr. Adekunle negotiate for transportation. As a Nigerian, I thought he'd get a better deal on the hiring of a car and driver for three days. We arranged to pay two thousand Naira, a bit less than three hundred dollars, to leave at noon on Sunday for Gboko, five hours to the south. We would spend the night in order to visit the NKST hospital on Monday, then drive to Makurdi and spend Monday night there, work at Makurdi General Hospital on Tuesday, and drive back to Jos, four hours north, on Tuesday evening.

*Chief of Tiv tribe demonstrates weaving.*

I particularly enjoyed the visit at NKST. Translated, that stands for "Universal Reformed Christian Church", a Christian Reformed church based in Nigeria. That was the denomination in which I had been raised. While in the office of the director, I noticed a framed diploma that indicated he had graduated from Calvin College, in Grand Rapids,

Michigan, the same college attended by many of my family and friends. The Christian Reformed Church of South Africa had sent missionaries to Benue State in 1911 to work with the people of the Tiv tribe. By 2011, the church had grown to over a million members, with over five hundred pastors in more than three thousand churches all over Nigeria.

During our visit, we were served lunch. It was a very large, old chicken cooked in a pot the same way my grandmother used to prepare it. I had not ever felt so close to my roots as I did out there in the bush. I think I can still taste that juicy old stewed bird.

The side trip went well. I finally met our regional director when he arrived in Jos late Tuesday about the time we returned. I learned that he had expected me to hire a car and driver without his assistance or guidance. Such confidence! In future visits I would know not to expect help.

Because I had been in Nigeria a few times before, I had no new insights about the people except to be reminded that telling an untruth was quite acceptable. Also, how unaccustomed the Nigerians are to people who are straight-forward. I read some newspaper articles that gave some evidence of this, which I saved as a reminder. For example, one columnist said "If you're a smoker visiting a non-smoking home and cannot go without a cigarette, the way to handle the situation would be to excuse yourself, saying you forgot to lock your car, go out and quickly smoke a half a cigarette and return".

I realized then how difficult it must have been for my Nigerian colleagues to hear me report a negative finding to them. Added to this was the hierarchical system, where junior staff must remain subservient to seniors or supervisors. I seemed to have no problem communicating with doctors directly; perhaps this was because we had the same concerns about quality and safety. However, the lay program staff seemed very nervous about what I might say to a person they considered their superior. They found it difficult to deal with a white female nurse offering suggestions to black male doctors. I trod on thin ice. The worst case example was that our East Africa Regional Office in Kenya had a medical officer working in a programmatic role. He seemed threatened by me. I believe his problem was that as a doctor, he felt he should have been in a superior position. But although I was a nurse, I was the Deputy Director of the International AVS Medical Division.

I stopped in London for an overnight rest and a look at the Frans Hals exhibit in the Royal Academy of Art. On the train from Gatwick airport, I noticed the old buildings that still looked sturdy and substantial. I saw the clothes and home furnishings in the Dutch paintings. I thought about Egyptian and Mexican pyramids and found myself wondering why, in so much of Africa, people were still living in mud huts. Why was Africa a thousand years behind?

# CHAPTER 33: NAIROBI, ZANZABAR, MOSHI, JULY 7 – 30, 1990

**ON ROUTE:** Little did I know I would be involved with a stow-away when I began this journey! I left New York with pleasant thoughts, and looking forward to my trip. I knew I would enjoy a brief stopover at our East African regional office in Nairobi, and had scheduled my return from Tanzania via The Netherlands. There, I planned to use my layover time to see the great Van Gogh retrospective exhibit in Otterlo.

I would have Grace Wambwa a companion in Tanzania, where I would be working with people I already knew. I would be taking part in a surgical training course, which seems to have become my special area of expertise in Africa.

As often happened, the Pan Am fight to Frankfort was delayed due to mechanical problems. I find it hard to remember when it left on time for these long trips. In Frankfort, there was the customary hold-over for baggage to be transferred to the aircraft that would take passengers continuing to Nairobi.

While at the ticket counter, verifying my seat assignment, I heard a woman talking to another agent about her stolen money, having no passport, a mother who would meet her, and her need to make this flight. I didn't pay close attention, but noticed she was probably in her mid-thirties, a bit scruffy, with dirty nails. She was wearing jeans and a green sweatshirt. She only carried a few unimportant-looking papers, such as a letter and a Lufthansa Airline time schedule.

Going about my own business, I got through my security check, and then, after showing my boarding pass yet again at the door, was allowed into the waiting room. To my surprise, as I sat down, this woman sat beside me. I figured she had made some arrangements with the agent, but was surprised to see she still carried nothing resembling a ticket or boarding pass.

As she had told the ticket agent, she began repeating her story to me, adding that her mother was a diplomat. They were originally from Cypress and Greece, but now living in Germany. Then she showed me an envelope with some names and addresses written on the back and edges. It had originally been mailed with Greek stamps to an address in Germany. She said, "This is my boarding pass. I can go anywhere in the world with it. See the names on here? We have connections with these people."

This all sounded very strange to me, but what did I know? Maybe her mother really could pull strings at an airport. But then the woman wanted to give me her envelope. As she was chattering away, I put it back with her other papers. I didn't want any part of whatever she was doing.

Near boarding time, she asked me to put her papers in my carry-on bag, because she did not have one. I told her I did not want to be responsible for them. Besides, I still had doubts she would get on the plane.

As the Pan Am agents were boarding the first and business class passengers, I went to the door and she followed. She continued behind me to the plane, where, for the fifth time, my boarding pass was checked. I walked to my assigned seat, she following behind me. Now this was very incredible to me. I put my carry-on bag in the front of me in the aisle seat I was in, making it more difficult for her to sit next to me. She paused, then moved to the first class section and sat down.

Soon I saw her return, apparently after the rightful person claimed the first class seat. She found an empty seat one row behind me, across the aisle. By this time, everyone had boarded and the attendants were serving juice while we were waiting to take off. The woman got up from her seat and came to me, saying "They told me you have my boarding pass".

Now sure the woman was a nut, I called the flight attendant and reported that the woman had no ticket or boarding pass, and that she was accusing me of holding them. Further, I said I did not know the woman, nor did I have anything of hers. Soon after, two German security agents entered. After speaking to her, and asking me if I had her boarding pass, they removed her from the plane.

Apparently, they questioned her at some length, because about forty-five minutes later, when we were taken off the plane with our belongings so the security force could check the aircraft, I again saw the woman being escorted from the interrogation room. We never heard anything else, but we were almost four hours late in taking off. Other passengers shared my shock that this woman could have simply walked past five checkpoints in what was considered one of the most secure airports in the world.

**NAIROBI:** On my way to Tanzania, I would be working a few preparatory days in our Regional office in Nairobi. When I finally arrived at the Nairobi airport, it was after midnight on the ninth of July instead of the evening before. By the time I changed currency, got through customs, hired a cab and got to the hotel, it was about two in the morning. On the way, the taxi had been checked by a security team on the road. That was when I learned that there had been rioting during the day, but I heard no details.

At the hotel, I found my reserved room had not been saved, and there was no room available. Checking in at the time was a fellow working with the US Centers for Disease Control's Malaria Unit who said he was leaving at five-thirty to fly to western Kenya. We made a deal. I'd lie on the sofa in the lobby until he checked out. Then he'd give me his key so I could go to his room to shower and get ready for work. It worked well; after a good breakfast, I left my baggage in what would be my room after cleaning, and set out for the office to start my work day. So, what I had thought would be an uneventful trip to Africa, turned out to be somewhat unusual.

I was always nice to return to Nairobi. I knew the staff, the city, the restaurants and shops. The weather was always great, the people pleasant to be with. I arranged lunch with Pam Lynam, a doctor on the regional staff, and Anil Kumar, a former NY staff now serving as a consultant auditor for AVS. We planned a trip to "Minar", a restaurant with an excellent Indian menu and lunch buffet. They both invited their spouses, so five of us enjoyed the feast and each other's company.

Walking back to the office through Parliament Square, we noticed it was very deserted and quiet. By this time, I had learned that the rioting was because some people were pressing for a two-party political system. President Moi had been insisting that until all Kenyans were unified instead of retaining loyalty to tribal groups, a multi-party system would be divisive. He feared parties would be formed on a tribal basis, and would lead to more internal strife.

We arrived at the back door of the office building and entered, still conscious of the deserted streets. All the offices were locked up, and corridors were dark. Pam had a key so we could get our things that we had left there. We learned that all buildings had been evacuated, buses and taxis had stopped, and people were told to stay at home. Pam's husband came with his car and took Anil and me to our hotels, but not before Anil and I had made plans to meet, if possible, for dinner at the Hilton later.

Although there were no hotel taxis available, the hotel was able to summon an operating taxi from downtown to come and take me to the Hilton. I met Anil and his wife Marian in the Residents' Lounge and we enjoyed an hour before settling for a coffee shop dinner. It was the only place open in the hotel - or maybe in the whole town. Everything had closed down earlier in the day.

Also in the lounge was an AID security staff person who had been sitting next to me on the now infamous "stow-away" flight. Another friend of his, the Administrative Officer for AID/Burundi, joined him, and all five of us ate together. There was instant rapport with everyone, and we continued swapping stories in the lounge till after midnight, when they saw me safely into a Hilton taxi, and I returned to the Fairview Hotel, located on a hillside on the edge of the city. I guess we should have felt guilty, what with all Nairobi locked inside while we had such fun, but we didn't.

The next day was a work-filled day at the office. The AVS office was open but most international organization offices remained closed. Our State Department and our Mission were nervous. Moi and government leaders favoring a continuation of the one-party system were making public statements against the US for having instigated moves toward a multi-party system. To make matters worse, one of the leaders of the rebellious group had gotten shelter in the US Embassy. The US was again being seen as the meddling body trying to tell other governments how their countries should be run.

By the time I left for Tanzania, buses and trucks had been overturned and set afire; cars, taxis, and some buildings had their windows smashed with rocks, and about twenty people had been killed. I collected a few newspaper clippings as reminders. In spite of all this, I actually saw nothing directly except the fear and extreme tension on people's faces. At one bus stop, I saw hundreds of people waiting for a bus that would probably never come. Not a sound. I thought that if someone dropped an empty Coke bottle, it would probably cause instant panic. Such public fear was a new experience for me.

**MOSHI:** In spite of the political unrest and rioting in Kenya, my partner Grace and I left for Dar-es-Salaam via an Air Tanzania Corporation airplane. Locally, "ATC" is defined as the Any Time Cancellation airline. Indeed, the schedule was all mixed up. Originally planned for a one o'clock afternoon flight, we were notified a day earlier that we should be at the airport early in the morning for an early departure. We left at noon, so in spite of the four hours standing in line, we were one hour early.

We met the Tanzanian Family Planning Association staff, and to my pleasant surprise, found that they had actually made the arrangements for the two-week course. I was pleased to feel confident that the two doctors I had identified on an earlier trip, Doctors Kapesa and Rukonge, were really going to be excellent leaders for the training center we hoped to establish in Tanzania. We would be training six doctor-nurse teams during the course, using a curriculum that I had been working on for some time. This would give us an opportunity to test the material and an opportunity for me to observe the training skills of the doctors. Grace would focus on the nurses being trained.

To our surprise, because the preparation work had been so well done, after Thursday evening, Grace and I had the weekend free. We decided to look into a trip to Zanzibar. We went to a travel office in the morning only to learn that tour groups were arranged for such trips on individual chartered planes, but at a very high price. Round trip for the two of us for one overnight stay would cost over four hundred dollars each. The cost would include a tour of Zanzibar Town plus a drive to the spice-growing area, but the hotel would be extra.

We moaned about our dilemma to our contact person at the USAID office during our initial briefing with her on Friday. She proposed another possible option. She suggested we might be able to arrange to hop on the Daily News plane that delivered newspapers to Zanzibar every morning at seven. The small plane had three seats for possible passengers.

We had already excluded the Air Tanzania flight, because even if we got a flight to Zanzibar, there would be no assurance that there would be a flight guaranteed to return us on time. We could not risk being absent for the training course. We had to return on time for the Monday morning session.

We found the Daily News distributing center in a little wooden shack behind the bigger office building. We were greeted ever so nicely by newsboys, and escorted past bundles of papers and magazines into the tiny office of their chief. The current weekend was already booked, but we could schedule the following Saturday. Grace would have to return to Kenya on Sunday, but she could book a flight from Zanzibar to Nairobi on Air Tanzania from there. I would be able to stay two nights in Zanzibar, returning with the newspapers on the dawn flight from Zanzibar to Moshi. The cost: seventy dollars for my round trip. Good deal!

**ZANZIBAR:** This twenty-four by fifty-mile-square island was fascinating. Before 1964, the island, along with its sister island, Pemba, formed the British Protectorate called Zanzibar. At that time, independence was gained by both Zanzibar and Tanganyika. Together, they formed the country now called Tanzania.

The people of Zanzibar originally came from Assyria, India, Egypt, Phoenicia, and Portugal. They were Hindus, Arabs, Chinese and Malays. By mid-nineteenth century, the Arab influence was so strong that the Sultan of Oman moved his capital to Zanzibar. These races and nationalities all left their marks. I enjoyed seeing the Moorish castellated buildings with arches, the intricate designs in the stucco of old Persian baths and the Arabian brass-studded carved doors in the narrow streets of the old city, called "Stone Town" because of the construction.

The Zanzibar Hotel, where we stayed, was in the midst of this old area, and cost twenty-four dollars for a twin-bedded room; fourteen for only me after Grace left. The total hotel cost for me for two nights on a tropical island was twenty-four dollars. It may not have been a Hilton, but it did have character.

I wish I could report that the hotel was clean and the food was excellent, but I cannot. The toilet seat and cover looked so bad, we decided to lift them both and just use the bowl. At least we could clean that. The place was just grubby and grimy.

On the first night, Grace and I ate at the African Hotel, a short walk from the hotel. We were attracted by the fact that the restaurant was two flights up, overlooking the Indian Ocean. The food was passable, but the sounds of the waves made up for any shortcomings.

The next day, we took a tour of historic places in and around Zanzibar Town. From there, the group went to see the ruins of the old Maruhubi Palace with its special area for the harem of ninety-nine women. From there, we went up the west coast of the island to see the Persian Baths.

*Zanzibar Architecture*

Next, we traveled east into the spice-growing area. We saw peppercorns growing on vines that climbed the trees. They were still green. When they got larger, they would turn reddish before they would be picked. I remembered one of my favorite restaurants in New Jersey that featured either pink or green peppercorn sauce on steaks. Now I know their source.

Cardamom grows at the roots of banana trees. The lowers look like miniature orchids, colored purple and white. Cinnamon trees are short and thin-trunked. After the bark is cut, it produces more. Cloves grow on tall trees. The buds are green and pink when harvested. After sun-drying, they turn brown as we see them. From the stems they make clove oil for liniment and toothache cures. When I heard about the "spice islands" as a child, I never thought I would ever visit here.

Continuing up the west coast, we reached the Mangapwani Slave Caves. There was where a sultan continued to keep slaves, even after slavery had been abolished, until he could ship them to Arabia. All blacks taken into slavery from East Africa went to Arab countries; those taken from West Africa went to the United States and other parts of the western hemisphere. Most of the East African slave trade went through either Mombasa or Zanzibar.

Just a bit further up the coast was a wonderful beach where we had an hour to swim. There we were, on a beautiful sand beach, crystal clear water, a couple boys with their fishing boats, and not another soul in sight but the eight of us in the tour group. This was a real treat before we drove back to town.

On Sunday, after Grace had taken the plane that was stopping in Zanzibar on its way to Kenya, I found my way over to the wharf area. I hoped I could get a boat ride to Prison Island for a day at the beach. I shared a boat with a Finnish couple and their two small children. My share was five dollars, round-trip.

We traveled in a crude wooden round-bottomed boat with an outboard motor. It was about twenty minutes until we arrived on a sandy spit of land. Altogether, there were perhaps twenty small groups or families there. We swam, sunned, read, had lunch, and went to see giant tortoises. It was lovely and peaceful, as we spent the time until our boat was to return at three-thirty.

I sat, watching the tide come in, eating up more and more of the beach. By three o'clock, most people had left. There was only a small dry spot on which we waited, and we were beginning to worry that the winds, which had really gotten very strong in the last hour or so, were going to make a rough trip back...if our "captain" ever showed up.

Finally! At four o'clock he arrived and those of us who were left got on board. It was really a rough, bumpy twenty-five minute ride. The boat was heading into the wind, so the front would rise on each wave and slap down into each "valley". Each slap brought sprays of water, so we were soaked by the time we reached Zanzibar Island again.

I covered my bathing suit with a skirt and tee-shirt, and walked through many narrow streets in the general direction of the hotel. I found it more interesting and cooler than the long coastal road. It was "Sunday quiet" but the people I did meet were friendly, and greeted me with "Jambo" or "Habari". A few kids said "Hello" or "Hi", practicing their English.

That night, I was alone, so I ate at the Hotel where I was staying. On the way to the restaurant, I saw a large mouse *(or was it a rat?)* scurry across the lobby floor. The presence of two cats in the restaurant reassured me. I ordered boiled lobster, which looked good, all cut up on my plate. It came with chips and spinach. The smell was strange. I said the missionary prayer: "Lord, I'll put it down; you keep it down".

After three or four bites, I knew – even with my faulty olfactory senses – that the lobster was foul. The waiter agreed, and substituted dried-out fried fish. Everything was not great in this tropical paradise. After dinner, I treated myself to some of my dwindling supply of Scotch. Surely, this was medicinal. I did not want to smell the lobster again on its way back up.

**BACK TO WORK:** The first week of the training course, before the Zanzibar side trip, had gone very well. We were working with six teams of doctors and operating room nurses, all from different sections of the country. In another six months, tubal ligation should be a common practice in Tanzania. A lot would depend on these initial providers. They really seemed highly motivated and excited about beginning services. It gave me a wonderful feeling to know that I have been a part of making a change in medical practice, in improving quality and safety, and in opening doors for women who no longer wished to be subject to unwanted pregnancies.

My plan was to return to see the effects of this initial training course. During the week, we had been reviewing early plans and drafted materials for a mini-lap training curriculum. If, when I came back, all was going well, we would field-test the completed curriculum with these trainers. At that time, we would use the new material to train more teams.

On one free Sunday, a couple of us enjoyed a trip to the Oyster Bay Hotel for lunch. The view of the Indian Ocean, from the restaurant veranda, was spectacular. Across the street was the beach lined with palm trees. We could hear the soft sounds of small waves while we ate Indian Ocean lobster.

After lunch, while I was strolling on the beach for a while, I met a painter who was working there under the palms. He was painting groups of Masai warriors or women. Some depicted the high jumps that the Masai men call "dancing". They were done with a palette knife instead of a brush. The colors were vibrant; the scenes depicted the spirit of the Masai perfectly. I could not go home without one. I bought a painting that was framed for a mere twenty-five dollars. To better travel with it, I had the artist keep the frame, rolling the canvas for me instead. It arrived safely and still pleases me every day.

The training course had progressed very well. The work was enjoyable, the co-workers were friendly and in good humor. One doctor from Arusha, Herman Hangu, urged me to return on a vacation so that he could arrange a safari into the Ngorongoro Crater or Serengeti Game Reserve. It seemed a good opportunity and I promised to considerate it the next year when I knew I would be returning to Mombasa in southern Kenya.

It was time to bid farewell to my new friends, and wish them well as they practiced their new skills and offered increasing options for Tanzanian women.

*The sands of time…and my well-traveled sandals.*

# CHAPTER 34: STOPOVER IN HOLLAND, JULY 28 – 30, 1990

After having worked two weeks in Tanzania, I was looking forward to a stopover in The Netherlands to see the Van Gogh Retrospective in Amsterdam and Otterlo. The overnight flight from Dar-es-Salaam was uneventful. I dozed a bit, but was not really rested when we landed just before dawn at Schiphol Airport. What a nice change from Africa! Everything was clean and efficient. My taxi looked new, unlike the junks I had been putt-putt-putting around in. An hour after touch-down I was at the Atlas hotel, a lovely former home of a merchant in the residential area near the museums and Vondel Park. I dropped off my luggage and started walking.

An hour later, I was in the center of the old city, at the Dam Square, with its conical monument, and the Royal Palace. The streets were quiet and the city was just beginning to come to life. I began my search for the restaurant "Cafe Scheltema". It had become my favorite restaurant in Amsterdam, and I wanted to be sure it was still there, providing a haven for writers, journalists, and script writers.

This cafe was where I had eaten with my mother when I took her back to the land of her birth in 1977. A well-known Dutch actor named Rijk de Gooyer and the movie crew that was finishing the editing of the film "Soldier of Orange" was there. They invited us to join them for a drink after dinner. Mom really enjoyed chatting with them in Dutch. An hour or so later, while I went to the ladies room, Rijk invited Mom to go home with him. She declined, but was pleased to think she could have. Since that occasion, I always tried to have dinner there... not in hopes of such an invitation, but because of the friendly atmosphere and home-style meals they served. It was not a place where I would see tourists.

After assuring myself that the restaurant was still functioning, I set off for the Central Rail Road Station to take a train to Haarlem in the hope of a visit to the Frans Hals Museum. I was soon trudging from Haarlem's station, through the city center square, and on towards the Museum that I found to be closed. The Hals Collection that had been there on tour was being replaced. My disappointment was tempered by the fact that I had seen the traveling collection in London in April, but I can never see too much of Hals, and would have enjoyed it in its own "home".

By mid-morning I was back at the Haarlem herring stall, and it was open. I enjoyed two *"nieuw harings"*, covered with chopped onions. Wonderful! Now, I really knew I was in Holland.

Back in Amsterdam, I headed for the ferry boats so I could enjoy an hour on the Ij, looking back at the city. Pleasant, comfortable free entertainment: a round trip on each of two boats. I spent the afternoon walking on all the old streets already familiar to me. How I loved this country!

I went to the Oude Hoogstraat, the street where I had rented an apartment on my first trip to Amsterdam. While it was fairly near the red light district, it was still a nice neighborhood then. It was not the same now. Vacationing back-packers crowded the street. The fish market, meat market, and wine shop where I bought my food and drink were gone, replaced by small noisy restaurants and cafes. Guess I'll just keep my memories and be glad I was there when I was.

I spent lots of time wandering on the shopping streets, Niewen Dijk and Kalver Straat, trying to find a shop that carried the old fashioned table covers seen in the seventeenth century paintings. No luck. It seems they are now only made on special orders from the cafes that still want to use them. They are considered antiques now, so I'm glad I have two already. Instead, I bought another rare cloth, made only in Zeeland in South Holland, which probably also will not be available in the future.

In Dar-es-Salaam, while I was in a bank changing traveler's checks, I was "bumped against". Later, I discovered my silver pill box missing. It had been a Dutch snuff box and had been in the family for perhaps a hundred years, thirty of them in my purse. I decided to look for a replacement. I finally found a modern copy of one for two hundred dollars. I saw an antique box from 1890 for an additional seventy-five dollars but resisted the temptation. Someone else's heirloom is not the same as my own.

On Saturday, after a stroll on the Leidsestraat, I headed for the Van Gogh Museum where I boarded the special bus to Otterlo, the location of Kroller-Muller Museum. The ride was lovely, on excellent roads, in a modern air-conditioned bus. We traveled through the flat countryside where I could see farm houses and barns, thatched and tiled roofs, corn fields, black and white cows, church steeples, and two little villages as we neared Otterlo.

The Kroller-Muller Museum sets well within a large wooded park famous for its sculptures. The park was so big that free bikes were available to borrow so visitors could get around. The exhibit was expansive and impressive. There was a separate building in the woods behind the museum that held the drawings and water colors. I spent the first two hours there.

After a snack of beer and a herring sandwich, I went into the Kroller-Muller to see the regular collection. To my surprise, there were at least twenty more Van Gogh's there: some great ones I didn't even know existed. Back on the bus, I paged through the catalogue that will help keep this wonderful day fresh my memory. On the way back to the Atlas Hotel, I stopped in a small restaurant for a genever (Dutch gin served ice cold in a small glass) and a big bowl of Dutch brown bean soup. Delicious!

I strolled along the canals, just enjoying the city. One house on the Herengracht was built in 1580. It was the oldest one I saw. Another house was three stories high but just the width of the door and windows above it. It could not have been more than eight feet wide. It held the record for the narrowest building, but I saw another, just a bit wider with a double door, five stories high.

There was a line a block long waiting to enter the Anne Frank House. This was not the case on either of the previous visits. How happy I was that I was here before this recent popularity. I was reminded of my previous trips to the Van Gogh Museum, where the exhibit rooms only had a few visitors each. I have especially fond memories of the first time I saw "The Potato Eaters". A teacher had school children, each seated on his or her portable stool while the teacher explained it. I was so impressed that Dutch children, even when very young, are exposed to such art, and have an early opportunity to learn to appreciate it.

This time, I was among the last group to enter the Van Gogh Museum before the special exhibit closed. The place was so chock full of people, it took great patience and lots of time to get in front of each painting, or at least near enough for an unobstructed view, but it was well worth the struggle.

My trip to Tanzania had definitely been one of the nicest trips I have made. The work was rewarding. The people I worked with were energetic and eager to learn. The stopover in Holland was icing on the cake!

*Dutch windmill*

# CHAPTER 35: LISBON AND BARCELONA, SEPT 26 – 30, 1991

**LISBON, PORTUGAL:** It was not often that my work took me to a developed country, and even less often did it take me to a seaside resort area. When the opportunity arose for me to attend a meeting in Barcelona, it seemed a wonderful opportunity to add a few days' vacation. Lisbon was the only choice because that was the one stop Pan Am made on its way to Barcelona. With a free ticket earned through the frequent flyer program, my Aunt Lois was able to make the trip, too.

We checked into a "pension", a small guest house that was actually a total of twenty rooms, located in a business building, half on the third floor and the rest on the fifth. Luckily, we were on the third floor because the elevator had periodic breakdowns. But the people were friendly and helpful, the room clean, and the sixty dollar price was a lot better than the two hundred dollars a night a real hotel would have charged.

Our first trip was a taxi ride to the Museum of Ancient Art. In addition to paintings, it had porcelain and furniture. There was a silver service made for King Joao V and some impressive tapestries. The people were quite proud of their Portuguese primitives, but I tend to prefer art done after the fifteenth century. I liked the Hals, Holbeins, and Durers and other Flemish, Dutch and Spanish works better.

Getting adventurous, we took a bus to the commercial center and had lunch in the shopping mall area. Wandering around later we followed signs to Castelo de Sao Jorge (St George's Castle). We started up a little winding road, followed the next sign and turned a corner only to find another hill, another sign, another corner, another hill and up and up. Each time we thought *"Well, we must be as high as we can get"*, there was another corner and another hill to climb.

We finally did make it to the castle. From the grounds there was a great view of the Tagus River, the waterway to the Atlantic Ocean. Also, we could see the new suspension bridge across the Tagus (one and a half miles across) looking very much like the Golden Gate Bridge in San Francisco. Lisbon, like San Francisco, is built on hills, and these hills could best be appreciated from the castle grounds.

White ducks, swans and geese were swimming in the moat. On one lawn were about six peacocks, one of which was albino. White deer were in a pen. The beautiful gardens, flowering trees, oleanders and hibiscus made a lovely peaceful setting. I wished I had taken my paints to create my own memory picture.

On the slopes, just below the castle was the section called Alfama, the area through which we had walked. It was the oldest part of Lisbon and the life styles of the local residents seemed to reflect that. Laundry hung out of windows over the narrow streets and alleys. Many houses had bird cages hanging near the doors and in windows, with finches, canaries, myna birds and various chirpers. Some old women sitting inside the windows smiled and greeted us as we walked by. Occasionally, we could glimpse at life in the courtyard, children playing, a woman washing, or dogs lazily sleeping.

The tile work was most fascinating to me. Some buildings in the older areas were entirely faced with ceramic tile squares. Other buildings were decorated with tile murals, or tiles around the doors and windows. On our trek up to the castle, we rested in a courtyard of a church. We sat on benches within an area covered by bougainvillea, and all the structures were tiled. Inside restaurants and museums there were more tiles decorating the walls. Some were the blue and white of the Chinese or Delft variety; others were multicolored. Tiles on the outside of buildings were usually of geometric designs in shades of blue, green or yellow-to-brown.

On our second day, we took an all day tour to Mafra, a city north of Lisbon, where we saw a monastery and a former palace all within one compound. I wondered about the possible relationship between those life styles. Part of the large building contained palace rooms and another part had the poorly furnished cells of the monks. The rough-hewn tables and benches of the monks were so different from the gilt, marble inlays and sumptuous furnishings of the palace.

We drove to Sintra, and visited the Pena Palace. In the town of Sintra we transferred to a smaller bus - one that could manage sixty sharp curves in the road on our way to the top of the hill where the palace perched. Actually, the palace looked like a castle from the outside, but was a charming home indoors. Totally furnished with antiques and belongings of the kings and queens who spent their summers on this cool hill, it had a cozy feeling. In contrast, the palace at Mafra had a corridor almost three hundred yards long between the king's and queen's bedrooms.

After lunch in the fishing village of Ericeira, we drove through the coastal resorts of Guincho, Cascais, and Estoril. We also went to the Queluz Palace, built to resemble Versailles. It, like the Mafra Palace, was expansive and cold. A section of it was not open to the public because visiting royalty is housed there. Queen Beatrix of the Netherlands was one of the more recent visitors.

I think I've always been interested in visiting Portugal because I associate its early days of navigation with Holland's past. I learned a bit of history on this visit, and I remembered that it was the Portuguese Vasco de Gama who rounded Africa, discovering the sea route to India in 1498. The Portuguese really ruled the seas, but during the years they were united with Spain (1580-1640), their overseas possessions were neglected by Spain. That enabled the Dutch to annex parts of the East Indies that were formerly Portuguese.

In 1755, an earthquake with accompanying fires and tidal waves destroyed most of Lisbon. On the morning of our third and last day, we walked downtown, took a cable car up a hill, took a tram down another hill and finally got to the ruins of the Carma monastery. When the city was being rebuilt, the people decided to leave these ruins as a reminder of the earthquake.

Now, feeling brave and eager for more exploration on our own, we descended from Carma in an outdoor elevator built by a follower of the man who did the Eiffel tower. Then we hunted for a tram to take us to Belem, a town west of Lisbon. We passed the great monastery of Jeronimos, but decided we didn't need to enter. The building was of the Manueline form of architecture and is one of the few examples still standing because the earthquake did not reach Belem.

Manueline architecture is characterized by the variety of motifs used around windows and doors. There are many motifs used simultaneously. For example, there can be anchors and chains to represent the sea, shells and strands of seaweed to represent the ocean, laurel branches and oak leaves as botanical symbols, and the cross of the Templar knights to represent Christianity. Interesting, but a bit confusing in its entirety, I thought.

We continued a bit further to the Belem Tower, standing off shore but accessible by a boardwalk. The tower looked like it belonged on a chess board. Attached, was a kind of patio one flight up, that had many turrets, domes and openwork balconies. It must have been quite an impressive sight to sailors returning home to this port, from which Vasco de Gama made his journeys.

In spite of showers that had us hiding until the sun peeked out again, we took a bus beyond our hotel to visit the Park of Eduardo VII. There was a statue of Pombal, the man who ordered the rebuilding after the earthquake, saying "Close the ports, bury the dead, and succor the living!"

I bought a "hot" gold bracelet from a man who claimed to be a stevedore from Angola, without money, with six children to feed, and who happened to have goods that presumably "fell off the boat". Lois thought I had gone bonkers but I said, *'I'd rather take a chance on this than the NY lottery or a bingo game. If it's gold, I have a good deal. If not, I have an expensive trinket as a wonderful reminder of three days in Portugal".*

**BARCELONA, SPAIN:** Thinking back on this stop-over in Lisbon, Portugal, I thought it was the most relaxing, evenly paced but full days of exploring I've had in a foreign country. Lois and I had just taken each day at a time, trying to cover priority areas first.

It was a contrast to a very busy recent trip to East Africa and Holland, in August, when I had planned a five-week vacation for a friend and two family members. On that occasion, I was to participate in an AVS conference in Mombasa, in southern Kenya for two weeks. I used that as an opportunity to arrange safaris for my guests while I worked. Then, we all traveled to Tanzania for another safari I had planned with the help of Dr. Herman Hangu, one of the trainees I had worked with from Arusha. He had connections for us to make a trip into Ngorongoro Crater and the Serengeti guided by a conservationist guide. On our way home, we spent a week in the Netherlands so I could introduce my oldest grand-daughter to my family's heritage.

Once in Barcelona, Lois and I set out to explore Las Ramblas - a great road for kiosks, strolling, local "tapas" bars, and for just looking at the people. We used the bus to get there.

The next day, we started out on the metro and found it very easy to use, except that there were some stairs involved. The Parc Guell, in the northern part of Barcelona, has patios, benches, terraces, and shelters designed by the outrageous architect, Antonio Gaudi. They looked like buildings out of "Alice in Wonderland", or like the Gingerbread Castle in Hamburg, New Jersey.

From the Parc, we went to the Gothic center and saw the cathedral and other old buildings. Next, we visited the Picasso Museum to see his works, starting from his drawings and paintings as a young lad, through his teens and early twenties. It was easy to see how, after he had mastered the traditional styles, he must have become bored.

During Picasso's teens, his work was similar to the sixteenth and seventeenth century masters. Then he seemed to experiment by following the impressionists. I could see touches of the styles of Van Gogh, Cezanne, Toulouse Lautrec, Seurat, and Manet. After that phase came his "color periods". This collection had a roomful of his blue paintings. Following period came the cubistic art with a collection of "Las Meninas", a name I didn't understand. Much to Lois' surprise, she enjoyed it!

The next day, we went to the more modern section of Barcelona where we saw more buildings designed by Gaudi. The famous landmark was the Church of the Holy Family, started in 1884, but still unfinished, and unlikely to be so in one hundred or more years, dependant as it is on public donations. I couldn't help but be fascinated by the wild creativity of the artist.

Until I arrived in Barcelona, I had never heard of Gaudi. His work created controversy among the citizens, so shocked were they at his unusual designs. One block, in fact, is called the "Block of Discord" because of the extreme styles. One building seems to undulate around the corner. The face of the building gives the impression of waves, and the balconies look like splashing surf. Another building has balconies that looked to me like half-masks (eye holes and the bridge of the nose).

Barcelona was quite cosmopolitan. I had envisioned more of a quiet city by the sea. The port area was very commercial and industrial, so swimming is that area was not recommended. The nearest beach is in Barceloneta, about eight miles away, so we had carried our bathing suits for nothing. No sun tan on this trip. The most memorable experience was our strolling in Las Ramblas area, generally just people-watching.

I was here to take part in the conference organized by the Society for the Advancement of Contraception. It was held on Thursday, Friday and Saturday, but with two hour lunch (or siesta) breaks from two to four o'clock. It really did not leave Lois with much "alone" time. The first day she just rested her back and legs. The second day, we went out for lunch together after she had toured the 1992 Olympic stadium, and the third day she had a mid-morning visit with the family of her friend from work. So the time went quickly.

On our last day, Sunday, we quickly went to the Spanish Village, built for the 1929 exhibition. The area was still full of streets and buildings typical of the various parts of Spain. We enjoyed it - especially all the little craft shops, cafes, narrow streets, little gardens and flower pots.

From there, we walked down the hill to the metro, taking it to Barceloneta. After a fabulous lunch of paella and a big pile of shrimp, we walked on the beach. It was Lois' first viewing of topless sunbathing. We took a cable car across to Barcelona. It left us off on Montjuic, so again we walked down the hill to the metro and back to our hotel.

With the late lunch hours, and a breakfast buffet that allowed us to take a sandwich, piece of fruit and a boiled egg, we only had dinner out one evening. The rest of the time we were only too happy to settle down with a picnic supper, supplemented by juice, cheese and nuts from the grocery shop.

It was a restful trip even though our days were full. Lois and I travel well together and it was certainly nice to have company on the exploratory visit to the Iberian Peninsula.

# CHAPTER 36: RETURN TO TANZANIA, MAR – APR, 1992

The purpose of this trip was to field-test a curriculum AVS had prepared for training doctors to perform mini-laparotomy under local anesthesia. On earlier trips, I had identified trainers. I had helped them to draft a curriculum during a subsequent visit. Upon return to the AVS office, I had worked with a staff person, Jim, who would oversee the programmatic aspects of the training. I had been responsible for the medical and surgical components, and had done the medical writing for the course.

Jim and I had flown together from NY and we arrived in Nairobi on a Saturday night. That gave us Sunday to get settled in and ready for work in the morning. I also had to walk to the market to buy an African dress because my suitcase had not arrived on the plane I had taken from Frankfort to Nairobi. One cotton dress would be sufficient until the baggage would arrive, hopefully the next day.

On Monday morning, we checked in at the office only to find the third member of our team would not be ready to work with us until Tuesday. After meeting with the office staff, we spent the rest of the afternoon trying to get return tickets reconfirmed. We also tried to arrange flights to and from the Kilimanjaro airport in northern Tanzania. We had expected the training session to be held in Dar-es-Salaam, but it had been moved to Moshi, so we would have to fly there from Dar.

Until you have tried to conduct business in the developing world, it is hard to imagine how long everything takes. Arranging our flights was not straightforward. We had to pay for the new flights with travel checks in dollars, but they had to give us change in Kenyan shillings. To get ten dollars' worth of shillings took almost forty-five minutes – in an office where selling tickets is their business.

While in Nairobi, Jim and I were invited to have dinner with a staff member, Virginia, at her house. It was outside the Nairobi city limits in a farming area and a nice change of scenery. Jim ended up stir-frying a great dinner. Virginia confessed she had no idea how to cook, and her young house girl had not yet learned yet either.

The pace of this entire trip so far could be described in the Swahili words, *"pole, pole"*, which means slowly, slowly or very slowly. Much of Wednesday was spent flying from Nairobi to Dar-es-Salaam. The next day, we spent about six hours waiting for the delayed plane to take us to the Kilimanjaro airport between Moshi and Arusha.

I spent the rest of the week going over the curriculum and the materials that were to be used. The Tanzanian doctors and I made revisions to the curriculum. Copies of the final papers were then duplicated for the trainees. By the time the course began on Monday, we were fairly well organized. As the week progressed, Jim and I continued the curriculum development while the others were in the operating room. There had not been a moment of pressure or urgency since we arrived, but a lot of work was getting done.

Each time I came to Tanzania, I had been impressed with the wonderful nature of the people. I think they are the most pleasant of all the African countries that I have visited. Everyone seemed to get along well. In the north, the Masai and the Meru tribes mingled with the others. There were both Hindu and Moslem Indians, each with their own place of worship in the little town of Moshi, and they, too, got along well. That was interesting to me because the inability of those two factions to get along was what caused Moslem Pakistan and Bangladesh to separate from Hindu India.

There were five doctor-nurse teams taking the course, and they were from various parts of Tanzania. No one knew another when they arrived on the weekend, but by the afternoon of the first day of the course, they were all friends, having fun as well as working together.

It was the month of Ramadan when we arrived, but I had not realized the month would end while we were working with the trainees. I had never been in a country for the Feast of *Id el Fitr*, which marks to end of the fasting period. During the first week of the course, a major topic of speculation was whether the moon would be sighted by the required "two devout Moslems" on Thursday night. If so, that would result in the two day Id holiday on Friday and Saturday and we would have a three-day holiday.

Jim and I were pleased that the moon was not sighted because our work would be delayed. It was a dark night Thursday, and the next night seemed to be the same. By the time we all went to our room about nine o'clock Friday, the moon had not been seen. By then, we began to think we would still have a three-day weekend from Saturday through Monday. About an hour later, I heard a wailing, shouting voice coming from the mosque, followed by noises of celebration in the streets. Good! The moon was seen on Friday night, and that meant we could get back to work on Monday.

On Saturday, all the participants packed into two vehicles and went to Arusha for the day. That city was once the capital of East Africa, the land that is now Uganda, Kenya and Tanzania. Arusha was a sizable city compared to the "one street" Moshi town. Along the way, we stopped in a game reserve. It was not a large wildlife refuge; it was more like the animal orphanage in Nairobi, where a variety of animals were kept in cages. It was a pleasant break for everyone, and I saw two serval cats at very close range, which was a treat. I could not help but think, however, that there was something strange about a group of native Africans looking at local animals in a zoo.

Sunday was one of the most interesting days of my life, thanks to Kunei, one of the trainees. He was a Masai, and was working as an assistant medical officer. A person who works as a doctor is called a medical officer. An assistant is one step lower, but these medics can qualify to be trained to do specific operations. Kunai was being trained to perform mini-laparotomies. Some assistant medical officers have been trained to practice general medicine where doctors are in short supply.

The Masai had only recently begun taking an interest in education for their children. Their culture had been pastoral, and they migrated with their cattle throughout southern Kenya and northern Tanzania. Kunei's father was well ahead of his time because he encouraged his children to go to school instead of herding cattle. The family was still a cattle family, with the extended family caring for the animals so the sons could be educated. Kunei told me he had a younger brother who was a medical officer in the area of his family's boma. He explained that a boma was a group of mud huts where the extended family lived with their cattle.

During the first week of the course, I got to know Kunei fairly well, primarily because I thought I'd probably never again have such an opportunity to learn about the Masai first-hand. By the end of the first week, Kunei had invited me to go with him to his family's boma on Sunday if we could arrange transportation. I offered to buy the petrol for one of the vehicles and to give the driver a tip, so all was arranged. Jim came along, too. At Kunei's suggestion, we stopped at a store to buy sugar, candy, gum, and some groceries to take to the family, which numbered about a hundred individuals.

We traveled on a paved road for about half an hour. After that was another hour of driving on a dirt path through a few small housing areas. We crossed creeks and drove through mud as I became increasingly doubtful that our four-wheel-drive vehicle would be able to cross the river. We had just had two nights of rain and it was the beginning of the rainy season. But we pressed ahead, slipping and sliding.

Finally, the river stopped us. There was no way to cross except by foot. So, off we went, crossing a river at a foot bridge made of rolling tree trunks. Then, for almost an hour more, we trudged in the hot sun, stepping over cow dung, sliding in mud, and jumping creeks.

I was wearing the closest garb I had to a Masai robe at the request of Kunei. It was an ankle length maroon robe with a floral print. The Masai color is red and their clothes are loose wraps. I was also wearing, as Masai women do, multiple strings of beads and old Tanzanian earrings. I carried a hidden gift for Kunei's mother in my bag, along with bug repellant, a camera, eight ounces of water in my emergency plastic bottle, and "sweat-wipers", cloth handkerchiefs I could rinse or let dry to reuse. My legs and feet were bare except for toe-strap sandals. I had learned that it was easier to wash my feet than to clean the insides of muddy shoes.

By the time we reached the boma, we were pooped and sunburned. One by one, and then group by group, we were greeted by the family and made to feel welcomed. They were all wearing red, except the small children who were wearing tan clothing. All were wearing loose robes or tied wraps. Little three-legged stools were brought for us to sit in the shade. Everybody shook hands and said their greetings in the Masai language; I returned greetings in Swahili, with a lot of "How are you?" and "Thank you"s thrown in. Smiles and holding hands go a long way.

Kunei distributed the sweets, telling the family it was our gift. The women admired my beads and dress. I admired their children, (so many of them!) even though flies usually surrounded them and crawled on their faces, especially around their eyes and mouth.

Kunei's brother offered us water and soda. He was the medical officer who had opened a small dispensary on the family's land. With the usual "missionary's prayer", I drank the water. How could I refuse...*from a doctor, it must be safe, right?* I also drank a bottle of warm Sprite and the cup of hot tea that followed later, grateful for the liquids after the dehydrating walk.

There was a lot of talk between Kunei and his family. They had not seen each other in six months. The younger brother, Moinget Ole Kuney, nicknamed Joseph in English, settled down next to me and we really had a good chance to get to know each other during the afternoon.

*Visiting at the boma of Dr Moinget Ole Kuney.*

Moinget and his entire family had been brought to Christianity through the Lutheran church many years ago. The church offered him an opportunity to go to medical school, but his response was "only if I can return to work with my people". The church first refused his condition, but later accepted, and Moinget was educated in a Lutheran hospital in Tanzania, the Kilimanjaro Christian Medical Center (KCMC).

After his medical education, he was posted to Machame, where there was a Lutheran hospital. It was about twenty miles north of Moshi. He served there for a while but was not happy because that was not really Masailand. As he described it, the number of Masai in Machame could be compared to the amount you can see of a hippo in the stream – a very small portion. So, Moinget was released from Machame and allowed to set up a dispensary on the Kuney boma.

Meanwhile, the brother who was our trainee, Karraine Kunei Kuney, constructed a church made of cement blocks so that the family and surrounding families would have more effective shelter than the trees they had been using for their worship area. Trees were not very protective in the rainy season. Consequently, the family now had a cement church, the dispensary, two out-houses and a building in which Moinget and the nurse and midwife lived. It was part of the dispensary unit.

All the rest of the family lived in mud homes of the traditional Masai style. Jim and I were invited into their homes. What impressed me most was the darkness. The only window was about six inches across. Otherwise, I thought it was quite a compact arrangement, cool, and quite livable, especially because I had the experience of living in a small tent before.

Every wife had her own hut. The children and any guests (should we have accepted their offer) would sleep in the next compartment, not as private as the wife's space where her husband could join her, and where she had room for her personal belongings. I even spotted a book in one home.

We met the entire clan and then visited the grave of Kunei's father, which was the only burial site in the boma. It was customary for only the head of the family to be buried in the boma. All other family members, when they died, were coated with animal fat and seated under a tree in the bush for the hyenas to eat.

Next, we visited with his mother. She was feeling depressed and was mourning the death of her brother the previous week. She was also enduring the effect of having eaten a lot of animal fat as a laxative so she could purge herself. I wondered to myself, "ex-lax" from cows?

Mama sat outside her hut in the shade. I gave her a long string of blue crystal beads in gold rims. She was very pleased, and the other family members were very complimentary. She immediately put them around her neck. Later, her youngest daughter was asking for them, but Mama proudly told the girl that the beads were my gift to her alone. I think I was happier than Mama.

Her younger brother was wearing a bracelet he had made of beads. He called it his "watch" as it had a circular cluster of beads that represented the face of the watch and a small bead on the side as the winding knob. After I gave Mama the beads, he took off his watch and gave it to me. I treasured it and have worn it often, even after I had washed off the cattle dung.

When I think of all the missionary centers I have seen in Africa, I cannot help but to compare them to this boma, which had lost its support from the Lutheran church because Moinget wanted to help his own people. So many missionary posts I have seen have been isolated from the people, mingling with the local residents only when preaching, or hiring them to work for the mission. I feel our missionary gifts may be misdirected. Here was this thirty-two-year old doctor, the age my son was when he died, trying to make life and health better for his people.

Moinget needed a way to get water from the spring up into a tank so it could flow by gravity to the boma and dispensary. He needed a bridge across the river so he could get to the source of supplies and so the people could get to his dispensary. He also needed a vehicle so he would not have to carry his patients all the way to the nearest "bus stop" about nine miles away. He needed medical supplies. He and his brother, Kunei, wanted to rid the area of the flies that are so endemic to the cattle-close life style of the Masai. They dreamed of a day when the cattle would be in an area a bit apart from the homes, where homes would have windows and screens to keep out the flies.

At the same time they were trying to change their life for the better, they were also struggling to preserve their Masai heritage. It is probably one of the most complex situations in the developing world. Hardly anything could be more primitive than the Masai boma life, yet I feel that would be where I would choose to live and work if I could.

The last week of the course was uneventful. Jim and I felt we could leave by midweek. All was going smoothly and we had no doubt the trainees were in good hands with the trainers. We returned to Dar-es-Salaam on Wednesday, after spending much of the day waiting at the airport for the one delayed plane to arrive at the Kilimanjaro airport. Air Tanzania had been reduced to operating only one plane. When we finally got to Dar, we decided to spend the night at the Oyster Bay hotel on the Indian Ocean.

On Thursday, there was a man selling coral on the beach across the street from our hotel and I bought a large piece as a reminder of my trip to Tanzania. The rest of the day I was occupied by trying to change my KLM flight from Friday to that night. Luckily for me, I finally succeeded and that meant I would have two full days in Holland before my scheduled flight from Amsterdam to New York.

Postscript: I never returned to Tanzania to volunteer in my retirement, but I did support Moinget for quite a while. He married the nurse and they had twin girls. I paid for them the get a pump and supply tank for their water and for the pipes needed to bring the water to the boma. I begged medicines from various pharmaceutical corporations but failed because I was not a recognized charity. I often wonder how they are. Part of my heart is in that boma.

# CHAPTER 37: NIGERIA AGAIN, DEC, 1992

Lagos: trying to modernize, yet some things seemingly doomed to continue. The first evidence of positive change was at the passport control booth where I noticed immediately that the one-way-view dark glass barriers separating visitors from the inspector had been removed since my last visit. I commented on it to the officer and he agreed it was an improvement. But then he asked, "So, what have you brought me?" I feigned a hearing difficulty and got him to repeat it twice more, though he was trying not to be heard by others. Then I laughed and replied, "What have I brought you? Nothing!" He got rid of me quickly. He obviously figured that a repeat visitor should know the airport employees expected tips, gifts, or bribes.

The currency declaration forms were no longer required so I just took $600 to the currency exchange window and asked for Naira. Because of the large amount, they asked me to enter the little booth from a back door. That meant dragging my luggage around a narrow path. Because the office was so small, I had to leave my bags where they could be stolen. Fortunately, I spotted a driver holding a card reading "Gonzagas" (*close enough to Gonzales*, I thought), so I indicated that I was his passenger, pointing to my luggage so he could keep an eye on it while I was in the booth.

The bank had a new bill-counting machine. They put $100 bills in the machine, which fanned them and electronically counted them. I was surprised by this new technology and the three employees huddled in the little cubicle, laughing at my amazement. I was handed a great bundle of Naira notes. Six hundred dollars equaled 12,000 Naira, twenty Naira for every dollar. Naira were only in N20 denominations then, so my dollars resulted in over six hundred Naira bills. My purse was not large enough so they all went into a plastic bag I had brought with me.

The driver had been sent by Family Health Services (FHS), a central coordinating group for all non-profit agencies working with USAID funds in Nigeria. He told me I was to be brought to the Eko Meridian Hotel, a switch from the Sheraton where I thought I had been booked. *"OK. Don't argue"*, I thought. *"Further evidence that Nigeria is still Nigeria"*. The Sheraton had refused to confirm my reservation anyway unless money had been deposited by 4 PM, and it was already four hours later, so I probably would not have gotten a room anyway. *"I'll work it out Monday when I meet our West Africa Director, Dr. Ade Adetunji."*

No stranger to the Eko, I knew I wanted to have dinner at their more formal dining room, the Restaurant of the Sun. The chef's special that night was Belgian mussels cooked in white wine, with French fries on the side. The mussels had been flown from Belgium on the same Sabena World Airlines plane that I had taken from Brussels that day. The big bowl of mussels was a great treat to start my journey. With a glass of cold Guilder beer it came to N270.

Of course, by selecting this special dinner, I did not get to enjoy the Nigerian specialty of the day: homemade *egusi* soup. That is a stew cooked in traditional style with fried fish, cow's foot, ox tripe, and beef. It is garnished with smoked fish and priced at N225. Nor did I get the chicken delicacy: fried chicken and gizzards cooked with stewed tomatoes, garnished with sautéed tomato and onion. Both of these Nigerian dishes could be accompanied by rice, pounded yam, *eba, fufu, amala, dodo, or semovita.* I knew both would also have been delicious because I have enjoyed many such meals.

Nigerian food seems very similar to me no matter what it is called. They tend to mix the beef and fish and vegetable into a stew served in a bowl. With that, they serve a large flat plate with the white starchy staple of the patron's choice, made from grain, cassava, or yam. While it is traditional to eat by using a ball of the staple as a spoon, restaurants will serve a fork for visitors.

I could not get to sleep until about two o'clock. In the morning, I was first awakened by some employee banging on the door, saying he was verifying that the room was empty. I assured him it was occupied. Next, I was awakened by a phone call for someone else. The caller was very insistent, and annoyed that I could not produce the man. Finally, I was awakened by a phone call from the floor attendant, asking if I did not want my room cleaned and my bed made. So, I finally got up and went to the pool in my bathing suit and robe, had lunch and lounged all afternoon. A quiet, relaxed way to start an assignment.

I was packed and ready early the next morning, expecting to be picked up by Ade, but when he had not arrived by 7:30, I took a cab to our West Africa office, near the airport, retracing the journey I had made two nights before. The open burning was continuing to create smog and smoke in the air. I was reminded of Secaucus, NJ, many years ago.

Ade, the AVS West Africa Director, was pleased to see me when I arrived at eight. He had been to the Sheraton to pick me up for a nine o'clock flight to Makurdi. FHS had messed everything up by sending me to the Eko Hotel. New plans had to be made. We left for the airport, planning to get a plane to almost anywhere, and then continue by road to our destination. We were able to get a noon flight to Enugu where we negotiated a driver and car for the three and a half hour road trip from Enugu to Makurdi.

Along the way, the gas tank got low, but gas was not readily available. Finally, we purchased five gallons on the black market for N60. It should have been N18.

No lunch opportunity. A small glass of ginger ale on the plane. No bathroom. I tried to use the bathroom at the airport when we landed in anticipation of the long road trip ahead of us. I opened the door to a stall and felt sticky fingers. I discovered that the place was being painted. Water was running in the sink, at least, so got most off. I was left with blue cuticles and a streak on my skirt, along with a full bladder. We proceeded with our long, hot, dry ride, arriving at the Benue Hotel by 4:30, when I finally got to a bathroom. Ade and I met again in the lounge to quench our thirst with the local beer, named "More". It was brewed in town, was rather flat, came in sixteen ounce bottles without labels, and was only slightly cooler than room temperature, but it was wet! It was also safer to drink than water.

The Benue Hotel was the best in town. I knew this because I had stayed in the other one a couple of times before. It was set up like garden apartments, some being two or three stories high. I had a room with a king-size bed, sofa, two chairs, a TV, air-conditioning and a small refrigerator. I hoped the electricity would not fail. The cost was the Naira equivalent of $30, just one dollar under my $31 allowance for that city. By comparison, the hotel in Lagos cost $165.50, just fifty cents below my allowance for that major center. Neither allowance left enough for meals.

There was no shower, but there was a hot water heater so I did not have to settle for a cold bath, at least. There was the inevitable five gallon bucket in the bathtub, and in it was a smaller bowl for scooping water to pour over my head and body. It was also an indication that the water might be shut off at any time so it would be best to fill the bucket, just in case.

The first stop was to the state hospital. All surgery had been cancelled because they had an infected case the previous day. They said they had washed the operating room with Lysol and now believed that they had to wait twenty-four hours for the bacteria to die before they could do more surgery. I learned that they had not cleaned thoroughly, probably counting on the Lysol without the use of soap and water. Also, I learned that there was not a single functioning autoclave that could be used to sterilize operating room linens, drapes, or towels.

To make matters worse, the one small malfunctioning autoclave was depended upon to sterilize linens for two other small hospitals in the state. No matter whatever may happen to me on one of these trips, I certainly hope that surgery is not required. Ade and I planned to return to observe surgery later in the week. Maybe the fumes will have gone; maybe they will have had another infected case. Meanwhile, all potential surgical clients were sent home.

The next stop was a day trip to Mkar, where the NKST (Reformed Church) hospital sets a fine example of health care. The folks there really try, and every time I have visited, I have been impressed. Once again, I met an employee who had gone to Calvin College in Michigan.

A thought occurred to me when I went into the hotel restaurant one evening. There was not a single place setting that was set up with a plate, utensils, napkin, salt and pepper, cup and saucer. When a guest needed a piece, it was "stolen" from another setting. The same thing happened in the operating room. The problem was never solved and there was never a complete set-up. Much the same thing happened when we hired a car for a trip. Invariably, we first had to go for gas. They were never prepared. No such thing as "anticipatory planning" in anything. Strange.

Ade left to return to Lagos on Thursday of my first week. From that time I would be "on my own". Friday was a travel day, and I had found a driver from FHS to take me to Jos, where I would have some free time on the weekend. Another week of work would follow.

Nathaniel was my driver. He asked me when I wanted to leave. I suggested he recommend the time, but it was clear he thought "Madame" should state her wish. I suggested nine o'clock, and he agreed. Later that day he saw me and asked me to show him my room so he would know where to pick up my bags. I took him there. When he left, he said, "I will pick you up at eight o'clock". I got the message. He wanted an earlier start. By seven-forty the next morning, he came into the dining room where I had just gotten coffee and breakfast after waiting since seven. He announced, "I am around". Interpreted, that means "Hurry. I am waiting for you". Of course, we then had to go to a gas station to "top it off". On the way, he wanted to stop for bananas and groundnuts (peanuts). It sounded like a good idea to me, too, so we could snack during the drive.

Each time we encountered a vendor selling bananas at a crossroad, he decided they were too expensive. They wanted N10 (about fifty cents) for a bunch and he refused. I gave him N15 and asked him to stop at the next place for bananas. He stopped at a market place, bought some fried food and a Sprite, sat on a bench to eat it, and then rinsed his eating hand with some of the soda. We took off again. Each time we saw bananas, I suggested he try again but he claimed none of them were fresh. Now that he had eaten, I was sure he just wanted to pocket what was left of the N15 I had given him.

A bit north of Makurdi was an area where the local people carved the large mortars and pestles used for pounding yams. I would have really loved to have one, but having picked one up once, I knew I could never mange the heavy wood. The bowl on its base would make a great waste basket for our patio, (or a high salad bowl – maybe a champagne cooler?) The pounder would be able to club an elephant, lion or bear if one could swing it. The women pound the yam in the same way women used to churn butter. The bowl on the ground, two hands on the pounder.

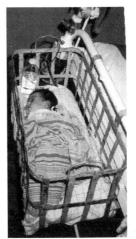

*Newborn in a rural district hospital.*

About half way to Jos, we went from flat Benue State to the hilly Plateau State. The difference in scenery was quite remarkable. The road gradually climbed, as Plateau State had the highest elevation and therefore the most pleasant weather. Mountains appeared, but as we got closer, they looked like all rock. Maybe that is why the local beverage was named Rock beer. There were heaps of rocks in hill formations. Some really strange configurations appeared to be an intentional stacking of smaller rocks on larger boulders. Sometimes there was a large rock balancing on a base of smaller rocks.

I was reminded of two things. First, of the way stones are piled in a Hebrew cemetery. The other memory was when I was once driving north of Phoenix to explore northern Arizona. I passed through a similar "rock garden" there, too. I think of it as a garden because it was so beautiful, amazingly peaceful in spite of the obvious force behind the rocks. It is no wonder that Zen utilizes rocks and sand for contemplation and rest.

We arrived in Jos at the Hill Station Hotel about one in the afternoon. I had to direct the driver because I was an old Jos visitor and he did not know the way. It was hard to believe I would have the rest of the afternoon and the weekend to rest in this pleasant area before the next assignment would start.

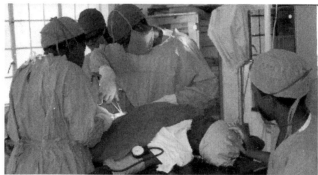

*Mini-lap training in Jos.*

Upon checking in, I had to leave a deposit of $365, equal to N7000, for a seven-day stay at N500 per day. The actual room charge should be N3500 for the week, but they required double. If I did not use up some of the extra deposit for meals, I would be checking out of the hotel with a lot of Naira and have difficulty exchanging them for dollars. I enjoyed grilled barracuda, very fresh bright green beans, deliciously sweet fresh carrots, and small boiled potatoes. I remembered the fresh vegetables from previous trips. They were a treat, and I charged the ten dollar dinner to my room account.

I spent a quiet afternoon reading out on the lawn and enjoying the breezes of Plateau State. The next day I decided to do some shopping. I wanted to avoid the hustle and bustle of the marketplace so went instead to the street where the traders had a few stalls. That was one of the benefits of returning to this city. I knew my way around. There were two vegetable stalls, three selling mostly wood or leather goods, and a few others with assortments of old trading beads, trinkets, jewelry, bone carvings, and old C-shaped bracelets that were once used as currency. I found that same shape carved into a walking stick I purchased. I also bought a carving of a man and a woman connected by a linked chain, believing it to be a marriage symbol.

Next, I headed to another street where clothing was available. I bought two dresses, one knee length and the other long. I'll be able to use them on other trips I'll be making in West Africa where the people appreciate the traditional clothing being worn – unlike Kenya, where they prefer polyester or rayon ruffles.

I enjoyed two hours of fun. I shop to enjoy the experience of bargaining and I hope I make it fun for the salesmen, too. It seems to work here as well as in Central America. There is a lot of kidding, laughing, and whispering offers so no one else will know the wonderful price we're discussing. When I reach my limit, I start to reduce my next offer. This is always met with shock and then laughter. A settlement usually follows with everyone pleased. For example, the two dresses I bought cost a total of twenty dollars. An antique silver Cross of Agadez cost ten dollars, which was a bargain because I saw fewer and fewer of these now rare pieces. The single piece of wood carving cost about ten also, and each walking stick was about eight. When I think about the many hours of labor that goes into each carving, they were cheap.

There was a meeting at the hotel on Saturday, attended by about three hundred people, all dressed in Nigerian finery. Men were in their flowing robes over matching pants and shirts, with hats to match. Women wore head wraps of all styles to coordinate with their dresses, all of which were very colorful. There were traditional dancers wearing not much more than cowry shells with rattles on their ankles. They were quite spectacular with the shiny white shells on their glistening chocolate colored skin. There was a small percussion band (mostly drums and rattles). There was also a modern band to play the National Anthem and to accompany the dignitaries as they entered. It was actually a fund-raising event to kick off a drive to build a hall where people now living in Plateau State, but originally from Osun State could meet. A list of seven reasons they should have such a meeting place was presented quite formally; most of reasons were social. The meeting lasted four hours, followed by continuing entertainment. The drums provided a different background sound for my sun-bathing that afternoon.

*Tribal dancer.*

Sunday was another restful day spent at the pool. That evening, a three-part TV series began: The Jackie Collins story, "Hollywood Wives". What an impression people form of us! It's no wonder the citizens of the third world want to go to the USA for their share of the world's wealth.

In Nigeria, there is a saying, "Everyone wants a piece of the National Cake". The meaning refers to the oil in Nigeria, which everyone considers to be a gift from God to all Nigerians. Everyone wants their share of all the benefits oil brought.

One of the Nigerian doctors I was working with believed that the oil and the money it brought spoiled everyone. In the earlier days of oil, too much money became available and there were no controls. No one could imagine an end to the profits. Now, the economy is not good, but people don't seem to have any concept of cutting back accordingly. They deserve a piece of the National Cake, so if money is short, they will steal, go on strike, withhold goods for the black market, and overcharge for everything.

Crime in the streets had increased (as if it had not been bad enough!) and it had spread well outside Lagos. Every day, the newspapers reported robberies on the main roads between cities. A number of stories were told to me by various people during this visit. Traders who used to go from city to city in cars became recognized by robber gangs. The traders then started to use the public buses, but soon the robbers learned of the switch, so now entire busloads of people were being robbed. When women were among the victims they were stripped because bras and panties had been used to conceal money. A nurse told me that a friend of hers hid her money under her large, bare, pendulous breasts and was thus able to fool the robbers!

Landlords were raising rents even in cases where the tenant had paid two or three year's rent in advance. When a tenant objected, the landlord removed all the doors and windows. If that didn't work, they took the tenant's property, including clothing and furniture. During my visit, there was a story in the papers. A landlord waited until his tenant was on a trip before he sent the notice of the increased rent. When the rent was due, he removed the windows and doors. To "officially" record the non-payment of the increased rent, he hired a tout to pose as the tenant, and got the court's permission to take possessions in lieu of the increased rent with the tout's agreement. The tenant came home to an empty house, and found that the courts had "approved" the action. The case was going to be appealed, but the tenant had little hope of anything being recovered.

This week celebrated the one-year anniversary of the President's move from Lagos to the new capital, Abuja. People were interviewed about what this had done to residents and businesses in Abuja. Some reactions were interesting. A student spoke of jam-packed classrooms where students struggled for seats. A journalist spoke of how the influx of people affected traffic and resulted in insufficient hospital facilities and services. A banker was pleased with the increased patronage. A laborer said that people got fired for almost no reason because there were so many unemployed ready to step in. He wanted the President to return to Lagos, saying "We don't need him here; he has made things difficult for us".

Best of all, I liked the fresh honesty of a lawyer who said that in spite of the influx of people, his law office had not yet witnessed a tremendous increase in clients. He said, "First, you have to understand that Abuja's crime level is low so not many arrests are made. Our legal business only booms when there are plenty of arrests, and through that, we receive invitations for court representations. But we still hope that as people continue to troop in, the crime rate might blow up, and with the effectiveness of the police, corresponding arrests would be made and there is where we lawyers come in!"

While in Jos, the work was often finished by mid-afternoon so I got into a bathing suit to cool off in the pool. Two teenage girls befriended me. Felicia, age seventeen, wanted to study law, and Cecelia, eighteen, wanted to become a journalist or novelist. They wanted to have photos to remember our times together so I promised to bring a camera the next day. They arrived all dressed up for the photo session and we spent time in the lounge talking that day as they were not dressed to swim. They were full of questions and so eager to learn. They were wonderful young ladies with high ambitions. I wished them well.

An experience with a young woman who was a hostess in the Hill Station Hotel restaurant was equally pleasant. I gave her a paperback I had finished. When I was missing from dinner two nights in a row, she called my room to find out if I was alright because she had missed me. I got a big hug and kiss when I left, and of course, I took more photos to send back to the staff.

Both the doorman and the driver I had hired to take me on a three day trip on my last trip had recognized me and greeted me warmly upon my arrival. I had sent them photos after the last trip. A little effort goes a long way. Meanwhile, I fully enjoyed the friendly attitudes.

Friday, the last day of my assignment, turned out to be a typical Nigerian travel nightmare! I left the Jos hotel at six in the morning, hitching a ride with two Nigerian men who happened to be going to the airport at that time. The car and driver I had hired the day before had failed to appear. I had to buy my ticket at the airport for a seven-thirty flight, but word spread while I was in line that the plane was fully booked. When I got to the head of the line, I got my ticket that I had assumed would be for the next flight, but the clerk assured me it was for the departing flight. My luggage was checked accordingly.

The boarding gate was padlocked and all the seats in the waiting room were filled. One man insisted he be allowed to go to the plane because his young child was already aboard. When the gate was unlocked for only him, the large crowd surged and I was caught in a stampede. I got three bruises on my arms and a pair of bent eye-glasses to show for it. Everyone started running for the plane, hoping for a seat. Half-way to the plane, it occurred to me that my luggage may not have been on it, so I stopped. A young attendant said, "Run, run, Madame! Your luggage is on the plane! Run! Run!"

So I ran, but all the seats were taken and we had to return to the waiting room. I knew that my two bags might very well "disappear" by the time I could get to Lagos. I went to the station manager and requested he call Lagos and have my bags held safely. He agreed. There was no more I could do but wait for the plane to return to Jos for its return trip to pick up those of us who were still waiting.

At ten-forty-five, people started to line up at the outer gate to the tarmac. Here, we had full force of the *harmattan* winds while we waited for the Okada Airline plane to arrive. Harmattan is an equivalent of winter in this sub-Saharan climate. It is accompanied by a lot of wind, hazy skies, and lower temperatures. It is the season when people wear sweaters and complain of *catarrh*, the common cold. Billboards advertise Vaseline-type products to keep lips and tissues soft in the harmattan season.

About half an hour after noon, the plane finally arrived. We all ran for it because it was another "first come, first seated" occasion. It was the way I had been introduced to plane travel in Nigeria more than five years earlier, but recently the situation had seemed to be improving. This time, the schools were being closed for Christmas holidays (called "ex-mas"). The airport was filled with over one hundred students trying to get home from boarding or military schools, adding to the confusion and overcrowding.

At the stairs to the plane there was another mob scene. No line could be formed. The ticket checker then selected a new spot for the line to form and the plane's stairs were lifted to prevent "climbers". Again, a mob formed at the new spot. Line busters again. More confusion. Arguments. I finally boarded the plane at one-thirty in the afternoon, knowing my appointment at the US Embassy would be missed and I could not contact them to explain.

The plane landed in Lagos an hour later. I was hot, dirty, and tired having had to deal with all these troubles since early morning. Besides, I had no breakfast or lunch. I had only one cup of tea at the airport before they ran out at eight o'clock.

More confusion awaited me at the small domestic airport where we landed. I had to pay off two helpers before my luggage could be located – but at least it was found. I immediately got a taxi to the USAID office for a debriefing, required after every visit. From there, I was taken to the Sheraton Hotel where I "negotiated with" (slipped some money to) the bell captain to hold my luggage for five hours. Then I went into the women's room in the lobby to wash up and change clothes. I felt like a homeless person washing up in New York's Port of Authority bus terminal when I did this, but it was preferable to remaining dirty. The problem with these newer bathrooms, however, is that they no longer have paper towels. I had to use my soiled skirt and blouse to dry myself before donning my clean clothes.

In a comfortable chair in the lounge, clean and refreshed, I was able to finish my trip report as well as the paperback I had been reading. I left for the international airport at nine that evening for a midnight departure to London where I would have a stop-over on my way home.

At the Nigerian customs clearance, I was asked about purchases. I told them I had one small carving, but I also had three clearly visible walking sticks in my hand. Two agents insisted I show a certificate from the museum giving me permission to take the carving out of the country. I argued, insisting this was a ridiculous suggestion.

I asked, "If I bought a carving at the airport shop where they sell similar carvings, would you send me back to a museum for a certificate?"

"No, but if you buy it outside the airport, you must produce it."

I replied, "No-one told me this policy when I arrived in Nigeria, nor on any trips I have made before."

"No matter, Madame. You must have it!"

Me: "Keep the carving! I don't want it!"

Agent: "I'll check with the supervisor."

To make a long story shorter, I got away with the carving that by then had stained the blouses it was wrapped in. What a waste! I left, threatening to never spend another unnecessary penny for a souvenir again.

From customs clearance, I had to proceed to passport clearance, then luggage identification. Between these steps, I spent a bit of time in the "First Class Waiting Room". What a joke! No air-conditioning, no cold drinks, no coffee or tea, no ice, no water. There were a few bottles of liquor on a shelf but no glasses. I found a coffee cup and poured a "finger" of brandy into it. I deserved it.

By ten-thirty, I had moved to the waiting room near the check-in gate, which was cooler than the "first class" lounge. We boarded about after midnight, only thirty-five minutes late. As soon as the "fasten seat belts" lights went out, I took my small carry-on bag to the lavatory and took another bath. At least I had paper towels this time. I put on make-up, deodorant, clean clothes; I brushed my teeth and my hair, donned clean clothes (again) and was ready for London.

All-in all, it was a good trip. I even found myself looking forward to returning in March, just three months later. I never thought I'd say I was eager to return, but the country was growing on me.

Postscript

I never made that return trip to Nigeria for AVS. In late February, 1993, I went one weekend to DeLancey, New York, located in the western foothills of the Catskill Mountains. I wanted to help my recently widowed friend, Richard Bowers, open his country home and begin to sort out all the medical records, mail and bills he had to face. When I was about to leave on Sunday evening, I tripped down two stairs and broke my leg. Richard nursed me for a week until the swelling went down and I could get a cast applied. By then he had convinced me to stay in the country for my recuperation. During the weeks it took until my bones healed, he succeeded in getting me to accept his marriage proposal. He also convinced me to retire from AVS. Given the realization that Dr. Amy Pollack really wanted to staff the medical division with new people, I was easily tempted to retire.

When I returned to the office in mid-May, I arranged for an early retirement, and had six weeks to finish up a few projects that I had been working on. I left the office in mid-July. Richard and I were married on July 30 on our wonderful mountain-top property in the country. When I returned for a farewell party at AVS in early August, I surprised everyone with the announcement of my recent wedding.

*Operating room nurse with supplies.*

# CHAPTER 38: THE PHILIPPINES, JAN, 1993

I knew when I left for this assignment that the trip would be different in that I anticipated possible social opportunities, but I didn't know how different until near the end of the two weeks, when I reflected on the experience.

The purpose of the trip was to field test a booklet I had written, a reference guide for both trainers and trainees in a course for mini-laparotomy under local anesthesia. My partners were Paul Blumenthal, a doctor affiliated with John's Hopkins, and Gary Bergthold, a training consultant, also sent by John's Hopkins. The joint venture was appropriate since they had developed the training guide and curriculum plan, and I had developed the "how to do it" reference book.

During the mini-lap course, we were going to field test a patient simulator, a life-sized doll that would permit simulated surgery. Johns Hopkins and AVS had collaborated on developing this model and we hoped it would provide new doctors and nurses an opportunity to learn the movements required to blindly reach into the pelvis through a very small incision and retrieve a loop of the Fallopian tube to tie off.

We would be conducting the training course in the Mary Johnston Hospital, a Methodist mission facility located in the center of the Tondo section of Manila, home of most of the indigent population and many slums.

Before setting off, I had been given names of two people to contact while in Manila. My friend, Dr. Cedric Porter, asked me to call his former classmate from Harvard Medical School, a doctor who was operating a large eye clinic in Manila. Another friend, Sandy Sorrell, asked me to try to find a former business contact with whom he had lost touch, someone named Mina Gabor, who had been the director of Lawin Industries when Sandy was a buyer for Lord and Taylor. So, I was prepared for possible social contacts outside the AVS circuit, and had packed some nicer clothes than I usually did.

On the plane from San Francisco, I sat next to a young woman, Vivian Yuchengco, who had her own stock brokerage firm in Manila, and was also the vice chair of the Makati Stock Exchange. We struck up quite a friendship during the trip and spent the two-hour layover in Incheon

Airport in Seoul, Korean airport together. When we arrived in Manila, she insisted on giving me currency for my taxi, so I did not have to go to the bank window to change money. She offered to help should I run into any need, and I promised I would let her know how things were going during my stay.

The work went well, with Paul, Gary and I working effectively together. I had known the director of the Fertility Control Center, Dr. Oblepias, since 1973. He was very pleased to have me there and even planned a farewell party for me on my last afternoon.

I called Ramon Batumbacal, the eye doctor, a day after I arrived, and delivered messages from Cedric Porter. Ramon invited me to go on Sunday to the Polo Club with him and his wife. I knew very little about the game and less about the high lifestyle of the polo club members, but was very willing to learn. I called Vivian, to let her know of the invitation and learned that she would be there, too. Next, I tried to locate Mina but she was not at Lawin anymore. She had taken a post in the Philippine Cabinet, and was now the Under-Secretary of the Department of Tourism. She was happy to get a message from Sandy after a ten year lapse in their contacts, and invited me to have dinner with her the following Monday.

On Saturday, Nelie Antigua, our doctor in charge of the AVS program in the Philippines, took me shopping and to a play. We saw "Noises Off", a British comedy. We had both lunch and dinner together and generally spent a pleasant time in each other's company. It was not too often I got a chance to spend a casual day with a co-worker in a non-work environment. Nelie and I had enjoyed a solid friendship since I worked with her on her first consulting assignment in Nepal, before she joined AVS staff.

Sunday was the big day at the Polo Club. I was to meet Ramon and Celing, his wife, at the club house at three o'clock. The club was in the exclusive Forbes Park section of Manila called Millionaires' Row because so many wealthy folks lived there. Celing was at the door to greet me. She introduced me to Ramon and to her friend who was in town, on leave from her job at the United Nations. Ramon was a recent past president so we were seated in special armchairs in the center of the section for officials, government ambassadors, and other former presidents of the club. Well-dressed waiters served us cocktails throughout the game.

Ramon explained the game to me. It was both very exciting and very beautiful. I had never seen such an array of young healthy horses. Each horse played in only one "chukker" and there are six chukkers to a game. That means each player has to have at least six horses, and with each horse costing about $25,000, it's no wonder that this is a millionaire's game. On the day of my visit, there was a round robin game, with three teams competing.

The American Ambassador threw in the first ball to start the match. He was seated next to the Ambassador from Russia, and I thought it was symbolic of the relationship between our two countries that had come far enough along for friendship.

Ramon and I chatted comfortably during the game. At one point, he commented on the fact that divorce is not legal in the Philippines. So, he said, "Instead of having serial monogamy like you do in the US, we have affairs". I liked the term "serial monogamy" and thought it was an appropriate description for the pattern of many people I could recall.

Vivian was there. She had quite a sense of humor, it seemed. She came up behind me and playfully covered my eyes. Of course, I guessed it was she, but Ramon was surprised I had another friend at the club. From their comradery, it was clear they had been friends.

After the games, a formal parade of waiters came in, bearing heavily-laden trays and serving dishes. The food was set out on large tables, meats were put on the grills, and a bar was opened. Musicians began playing. Soup and shrimp cocktails were served while the meats cooked. The party had begun. Everybody circulated, and I got to speak to quite a few, including the American Ambassador, Mr. Solomon.

After the party, Ramon and Celing took me to their home, also in Forbes Park. It was lovely, with a cocktail lounge and bar near the front entrance where we settled down with a nightcap and talked a while. They insisted that their driver take me back to the hotel rather than my calling a taxi.

The next night was Monday, and I was paged in the hotel lobby to meet a man who turned out to be Mina's body guard. She was waiting in the car with her driver. She said there was a slight change of plans. We were to go to a birthday party instead of to dinner. Mina had told her hostess that she had a guest and was encouraged to bring me along. "Whose birthday?" I asked.

"Corey Aquino's", was Mina's reply! I could hardly believe it. It was not as if I got invited to a president's birthday party every day. I was certainly glad I had dressed up for the occasion.

Although Cory was not the current president, having lost the recent election, the party was still special in that the Cabinet members who had worked with her were all there to celebrate her first birthday since leaving office. Mina had served as the Under-Secretary for the Department of Trade under Corazon Aquino's administration. In fact, she had taken her first government post under Marcos about ten years before, not too long after my friend Sandy had last been in touch, so he knew nothing of her elevated positions during these years.

Cory was most gracious. She personally greeted everyone as guests arrived and she welcomed me most warmly. A long table laden with goodies filled a large reception room at the front of the house. A chef was heating cheese and warming little rolls on a hot plate. As soon as we entered, we were given a little sandwich. A band of five musicians entertained us while we nibbled and mingled.

Outside, on a terrace, tables had been set up, each with about eight chairs. A variety of meats were cooking on the barbecue grills; tables displayed a wide choice of foods, both hot and cold. One dish was a whole cooked fish with a tasty sauce that I remember to be unique even if I cannot recall its exact flavor these many years later. As soon as the fish was almost all forked up, another platter with a fresh fish appeared. One grill had some German sausage that many guests seemed to think was a special attraction. It didn't strike me as anything unusual, but German food may not be as readily available in the Philippines as it is in the US.

The party was held in the family home in Forbes Park. Cory referred to it as her mother's home. Cory, herself, lives in Queson City, which was the capital during her administration. Two daughters were there, and I met both of them. One daughter and some of her friends sat at the table where Mina and I were seated.

I met and spoke to a number of people, especially enjoying the sense of humor of Nieves, the woman who was the Secretary of Labor. There was also a Secretary (maybe the Department of Public Works) whose last name was Gonzales, so there was a fair amount of kidding about our being in-laws. I met the head of the national TV network who, I believe, was anti-family planning, but who did not seem to object when she heard about the kind of work I was doing. I also enjoyed talking to a woman who headed a program called "Peso-peso", which encouraged savings by the poor. It was run by a group of professional women, who taught other women how to better manage their money. I believe there is also a small loan fund in the program, but whatever the details, it seemed to be a program going in the right direction.

Mina introduced me as a nurse who helps teach doctors how to do surgery. Of course, that raised questions about my work. When I briefly told of how we were giving technical assistance at the Fertility Control Center at the Mary Johnston Hospital, everyone seemed to be very supportive, acknowledging the need for family planning in their country. The Roman Catholic Church was very much in control, however, so family planning had not had governmental support under Marcos or Aquino. New President Ramos apparently felt differently, and the current Secretary of Health was definitely in favor. He and the humorous Nieves handed around condoms at a recent cabinet meeting, I was told. I was sorry he was not at the party so I could meet him.

Waiters served drinks during the dinner. When dessert time came, there were many pastry selections, but someone asked if some fruit with cheese could be brought to us on a platter. A tray soon came, piled high with large juicy strawberries, grapes and other fruits, including sections of grapefruit, all peeled neatly and easy to eat. I had never thought of grapefruit as a dessert fruit, but it was a nice touch after all the heavier foods. With the cheese and fruits came port wine. Espresso coffee followed. These millionaires certainly knew how to throw a party.

On my last night in Manila, my Johns Hopkins colleagues and I were joined by two more. The new Medical Director for AVS, Dr. Amy Pollack, had arrived in Manila, along with Dr. John Naponick, AVS regional medical advisor for Asia. They were in the country on another assignment, so we all decided to go to dinner and to a night club together. Because it was Chinese New year, we started with a Chinese restaurant for dinner.

After dinner, we went to a night club called "The Hobbit House", a place with low ceilings, small chairs one might find in a kindergarten, and low tables. It was owned and operated by little people, both midgets and dwarfs. John was seven feet tall, which was why I had suggested that club. What a laugh when we entered, with poor John having to walk bending over. The little people were so amused and amazed at his height. They brought a special chair for him. Actually, we would call it a regular chair, but to them it was special because it was so big. One woman, especially, kept coming to the table to talk to John. She was fascinated by the size of his feet, and she had great fun stepping over his shoe as though she were going over a big hurdle.

There was a music group, also of little people. Two young folks danced with the rock music and put on quite a show with their thrusting pelvises. It seemed so unbelievable that such small human being could move in such adult ways. I still can't figure out how old they were. I guess maybe they were in their teens or pre-teens. But so tiny!

Well, the work was finished. I was the first to leave the country, having to get home to put in a week of work before leaving for a scheduled month in Africa. The return trip was a long one; thirty-one hours door to door. When I got back to the office I learned that my trip to Africa had been cancelled, so that I could write the extra chapters of the reference book wanted by the Philippines, and oversee the completion of the book.

The day of my return, I had lunch with one of the program staff who had just come back from a trip to Iran. Our two trips had been so different. She had to wear a head cover and veil from the time the plane landed until she left the country. Even in the hotel room, she had to cover up before she opened the door to let someone in. There were signs on all the buildings saying "Down with the U.S.", left over from the last regime under the Ayatollah. No parties for her.

I enjoyed working on this project. It gave me a real sense of accomplishment to have been able to put together all the didactic medical material necessary to teach this surgical procedure. It included information that would help guide the trainees when they arrived at their home base and initiated services. It covered everything from how to set up services, perform the surgery, treat complications, analyze problems (including deaths if they happen), monitor the quality of the service, prevent infections, and eventually teach others, again using my book. The document would be the official reference book for the government programs. AVS had established a foothold in the Philippines.

Unexpectedly, it turned out that this trip to the Philippines was my last AVS project, but it was a high point on which to retire. Accustomed to working in very poor areas of the world and having very few opportunities to socialize with any other than my colleagues, it was a drastic change to have been hob-knobbing with the *crème de la crème* of Manila.

*With Corazon Aquino in Manila.*

# Part Three: Consulting After Retirement From AVS

# MY CONSULTING YEARS
## INTRODUCTION

It was strange to leave AVS. The organization had filled my life for thirty years and I wondered how I would feel, having no office to go to, no assignments, and no new projects to look forward to. As I contemplated these factors, I decided that I really wanted to try serving as a consultant for a while. I thought that would help me make the transition from employment to retirement. I worked with an agency that helped me prepare my resume and get me started on this next phase of my life.

At the same time, I was adjusting to my new home, having married Richard Bowers in July. We lived on 125 acres on top a mountain in the western foothills of the Catskills. Part of the property had fields planted with crops for a local dairy farmer; part was woods with trails that needed to be tended and kept clear for hiking. Additionally, there was a very large garden for which Richard and I had started seedlings of the vegetables that we would be planting soon. This was far different than the small apartment I had lived in for the past ten years in Manhattan.

By the end of the year, I had done a bit of work for the Johns Hopkins program in India and had been contacted for possible work in Nigeria. I was particularly pleased to take the assignment in Nigeria as I had spent so many weeks there and enjoyed the people of that country.

Another assignment took me to Zimbabwe. I had not been that far south in Africa before and was very pleased to have two weekends of my twenty-one day trip free so that I could be a tourist for a little while. It was wonderful to see that there had once been a thriving civilization in that area, unknown to most of the world, I fear.

The final significant task I took on was to conduct a week-long workshop for the outreach workers on the Nigerian Family Planning Association. It was exactly what I had always thought AVS should have been offering to the countries that were initiating sterilization services. When I first began my volunteer work with AVS, we were creating a popular demand for services. Over the years, I had been further convinced that doctors would provide a service if there were people asking for it. But AVS, in its International Project, set about to train doctors and had never followed what had been successful in our own country.

Today, as I listen to television ads, I note that a majority of them seem to be saying, "Ask your doctor if this medication might be good for you", or some such message. The drug companies, even those clearly selling drugs that require a prescription, are stimulating a client demand for their product. When the patient asks the doctor for a specific pill or brand, the doctor is more apt to comply. At least that is what the drug manufacturers are hoping when they pitch the ads to the public.

I was very pleased to have had this opportunity to share my knowledge of publicity, public relations, client education and outreach to the family planning workers in Nigeria. They seemed delighted with their increased knowledge of such things as writing press releases, holding press conferences, and various out-reach activities.

After three years of doing consulting work, I was ready for full time retirement. Richard and I had purchased a motor-home and were going south in the winter. With our home being at an elevation of twenty-two hundred feet, with a mile long driveway, snow plowing was a task we were not enjoying. We continued our gardening and I thoroughly loved living there until Richard's death in 2006. Our mutual interests in population and environmental issues added purpose to both our lives.

*Our retirement home.*

# CHAPTER 1: ZIMBABWE, NOV, 1994

Serving as a consultant after I left AVS, I had the opportunity to work for JHPIEGO, which once stood for the Johns Hopkins Program for International Education in Gynecology and Obstetrics. It has since expanded its work to include many issues that affect health and reproductive wellbeing, and simply uses the acronym now. In the same way, AVS has expanded its role and now calls itself EngenderHealth.

The assignment that I undertook for JHPIEGO was to facilitate a supervision workshop in Zimbabwe for the national family planning organization. The workshop was to be two weeks in length, but I had arrived one week earlier to prepare for it. That gave me two weekends in the country for an opportunity to be a tourist. There were two sites I felt compelled to visit.

On my first weekend, I flew to Victoria Falls. Dr. David Livingstone, the first white man to see the falls, said that "scenes so lovely must have been gazed upon by angels in their flight". He came upon them in 1855 and named them in honor of his queen.

The falls were amazing. I had not imagined how broad the cliffs were. It seemed I walked for miles along the ridge. Splashing water caused mist to moisten me as I trudged along in wonder at the sight. The water also resulted in a rainbow that was always visible, adding to the beauty of the scenery.

At last, I arrived at the bridge that spans the gorge separating Zimbabwe from Zambia. There, far below, was the rushing Zambezi River. To my surprise, there were bungee jumpers hurling themselves off the bridge. My stomach still flips as I recall the scene in my mind.

On the weekend between the two weeks of the workshop, I was able to catch a ride with a couple of participants who had a vehicle at their disposal so that they could return to their children for the weekend. They lived in Masvingo, the nearest city to the second site I wanted to see. Zimbabwe's most renowned attraction is the Great Zimbabwe, considered the center of the Kingdom of the Ancients. I stayed at a hotel in Masvingo and hired a taxi to take me to the ruins.

Great Zimbabwe was once a citadel and a holy place. There are no kings or high priests anymore, but the atmosphere was awe-inspiring. My first

332

sight was the remnants of a mighty wall on the edge of a sheer granite cliff. Below that was the Great Enclosure, thought to be the dwelling place of the king's wives. All the structures were of granite blocks that were cut and fitted together without the use of any mortar. Carbon dating indicates that the oldest walls were built between the years 1100 and 1500. The newer sections are estimated to have been built in the fourteenth century. There may have been as many as thirty thousand people living in the area at its height. With that density, there may have been environmental problems that resulted in the doom of the kingdom. Underbrush, tall grasses and shrubs gradually covered over the structures until a hunter stumbled on the ruins in 1867.

Part of the supervision workshop was to draft a personnel plan for a family planning organization. The exercise demonstrated to me their concept of organizational structure and how it differed from mine. The family planning workers, all women, started at the top of the staff pyramid. The person in charge should have three or four people reporting to the director, they said. Next, each of those on that second level should have a number of people reporting to them. And so it went, down the line, with the participants trying to devise titles for each level, and deciding what each person's responsibility would be. The result was a top-heavy organization with more chiefs than workers.

I proposed that they start with the basic tasks that needed to be done to operate the family planning service. For example, they would need a receptionist, staff to interview the clients, someone to do physical examinations, and so forth. They would need auxiliary help as well, perhaps a cleaning person, a collector of fees, and someone to schedule appointments. I next had them consider how those basic providers of service would be supervised. The result was a far leaner staff. I often wondered how the supervision system survived over the next years.

The workshop was held in Harare, the capital of Zimbabwe, in the office space of the family planning organization. We worked while seated around a large table. For efficiency, the director had ordered lunches to be brought into the conference room. Nearby, there was a small sidewalk shop where a woman cooked food in pots set over a small fire. There was no running water or plumbing as the structure was not much more than a roof and three sidewalls. Inside were a small table and a few stools. I had seen the facility and marveled at her ability to cook in such a limited kitchen.

Every morning a staff person would ask each participant if she wanted the cow's foot stew or the mixed meats for lunch. Every day we were offered the same two choices and I always selected the cow's foot stew. I had many such meals in my years of working in West Africa and I had gotten to like the dish. On the last day, just for a change, I ordered the mixed meats, not having any idea what would it might contain. On other trips, I had found chunks of mystery meat, sections of bones, pieces of hide, and even teeth on a jaw bone in my mixed meat. I knew that animals caught in the wild were referred to as bush meat, and that such meat often included monkey or an animal called a grass-cutter that had a jaw like a rat.

When my plate arrived, I was eager to see what it was going to be this time. To my surprise, I found among the meats and vegetables, cross sections of what looked like calamari. White rings, about an inch in length. I ate a few pieces, trying to guess what I was eating, knowing it could not possibly have been octopus or squid. It had no particular taste and was a bit chewy.

I finally asked one of the ladies who also had the mixed meats, "What are these white rings?" She replied, nonchalantly, "Rectum". I never got clarification, but suspect they were sections of gut that had been added to the pot. I think I will stick with the cow's foot stew in the future.

# CHAPTER 2: THE NIGERIA PROJECT,
# MAR – APR, 1995

This was my second trip to Nigeria as a consultant. I was working with the Planned Parenthood Federation of Nigeria (PPFN), developing a Clinic Manual to be used as the standard for all services offered at their clinics. Afterward, they hope that the Nigerian family planning clinics outside the Planned Parenthood system will also use it as the national set of standards and procedures. I was proud to be the one to initiate the project and see it through its development.

Last March, I made my first trip for this project, spending over three weeks in Nigeria. During the summer I worked at home for another three weeks. This second trip was originally scheduled for later in the spring, but suddenly there was a risk that the US Agency for International Development funds for Nigeria might be cut off, so I was summoned to get there as soon as possible. I learned that if a project is underway, funds could be "continued" as long as they had been obligated before the de-funding.

When the call came, my husband and I were in California in our motor home. We had to rush back, driving straight across the country so I could leave within two weeks of getting the news. Meanwhile, my visa was being processed, tickets were being purchased, and my contract being approved by USAID. My task for this trip was to field test the manual with local personnel. Then, after some changes and fine tuning, I would again return to teach the course to the people who will be the trainers.

These plans would return me to Nigeria in July. At that time, I was scheduled to conduct a six-day course in public relations and publicity for the Nigerian outreach workers. I was excited about this added task. I had long believed that AVS had erred in not including such projects in their international programs. Although AVS had originally had such success in the United States in their outreach activities, especially in the 60s and 70s, the International Project of AVS seemed not to have any idea that they might offer such ideas overseas. I was finally going to be able to put my theory into action.

As I was writing these notes about half way through the visit, I found myself thinking that I was again in another country, another culture, doing things so totally removed from the USA and home. I frequently felt somewhat schizophrenic in the two worlds I lived in.

I was also having mixed feelings about whether or not, or for how long, I should continue consulting. At first, when I left AVS, I needed to prove to myself I could get work outside that agency. Now I knew that I could and it was going well. Getting more than three hundred dollars a day plus all expenses was nice, but I no longer felt I had to prove anything to anyone – or to myself.

Sometimes I wondered, was I really making a difference? I decided to put all decisions on hold for at least six months to see how this long-term PPFN project works out. If there was any indication that services in Nigeria have improved either in quality or quantity, I would have the extra push to do more. But some days it seemed as if no matter what outside agencies were trying to help accomplish in a country, the internal capability, urgency, or interest, was not obvious. I liked to believe that the situation was not without hope.

This morning, as every other day, the driver picked me up at the five-star Sheraton Hotel, and drove me through traffic "go-slows" on the main roads. Then he took a detour to avoid the greater traffic and proceeded through narrow round-about streets in a residential area to approach PPFN from what he called "the back door". These areas were not purely residential. There were always women or families trying to sell food, candy, or basic supplies on the streets. There were men selling papers, magazines, and automotive goods. Interspersed with homes there were tailors, business centers where a photocopier or a fax machine would be available, and anything else that might bring some income.

As I passed through the streets between seven and eight in the morning, the roads were narrowed to single car width because of all the children going to school. The streets were full of these similarly-clad uniformed boys and girls from three to five feet in height. It was like a moving cloud or a herd crossing fields in search of something they all needed. It left an indelible impression. Half of Nigeria's population was under the age of fifteen. One could not help but think what that meant in terms of childbearing in the next twenty years. There was such a need here, but, I wondered, is change possible? And will it happen in time? Yet, the children were all clean and wearing fresh clothes. The parents clearly cared about their children and did their best. I had never seen a poorly-cared-for child or baby here, unlike India or Bangladesh where infants crawled about in the dirt, often covered in flies and sores.

My colleague here, Susan Aradeon, had been under stress this week because her house was broken into. She was trying to be stoic about it, but was obviously worried. Once the robbers had discovered that no security responded when the alarms went off on the University campus where they lived, it would be only a matter of time until they would break into the house. This time, they only entered and harmed the house staff that lived in the auxiliary building a few feet from the house. She only hoped they will not use their weapons on her family.

At lunch today at the USAID cafeteria, two other women were giving her advice. One sleeps with a loaded pistol at her bedside and she advised Susan to do the same. She offered her farm for Susan to practice shooting. The other woman has a rifle loaded and ready, but out of reach of her young son. She recommended Susan get an oozie so she could just "sweep" the gun and be sure to hit at least some. Susan could not bring herself to the idea of shooting anyone, but the person who recommended the oozie told her how armed robbers had held her captive for two hours while she was pregnant. The experience left her convinced she would do anything to prevent armed robbers from entering again. Susan thinks her family might have been targeted because the name of her husband (a professor at the University of Lagos) was on a petition seeking better work conditions for professors. He also had opposed promotion of some male students. Either could have been the reason. She said, "Either you learn to live this way, or leave Nigeria".

One of the issues that was raised at the USAID meeting today was the impending "decertification" of Nigeria, meaning funds will be cut off – possibly by the end of March. The USAID Director, Stephen Spielman, said he intended to ignore the message and would continue until forced to stop. The Washington Office at AID had "signed off" on Spielman's request for extended funding, "Now it is up to Congress and", he says, "who knows what those Republicans might do?"

*Planned Parenthood Federation of Nigeria.*

# CHAPTER 3: MEMORIES OF LAGOS, 1995

The sight of black exhaust from vehicles, with the resulting grey atmosphere.

The smell of rotting vegetation near the port, where the squatters live.

The sight of circular plantings in the bay, where fishermen have created their own fish nurseries.

The sight of crippled, deformed people on street corners, waving their broken limbs and deformities to ask for alms.

The sight of thousands of children in school uniforms going to school in the early morning.

The awareness of the lack of books in the hands of the school children. Except for the occasional note book, there seemed to be little to read outside of school. In class, there was probably a similar situation. The teacher had the books, reading or lecturing to the students who took notes.

The smell of open, green slimy sewers along the road competing with the sweet smell of cactus flowers and lilies.

The feel of climbing or descending steps where all the stair widths, heights, and depths were different.

The sight of mothers sitting on the roadside, nursing their babies while other children were napping or playing.

The sight of young boys selling newspapers, magazines, and all sorts of goods in the road during the "go-slows" (traffic jams).

The sight of "bus conductors" hanging from the side doorways of Volkswagen vans, putting their lives at great risk of being crushed between vehicles.

The driving patterns. Lanes in the road? Forget it. That would take away the fun and challenge of Lagos streets. To prepare for a trip to Lagos, it should be mandatory to spend a few days driving bumper cars in the "Dodge-em" ride of an amusement park.

The taste of bush meat, more bush meat, and even more bush meat.

The sight of bush meat. All sorts of things could be found in the food. The animals were chopped into chunks. One day, I found in my soup the upper jaw of a rodent (musk rat, probably), buck teeth and all. Hairy lips, tongue parts, hide with the hair still on, and innards have all found their way to my plate.

The smell of sweat, especially in closed rooms.

The sound of Pidgin English, local languages and accents, all different, it seems. One word was universal: Fuel, but pronounced fo-ol, or fu-ool. It threw me off, thinking of people, not gasoline.

The power failures. "NEPA is out" or "No NEPA," were common reports, meaning the Nigerian Electric Power Authority was out of commission.

The lack of electricity even when NEPA was not out. Poor wiring, overburdened circuit boxes, hot wires, generators that didn't step in because they were flooded or out of gas, (sorry, fu-ool), means that nothing electrical could be depended upon, including water supply.

The sight of dirty floors. I wondered if some had ever been scrubbed.

The sight of cleaning women, bending over with a bunch of twigs in hand, sweeping floor dust into a dust pan. This was for carpets as well as bare floors. A lot of dust was raised before it settled in again.

The sound of the same songs being played by the Sheraton lobby band every evening, month after month, year after year.

The taste of strong coffee, perhaps boiled, that demanded milk be added to sooth the stomach lining.

The sounds of friendly greetings, everywhere, every day.

The refreshing taste of a cold Harp beer after coming in hot and sweaty and dehydrated.

The sight of Nigerian men dressed in white or pastel robes trimmed with eyelet, lace, and rhinestones, wearing caps that match their clothing.

The sight of colorful head wraps on the women, matching their dresses.

The sight of a child bathing and brushing his teeth at the roadside where he could dump the water and spit into the sewer. He was there almost every morning last year. This year, there was no sight of him. Did his family move? Or, is he dead?

The client records, listing the number of children born alive to the mother seeking to have her tubes tied. The number of her children still living. The totals were never the same.

The variety of hairdos on the women. Some almost bald, others covered with corn row braids. One "do" had such narrow braids that her hair looked like corduroy. One head was covered with squiggly twists of hair that resembled a nest of worms.

The sadness of saying goodbye to colleagues.

The insecure feeling when I was transported to and from the Mohammed Murtala International Airport in Lagos in an armored vehicle.

The heat of the airport, and the knowledge that for a midnight departure, the misery started six hours earlier.

The feeling of frustration and furious anger when told (though the ticket had been confirmed a week ago) that there was no seat available. The explanation: because I had confirmed so long ago, they took my name off the list.

The slight sense of satisfaction after two hours of "fighting", to have an official at the airport "find" a seat for me, without my having given him a payment.

The feeling of waiting two or more hours till boarding time in a hot room. The resulting dirty feeling of being drenched again in sweat for the final hour at the gate.

The refreshing air upon entering the plane – finally.

The speed to the plane's bathroom to strip down, wash with soap and water, dry with paper towels, change clothes, and feel a bit refreshed.

The joy of arriving home with the satisfaction of having accomplished something Nigeria felt was valuable and long-lasting.

These memories will stay forever with me.

# CHAPTER 4: A COUNTRY IN TRANSITION: NIGERIA

This article was published in the Delaware County Register & Review Newspaper, NY; August, 1995.

General Sani Abacha, Moshood Abiola: these names are not heard in Delaware County. They mean little to most local residents, yet they are important characters in one of the most corrupt political struggles in the world: Nigeria's attempt to become a democratic nation.

In Nigeria's June, 1993 first democratic election in many years, the winner was a wealthy businessman, Moshood Abiola. The people rejoiced in what they thought was the beginning of a popular government. But Abiola never took office. Instead, military leaders accused him of treason, had him sentenced in secret trials, and imprisoned him, where it is feared he is being tortured. All this for simply saying "I am the President", after a majority vote in the election. So, the pattern of military dictatorship continues.

General Sani Abacha, the current military ruler, claims he is planning a transition to democratic government, but the people see no evidence of that. October, 1995, the thirty-fifth anniversary of Nigeria's independence from Great Britain, is the date Abacha claims the transition from military to civilian government will occur.

Earlier this year, there was an attempt to overthrow the military government, but it failed. Now there are forty more prisoners in addition to General Olusegun Obasanjo who have been accused of participating in the coup. Families of the accused beg for their release; foreign governments including the United States have made pleas for their release, or at least a fair trial, but the imprisonment and probable mistreatment continues.

Daily, Nigerians listen to radios and read the newspapers to learn what is happening to the prisoners, but they know that the military government controls the press and broadcast media. Some newspapers that took a stand to try to be truthful have been closed down by the government. Only the "approved" news is released. Much of that is better called "disinformation" – outright falsehoods made up by the leaders.

Nigeria, once considered the hope of sub-Saharan Africa, is one rich in minerals and oil. It is twice the size of California. With 110,000,000 citizens, it is the most heavily populated country of the continent. One quarter of all Africans is Nigerian. The country is $37 billion in debt. The average annual income is $320. The people of Nigeria deserve a better world to live in.

Betty Gonzales Bowers

# CHAPTER 5: NICARAGUA, APRIL, 1997

For two weeks, Richard Bowers and I were part of a small group that visited Nicaragua in Central America. By coincidence, the five participants were all from New York State, though the joint sponsors of the trip were two Connecticut organizations: Promoting Enduring Peace, and the New Haven/Leon Sister City Project.

The theme of the delegation's visit was sustainable community development and sustainable agriculture. In a country that has been denied so much foreign aid because of their political problems, it was essential that any aid or local development projects be of the enduring kind: projects that could be sustained within the country without continuing outside support.

We were met at the airport by Lee Cruz, the director of the New Haven/Leon Sister City Project. From our base in the city of Leon on the Pacific coast, fifty-seven miles northwest of Managua, we visited various agencies, micro-credit unions, farms, businesses, and schools. We also visited "new neighborhoods" that were just crude cardboard and wooden shelters occupied by squatters". All were examples of efforts being made for improvement of the quality of life for the people.

**Medical Issues** – On the road that we traveled from the airport to Leon, we encountered an accident that was a cruel introduction to the unavailability of medical assistance. A truck had collided with a bus, and at least one other vehicle had also crashed. As we approached the scene, the driver detoured off the road in our four-wheel-drive amphibian Toyota Land Cruiser. We saw people crying in the roads, some attempting to walk away. There were no police or medical assistants. Our escort told us that if anyone would come to the scene, it would be the Red Cross, **if** they heard about it, which would be unlikely because of lack of phones, and **if** there were any fuel in their vehicle to get to the scene. Accident victims were, therefore, expected to help each other. We learned the next day that nine persons had been killed, in addition to an unknown number injured.

In speaking to women, we found them open to discussing their needs and strong desires for birth control information and service. Nicaragua has had an astoundingly high birth rate. The median age was sixteen. Family planning services have not been funded by the US Agency for International Development because of our foreign aid policy. The shame of this is hard

344

to comprehend, as America has a long history of interfering with the governing of Nicaragua.

**United States' Involvement in Nicaragua** - We have had a presence in the country since the 1850s when a Tennessee native, William Walker, established himself as President of Nicaragua. President Howard Taft, continuing the control of the Nicaraguans, sent in our Marines, who stayed on till the 1930s when Anastasio Somoza Garcia took over the leadership in a way that satisfied the US. After twenty years, one of Somoza's sons took over. He carried on the frauds and tortures until tension built to the point where the Sandinista guerrilla movement started in 1962. The final overthrow of the Somoza regime took place in 1979, a time that the people there refer to as the "Triumph of the Revolution".

We especially appreciated the opportunity to hear about the revolution from Harold Chavarra, who took us to see the fortress where he had been held prisoner by the Somoza National Guard, in cells that were mostly below ground. Reminders of that time have left him with permanent scars, both inside and outwardly.

The Sandinistas redistributed land to the poor, who were not prepared to work a productive farm. The National Autonomous University of Nicaragua was now trying to rectify this by offering training for sustainable organic vegetable and fruit farming.

The Sandinistas were not prepared to lead the country. Soon the US, under Ronald Reagan, organized a band of Contras to bring the Sandinistas down. In 1990, Centralist Violeta de Chamorro defeated the Sandinista Daniel Ortega, and the contra civil war slowly wound down. Conservative Arnoldo Aleman became president in October, 1996, though the Sandinistas remained a near majority in local offices.

**Living Conditions** - While in the country, we lived with a family on the outskirts of Leon. Two others of the delegation lived with a family next door. As the local families did not speak any English, and four members of the delegation spoke no Spanish, I became the translator after our leader, Lee Cruz, had left us each day. Sharing a home with an extended family definitely added to our understanding of the country and its people.

We shared one bathroom that had only a cold water faucet. We ate the local dishes that were prepared - mostly rice and beans. We supplemented the diet by shopping in the central market stalls for fruits and vegetables to be shared by the family. Fresh fruit was a real treat. A huge papaya, the size of a watermelon, cost only a dollar. Pineapples, bananas, and other tropical fruits were a treat, often being turned into cool, refreshing drinks, *"refrescas"*.

Laundry was a challenge. Washing was done in a *"pila"*. This was a cement sink with a corrugated bottom that served as a scrub board. The plumbing and sewage treatment systems were primitive, not allowing paper to be flushed. Adjusting to these changes was a bit of a strain, but not as bad as the constant heat. Fortunately, we were given the only household fan for our bedroom for some relief.

**Local Industries** - Tanneries were a risky business. Traditionally, the tanners have stomped on the hides in vats of chemicals that eventually harm their central nervous system. The chemical runoffs fed into the local river that was the only source of water for many. Tanneries were being moved to a separate area and there were some attempts to wash the hides in mechanical tumblers.

A rope pump factory was a successful industry. With lack of electricity, a pump powered by hand or by feet could be used to supply farms and businesses with water. The Nicaraguans who developed this efficient system utilizing old bicycle wheels are now transferring this low-technological method to other countries.

Micro-loan funds were available, some through the Center for the Promotion of Local Development (CEPRODEL) under the direction of Harold Chavarra. Other funds were available through the Presbyterian supported international relief agency, the Evangelical Council of Churches (CEPAD). Small, short-term loans were granted, many to women, to finance the development of small businesses, shops, shoe-makers, clothing distributors, weavers, etc. We visited many of these, and were impressed with the results, including the remarkable loan default rate of only 1.2%.

**Schools** - The typical school buildings in the poor neighborhoods have been almost solid walls. Because of the lack of construction skills, the absence of windows was thought to result in sturdier buildings. With technology now spreading, safer schools are being built, some of wood construction in an earthquake resistant manner. Others were of rammed earth, where walls of moist dirt are pounded between temporary wood frames. These allow for lighter, brighter, cooler classrooms. While in Leon, we helped in a school construction project, under the leadership of a young woman volunteer carpenter.

The average teacher's monthly salary was the equivalent of sixty-five dollars. School supplies were meager. Teachers we met were always hoping some foreign assistance would be offered. The history, however, had been that international aid would pay for teachers' salary and materials for a while, but when the aid stopped, the schools stopped. Now the emphasis was on preparing the local people to provide better school buildings, on building and selling bicycles for the teachers' transportation, and on charging some tuition for the improved education. All this was an attempt to be self-sufficient.

**Church Life** - In traditionally Roman Catholic Central America, the fastest growing church was that of the Pentecostals. Explained by the Presbyterian theologian, Rev. Richard Shaull, this religion, centered in the other-world, sustains people trying to survive in this world. Those who cannot count on getting medical care go to services of divine healing. Those who feel their lives and society are possessed by demonic forces discover a spiritual help for overcoming these forces. For those who can't find work, or are completely abandoned, the experience of conversion and the support of a church "family" helps them survive and maybe start over again.

Worship in the mainline churches is better suited to a literate culture. A more effective worship for the poor is needed to appeal to those with an oral culture. Music and songs of praise appeal to emotions. Telling stories in testimonies touches the hearts of parishioners. If mainline denominations are to contribute to the future of Christianity in Latin America, we must recognize a need to relate more fully with the poor majority.

While in Nicaragua, we were able to obtain a Protestant Bible, written in Spanish, for one local poor church that could not afford one. We were also very touched by the words and music of the ecumenical Peasant's Mass of Nicaragua, freely translated into English by Linda McCrae and the Inter-Religious Task Force on Central America.

### You Are the God of the Poor
Chorus
You are the God of the poor
Human and humble and gracious.
The God at work in the factory
In your face the wisdom of ages.
That's why I can talk to you
The way I talk with my people
Because you are the God, the worker
And Christ is a worker too.
Verse 1.
You go hand in hand with all my people
You struggle in country and in town.
At the corner store you ask "how much?"
Waiting long for the prices to come down.
You eat snow cones in the park
With Mary and Rose and Juan Jose'.
You even complain about the snow cones
When they're not as sweet as yesterday. (Chorus)
Verse 2.
I have seen you standing at the corner store
My friend, there I call you by your name.
I have seen you selling lottery tickets
With no embarrassment or shame.
I have seen you at the service station
Looking under hoods and fixing cars.

Even filling holes along the highway
In old leather gloves and overalls. (Chorus)

**View of a tourist** - Nicaragua was not about to become a tourist Mecca in the near future, we were sure. We travelers from the developed world would not be eager to vacation in poor countries with few of the conveniences we are so accustomed to. In addition, transportation would be difficult.

The environment was not entirely friendly. Nicaragua's largest freshwater lake was full of sharks (like the Somoza generations who fed on the people for so many years). The beach where we spent a free day had such severe undertow that signs warned that ninety-two persons had been drowned in the last year. There were no life guards there.

It is a country with many volcanoes, two of which we visited. One had erupted twice since 1992. The ash was so thick that as we tried to climb the slope, the vehicle got stuck. What looked like bushes in the distance were actually buried trees.

We experienced a minor earthquake; a common occurrence. A big one occurred in 1972 and left the city of Managua in rubble. It killed six thousand people. The largest Cathedral in Central America still stood as a reminder, damaged and unused, in the central plaza of Managua.

The trip, although short in duration, provided a great amount of experience for us. We enjoyed the Nicaraguan people, who, though speaking a different language, never-the-less were much like people everywhere. The world is indeed a smaller place than once imagined, and the struggles of the poor are the same, whether in our own country or in another land. We hope that by our participation in this delegation, we have helped promote a more enduring peace with the people of Nicaragua.

# CHAPTER 6: REFLECTION ABOUT AFRICA, JAN, 1998

Many years after my last journal notes, as I was reminiscing about my many assignments that took me to Africa, I added the following reflections of trips that stood out in my memory.

The first was the one that enabled me to take my aunt on a safari to Kenya. Lois was my mother's youngest sister, and I had grown up in the same house with her. After my parents were divorced, when I was seven, I was under the care of my maternal grandparents. Lois and I were more like sisters. I was delighted to find I had accumulated enough frequent flyer miles to obtain a round trip Pan-Am flight for Lois.

For the first week, while I was working at the AVS office in Nairobi, we were able to visit local or nearby places. On the weekend, I hired a car and driver so we could visit a mission she had been supporting in the Lake Naivasha area. During the week while I was at the office, she was free to wander in the shopping and hotel area in mid-town.

The second week, we flew to Mombasa on the south-east coast of Kenya, for a two week curriculum development conference, the reason I had been sent to Kenya. We stayed at a lovely hotel on the beach, and Lois could enjoy the resort-like atmosphere while I was busy at the conference.

When we were to return to Nairobi, we took an overnight train from Mombasa, which was a new experience for me, too. We enjoyed having dinner served in the old style dining car, and the fun of trying to sleep in the noisy railroad bunks. A special treat was having breakfast early in the morning as we were riding through the vast savannah with free-roaming animals everywhere in sight. I am sure that this African trip was a major highlight in Lois' life.

I made many trips subsequent to the drafting of the surgical curriculum, spending a considerable amount of my time in the New York office doing further writing and development of the medical components of the material. Some of these subsequent trips were for the purpose of field testing the material. Finally, we held another conference in Mombasa, where doctors and nurses from all over Africa were invited. They reviewed the curriculum and training material, and began to develop plans for training courses in their countries. Thus, the work I did had direct impact on the development of surgical skills and training courses in the entire continent.

When I was to return to Mombasa for this second conference, I invited my friend Vivian, my oldest grand-daughter Sherean, and my husband to accompany me. Again, I bought all the tickets through frequent flyer credits. While I was at work during the conference, I had arranged for escorted safaris for the three of them. They went to many game reserves, visited coastal towns on guided tours, and had their own driver and car for all of this. Some days they just stayed at the hotel and enjoyed the beach.

After the conference, we traveled by the overnight train that Lois and I had taken to Nairobi. After a day or two to repack and "do the town", we flew to the Kilimanjaro airport in northern Tanzania, where again, I had made all tour arrangements. We were met by a driver and guide who took us over very difficult roads, for a long journey to Ngorongoro Crater, a naturally enclosed area where animals live in relative peace and safety from poachers. Our guide was an environmentalist, and he had arranged an additional opportunity for us to spend time with the manager of the crater's reserve. He supplied a great amount of information we never would have gotten otherwise, and then gave all his notes and papers to Sherean so she could use them for school.

After we flew back to Kenya from Tanzania we went to "Treetops", a hotel built up in the trees. The Queen of England actually became Queen here, as she was on safari and staying there when her father died. Like "The Ark", where I had gone on an earlier trip myself, it was an all-night animal watch.

On the way back to the US, we flew into Germany, took a train to the Netherlands, and spent a week visiting that country with a rented car. I wanted Sherean to see my family's country of origin. All together, we spent five weeks traveling together.

One of the other trips to Kenya entailed my teaching infection prevention practices to staffs at various hospitals. This was a critical and important task because of the high risk to the operating room staff who might be at risk of contracting AIDS from a needle prick or surgical wound. It was also meant to protect the helpers who washed the instruments and linens in the absence of proper precautionary disinfecting measures. As a result, an entire chapter on infection prevention was added to the curriculum that was in development.

Upon reflection, I believe I helped to improve medical standards in Kenya that had unending effects in all of Africa because Kenya was the primary training ground for other countries. These changes included improving the safety of surgery, prevention of the spread of AIDS, and the developing the knowledge and the skills of doctors and nurses. I am proud of my role in all of this.

After I left AVS in 1993, I served as a consultant for a few years. A major contract was with the Family Planning Association of Nigeria. The assignment was to help develop a manual to be used as a guide for all the activities of a family planning clinic. It encompassed the entire experience of a client, starting with the initial visit. It included the processing of data to be collected, counseling, the contraceptive methods offered and provided, treatment of any side effects, infection control and prevention, financial records, and community outreach activities.

An extra task was to teach a week-long course on public relations and publicity to the outreach workers of the clinic. This had never been done in any program before. The staff members who attended the course were excited to learn how to write a press release, how to promote the family planning program in the media, and to conduct other activities to promote their services.

This kind of program was what I had always thought AVS was supposed to have done internationally, but it had been totally ignored by the leadership of the International Project of AVS: Dr. Lubell, Marilyn Schima, and those who came after their departure. Because they had not been involved with those activities in the United States, such concepts were outside their field of knowledge or expertise. I was especially happy that I could share the US experience with West Africa, and hope it was effective.

My final achievement was to initiate an outreach program for voluntary sterilization overseas, using the skills I had acquired when I first began my work with AVS. My public health journey to provide safe, voluntary permanent contraception had come full circle.

# APPENDIX

**Betty Gonzales, R.N.**
**International Health/Family Planning Consultant**
*Specialist in Surgical Services*

Route 1, Box 28, DeLancey, New York, 13752
Phone and Fax (607) 746-3872

## Summary

Highly experienced, international family planning consultant with major accomplishments and publications in the areas of medical quality assurance, curriculum development, training, and professional education, country needs assessments, infection prevention, and public information.

Over twenty years of direct experience in all areas of voluntary sterilization, culminating in the positions of Deputy Director of the Medical Division and Medical Program Advisor for the Association for Voluntary Surgical Contraception (AVSC). Numerous international consulting assignments have resulted in a strong knowledge base and accomplishments in the following areas:

## Medical Quality Assurance

Examples:

* Conducted medical quality assurance visits in over forty countries.

* Monitored the progress and provided technical assistance for the development of guidelines for surgical services in sub-Saharan Africa, Asia, Central and South America, and the Caribbean.

* Drafted and field tested the medical the medical guidelines for mini-laparotomy and local anesthesia for the Government of The Philippines.

* Evaluated the complications in a Central American country's laparoscopic program, identified causes, and made recommendations that resulted in decreased incidence of surgical problems.

* In many countries, evaluated methods used for disinfection and sterilization of surgical instruments, techniques used, and areas needing improvement.

* Trained doctors in numerous countries to do medical monitoring, supervision, and quality assurance for both governmental programs and for non-governmental organizations (NGOs).

* Analyzed, on an annual basis, all complications and mortalities that were associated with AVSC funded programs, world-wide.

* Made frequent site visits for evaluation of program needs, services, skills, and training courses.

## Curriculum Development, Training, and Professional Education
Examples:

* Participated in surgical training in the U.S. for minilaparotomy, laparoscopy under local anesthesia, and no-scalpel vasectomy.

* Participated in surgical training throughout the developing world, introducing the concept of surgical team training to involve the nursing and paramedical workers.

* Wrote the medical components for two international curricula, one for vasectomy and one for minilaparotomy under local anesthesia. The modules in both included preoperative assessment, surgical techniques and procedures, local anesthesia techniques, postoperative care and follow-up, prevention, diagnosis and treatment of complications, record keeping, case studies, and analysis of complications and mortalities.

* Provided the technical information and supervised the medical contents of a film developed in Kenya for the introduction of post-partum tubal ligation for all sub-Saharan counties.

* Authored articles and made numerous presentations on counseling and informed consent for permanent birth control.

* Wrote reference materials to be used by both trainers and trainees in minilaparotomy courses.

* Was the primary author of *No-scalpel Vasectomy: An Illustrated Guide for Surgeons*.

* Wrote the reference materials to be used in vasectomy courses.

* Wrote published articles for professional education in voluntary sterilization.

### Country Needs Assessments
Examples:

* In Nepal, assessed the potential for introducing post-partum tubal ligation and integrating these services into the existing maternity hospitals.

* In Guatemala, was the team leader for an assessment of all voluntary sterilization services, both in the public and private sectors. This included both a medical and voluntarism review, and assessment of problems, and recommendations for future directions.

* In Honduras, was team leader for a needs assessment similar to that of Guatemala.

* In Nepal, was leader of a team evaluating both counseling and surgical training needs. Trained a local doctor to do quality assurance supervision during that visit.

* In Kenya, was a member of a team assessing voluntarism and levels of public information about surgical contraception.

* In Sri Lanka, assessed counseling skills and voluntarism of sterilization

clients for the national program.

## Infection Prevention

Examples:

* Member of the international infection prevention review task force that resulted in the publication and worldwide acceptance of the problem-solving guide *Infection Prevention for Family Planning Service Programs.*

* Helped introduce infection prevention activities into the AVSC programs.

* Evaluated post-surgical complications in a West African country, identified problems, and recommended changes to reduce the numbers of infections.

* Introduced new disinfection procedures in some West African programs to help prevent spread of HIV and HBV.

* Conducted training in infection prevention, trained a future trainer and medical monitor of infection prevention in Nigeria.

## Public Information

Examples:

* Increased public awareness of voluntary sterilization as a family planning method, and played a leading role in changing restrictive hospital and medical insurance policies in the United States.

* Operated the AVS speakers bureau for the U.S. public information campaign in the 1970s.

* Co-authored the client information booklets used for sterilization clients, and worked with the U.S. Department of Health and Human Services in the preparation of the regulations for Federally-funded sterilizations.

* Developed and wrote client information packets for use by the national AVS public information staff.

* Developed brochures that served as models for many other regions and countries.

* Spokesperson on hundreds of radio and television programs, to help create a client demand for sterilization services, and to educate the public.

* Supervised and was primary medical advisor for the nation-wide AVS information and referral service.

## Work History

The Association for Voluntary Surgical Contraception, Inc. (formerly The Association for Voluntary Sterilization). New York. Employed July, 1971 until retirement in July, 1993.

From 1983, served as Deputy Director of the newly organized Medical Division of AVS.

**Education**
* Received a Registered Nurse degree in 1952
* Took varied courses in Public Health at Seton Hall and Fairleigh Dickenson Universities in New Jersey;
* Studied public relations and publicity at New York University;
* Received yearly continuing medical education credits for courses, conferences and seminars in Gynecology, Laparoscopy, Family Planning, Contraceptive Technology and Nursing.
* Studied and practiced microsurgery at the animal lab of the University of Louisville Microsurgical Center.

**Professional Activities**
* Edited the *AVS News* for the U.S. donors, members and international providers.
* Created and Edited the *AVS Biomedical Bulletin* to educate professionals in the newest scientific findings and surgical innovations in the field of voluntary sterilization.
* Proof-reader and editor of hundreds of drafts of articles and books pertaining to voluntary sterilization.

**OTHER**
* July, 1993: Upon retirement, received a Certificate of Recognition in *"acknowledgment of the extraordinary achievements and contributions that Betty Gonzales has made to the Association for Voluntary Surgical Contraception and to the field of reproductive health, beginning as a consultant and lecturer for the Association for Voluntary Sterilization in 1961, when she learned how difficult it was for women to get sterilization services, and joining the staff in 1971, Betty played a key role in making voluntary sterilization a real choice for women and men in the United States. Along the way, Betty produced an impressive array of publications and papers on various aspects of voluntary sterilization and Health. She then took her network and what she had learned to the newly established Medical Division of AVS, helping to make safe and voluntary sterilization services available to other countries. Betty made substantial contributions to a whole range of manuals and guides from the World Health Organization's Vasectomy guidelines to the minilaparotomy curriculum, while making field trips to sites from Mombasa to Manila. This certificate cannot give adequate recognition to Betty Gonzales' achievements; the real recognition is the better lives that her work and the work of people like her have made possible."*

* December, 1989: Received the AVS Meritorious Service *Award "for extraordinary achievements in making surgical contraception available to men and women in the United States through public education, hospital policy changes, and professional education, and for providing practical and sound medical guidance to the Medical Division for surgical contraception services around the world".*

356

* 1961-1971, was a volunteer consultant to AVS, and a national spokesperson for voluntary sterilization in the U.S. Did hundreds of radio and television talks shows, news programs, and presentations to both public and professional groups across the country.

*During this period, was also a hospital obstetrical nurse and a N.J. Public Health Nurse in a community of 6,000 residents, for nine years.

September, 1993

## PUBLICATIONS by BETTY GONZALES

Khairullah Z, Huber DH, Gonzales B, "Declining mortality in international sterilization services". International Journal of Gynecology and Obstetrics, 1992, 39:41-50.

Gonzales B, Marston-Ainley S. Vansintejan G, "No-Scalpel Vasectomy: An Illustrated Guide for Surgeons". Association for Voluntary Surgical Contraception, New York, 1991.

Kendrick JS, Gonzales B, Huber DH, Grubb GS, Rubin GL, "Complications of vasectomies in the United States". Journal of Family Practice. 1987 Sep; 25(3):245-8.

Kornhaber R, Thompson L, Gonzales B, "Female voluntary sterilization: New York, Association for Voluntary Sterilization, 1985. 221p. (Training Course for Health Clinicians: Module Eight)

Gonzales B, Psychosexual responses to female sterilization". In Van Lith DA, Keith LG, Van Hall EV, ed. New Trends in Female Sterilization. Chicago, Year Book Medical publishers, 1983: 195-201

Gonzales B "Counseling for sterilization." In Phillips JM, ed. Endoscopic Female Sterilization. Downey, California, American Association of Gynecologic Laparoscopists, 1983.

Gonzales B, "The international medicolegal status of sterilization for mentally handicapped people" Journal of Reproductive Medicine" 1982 May; 27(5):257-8.

Gonzales B, "Voluntary sterilization: counseling as a prerequisite to informed consent." Medicine and Law. 1982; 1:29-32.

Gonzales B, Sansoucie RW. "Sterilization: issues in conflict." In Hiller MD, ed. Medical Ethics and the Law: Implications for Public Policy. Cambridge, Massachusetts, Ballinger, 1981. 18 p.

Gonzales B, "Counseling for sterilization." Journal of Reproductive Medicine. 1981 Oct; 26(10):538-40.

Gonzales B, "Psychosexual aftermath of voluntary sterilization." Advances in Planned Parenthood. 1979; 14(4):137-43.

Gonzales B, "Physicians' attitudes toward sterilization reversal." In Phillips JM, ed. Endoscopy in Gynecology: the proceedings of the Third International Congress on Gynecologic Endoscopy, San Francisco. Downey, California, American Association of Gynecologic Laparoscopists, 1978. :1667.

Gonzales B, "Vasectomy defended." Family Planning Perspectives 6(1): 3-4. Winter 1974

Gonzales B, "Voluntary sterilization." In Human Sexuality: Nursing Implications, New York, The American Journal of Nursing Company, 1973: 134-140

Gonzales B, "Voluntary sterilization." American Journal of Nursing 70(12): 2581-2583. Dec 1970.

## PRESENTATIONS

Gonzales B, "The role of paramedics in assuring safe practices." Fifth International Congress of the Society for the Advancement of Contraception, Voluntary Surgical Contraception Workshop, Caracas, Venezuela, October 5, 19987.

Huber DH, Khairullah Z, Gonzales B, "Mortality attributable to voluntary surgical contraception in international programs." Society for the Advancement of Contraception, Fourth Annual Meeting, Chicago, Illinois, September, 1986.

Gonzales B, "Transcervical installation of phenol-mucilage." *Simposio Nacional sobre Oclusion Tubaria*, held in *Instituto Nacianal de las Nutricion Salvador Zubiran*, Mexico City, Mexico, January 7-8. 1985.

Khairullah ZE, Gonzales B, "Training for voluntary surgical contraception." International Scientific and Medical Conference, Jakarta, Indonesia, 26-30 November, 1984.

Kendrick JS, Gonzales B, Huber DH, Grubb GS, Rubin GL, Flock ML, "Vasectomies in the United States, 1982" Association of Planned Parenthood Professionals, November 3, 1984.

Gonzales B, "The international medical-legal status of sterilization for mentally handicapped persons." International Congress on Gynecologic Endoscopy and Microsurgery (AAGL), Phoenix, Arizona, Nov. 4-8, 1981.

Gonzales B, "Sterilization: legal status and legislative trends". International Congress on Gynecologic Endoscopy and Microsurgery, Phoenix, Arizona, Nov. 4-8, 1981

Gonzales B, "Sterilization" Third Annual "Women in Crisis" conference, New York, June 30, 1981

Gonzales BL, "Psychosexual relationships to female sterilization." Boerhaave Course, in New Trends in Female sterilization Techniques, University of Leiden, Netherlands, May 14-15, 1981.

Gonzales B, "Sterilization: an option for the disabled." National Conference of Israel Society for Rehabilitation of the Disabled, Tel Aviv, Israel. Feb 22, 1981

Gonzales B, "Medico-legal aspects of sterilization for mentally disabled persons." First International Convention: Medico-legal Aspects of Disability, Tel Aviv, Israel, Feb. 15-19, 1981.

Gonzales B, "Voluntary sterilization: can retarded young adults choose it?" American Association of Psychiatric Services for Children, 32nd Annual Meeting, New Orleans, Nov 16-20, 1980.

Gonzales BL, "Counseling for prospective sterilization patients." Clinical Symposium on Gynecologic Endoscopy, New Orleans, Nov 19-23, 1980.

Gonzales B, "Role of the nurse-midwife in counseling for sterilization." American College of Nurse-Midwives, Minneapolis, May 11-15, 1980.

Gonzales B, "Voluntary sterilization: beyond the letter of the law." National Family Planning and Reproductive Health Association Annual Meeting, Washington, D.C., Feb 28, 1980.

Gonzales B, "Psychosexual aspects of voluntary sterilization." Fourth International Congress on Gynecological Endoscopy, Las Vegas, Nevada. Nov. 4-9, 1979.

Gonzales B, "Counseling women for voluntary sterilization." Clinical Symposium on Gynecologic Endoscopy, Las Vegas, Nevada, Nov. 1979

Gonzales B, "Voluntary sterilization: counseling as a prerequisite to informed consent." Fifth World Congress on Medical Law, Ghent, Belgium, August 19-23, 1979

Gonzales B, "Psychosexual aftermath of female sterilization." Clinical Symposium on Gynecologic Endoscopy, Hollywood, Florida, Nov. 1978.

Gonzales B, "Sterilization trends: a radical change." Clinical Symposium on Gynecologic Laparoscopists Nurses Section, Hollywood, Florida, Nov. 17, 1978.

Gonzales B, "New DHEW regulations for sterilization." American Association of Gynecologic Laparoscopists Nurses Section, Hollywood, Florida, Nov. 17, 1978

Gonzales B, "Psychosexual aftermath of voluntary sterilization." The National Council on Family Relations Round-table, Philadelphia, Pennsylvania, October 19, 1978.

Gonzales B, "Voluntary sterilization: counseling for informed consent." International Conference on Venereal Disease, Family Planning and Human Sexuality, Honolulu, Hawaii, June 11-18, 1978.

Gonzales B, "Sterilization abuse". National Organization of Women, Queens, New York, April 1, 1978.

Gonzales B, "Voluntary sterilization: available for all, imposed on none". National Association for the Advancement of Colored People, New York, NY, March 19, 1978.

Gonzales B, "Enlisting community support." Mini-lap Seminar, Syracuse, NY, Sept. 18-19, and San Francisco, Dec. 11-12, 1977

Gonzales B, "Voluntary sterilization: the role of the health professional on counseling". American Public Health Association Annual Meeting, Washington, D.C. Oct. 30-Nov. 3. 1977.

Gonzales B, "Voluntary sterilization: freedom of choice for the sexually mature retarded person." American Association on Mental Deficiency, New Orleans, June 7, 1977.

## PAPERS

Gonzales B, "Broadcast programming for voluntary sterilization".

Gonzales B, "Estimate of number of voluntary sterilizations performed" Association for Voluntary Sterilization, New York. Published annually from 1971 to 1981.

**Betty Gonzales, R.N.**
**International Health/Family Planning Consultant**
*Specialist in Surgical Services*

Route 1, Box 28, DeLancey, New York, 13752
Phone and Fax (607) 746-3872

## ADDENDUM TO RESUME: CONSULTANCIES

| Dates | # Days | Employer | Services Provided |
|---|---|---|---|
| 1993 | | | |
| November | 1 | JHPIEGO | Surgical Guidelines for India |
| December | 5 | JHPIEGO | Surgical Guidelines for India |
| | | | |
| 1994 | | | |
| January | 5 | MSH | Clinic Management Background for Nigeria |
| March/April | 23 | MSH | Clinic Management Workshop in Nigeria |
| April | 1 | Gyno-Pharma | Market Research for Laparoscopic Instruments |
| May-July | 20 | MSH | Development of Clinical Procedures for Nigeria |
| August | 1 | MSH | Additional Clinic Procedures for Nigeria |
| November | 21 | JHPIEGO | Supervision Workshop Facilitator in Zimbabwe |
| | | | |
| 1995 | | | |
| March | 28 | MSH | Initiate Clinic Management Procedures in Nigeria |
| May | 3 | MSH | Publication/Editing Procedures Manual |

| | | | |
|---|---|---|---|
| June | 15 | Pathfinder | Drafted a General Equipment Manual |
| July | 20 | MSH | Implement Clinic Procedures Manual |
| July | 6 | MSH | Conduct Workshop: Public Relations, Patient Information and Client Recruitment in Nigeria |

1996

| | | | |
|---|---|---|---|
| September | 4 | Femcare | Introduction of Filshie Clip in USA |
| October | 1 | Avalon | Write Product description for publications |
| November | 1 | Avalon | Make Contact Calls and Draft Client Information brochure. |

Made in the USA
Middletown, DE
02 December 2014